Bloom's Modern Critical Views

Bloom's Modern Critical Views

JANE AUSTEN
New Edition

Edited and with an introduction by
Harold Bloom
Sterling Professor of the Humanities
Yale University

BLOOM'S
LITERARY CRITICISM
An imprint of Infobase Publishing

Bloom's Modern Critical Views: Jane Austen, New Edition

Copyright © 2009 by Infobase Publishing
Introduction © 2009 by Harold Bloom

All rights reserved. No part of this publication may be reproduced or utilized in any form or by any means, electronic or mechanical, including photocopying, recording, or by any information storage or retrieval systems, without permission in writing from the publisher. For more information contact:

Bloom's Literary Criticism
An imprint of Infobase Publishing
132 West 31st Street
New York NY 10001

Library of Congress Cataloging-in-Publication Data
Jane Austen / edited and with an introduction by Harold Bloom. — New ed.
   p. cm. — (Bloom's modern critical views)
   Includes bibliographical references and index.
   ISBN 978-1-60413-397-4 (hardcover)
   1. Austen, Jane, 1775–1817—Criticism and interpretation. 2. Women and litera-ture—England—History—19th century. 3. Love stories, English—History and criticism. I. Bloom, Harold. II. Title. III. Series.

   PR4037.J28 2009
   823'.7—dc22

                              2008044616

Bloom's Literary Criticism books are available at special discounts when purchased in bulk quantities for businesses, associations, institutions, or sales promotions. Please call our Special Sales Department in New York at (212) 967-8800 or (800) 322-8755.

You can find Bloom's Literary Criticism on the World Wide Web at http://www.chelseahouse.com.

Contributing editor: Pamela Loos
Cover design by Takeshi Takahashi

Printed in the United States of America
IBT EJB 10 9 8 7 6 5 4 3 2 1

This book is printed on acid-free paper.

All links and Web addresses were checked and verified to be correct at the time of publication. Because of the dynamic nature of the Web, some addresses and links may have changed since publication and may no longer be valid.

Contents

Editor's Note

My introduction centers on Jane Austen's relationships to Shakespeare, Samuel Richardson, and Dr. Samuel Johnson, while narrating the fortunes of the Protestant will in four great novels: *Pride and Prejudice*, *Mansfield Park*, *Emma*, and *Persuasion*.

Mary Poovey traces a dialectic between Austen's aesthetic wit and the ideological paradoxes of Austenian society.

Richardson's influence on *Persuasion* is emphasized by E.B. Moon, after which Anne K. Mellor analyzes the contrast between Mary Shelley and Austen in their stances toward romanticism.

For Cynthia Wall, spatial relations between Elizabeth and Darcy in *Pride and Prejudice* mirror their eventual accommodation, while William Deresiewicz adroitly suggests that erotic love in Austen essentially is a form of friendship.

Mansfield Park is seen by Jo Alyson Parker as a double-voiced work, both upholding tradition yet also criticizing the constructions of patriarchal order.

Ivor Morris charmingly praises the sincerity of the sublimely egregious Mr. Collins of *Pride and Prejudice*, after which Paula Byrne demonstrates the art of the theater in *Emma*.

Persuasion, to Gloria Sybil Gross, manifests Dr. Johnson's fierce realism in regard to marriage, while both *Mansfield Park* and *Sense and Sensibility* impress Patricia Menon as possessing aspects at once comic and darkening toward the tragic.

Emily Auerbach wisely searches *Sense and Sensibility* for "reasons of the heart" that, in Austen, reason does know, after which Sarah Emsley concludes this volume with an acute reading of friendship and tolerance in *Emma*.

HAROLD BLOOM

Introduction

The oddest yet by no means inapt analogy to Jane Austen's art of representation is Shakespeare's—oddest, because she is so careful of limits, as classical as Ben Jonson in that regard, and Shakespeare transcends all limits. Austen's humor, her mode of rhetorical irony, is not particularly Shakespearean, and yet her precision and accuracy of representation is. Like Shakespeare, she gives us figures, major and minor, utterly consistent each in her or his own mode of speech and being, and utterly different from one another. Her heroines have firm selves, each molded with an individuality that continues to suggest Austen's reserve of power, her potential for creating an endless diversity. To recur to the metaphor of oddness, the highly deliberate limitation of social scale in Austen seems a paradoxical theater of mind in which so fecund a humanity could be fostered. Irony, the concern of most critics of Austen, seems more than a trope in her work, seems indeed to be the condition of her language, yet hardly accounts for the effect of moral and spiritual power that she so constantly conveys, however implicitly or obliquely.

Ian Watt, in his permanently useful *The Rise of the Novel*, portrays Austen as Fanny Burney's direct heir in the difficult art of combining the rival modes of Samuel Richardson and Henry Fielding. Like Burney, Austen is thus seen as following the Richardson of *Sir Charles Grandison*, in a "minute presentation of daily life," while emulating Fielding in "adopting a more detached attitude to her narrative material, and in evaluating it from a comic

1

and objective point of view." Watt goes further when he points out that Austen tells her stories in a discreet variant of Fielding's manner "as a confessed author," though her ironical juxtapositions are made to appear not those of "an intrusive author but rather of some august and impersonal spirit of social and psychological understanding."

And yet, as Watt knows, Austen truly is the daughter of Richardson, and not of Fielding, just as she is the ancestor of George Eliot and Henry James, rather than of Dickens and Thackeray. Her inwardness is an ironic revision of Richardson's extraordinary conversion of English Protestant sensibility into the figure of Clarissa Harlowe, and her own moral and spiritual concerns fuse in the crucial need of her heroines to sustain their individual integrities, a need so intense that it compels them to fall into those errors about life that are necessary for life (to adopt a Nietzschean formulation). In this too they follow, though in a comic register, the pattern of their tragic precursor, the magnificent but sublimely flawed Clarissa Harlowe.

Richardson's *Clarissa*, perhaps still the longest novel in the language, seems to me also still the greatest, despite the achievements of Austen, Dickens, George Eliot, Henry James, and Joyce. Austen's Elizabeth Bennet and Emma Woodhouse, Eliot's Dorothea Brooke and Gwendolyn Harleth, James's Isabel Archer and Milly Theale—though all these are Clarissa Harlowe's direct descendants, they are not proportioned to her more sublime scale. David Copperfield and Leopold Bloom have her completeness; indeed Joyce's Bloom may be the most complete representation of a human being in all of literature. But they belong to the secular age; Clarissa Harlowe is poised upon the threshold that leads from the Protestant religion to a purely secular sainthood.

C.S. Lewis, who read Milton as though that fiercest of Protestant temperaments had been an orthodox Anglican, also seems to have read Jane Austen by listening for her echoings of the New Testament. Quite explicitly, Lewis named Austen as the daughter of Dr. Samuel Johnson, greatest of literary critics, and rigorous Christian moralist:

> I feel . . . sure that she is the daughter of Dr. Johnson: she inherits
> his commonsense, his morality, even much of his style.

The Johnson of *Rasselas* and of *The Rambler*, surely the essential Johnson, is something of a classical ironist, but we do not read Johnson for his ironies, or for his dramatic representations of fictive selves. Rather, we read him as we read Koheleth; he writes wisdom literature. That Jane Austen is a wise writer is indisputable, but we do not read *Pride and Prejudice* as though it were Ecclesiastes. Doubtless, Austen's religious ideas were as profound as Samuel Richardson's were shallow, but *Emma* and *Clarissa* are Protestant novels without being in any way religious. What is most original about the representation of Clarissa Harlowe is the magnificent intensity of her slowly described dying, which goes on for about the last third of Richardson's vast novel, in a Puritan ritual that celebrates the preternatural strength of her will. For that is Richardson's sublime concern: the self-reliant apotheosis of the Protestant will. What is tragedy in *Clarissa* becomes serious or moral comedy in *Pride and Prejudice* and *Emma*, and something just the other side of comedy in *Mansfield Park* and *Persuasion*.

Pride and Prejudice
Rereading *Pride and Prejudice* gives one a sense of Proustian ballet beautifully working itself through in the novel's formal centerpiece, the deferred but progressive mutual enlightenment of Elizabeth and Darcy in regard to the other's true nature. "Proper pride" is what they learn to recognize in one another; propriety scarcely needs definition in that phrase, but precisely what is the pride that allows amiability to flourish? Whatever it is in Darcy, to what extent is it an art of the will in Elizabeth Bennet? Consider the superb scene of Darcy's first and failed marriage proposal:

> While settling this point, she was suddenly roused by the sound of the doorbell, and her spirits were a little fluttered by the idea of its being Colonel Fitzwilliam himself, who had once before called late in the evening, and might now come to inquire particularly after her. But this idea was soon banished, and her spirits were very differently affected, when, to her utter amazement, she saw Mr. Darcy walk into the room. In an hurried manner he immediately began an inquiry after her health, imputing his visit to a wish of hearing that she were better. She answered him with cold civility. He sat down for a few moments, and then getting up, walked about the room. Elizabeth was surprised, but said not a word. After a silence of several minutes, he came towards her in an agitated manner, and thus began:
>
> "In vain have I struggled. It will not do. My feelings will not be repressed. You must allow me to tell you how ardently I admire and love you."
>
> Elizabeth's astonishment was beyond expression. She stared, coloured, doubted, and was silent. This he considered sufficient encouragement; and the avowal of all that he felt, and had long felt for her, immediately followed. He spoke well; but there were feelings besides those of the heart to be detailed, and he was not more eloquent on the subject of tenderness than of pride. His sense of her inferiority—of its being a degradation—of the family obstacles which judgment had always opposed to inclination, were dwelt on with a warmth which seemed due to the consequence he was wounding, but was very unlikely to recommend his suit.

In spite of her deeply-rooted dislike, she could not be insensible to the compliment of such a man's affection, and though her intentions did not vary for an instant, she was at first sorry for the pain he was to receive; till, roused to resentment by his subsequent language, she lost all compassion in anger. She tried, however, to compose herself to answer him with patience, when he should have done. He concluded with representing to her the strength of that attachment which, in spite of all his endeavours, he had found impossible to conquer; and with expressing his hope that it would now be rewarded by her acceptance of his hand. As he said this, she could easily see that he had no doubt of a favourable answer. He *spoke* of apprehension and anxiety, but his countenance expressed real security. Such a circumstance could only exasperate farther, and, when he ceased, the colour rose into her cheeks, and she said:

"In such cases as this, it is, I believe, the established mode to express a sense of obligation for the sentiments avowed, however unequally they may be returned. It is natural that obligation should be felt, and if I could *feel* gratitude, I would now thank you. But I cannot—I have never desired your good opinion, and you have certainly bestowed it most unwillingly. I am sorry to have occasioned pain to anyone. It has been most unconsciously done, however, and I hope will be of short duration. The feelings which, you tell me, have long prevented the acknowledgment of your regard, can have little difficulty in overcoming it after this explanation."

Mr. Darcy, who was leaning against the mantelpiece with his eyes fixed on her face, seemed to catch her words with no less resentment than surprise. His complexion became pale with anger, and the disturbance of his mind was visible in every feature. He was struggling for the appearance of composure, and would not open his lips till he believed himself to have attained it. The pause was to Elizabeth's feelings dreadful. At length, in a voice of forced calmness, he said:

"And this is all the reply which I am to have the honour of expecting? I might, perhaps, wish to be informed why, with so little *endeavour* at civility, I am thus rejected. But it is of small importance."

Stuart M. Tave believes that both Darcy and Elizabeth become so changed by one another that their "happiness is deserved by a process of mortification begun early and ended late," mortification here being the wounding of pride.

Tave's learning and insight are impressive, but I favor the judgment that Elizabeth and Darcy scarcely change, and learn rather that they complement each other's not wholly illegitimate pride. They come to see that their wills are naturally allied, since they have no differences upon the will. The will to what? Their will, Austen's, is neither the will to live nor the will to power. They wish to be esteemed precisely where they estimate value to be high, and neither can afford to make a fundamental error, which is both the anxiety and the comedy of the first proposal scene. Why after all does Darcy allow himself to be eloquent on the subject of his pride, to the extraordinary extent of conveying "with a warmth" what Austen grimly names as "his sense of her inferiority"?

As readers, we have learned already that Elizabeth is inferior to no one, whoever he is. Indeed, I sense as the novel closes (though nearly all Austen critics, and doubtless Austen herself, would disagree with me) that Darcy is her inferior, amiable and properly prideful as he is. I do not mean by this that Elizabeth is a clearer representation of Austenian values than Darcy ever could be; that is made finely obvious by Austen, and her critics have developed her ironic apprehension, which is that Elizabeth incarnates the standard of measurement in her cosmos. There is also a transcendent strength to Elizabeth's will that raises her above that cosmos, in a mode that returns us to Clarissa Harlowe's transcendence of her society, of Lovelace, and even of everything in herself that is not the will to a self esteem that has also made an accurate estimate of every other will to pride it ever has encountered.

I am suggesting that Ralph Waldo Emerson (who to me is sacred) was mistaken when he rejected Austen as a "sterile" upholder of social conformities and social ironies, as an author who could not celebrate the soul's freedom from societal conventions. Austen's ultimate irony is that Elizabeth Bennet is inwardly so free that convention performs for her the ideal function it cannot perform for us: it liberates her will without tending to stifle her high individuality. But we ought to be wary of even the most distinguished of Austen's moral celebrants, Lionel Trilling, who in effect defended her against Emerson by seeing *Pride and Prejudice* as a triumph "of morality as style." If Emerson wanted to see a touch more Margaret Fuller in Elizabeth Bennet (sublimely ghastly notion!), Trilling wanted to forget the Emersonian law of Compensation, which is that nothing is got for nothing:

> The relation of Elizabeth Bennet to Darcy is real, is intense, but it expresses itself as a conflict and reconciliation of styles: a formal rhetoric, traditional and rigorous, must find a way to accomodate a female vivacity, which in turn must recognize the principled demands of the strict male syntax. The high moral import of the novel lies in the fact that the union of styles is accomplished without injury to either lover.

Yes and no, I would say. Yes, because the wills of both lovers work by similar dialectics, but also no, because Elizabeth's will is more intense and purer, and inevitably must be dimmed by her dwindling into a wife, even though Darcy may well be the best man that society could offer to her. Her pride has playfulness in it, a touch even of the Quixotic. Uncannily, she is both her father's daughter and Samuel Richardson's daughter as well. Her wit is Mr. Bennet's, refined and elaborated, but her will, and her pride in her will, returns us to Clarissa's Puritan passion to maintain the power of the self to confer esteem, and to accept esteem only in response to its bestowal.

Mansfield Park

John Locke argues against personifying the will: persons can be free, but not the will, since the will cannot be constrained, except externally. While one sleeps, if someone moved one into another room and locked the door, and there one found a friend one wished to see, still one could not say that one was free thus to see whom one wished. And yet Locke implies that the process of association does work as though the will were internally constrained. Association, in Locke's sense, is a blind substitution for reasoning, yet is within a reasoning process, though also imbued with affect. The mind, in association, is carried unwillingly from one thought to another, by accident as it were. Each thought appears, and carries along with it a crowd of unwanted guests, inhabitants of a room where the thought would rather be alone. Association, in this view, is what the will most needs to be defended against.

Fanny Price, in *Mansfield Park*, might be considered a co-descendant, together with Locke's association-menaced will, of the English Protestant emphasis upon the will's autonomy. Fanny, another precursor of the Virginia Woolf of *A Room of One's Own*, was shrewdly described by Lionel Trilling as "overtly virtuous and consciously virtuous," and therefore almost impossible to like, though Trilling (like Austen) liked Fanny very much. C.S. Lewis, though an orthodox moralist, thought Fanny insipid: "But into Fanny, Jane Austen, to counterbalance her apparent insignificance, has put really nothing except rectitude of mind; neither passion, nor physical courage, nor wit, nor resource." Nothing, I would say, except the Protestant will, resisting the powers of association and asserting its very own persistence, its own sincere intensity, and its own isolate sanctions. Trilling secularized these as "the sanctions of principle" and saw *Mansfield Park* as a novel that "discovers in principle the path to the wholeness of the self which is peace." That is movingly said, but secularization, in literature, is always a failed trope, since the distinction between sacred and secular is not actually a literary but rather a societal or political distinction. *Mansfield Park* is not less Protestant than *Paradise Lost*, even though Austen, as a writer, was as much a sect of one as John Milton was.

Fanny Price, like the Lockean will, fights against accident, against the crowding out of life by associations that are pragmatically insincere not because they are random, but because they are irrelevant, since whatever is not the will's own is irrelevant to it. If Fanny herself is an irony it is as Austen's allegory of her own defense against influences, human and literary, whether in her family circle or in the literary family of Fanny Burney, Fielding, and Richardson. Stuart Tave shrewdly remarks that: "*Mansfield Park* is a novel in which many characters are engaged in trying to establish influence over the minds and lives of others, often in a contest or struggle for control." Fanny, as a will struggling only to be itself, becomes at last the spiritual center of *Mansfield Park* precisely because she has never sought power over any other will. It is the lesson of the Protestant will, whether in Locke or Austen, Richardson or George Eliot, that the refusal to seek power over other wills is what opens the inward eye of vision. Such a lesson, which we seek in Wordsworth and in Ruskin, is offered more subtly (though less sublimely) by Austen. Fanny, Austen's truest surrogate, has a vision of what Mansfield Park is and ought to be, which means a vision also of what Sir Thomas Bertram is or ought to be. Her vision is necessarily moral, but could as truly be called spiritual, or even aesthetic.

Perhaps that is why Fanny is not only redeemed but can redeem others. The quietest and most mundane of visionaries, she remains also one of the firmest: her dedication is to the future of Mansfield Park as the idea of order it once seemed to her. Jane Austen may not be a Romantic in the high Shelleyan mode, but Fanny Price has profound affinities with Wordsworth, so that it is no accident that *Mansfield Park* is exactly contemporary with *The Excursion*. Wordsworthian continuity, the strength that carries the past alive into the present, is the program of renovation that Fanny's pure will brings to Mansfield Park, and it is a program more Romantic than Augustan, so that Fanny's will begins to shade into the Wordsworthian account of the imagination. Fanny's exile to Portsmouth is so painful to her not for reasons turning upon social distinctions, but for causes related to the quiet that Wordsworth located in the bliss of solitude, or Virginia Woolf in a room of one's own:

> Such was the home which was to put Mansfield out of her head, and teach her to think of her cousin Edmund with moderated feelings. On the contrary, she could think of nothing but Mansfield, its beloved inmates, its happy ways. Everything where she now was was in full contrast to it. The elegance, propriety, regularity, harmony, and perhaps, above all, the peace and tranquillity of Mansfield, were brought to her remembrance every hour of the day, by the prevalence of everything opposite to them *here*.

The living in incessant noise was, to a frame and temper delicate and nervous like Fanny's, an evil which no super-added elegance or harmony could have entirely atoned for. It was the greatest misery of all. At Mansfield, no sounds of contention, no raised voice, no abrupt bursts, no tread of violence, was ever heard; all proceeded in a regular course of cheerful orderliness; everybody had their due importance; everybody's feelings were consulted. If tenderness could be ever supposed wanting, good sense and good breeding supplied its place; and as to the little irritations, sometimes introduced by Aunt Norris, they were short, they were trifling, they were as a drop of water to the ocean, compared with the ceaseless tumult of her present abode. Here, everybody was noisy, every voice was loud (excepting, perhaps, her mother's, which resembled the soft monotony of Lady Bertram's, only worn into fretfulness). Whatever was wanted was halloo'd for, and the servants halloo'd out their excuses from the kitchen. The doors were in constant banging, the stairs were never at rest, nothing was done without a clatter, nobody sat still, and nobody could command attention when they spoke.

In a review of the two houses, as they appeared to her before the end of a week, Fanny was tempted to apply to them Dr. Johnson's celebrated judgment as to matrimony and celibacy, and say, that though Mansfield Park might have some pains, Portsmouth could have no pleasures.

The citation of Dr. Johnson's aphorism, though placed here with superb wit, transcends irony. Austen rather seeks to confirm, however implicitly, Johnson's powerful warning, in *The Rambler*, number 4, against the overwhelming realism of Fielding and Smollett (though their popular prevalence is merely hinted):

But if the power of example is so great, as to take possession of the memory by a kind of violence, and produce effects almost without the intervention of the will, care ought to be taken, that, when the choice is unrestrained, the best examples only should be exhibited; and that which is likely to operate so strongly, should not be mischievous or uncertain in its effects.

Fanny Price, rather more than Jane Austen perhaps, really does favor a Johnsonian aesthetic, in life as in literature. Portsmouth belongs to representation as practiced by Smollett, belongs to the cosmos of Roderick Random.

Fanny, in willing to get back to Mansfield Park, and to get Mansfield Park back to itself, is willing herself also to renovate the world of her creator, the vision of Jane Austen that is *Mansfield Park*.

Emma

Sir Walter Scott, reviewing *Emma* in 1815, rather strangely compared Jane Austen to the masters of the Flemish school of painting, presumably because of her precision in representing her characters. The strangeness results from Scott's not seeing how English Austen was, though the Scot's perspective may have entered into his estimate. To me, as an American critic, *Emma* seems the most English of English novels, and beyond question one of the very best. More than *Pride and Prejudice*, it is Austen's masterpiece, the largest triumph of her vigorous art. Her least accurate prophecy as to the fate of her fictions concerned *Emma*, whose heroine, she thought, "no one but myself will much like."

Aside from much else, Emma is immensely likable, because she is so extraordinarily imaginative, dangerous and misguided as her imagination frequently must appear to others and finally to herself. On the scale of being, Emma constitutes an answer to the immemorial questions of the Sublime: More? Equal to? Or less than? Like Clarissa Harlowe before her, and the strongest heroines of George Eliot and Henry James after her, Emma Woodhouse has a heroic will, and like them she risks identifying her will with her imagination. Socially considered, such identification is catastrophic, since the Protestant will has a tendency to bestow a ranking upon other selves, and such ranking may turn out to be a personal phantasmagoria. G. Armour Craig rather finely remarked that: "society in *Emma* is not a ladder. It is a web of imputations that link feelings and conduct." Yet Emma herself, expansionist rather than reductionist in temperament, imputes more fiercely and freely than the web can sustain, and she threatens always, until she is enlightened, to dissolve the societal links, in and for others, that might allow some stability between feelings and conduct.

Armour Craig usefully added that: "*Emma* does not justify its heroine nor does it deride her." Rather it treats her with ironic love (not loving irony). Emma Woodhouse is dear to Jane Austen, because her errors are profoundly imaginative, and rise from the will's passion for autonomy of vision. The splendid Jane Fairfax is easier to admire, but I cannot agree with Wayne Booth's awarding the honors to her over Emma, though I admire the subtle balance of his formulation:

> Jane is superior to Emma in most respects except the stroke of
> good fortune that made Emma the heroine of the book. In matters
> of taste and ability, of head and heart, she is Emma's superior.

Taste, ability, head, and heart are a formidable fourfold; the imagination and the will, working together, are an even more formidable twofold, and clearly may have their energies diverted to error and to mischief. Jane Fairfax is certainly more *amiable* even than Emma Woodhouse, but she is considerably less interesting. It is Emma who is meant to charm us, and who does charm us. Austen is not writing a tragedy of the will, like *Paradise Lost*, but a great comedy of the will, and her heroine must incarnate the full potential of the will, however misused for a time. Having rather too much her own way is certainly one of Emma's powers, and she does have a disposition to think a little too well of herself. When Austen says that these were "the real evils indeed of Emma's situation," we read "evils" as lightly as the author will let us, which is lightly enough.

Can we account for the qualities in Emma Woodhouse that make her worthy of comparison with George Eliot's Gwendolen Harleth and Henry James's Isabel Archer? The pure comedy of her context seems world enough for her; she evidently is not the heiress of all the ages. We are persuaded, by Austen's superb craft, that marriage to Mr. Knightley will more than suffice to fulfill totally the now perfectly amiable Emma. Or are we? It is James's genius to suggest that while Osmond's "beautiful mind" was a prison of the spirit for Isabel, no proper husband could exist anyway, since neither Touchett nor Goodwood is exactly a true match for her. Do we, presumably against Austen's promptings, not find Mr. Knightley something of a confinement also, benign and wise though he be?

I suspect that the heroine of the Protestant will, from Richardson's Clarissa Harlowe through to Virginia Woolf's Clarissa Dalloway, can never find fit match because wills do not marry. The allegory or tragic irony of this dilemma is written large in Clarissa, since Lovelace, in strength of will and splendor of being, actually would have been the true husband for Clarissa (as he well knows) had he not been a moral squalor. His death-cry ("Let this expiate!") expiates nothing, and helps establish the long tradition of the Anglo-American novel in which the heroines of the will are fated to suffer either overt calamities or else happy unions with such good if unexciting men as Mr. Knightley or Will Ladislaw in *Middlemarch*. When George Eliot is reduced to having the fascinating Gwendolen Harleth fall hopelessly in love with the prince of prigs, Daniel Deronda, we sigh and resign ourselves to the sorrows of fictive overdetermination. Lovelace or Daniel Deronda? I myself do not know a high-spirited woman who would not prefer the first, though not for a husband!

Emma is replete with grand comic epiphanies, of which my favorite comes in volume 3, chapter 11, when Emma receives the grave shock of Harriet's disclosure that Mr. Knightley is the object of Harriet's hopeful affections:

When Harriet had closed her evidence, she appealed to her dear Miss Woodhouse, to say whether she had not good ground for hope.

"I never should have presumed to think of it at first," said she, "but for you. You told me to observe him carefully, and let his behavior be the rule of mine—and so I have. But now I seem to feel that I may deserve him; and that if he does choose me, it will not be any thing so very wonderful."

The bitter feelings occasioned by this speech, the many bitter feelings, made the utmost exertion necessary on Emma's side to enable her to say in reply,

"Harriet, I will only venture to declare, that Mr. Knightley is the last man in the world, who would intentionally give any woman the idea of his feeling for her more than he really does."

Harriet seemed ready to worship her friend for a sentence so satisfactory; and Emma was only saved from raptures and fondness, which at the moment would have been dreadful penance, by the sound of her father's footsteps. He was coming through the hall. Harriet was too much agitated to encounter him. "She could not compose herself—Mr. Woodhouse would be alarmed—she had better go;"—with most ready encouragement from her friend, therefore, she passed off through another door—and the moment she was gone, this was the spontaneous burst of Emma's feelings: "Oh God! that I had never seen her!"

The rest of the day, the following night, were hardly enough for her thoughts.—She was bewildered amidst the confusion of all that had rushed on her within the last few hours. Every moment had brought a fresh surprise; and every surprise must be matter of humiliation to her.—How to understand it all! How to understand the deceptions she had been thus practising on herself, and living under!—The blunders, the blindness of her own head and heart!—she sat still, she walked about, she tried her own room, she tried the shrubbery—in every place, every posture, she perceived that she had acted most weakly; that she had been imposed on by others in a most mortifying degree; that she had been imposing on herself in a degree yet more mortifying; that she was wretched, and should probably find this day but the beginning of wretchedness.

The acute aesthetic pleasure of this turns on the counterpoint between Emma's spontaneous cry: "Oh God! that I had never seen her!" and the exquisite comic touch of: "She sat still, she walked about, she tried her own room, she tried the shrubbery—in every place, every posture, she perceived that she had acted most weakly." The acute humiliation of the will could not be better conveyed than by "she tried the shrubbery" and "every posture." Endlessly imaginative, Emma must now be compelled to endure the mortification of reducing herself to the postures and places of those driven into corners by the collapse of visions that have been exposed as delusions. Jane Austen, who seems to have identified herself with Emma, wisely chose to make this moment of ironic reversal a temporary purgatory, rather than an infernal discomfiture.

Persuasion

"Persuasion" is a word derived from the Latin for "advising" or "urging," for recommending that it is good to perform or not perform a particular action. The word goes back to a root meaning "sweet" or "pleasant," so that the good of performance or nonperformance has a tang of taste rather than of moral judgment about it. Jane Austen chose it as the title for her last completed novel. As a title, it recalls *Sense and Sensibility* or *Pride and Prejudice* rather than *Emma* or *Mansfield Park*. We are given not the name of a person or house and estate, but of an abstraction, a single one in this case. The title's primary reference is to the persuasion of its heroine, Anne Elliot, at the age of nineteen, by her godmother, Lady Russell, not to marry Captain Frederick Wentworth, a young naval officer. This was, as it turns out, very bad advice, and, after eight years, it is mended by Anne and Captain Wentworth. As with all of Austen's ironic comedies, matters end happily for the heroine. And yet each time I finish a rereading of this perfect novel, I feel very sad.

This does not appear to be my personal vagary; when I ask my friends and students about their experience of the book, they frequently mention a sadness which they also associate with *Persuasion*, more even than with *Mansfield Park*. Anne Elliot, a quietly eloquent being, is a self-reliant character, in no way forlorn, and her sense of self never falters. It is not *her* sadness we feel as we conclude the book: it is the novel's somberness that impresses us. The sadness enriches what I would call the novel's canonical persuasiveness, its way of showing us its extraordinary aesthetic distinction.

Persuasion is among novels what Anne Elliot is among novelistic characters—a strong but subdued outrider. The book and the character are not colorful or vivacious; Elizabeth Bennett of *Pride and Prejudice* and Emma Woodhouse of *Emma* have a verve to them that initially seems lacking in Anne Elliot, which may be what Austen meant when she said that Anne was "almost too good for me." Anne is really almost too subtle for us, though not for Wentworth, who has something of an occult wavelength to her. Juliet

McMaster notes "the kind of oblique communication that constantly goes on between Anne Elliot and Captain Wentworth, where, though they seldom speak to each other, each constantly understands the full import of the other's speech better than their interlocutors do."

That kind of communication in *Persuasion* depends upon deep "affection," a word that Austen values over "love." "Affection" between woman and man, in Austen, is the more profound and lasting emotion. I think it is not too much to say that Anne Elliot, though subdued, is the creation for whom Austen herself must have felt the most affection, because she lavished her own gifts upon Anne. Henry James insisted that the novelist must be a sensibility upon which absolutely nothing is lost; by that test (clearly a limited one) only Austen, George Eliot, and James himself, among all those writing in English, would join Stendhal, Flaubert, and Tolstoy in a rather restricted pantheon. Anne Elliot may well be the one character in all of prose fiction upon whom nothing is lost, though she is in no danger of turning into a novelist. The most accurate estimate of Anne Elliot that I have seen is by Stuart Tave:

> Nobody hears Anne, nobody sees her, but it is she who is ever at the center. It is through her ears, eyes, and mind that we are made to care for what is happening. If nobody is much aware of her, she is very much aware of everyone else and she perceives what is happening to them when they are ignorant of themselves . . . she reads Wentworth's mind, with the coming troubles he is causing for others and himself, before those consequences bring the information to him.

The aesthetic dangers attendant upon such a paragon are palpable: how does a novelist make such a character persuasive? Poldy, in Joyce's *Ulysses*, is overwhelmingly persuasive because he is so complete a person, which was the largest of Joyce's intentions. Austen's ironic mode does not sanction the representation of completeness: we do not accompany her characters to the bedroom, the kitchen, the privy. What Austen parodies in *Sense and Sensibility* she raises to an apotheosis in *Persuasion*: the sublimity of a particular, inwardly isolated sensibility. Anne Elliot is hardly the only figure in Austen who has an understanding heart. Her difference is in her almost preternatural acuteness of perception of others and of the self, which are surely the qualities that most distinguish Austen as a novelist. Anne Elliot is to Austen's work what Rosalind of *As You Like It* is to Shakespeare's: the character who almost reaches the mastery of perspective that can be available only to the novelist or playwright, lest all dramatic quality be lost from the novel or play. C.L. Barber memorably emphasized this limitation:

The dramatist tends to show us one thing at a time, and to realize that one thing, in its moment, to the full; his characters go to extremes, comical as well as serious; and no character, not even a Rosalind, is in a position to see all around the play and so be completely poised, for if this were so the play would cease to be dramatic.

I like to turn Barber's point in the other direction: more even than Hamlet or Falstaff, or than Elizabeth Bennet, or than Fanny Price in *Mansfield Park*, Rosalind and Anne Elliot are almost completely poised, nearly able to see all around the play and the novel. Their poise cannot transcend perspectivizing completely, but Rosalind's wit and Anne's sensibility, both balanced and free of either excessive aggressivity or defensiveness, enable them to share more of their creators' poise than we ever come to do.

Austen never loses dramatic intensity; we share Anne's anxiety concerning Wentworth's renewed intentions until the novel's conclusion. But we rely upon Anne as we should rely upon Rosalind; critics would see the rancidity of Touchstone as clearly as they see the vanity of Jacques if they placed more confidence in Rosalind's reactions to everyone else in the play, as well as to herself. Anne Elliot's reactions have the same winning authority; we must try to give the weight to her words that is not extended by the other persons in the novel, except for Wentworth.

Stuart Tave's point, like Barber's, is accurate even when turned in the other direction; Austen's irony is very Shakespearean. Even the reader must fall into the initial error of undervaluing Anne Elliot. The wit of Elizabeth Bennet or of Rosalind is easier to appreciate than Anne Elliot's accurate sensibility. The secret of her character combines Austenian irony with a Wordsworthian sense of deferred hope. Austen has a good measure of Shakespeare's unmatched ability to give us persons, both major and minor, who are each utterly consistent in her or his separate mode of speech, and yet completely different from one another. Anne Elliot is the last of Austen's heroines of what I think we must call the Protestant will, but in her the will is modified, perhaps perfected, by its descendant, the Romantic sympathetic imagination, of which Wordsworth, as we have seen, was the prophet. That is perhaps what helps to make Anne so complex and sensitive a character.

Jane Austen's earlier heroines, of whom Elizabeth Bennet is the exemplar, manifested the Protestant will as direct descendants of Samuel Richardson's Clarissa Harlowe, with Dr. Samuel Johnson hovering nearby as moral authority. Marxist criticism inevitably views the Protestant will, even in its literary manifestations, as a mercantile matter, and it has become fashionable to talk about the socioeconomic realities that Jane Austen excludes, such as the West Indian slavery that is part of the ultimate basis for the financial security most of her characters enjoy. But all achieved literary works are founded upon exclusions, and no one has demonstrated that increased consciousness of the relation between culture and imperialism is of the slightest benefit whatsoever in learning to read *Mansfield Park*. *Persuasion* ends with a tribute to the British navy, in which Wentworth has an honored place. Doubtless Wentworth at sea, ordering the latest batch of disciplinary floggings, is not as pleasant as Wentworth on land, gently appreciating the joys of affection with Anne Elliot. But once again, Austen's is a great art founded upon exclusions, and the sordid realities of British sea power are no more relevant to *Persuasion* than West Indian bondage is to *Mansfield Park*. Austen was, however, immensely interested in the pragmatic and secular consequences of the Protestant will, and they seem to me a crucial element in helping us appreciate the heroines of her novels.

Austen's Shakespearean inwardness, culminating in Anne Elliot, revises the moral intensities of Clarissa Harlowe's secularized Protestant martyrdom, her slow dying after being raped by Lovelace. What removes Clarissa's will to live is her stronger will to maintain the integrity of her being. To yield to the repentant Lovelace by marrying him would compromise the essence of her being, the exaltation of her violated will. What is tragedy in Clarissa is converted by Austen into ironic comedy, but the will's drive to maintain itself scarcely alters in this conversion. In *Persuasion* the emphasis is on a willed exchange of esteems, where both the woman and the man estimate the value of the other to be high. Obviously outward considerations of wealth, property, and social standing are crucial elements here, but so are the inward considerations of common sense, amiability, culture, wit, and affection. In a way (it pains me to say this, as I am a fierce Emersonian) Ralph Waldo Emerson anticipated the current Marxist critique of Austen when he denounced her as a mere conformist who would not allow her heroines to achieve the soul's true freedom from societal conventions. But that was to mistake Jane Austen, who understood that the function of convention was to liberate the will, even if convention's tendency was to stifle individuality, without which the will was inconsequential.

Austen's major heroines—Elizabeth, Emma, Fanny, and Anne—possess such inward freedom that their individualities cannot be repressed. Austen's art as a novelist is not to worry much about the socioeconomic genesis of that inner freedom, though the anxiety level does rise in *Mansfield Park* and *Persuasion*. In Austen, irony becomes the instrument for invention, which Dr. Johnson defined as the essence of poetry. A conception of inward freedom that centers upon a refusal to accept esteem except from one upon whom one has conferred esteem, is a conception of the highest degree of irony. The supreme comic scene in all of Austen must be Elizabeth's rejection of Darcy's first marriage proposal, where the ironies of the dialectic of will and esteem become very nearly outrageous. That high comedy, which continued in *Emma*, is somewhat chastened in *Mansfield Park*, and then becomes something else, unmistakable but difficult to name, in *Persuasion*, where Austen has become so conscious a master that she seems to have changed the nature of willing, as though it, too, could be persuaded to become a rarer, more disinterested act of the self.

No one has suggested that Jane Austen becomes a High Romantic in *Persuasion*; her poet remained William Cowper, not Wordsworth, and her favorite prose writer was always Dr. Johnson. But her severe distrust of imagination and of "romantic love," so prevalent in the earlier novels, is not a factor in *Persuasion*. Anne and Wentworth maintain their affection for each other throughout eight years of hopeless separation, and each has the power of imagination to conceive of a triumphant reconciliation. This is the material for a romance, not for an ironical novel. The ironies of *Persuasion* are frequently pungent, but they are almost never directed at Anne Elliot and only rarely at Captain Wentworth. There is a difficult relation between Austen's repression of her characteristic irony about her protagonists and a certain previously unheard plangency that hovers throughout *Persuasion*. Despite Anne's faith in herself she is very vulnerable to the anxiety, which she never allows herself to express, of an unlived life, in which the potential loss transcends yet includes sexual unfulfillment. I can recall only one critic, the Australian Ann Molan, who emphasizes what Austen strongly implies, that "Anne ... is a passionate woman. And against her will, her heart keeps asserting its demand for fulfillment." Since Anne had refused Wentworth her esteem eight years before, she feels a necessity to withhold her will, and thus becomes the first Austen heroine whose will and imagination are antithetical.

Although Austen's overt affinities remained with the Aristocratic Age, her authenticity as a writer impelled her, in *Persuasion*, a long way toward the burgeoning Democratic Age, or Romanticism, as we used to call it. There is no civil war within Anne Elliot's psyche, or within Austen's; but there is the emergent sadness of a schism in the self, with memory taking the side of imagination in an alliance against the will. The almost Wordsworthian power of memory in both Anne and Wentworth has been noted by Gene Ruoff. Since Austen was anything but an accidental novelist, we might ask why she chose to found *Persuasion* upon a mutual nostalgia. After all, the rejected Wentworth is even less inclined to will a renewed affection than Anne is, and yet the fusion of memory and imagination triumphs over his will also. Was this a relaxation of the will in Jane Austen herself? Since she returns to her earlier mode in *Sanditon*, her unfinished novel begun after *Persuasion* was completed, it may be that the story of Anne Elliot was an excursion or indulgence for the novelist. The parallels between Wordsworth and *Persuasion* are limited but real. High Romantic novels in England, whether of the Byronic kind like *Jane Eyre* and *Wuthering Heights* or of a Wordsworthian sort like *Adam Bede*, are a distinctly later development. The ethos of the Austen heroine does not change in *Persuasion*, but she is certainly a more problematic being, tinged with a new sadness concerning life's limits. It may be that the elegant pathos *Persuasion* sometimes courts has a connection to Jane Austen's own ill health, her intimations of her early death.

Stuart Tave, comparing Wordsworth and Austen, shrewdly noted that both were "poets of marriage" and both also possessed "a sense of duty understood and deeply felt by those who see the integrity and peace of their own lives as essentially bound to the lives of others and see the lives of all in a more than merely social order." Expanding Tave's insight, Susan Morgan pointed to the particular affinity between Austen's *Emma* and Wordsworth's great "Ode: Intimations of Immortality from Recollections of Earliest Childhood." The growth of the individual consciousness, involving both gain and loss for Wordsworth but only gain for Austen, is the shared subject. Emma's consciousness certainly does develop, and she undergoes a quasi-Wordsworthian transformation from the pleasures of near solipsism to the more difficult pleasures of sympathy for others. Anne Elliot, far more mature from the beginning, scarcely needs to grow in consciousness. Her long-lamented rejection of Wentworth insulates her against the destructiveness of hope, which we have seen to be the frightening emphasis of the earlier Wordsworth, particularly in the story of poor Margaret. Instead of hope, there is a complex of emotions, expressed by Austen with her customary skill:

> How eloquent could Anne Elliot have been,—how eloquent, at least, were her wishes on the side of early warm attachment, and a cheerful confidence in futurity, against that over-anxious caution which seems to insult exertion and distrust Providence!—She had been forced into prudence in her youth, she learned romance as she grew older—the natural sequel of an unnatural beginning.

Here learning romance is wholly retrospective; Anne no longer regards it as being available to her. And indeed Wentworth returns, still resentful after eight years, and reflects that Anne's power with him is gone forever. The qualities of decision and confidence that make him a superb naval commander are precisely what he condemns her for lacking. With almost too meticulous a craft, Austen traces his gradual retreat from this position, as the power of memory increases its dominance over him and as he learns that his jilted sense of her as being unable to act is quite mistaken. It is a beautiful irony that he needs to undergo a process of self-persuasion while Anne waits, without even knowing that she is waiting or that there is anything that could rekindle her hope. The comedy of this is gently sad, as the reader waits also, reflecting upon how large a part contingency plays in the matter.

While the pre-Socratics and Freud agree that there are no accidents, Austen thinks differently. Character is fate for her also, but fate, once activated, tends to evade character in so overdetermined a social context as Austen's world. In rereading *Persuasion*, though I remember the happy conclusion, I nevertheless feel anxiety as Wentworth and Anne circle away from each other in spite of themselves. The reader is not totally persuaded of a satisfactory interview until Anne reads Wentworth's quite agonized letter to her:

> "I can listen no longer in silence. I must speak to you by such means as are within my reach. You pierce my soul. I am half agony, half hope. Tell me not that I am too late, that such precious feelings are gone for ever. I offer myself to you again with a heart more your own, than when you almost broke it eight years and a half ago. Dare not say that man forgets sooner than woman, that his love has an earlier death. I have loved none but you. Unjust I may have been, weak and resentful I have been, but never inconstant. You alone have brought me to Bath. For you alone I think and plan.—Have you not seen this? Can you fail to have understood my wishes?—I had not waited even these ten days, could I have read your feelings, as I think you must have penetrated mine. I can hardly write. I am every instant hearing something which overpowers me. You sink your voice, but I can distinguish the tones of that voice, when they would be lost on others.—Too good, too excellent creature! You do us justice indeed. You do believe that there is true attachment and constancy among men. Believe it to be most fervent, most undeviating in
>
> F.W.
>
> "I must go, uncertain of my fate; but I shall return hither, or follow your party, as soon as possible. A word, a look will be enough to decide whether I enter your father's house this evening or never."

I cannot imagine such a letter in *Pride and Prejudice*, or even in *Emma* or *Mansfield Park*. The perceptive reader might have realized how passionate Anne was, almost from the start of the novel, but until this there was no indication of equal passion in Wentworth. His letter, as befits a naval commander, is badly written and not exactly Austenian, but it is all the more effective thereby. We come to realize that we have believed in him until now only because Anne's love for him provokes our interest. Austen wisely has declined to make him interesting enough on his own. Yet part of the book's effect is to persuade the reader of the reader's own powers of discernment and self-persuasion; Anne Elliot is almost too good for the reader, as she is for Austen herself, but the attentive reader gains the confidence to perceive Anne as she should be perceived. The subtlest element in this subtlest of novels is the call upon the reader's own power of memory to match the persistence and intensity of the yearning that Anne Elliot is too stoical to express directly.

The yearning hovers throughout the book, coloring Anne's perceptions and our own. Our sense of Anne's existence becomes identified with our own consciousness of lost love, however fictive or idealized that may be. There is an improbability in the successful renewal of a relationship devastated eight years before which ought to work against the texture of this most "realistic" of Austen's novels, but she is very careful to see that it does not. Like the author, the reader becomes persuaded to wish for Anne what she still wishes for herself. Ann Molan has the fine observation that Austen "is most satisfied with Anne when Anne is most dissatisfied with herself." The reader is carried along with Austen, and gradually Anne is also persuaded and catches up with the reader, allowing her yearning a fuller expression.

Dr. Johnson, in *The Rambler* 29, on "The folly of anticipating misfortunes," warned against anxious expectations of any kind, whether fearful or hopeful:

> because the objects both of fear and hope are yet uncertain, so we ought not to trust the representations of one more than the other, because they are both equally fallacious; as hope enlarges happiness, fear aggravates calamity. It is generally allowed, that no man ever found the happiness of possession proportionate to that expectation which incited his desire, and invigorated his pursuit; nor has any man found the evils of life so formidable in reality, as they were described to him by his own imagination.

This is one of a series of Johnsonian pronouncements against the dangerous prevalence of the imagination, some of which his disciple Austen had certainly read. If you excluded such representations, on the great critic's advice, then Wordsworth could not have written at all, and Austen could not have written *Persuasion*. Yet it was a very strange book for her to write, this master of the highest art of exclusion that we have known in the Western novel. Any novel by Jane Austen could be called an achieved ellipsis, with everything omitted that could disturb her ironic though happy conclusions. *Persuasion* remains the least popular of her four canonical novels because it is the strangest, but all her work is increasingly strange as we approach the end of the Democratic Age that her contemporary Wordsworth did so much to inaugurate in literature. Poised as she is at the final border of the Aristocratic Age, she shares with Wordsworth an art dependent upon a split between a waning Protestant will and a newly active sympathetic imagination, with memory assigned the labor of healing the divide. If the argument of my book has any validity, Austen will survive even the bad days ahead of us, because the strangeness of originality and of an individual vision are our lasting needs, which only literature can gratify in the Theocratic Age that slouches toward us.

MARY POOVEY

Ideological Contradictions and the Consolations of Form: The Case of Jane Austen

Reading Jane Austen's novels in the context of the works of Mary Wollstonecraft and Mary Shelley reminds us that Austen also lived through and wrote about the crisis of values that dominated late eighteenth- and early nineteenth-century English society. Austen's perspective on this crisis was, of course, markedly different from those of the other two women, for whereas both the lower middle-class Wollstonecraft and the emigrée Shelley witnessed the radicals' challenge to propriety from outside its eminent domain, Austen spent her entire life in the very heart of propriety. Austen never traveled as widely as either Wollstonecraft or Shelley, she never flamboyantly defied propriety, and she never wrote to support herself or anyone else. Perhaps partly as a consequence of her limited experience, Austen did not choose to write about politics, nature, or metaphysics, and she assiduously avoided the highly imaginative, melodramatic incidents that so fascinated her contemporaries.

Yet for all the obvious differences between her life and aesthetic interests and theirs, Jane Austen did concern herself with many of the same issues as Wollstonecraft and Shelley—with the process of a young girl's maturation, for example, and, more important, with the complex relationship between a woman's desires and the imperatives of propriety. Considering Austen's novels from the perspective of these issues and in terms of the debate already set

From *The Proper Lady and the Woman Writer: Ideology as Style in the Works of Mary Wollstonecraft, Mary Shelley, and Jane Austen*, pp. 172–207, 265–267. © 1984 by the University of Chicago.

21

out in the works of Wollstonecraft and Shelley enables us to recognize what the challenge to traditional values looked like from the inside and how an artistic style could constitute part of a defense against this challenge. As we will see, Austen's class position placed her firmly in the middle of the crisis of values we have been examining. As with Wollstonecraft and Shelley, Austen's gender and her decision to write professionally focused the contradictions inherent in this crisis. What is new is that Austen's aesthetic choices—her style and her subject matter—can be seen as "solutions" to some of the problems that neither Wollstonecraft nor Shelley could solve. My analysis of Austen's work therefore comes last not because this order is faithful to chronology but because her novels culminate a sequence of stages of female insight and artistic achievement. We can never fully "explain" genius, but in considering the ways in which Austen both completes Wollstonecraft's analysis of female inhibition and perfects Shelley's attempt to make propriety accommodate female desire, we can better understand her accomplishment and some of the functions her artistic strategies served.[1]

Our access to Jane Austen's personal attitudes to historical events and to propriety will always be blocked by her sister Cassandra, who destroyed many of Austen's letters and censored numerous others; moreover, the letters that did survive at times convey contradictory opinions and, what is perhaps even more confusing, almost always employ a decidedly ambiguous tone.[2] When an individual work by Wollstonecraft or Shelley seems morally or stylistically ambiguous, surviving letters or journals help provide a background for interpretation; and the psychological or aesthetic complexities that appear in their fiction and nonfiction alike can be clarified in the same way. But the incompleteness and opacity of Austen's personal record often compound the notorious instability of her novelistic irony, thus leading us further into confusing (if delightful) ambiguity. When Austen tells the obsequious James Stanier Clarke, for example, that "I think I may boast myself to be, with all possible vanity, the most unlearned and uninformed female who ever dared to be an authoress" (*JAL*, 2:443; 11 December 1815), we feel certain that she pretends to diminish herself at her silly correspondent's expense. But when she tells her nephew that she cannot manage his "strong, manly, spirited Sketches" upon the canvas of her art—"the little bit (two inches wide) of Ivory on which I work with so fine a Brush, as produces little effect after much labour" (*JAL*, 2:468–69; 16 December 1816)—it is difficult to determine exactly how much of her self depreciation is genuine, how much is simply encouragement for the young writer, and how much is the mock vanity of a self-confident miniaturist. The Austen legacy has been further complicated, of course, by the officious concern of her relatives. In addition to Cassandra's excessive concern for propriety, the efforts of her brother and nephews to beatify "Aunt Jane" for Victorian readers has also blurred our hindsight and has no doubt generated, in some cases, as much overcompensation as accurate evaluation.

Lady Susan

In the absence of extensive biographical documentation, then, Austen's juvenilia provide a logical point of departure. Indeed, her most extended early work, *Lady Susan* (composed c. 1793–94),[3] places her precisely "between" Wollstonecraft and Shelley and broadly establishes the aesthetic and ethical issues that were to occupy her for the remainder of her career. *Lady Susan* is an epistolary satire that takes to task both the ideal of "natural" propriety, which Mary Wollstonecraft also challenged, and the suggestion, similarly rejected by Mary Shelley, that individual desire is, automatically, socially constructive. In the course of *Lady Susan*, Austen seems to agree with *both* Wollstonecraft and Shelley; for, like Shelley, she insists on the destructive potential of individual desire, and, like Wollstonecraft, she points to the way in which the contradictions of social manners may distort the constructive energies women do possess. Because of the hypocrisy implicit in propriety, Austen suggests, there can be no victors: society cannot afford to unleash the energy inherent in female desire, yet the morality by which society controls desire destroys the individual and threatens society itself. In many ways the "heroine" of *Lady Susan* is Austen's version of the energy that Shelley was to call a "monster"; but because Lady Susan's society is almost as repressive and barren as the one depicted in Wollstonecraft's *Maria*, Austen's presentation of this creature is even more ambiguous than Shelley's dramatization of the monster in 1818.

The first two letters that appear in *Lady Susan* establish the unmistakable tone and range of the heroine's voice. Recently widowed, immediately ejected from her "particular" friend's house for her outrageous flirtations, Lady Susan Vernon writes first to her brother, Charles Vernon, to whom she displays only her "winningly mild" countenance. "My kind friends here are most affectionately urgent with me to prolong my stay," she assures him, "but their hospitable & chearful dispositions lead them too much into society for my present situation & state of mind."[4] She is looking forward, she says, to meeting her new "Sister" in the "delightful retirement" of the country. But the reader, more privileged than Mr. Vernon, immediately receives another version of these "facts." In the next letter, addressed to her confidential friend, Alicia Johnson, Lady Susan explains that "the Females of the Family are united against me"; "the whole family are at war" (pp. 244, 245). "Charles Vernon is my aversion, & I am afraid of his wife," she acknowledges; nevertheless, out of necessity, she is off to visit them in "that insupportable spot, a Country Village" (pp. 246, 245–46). Already we see that Lady Susan uses her letters to manipulate reality—to create it, in fact; for we can assume that she plays on Mrs. Johnson's prejudices against propriety almost as consistently as she plays on her brother's simpleminded belief that "truth" has only one face and a single voice.

In Lady Susan's adroit manipulation of "truth" Austen is dramatizing the way that the gap between appearance and reality, which is intrinsic to the paradoxical configuration of propriety, generates a crisis of moral authority. And the remarkable success Susan enjoys with most of her audience for most of the novel suggests the gravity of this crisis. Because her retreat to the country enhances the impression she cultivates of being both virtuous and unavailable, Susan sustains the interest of both of her town admirers and adds to them Reginald De Courcy, Mrs. Vernon's brother and the heir to his family's estate. Susan is able to manipulate others chiefly because she knows that the use of language is an art capable of generating plausible, internally consistent, but wholly malleable fictions just as the manners of propriety can. Thus she reverses Reginald's initial prejudices against her simply by revising the "facts" on which her notoriety is based, and she prejudices the Vernons against her own daughter Frederica so as better to control the child and then almost manages to make this timid daughter marry the man she herself has chosen for her—her own cast-off suitor, Sir James Martin. Lady Susan freely admits to the pleasure her quick wit and creative pen afford: "If I am vain of anything," she preens, "it is of my eloquence. Consideration & Esteem as surely follow command of Language, as Admiration waits on Beauty" (p. 268). In the end she fails to control reality completely only because the people she has successfully duped—Mrs. Manwaring and Reginald, Frederica and Mrs. Vernon—escape the closed system of her rhetoric by talking to each other. "Horrid" facts obtrude, and her victims conspire to drive Susan out of both family circles. Ultimately, Susan, without a pen or audience, has no influence because she has no vehicle or context by which to create her "self."

Throughout the novel, Lady Susan also aspires to maintain a related but equally precarious balance: she wants to retain the power to exercise her aggressive energies and, at the same time, the reputation for propriety that gives her that power. "Those women are inexcusable," she scoffs, "who forget what is due to themselves & the opinion of the World" (p. 269). The principle that Lady Susan overlooks but that Jane Austen underscores is that, given the nature of female desire, these two "dues" are incompatible. Susan's fidelity to herself would entail indulging her apparently insatiable appetite for attention; yet the "World" will not grant that appetite free expression or substantial gratification. Lady Susan, in other words, is trapped in the very paradox of propriety that she thought she could exploit; because it demands indirection, propriety effectively distorts the desires it seemed to accommodate.

Despite her apparently indomitable wit, Lady Susan also finds herself thwarted by another irony of the female situation. She seems to be a woman of the mind and to pride herself on her ability to dominate not only other people and their perceptions of reality but emotion itself. Susan's sharpest comments are reserved for women who, like her own daughter and Mrs. Manwaring, experience and express strong feeling without inhibition or art. Of her daughter Susan despairs: "I never saw a girl of her age, bid fairer to be the sport of Mankind. Her feelings are tolerably lively & she is so charmingly artless in their display, as to afford the most reasonable hope of her being ridiculed & despised by every Man who sees her." "Artlessness will never do in Love matters," she continues, "& that girl is born a simpleton who has it either by nature or affectation" (p. 274). Yet despite her professed preference for art over spontaneity, Austen hints that Susan yearns for a genuine contest— perhaps even for defeat by an emotion that prudence cannot master. She will not marry the "contemptibly weak" Sir James, she vows, for all his wealth: "I must own myself rather romantic in that respect, & that Riches only, will not satisfy me" (p. 245). Initially she is aroused by Reginald precisely because he seems a worthy antagonist. "There is something about him that rather interests me," she admits; "a sort of sauciness, of familiarity which I shall teach him to correct. . . . There is exquisite pleasure in subduing an insolent spirit, in making a person predetermined to dislike, acknowledge one's superiority" (p. 254). The problem here is that even though Susan insists that power resides in the mind, she fears that it may actually originate in emotion. Noting the perceptible increase in Frederica's affection for Reginald, Susan admits to "not feeling perfectly secure that a knowledge of that affection might not in the end awaken a return. Contemptible as a regard founded only on compassion, must make them both, in my eyes, I [feel] by no means assured that such might not be the consequence" (p. 280).

Beneath Lady Susan's artful self-presentation, then, lurk fears and desires she can neither conceal nor acknowledge. Her boasts of the power of art belie a fascination not only with the "romantic" love that drives her daughter to defy her but even with the fear that compels Frederica to run away from Sir James. Similarly, Susan's need to be flattered hides her persistent anxiety that neither she nor the "World" is as admirable as she wants to believe, and her impatience with spontaneity cloaks her fear that its real liability is just what she says it is: if one is not loved in return, the lover may ridicule, despise, and make sport of a woman's heart.

Despite her aggressive hostility to feminine stereotypes, Lady Susan conforms precisely to the typical female the mid-eighteenth-century moralists described: she is vain, obsessed by men, dominated by her appetites, and, finally, incapable of creating any identity independent of the one she tries to denounce.[5] Ironically, her aggressiveness only affirms the vulnerability she prides herself on having overcome, and she is finally caught in the most fatal paradox of female feeling: to express love is to risk rejection, yet never to acknowledge feeling is to court isolation and the hollow victory of having successfully repressed desire.

Part of the problem, Austen implies, is that society fails to provide any power adequate to Lady Susan. Even in this patriarchal society there are simply no men strong enough either to engage or resist her irrepressible energy. The novel is consistently dominated by women, despite Susan's preoccupation with men. Mr. Vernon seems oblivious to what is happening beneath his roof, Reginald's father, even when told of Susan's plot, refuses to believe that such women exist; Sir James, Mr. Manwaring, and Reginald are simply dupes of Susan's wiles. Only the women are capable of grasping the implications of her exuberance or of doing anything about it. Even timid Frederica three times defies her mother; Mrs. Manwaring finally overthrows Susan by pursuing her husband to London; and Mrs. Vernon consistently proves herself capable not only of understanding Susan's art but of matching it with machinations of her own. As Lloyd W. Brown has noted, the only real contest in *Lady Susan* is between the heroine and Mrs. Vernon; Reginald and Frederica constitute the pawns and the spoils. Like Lady Susan, Mrs. Vernon seeks to control the emotions and the fixtures of these two young people; both women are egotists, who use their epistolary art to manipulate "reality," and only they can fully comprehend any desire other than avarice.[6]

By the end of the story, the failure of every moral authority in Susan's society threatens to subvert any didactic effect this novel might have seemed to promise. On the one hand, *Lady Susan* constitutes an attack on propriety, which, paradoxically, Austen presents as both restrictive and permissive. Such morality, Austen suggests, is inadequate not because it has misrepresented female nature but because its attempt to control desire has served only to distort this powerful force, to drive it into artful wiles and stratagems that are often both socially destructive and personally debilitating. On the other hand, because the world Austen depicts contains neither adequate outlets for this energy nor a paternal authority capable of mastering it, we cannot imagine what constructive form Susan's exuberance could take—or, for that matter, what social or moral institution could control it. Because Susan's energy exceeds the capacity of the world she inhabits, it is necessarily destructive—not only of the foolish men but of innocent young persons like Frederica and, ultimately, of Lady Susan herself.[7]

Despite its destructive tendencies and effects, however, Lady Susan's energy—like that of Shelley's monster—remains the most attractive force in this novel. And, as in *Frankenstein*, the power of this attraction is reinforced by the epistolary form, which allows us not only to engage ourselves with Lady Susan's intellect but to sympathize with her conflicting feelings as well. Even though the letters Mrs. Vernon writes supply another perspective on Susan's schemes, her judgments are no more "objective" or authoritative than

Susan's whims—especially given her personal grudge against Susan. Similarly, the final agent of "justice"—Mrs. Manwaring—comes from the household that was, initially, so easily duped, and she too, like Mrs. Vernon, retaliates from personal motives, not to save some absolute system of disinterested values. In a novel that lacks a spokesperson for such values, the epistolary form generates moral anarchy; Austen does not establish a genuinely critical position within the fiction but depends instead on an implicit contrast between the values presented and those the satire presumes but does not formulate. Within the moral consensus of a family such allusiveness might well suffice, and we can imagine Austen reading *Lady Susan* to her amused family circle. But without this consensus there is no moral authority because there is no narrative authority. In the laissez-faire competition the epistolary *Lady Susan* permits, the reader will identify with whatever character dominates the narration or most completely gratifies the appetite for entertainment. In *Lady Susan* this character is, of course, the dangerous heroine.

So compelling and so complete is this heroine's artful power that the only way Austen can effectively censure her is to impose punishment by narrative fiat. Predictably, this entails disrupting the epistolary narrative and ridiculing not just the correspondents but the morally anarchic epistolary form itself. "This Correspondence," Austen playfully announces in the "Conclusion," ". . . could not, to the great detriment of the Post office Revenue, be continued longer. Very little assistance to the State could be derived from the Epistolary Intercourse of Mrs. Vernon & her niece" (p. 311). She then abruptly summarizes the fate of the characters: Mrs. Vernon and Mrs. Manwaring triumph, and Frederica and her mother reverse positions in almost every important respect: the daughter marries Reginald, and Lady Susan is reduced to marrying the suitor whom Frederica has now cast off, Sir James Martin. But Austen will not allow even this summary to have final authority, for in her final reference to Lady Susan she leaves her in exactly the same moral vacuum in which we found her: "Whether Lady Susan was, or was not happy in her second Choice—I do not see how it can ever be ascertained—for who would take her assurance of it, on either side of the question?" (p. 313).

Austen's final ambivalence here suggests an attempt to accomplish the same feat to which Lady Susan aspired: to obtain both "what is due to [herself] & the opinion of the World." What is due to herself as an artist is uninhibited self-expression; the "opinion of the World" requires conclusive moral order. Austen seems reluctant to deny the power or attraction of female energy, perhaps because it is too close to the creative impulse of her own wit; nor does she fully condone the indulgence of that energy, for its destructive potential is undeniable. By allowing herself and her reader imaginative engagement with her heroine, Austen seems to satisfy the prerogatives of desire;

by abruptly severing that engagement, she aspires to reassert the system of social principles whose authority Lady Susan has so effectively challenged.

The narrative impasse at the conclusion of *Lady Susan* is in many ways reminiscent of the problems that beset Wollstonecraft's *Maria*: the appeal of female feeling competes with Austen's reservations about it almost as dramatically as Wollstonecraft's attraction to "romantic expectations" jeopardizes her critique of sentimentalism. In both cases, one consequence of this aesthetic ambiguity is uncertainty for the reader as to the moral ground of the novels. Just as *Maria* seems to hover between irony and wholehearted sentimentalism, so *Lady Susan* occupies the gray area between satire and direct social criticism. But the intervention of the unmistakable narrative voice at the end of *Lady Susan*, while necessitated by a version of *Maria*'s tonal uncertainty, points to one essential difference between these two writers—a difference that becomes more marked during Austen's subsequent career. The "solution" Wollstonecraft offers in *Maria* involves two extreme gestures: on the one hand, she rejects social institutions that inhibit individual feeling; on the other hand, she redefines human emotions so that they transcend social institutions altogether. By contrast, Austen brings individual desire into confrontation with social institutions in order first to discipline anarchic passion and then to expand the capacity of such institutions to accommodate educated needs and desires. One reason *Maria*'s conclusion remains blocked is that everything in the sections Wollstonecraft finished suggests her desire to segregate the realistic depictions of corrupt society from her romantic effusions of passion. The conclusion of *Lady Susan*, on the other hand, for all its contrivance, suggests an impulse to contain even momentary fantasies of unmitigated power within the twin controls of aesthetic closure and social propriety. In this sense, Jane Austen resembles Mary Shelley more than Mary Wollstonecraft. But the balance of her sympathies, along with the aesthetic solutions she developed to convey them, take her beyond the artistic achievement of either of the other two.

The division of sympathies we see in *Lady Susan* bears a particularly interesting relationship to Jane Austen's complex social and economic position during this period of change. As we have already seen, the period between 1775 and 1817, the years of Austen's life, was punctuated by challenges to the traditional hierarchy of English class society and, as a consequence, to conventional social roles and responsibilities. William Wordsworth's 1817 survey of the preceding thirty years summarizes the chaotic impact of these changes:

> I see clearly that the principal ties which kept the different classes
> of society in a vital and harmonious dependence upon each other

have, within these 30 years, either been greatly impaired or wholly dissolved. Everything has been put up to market and sold for the highest price it would buy.... All ... moral cement is dissolved, habits and prejudices are broken and rooted up, nothing being substituted in their place but a quickened self interest.[8]

In England, the decisive agent of this change was not just the French Revolution but the more subtle, more gradual, dissemination of the values and behavior associated with capitalism—first, agrarian capitalism in the mid- and late eighteenth century, then, in the early nineteenth century, industrial capitalism, as money made itself felt in investment and capital return. As we have seen, by the first decades of the nineteenth century, birth into a particular class no longer exclusively determined one's future social or economic status, the vertical relationships of patronage no longer guaranteed either privileges or obedience, and the traditional authority of the gentry, and of the values associated with their life-style, was a subject under general debate. In the midst of such changes, the assumptions that had theoretically been shared by eighteenth-century moralists and their audiences seemed increasingly problematic, requiring refinement and defense if not radical change. As the literature and political debates of this period unmistakably reveal, the crisis in imaginative and moral authority was pervasive and severe; even conservative writers generally abandoned arguments about absolute truths in favor of discussions in which one set of principles was defended against a contrary but equally coherent system of values.[9]

As the daughter of a country clergyman with numerous and strong ties to the landed upper gentry, Jane Austen was involved in this crisis of authority in an immediate and particularly complex way. As Donald J. Greene has conclusively demonstrated, Jane Austen was acutely aware of her kinship to several prominent families, among them the Brydges, who were earls and lords of Chandos, and the lords Leigh of Stoneleigh.[10] More immediately, as a clergyman Austen's father belonged to the lesser realms of the gentry, and Jane and her siblings all benefited more or less directly from the patronage that traditionally reinforced the gentry's hegemony. One of Austen's brothers, Edward, was adopted by the wealthy Knight family, of Kent, and, as heir to the valuable estate of Godmersham, he was eventually able to provide a home at Chawton Cottage for Jane, her mother, her sister, and their friend Martha Lloyd. Two of Austen's other brothers, James and Henry, became clergymen, and her two youngest brothers, Francis and Charles, entered the British navy and eventually became admirals; Francis in fact became a knight. Thus Jane Austen was raised in the heart of middle-class society; she shared its values, and she owed her own position to the bonds of patronage that cemented traditional society, even though her immediate resources never permitted her fully to emulate the gentry's life-style.

In keeping with this class affiliation, Jane Austen's fundamental ideological position was conservative; her political sympathies were generally Tory, and her religion was officially Anglican; overall, she was a "conservative Christian moralist," supportive of Evangelical ethical rigor even before she explicitly admitted admiring the Evangelicals themselves.[11]

But neither the external evidence of Austen's social position nor the internal evidence of her novels supports so strict a delineation of her sympathies. In the first place, even the traditional practices of paternalism were influenced during this period by the rhetoric and practices of individualism. (To give but one relevant example: promotion in such prestigious professions as the navy could result from individual effort and merit [as *Persuasion* indicates]; at other times it depended on the interest of a patron [as William Price learns in *Mansfield Park*]). In the second place, the role played by Austen's class in the rise of capitalism was particularly complicated; for the agricultural improvements that preceded and paved the way for early industrial capitalism were financed and initiated in many cases by the landowning gentry, yet the legal provisions of strict settlement and entail were expressly designed to prohibit land from becoming a commodity susceptible to promiscuous transfer or easy liquidation. Despite the fact that the landowning gentry participated in the expansion of agrarian capitalism, their role was passive, not active; as a consequence, their values and life-style were not extensively altered until the more radical and rapid expansion of industrial capitalism began in the first decades of the nineteenth century. When that occurred, the gentry were suddenly awakened to the implications of the changes to which their patterns of expenditure had contributed.[12] From the more vulnerable position of the lower levels of the gentry, Jane Austen was able to see with particular clarity the marked differences between the two components of the middle class: the landed gentry and the new urban capitalist class.[13] The division of sympathies that occurs in her novels when middle-class daughters get rewarded with the sons of landed families emanates at least partly from Austen's being both involved in and detached from these two middle-class groups at a moment when they were implicitly competing with each other.

In Austen's very early works, like *Lady Susan*, this division of sympathies characteristically leads either to broad farce or to the tonal uncertainties of parody.[14] As her career progresses, however, we see Austen gradually develop aesthetic strategies capable of balancing her attraction to exuberant but potentially anarchic feeling with her investment in traditional social institutions. This balance is embodied in the thematic material she chooses and the rhetorical stance she adopts. At their most sophisticated, Austen's rhetorical strategies harness the imaginative energy of her readers to a moral design; she thus manages to satisfy both the individual reader's desire for emotional gratification and the program of education prescribed by traditional moral aestheticians.

To understand why Austen assumed that a novel could simultaneously gratify the cravings of the imagination and provide moral instruction, it is useful to turn to Samuel Johnson, Austen's favorite eighteenth-century essayist. According to Johnson, novel-reading is an active, not passive, enterprise, for it aggressively engages the imagination of its young reader. Novels, Johnson explains,

> are the entertainment of minds unfurnished with ideas, and therefore easily susceptible of impressions; not fixed by principles, and therefore easily following the current of fancy; not informed by experience, and consequently open to every false suggestion and partial account.... If the power of example is so great, as to take possession of the memory by a kind of violence, and produce effects almost without the intervention of the will, care ought to be taken that, when the choice is unrestrained, the best examples only should be exhibited; and that which is likely to operate so strongly, should not be mischievous or uncertain in its effects.[15]

Johnson's wariness about the power of the imagination should remind us of Mary Shelley; for, as different as these two writers were, they shared a profound anxiety about the insatiable hunger of the imagination. Johnson's answer to this anxiety was to compose not novels but moral essays that were characterized by a tremendous respect for reason's antagonist. Mary Shelley's solution, as we have seen, was simultaneously less evasive and less effective. In fact, her novels represent the two dangers to which imaginative engagement might lead. At one extreme, as the 1818 *Frankenstein* proves, a "romantic" novel might so thoroughly activate the imagination as to undermine all moral authority; at the other extreme, as in *Falkner*, the moral novel might so dogmatically focus the imagination that all subversive exuberance would be driven into the background of the fiction, only to return to the forefront in troubling reminders of what cannot be contained.

To a certain extent, Jane Austen shared this ambivalence with regard to the imagination. When Anne Elliot advises Captain Benwick in *Persuasion* to admit "a larger allowance of prose in his daily study" so as to "rouse and fortify" a mind made "tremulous" by immersion in Romantic poetry, she is warning against the "susceptibility" of the indulged imagination.[16] But while Austen might well agree with Johnson that novels should "serve as lectures of conduct, and introductions into life," her major works are not as defensive as either his *Rasselas* or Shelley's *Falkner*; they do not, that is, "initiate youth by mock encounters in the art of necessary defence."[17] Instead, Austen attempts to convert the pleasure generated by imaginative engagement into a didactic tool. As the "productions" that provide "more extensive and unaffected pleasure than those of any other literary corporation in the world," novels are best suited for such education. For in the best novels, Austen continues in *Northanger Abbey*, "the greatest powers of the mind are displayed, . . . the most thorough knowledge of human nature, the happiest delineation of its varieties, the liveliest effusions of wit and humour are conveyed to the world in the best chosen language."[18]

Sense and Sensibility

The narrative impasse reached in Wollstonecraft's *Maria* and the Scylla and Charybdis of Shelley's aesthetic choices remind us that achieving such a balance was not easy. Jane Austen's first published novel, *Sense and Sensibility* (1811), suggests how persistent this problem proved to be for her early in her career.[19] *Sense and Sensibility* is a much darker novel than any of the juvenilia or the parodic *Northanger Abbey* (1818), and we might speculate that one origin of its somber tone and the eruptions of anarchic feeling that punctuate it lies in the anxiety with which Austen viewed individualism's challenge to paternalism. For in *Sense and Sensibility*, as, in a slightly different way, in *Lady Susan* and *Northanger Abbey*, the most fundamental conflict is between Austen's own imaginative engagement with her self-assertive characters and the moral code necessary to control their anarchic desires.

In the greater part of *Sense and Sensibility*, Austen's aesthetic strategies endorse the traditional values associated with her "sensible" heroine, Elinor Dashwood. One of these strategies consists in measuring all of the characters (including Elinor) against an implicit, but presumably authoritative, moral norm. As early as the second chapter, in that free, indirect discourse that is the hallmark of her mature style, Austen shadows the opinion of a single fallible character with this implicit moral standard.[20] Irony in *Sense and Sensibility* arises for the most part from the novel's action; the dialogue between Mr. and Mrs. John Dashwood points up as surely as any overt narrative commentary the parsimony behind their dwindling good will. But our response to this dialogue is initially shaped by such sentences as the following: "To take three thousand pounds from the fortune of their dear little boy, would be impoverishing him to the most dreadful degree"; "How could he answer it to himself to rob his child, and his only child too, of so large a sum?"[21] The hyperbole expressed in the words "impoverishing," "dreadful," and "rob" conveys both the strategy of Mrs. Dashwood's rhetoric and its absurdity, and the repeated use of the word "child" suggests how effective she is in manipulating John Dashwood's generosity. Because these sentences belong to the narrative and not to direct dialogue, they mimetically convey the tone of the conversation and simultaneously judge it by reference to an implicit system of more humane values—the undeniably Christian values that one should love one's neighbor as one's self and that the man who hoards treasures in this world (or the woman who encourages him to do so) will never get into the kingdom of heaven.

But despite this ground of Christian principles, nearly everything in the plot of *Sense and Sensibility* undermines the complacent assumption that they are principles generally held or practically effective. Almost every action in the novel suggests that, more often than not, individual will triumphs over principle and individual desire proves more compelling than moral law. Even the narrator, the apparent voice of these absolute values, reveals that moral principles are qualified in practice. The narrator's prefatory evaluation of John Dashwood, for example—"he was not an ill-disposed young man, unless to be rather cold hearted, and rather selfish, is to be ill-disposed" (p. 5)—directs our attention most specifically to the way in which what should, in theory, be moral absolutes can, and in practice do, shade off into infinite gradations and convenient exceptions. Is it always morally wrong to be "rather" selfish, especially in a society in which such selfishness is the necessary basis for material prosperity? What efficacy will moral absolutes have in such a society? How could Elinor's patient, principled fidelity win the passive, principled Edward if it were not, finally, for Lucy Steele's avarice?

A second strategy that is apparently designed to forestall such questions by aligning the reader's sympathies with Elinor's "sense" involves the juxtaposition of Elinor and her sister Marianne at nearly every critical juncture in the novel. Consistently, Elinor makes the prudent choice, even when doing so is painful; almost as consistently, Marianne's decisions are self-indulgent and harmful, either to herself or to someone else. But this neat design is less stable than an absolute and authoritative moral system would seem to require. Many readers have found Marianne's "spirit" more appealing than Elinor's cautious, prim, and even repressive reserve, and they have found Marianne's passionate romance with Willoughby more attractive than the prolonged frustration to which Elinor submits. That such preferences may be in keeping with at least one countercurrent of the novel is suggested by the fact that whenever Austen herself explicitly compares the two putative heroes—Colonel Brandon and Edward Ferrars—with the less moral, more passionate Willoughby, it is Willoughby who is appealing. On two occasions when Willoughby is expected but one of the more subdued lovers appears instead, the disappointment is unmistakable; and when the reverse situation occurs, in the climactic final encounter between Elinor and Willoughby, Elinor is aroused to a pitch of complex emotion we never see Edward inspire in anyone. Moreover, Willoughby repeatedly bursts into the narrative with "manly beauty and more than common gracefulness," but Edward and Brandon seem inert fixtures of the plot, incapable of energetic gallantry and attractive only to the most generous observer. The initial description of each of them is dominated by negative constructions and qualifying phrases, and even Elinor cannot unreservedly praise the man she wants to marry. "At first sight," she admits, "his address is certainly not striking; and his person can hardly be called handsome, till the expression of his eyes, which are uncommonly good, and the general sweetness of his countenance, is perceived. At present, I know him so well, that I think him really handsome; or, at least, almost so" (p. 20). Colonel Brandon, "neither very young nor very gay," is "silent and grave" much of the time (p. 34), and his "oppression of spirits," like Edward's chronic depression, can scarcely compete with Willoughby's charm.

The most telling dramatization of the contest between the potentially anarchic power of feeling and the restraint that moral principles require takes the form of a conflict within Elinor herself. This scene, in the final volume, owes much to conventional eighteenth-century didactic novels, but Austen's placing it at a moment when the generally self-disciplined Elinor is unusually susceptible to emotion gives it a particularly complicated effect. Colonel Brandon has presented a living to Edward Ferrars, and Elinor is finally, but sadly, reconciled to the fact that her lover will marry someone else. In the midst of this personal disappointment, she is also particularly sensitive to her sister's condition, for Marianne, whose own romantic disappointment had sent her into a dangerous decline, has just been declared out of danger. Elinor's "fervent gratitude" for this news is especially great because of the joy and relief it will bring to her mother, whose arrival is expected at any moment. It is this hectic peace—as Marianne sleeps quietly upstairs and a violent storm assaults the house—that Willoughby invades when he melodramatically steps into the drawing-room.

Elinor's first response is "horror" at his audacious intrusion; but before she can leave the room, Willoughby appeals to something even more powerful than Elinor's "honour": her curiosity. Elinor is momentarily captivated by Willoughby's "serious energy" and "warmth," and she listens "in spite of herself" to the story he unfolds—the chronicle of his passions, both honorable and base. At the end of his dramatic recital, Willoughby asks Elinor for pity, and, even though she feels it is her "duty" to check his outburst, she cannot repress her "compassionate emotion." It is this emotion that governs her judgment of Willoughby—a judgment that verges disconcertingly on rationalization:

> Elinor made no answer. Her thoughts were silently fixed on the irreparable injury which too early an independence and its consequent habits of idleness, dissipation, and luxury, had made

in the mind, the character, the happiness, of a man who, to every advantage of person and talents, united a disposition naturally open and honest, and a feeling, affectionate temper. The world had made him extravagant and vain—Extravagance and vanity had made him cold-hearted and selfish. [p. 331]

When Willoughby departs, he leaves Elinor in an even greater "agitation" of spirits, "too much oppressed by a croud of ideas . . . to think even of her sister."

> Willoughby, in spite of all his faults, excited a degree of commiseration for the sufferings produced by them, which made her think of him as now separated for ever from her family with a tenderness, a regret, rather in proportion, as she soon acknowledged within herself—to his wishes than to his merits. She felt that his influence over her mind was heightened by circumstances which ought not in reason to have weight; by that person of uncommon attraction, that open, affectionate, and lively manner which it was no merit to possess; and by that still ardent love for Marianne, which it was not even innocent to indulge. But she felt that it was so, long, long before she could feel his influence less. [p. 833]

One purpose of this episode is clearly to dramatize the odds against which Elinor's "sense," or reason, ultimately triumphs and therefore to increase, not undermine, our admiration for that faculty. But a second effect of the passage is to subject the reader to the same temptation that assails Elinor. Because the presentation is dramatic and because, for a moment at least, the character whose judgment has thus far directed our own hesitates in her moral evaluation, the reader is invited to judge Willoughby not by reference to an objective standard but by his immediate appeal to our imaginative, sympathetic engagement. As Elinor temporizes, the moral principle for which she otherwise speaks seems dangerously susceptible to circumstances, to the appeal of "lively manners," and to the special pleading of aroused female emotion.

Jane Austen seems anxious to control the moral anarchy that strong appeals to feeling can unleash; yet, significantly, she does not exclude passion from the novel, nor does she so completely qualify it as to undermine its power. Instead, Austen attempts to bend the imaginative engagement it elicits in the reader to the service of moral education. To do so, she restricts the reader's access to the romantic plot by conveying its details and its emotional affect only through indirect narration. At the beginning of the novel, for example, the incident in which Willoughby rescues Marianne is summarized by the dispassionate narrative persona, who supplies sentimental clichés but not Marianne's response to her rescue: "The gentleman offered his services, and perceiving that her modesty declined what her situation rendered necessary, took her up in his arms without farther delay" (p. 42). Similarly, the episode in which Willoughby cuts and kisses a lock of Marianne's hair is given to Margaret to relate (p. 60), and the emotional specifics of Willoughby's farewell at Barton Cottage can be deduced only from their aftermath (p. 82). Most of Marianne's outbursts of passion to Willoughby are confined to letters, which are concealed from the reader until after Willoughby has snubbed Marianne. In fact, the only emotionally charged encounter between the lovers that Austen presents dramatically is their final meeting at the London ball, and there Marianne's passion is transmuted by Willoughby's silence into the terrible muffled scream that both voices and symbolizes her thwarted love. So careful is Austen to keep the reader on the outside of such "dangerous" material that she embeds the most passionate episodes within other, less emotionally volatile stories. Thus the story of the two Elizas—related, as we will see, by a character whose relationship to the tale immediately activates our judgment—is contained within the story of Marianne's passion for Willoughby—a relationship whose emotional content is conveyed to the reader more by innuendo, summary, and indirection than by dramatic presentation. And this second story, in turn, is contained within the story of the relationship that opens and closes the novel—Elinor's considerably less demonstrative affection for Edward. By embedding these stories in this way, Austen seeks to defuse their imaginative affect and increase their power to educate the reader: from the fates of the two Elizas we learn to be wary of Marianne's quick feelings, and from the consequences of Marianne's self-indulgent passion we learn to value Elinor's reserve.

Instead of being allowed to identify with Marianne, then, for most of the novel we are restricted to Elinor's emotional struggles. This enables Austen to dramatize the complexities of what might otherwise seem an unattractive and unyielding obsession with propriety; it also permits her to filter the two stories of illicit passion through a character whose judgment generally masters emotion. That the passion bleeds from the narrators of these two tales into Elinor's "sense" attests to the power of this force and to the dangerous susceptibility that, without proper control, might undermine the judgment of even the most rational reader.

Austen also attempts to control the allure of Marianne's romantic desires by refusing to consider seriously either their social origin or their philosophical implications. As Tony Tanner has pointed out, Austen really avoids the systematic examination of "sensibility" that the novel seems to promise.[22] The novel begins like a novel of social realism. In the first paragraphs the narrator sounds like a lawyer or a banker; family alliances, the estate that is the heart of

paternalistic society, even the deaths of loved ones, are all ruthlessly subordinated to the economic facts. Given this introduction, the reader has every reason
to believe that the most important fact—that Mrs. Dashwood will have only
five hundred pounds a year with which to raise and dower her daughters—will
govern the futures of Elinor, Marianne, and Margaret. And given this probable
development, the reader can understand why romantic fantasies are appealing.
It is no wonder that Marianne—facing a life of poverty, the spiritual banal-
ity of relatives like the John Dashwoods, and the superficial urbanities of a
neighborhood composed only of the Middletons and Mrs. Jennings—turns to
Cowper for imaginative compensation; nor is it surprising that she fancies (in
accordance with the promises of romantic novels) that her beauty will win the
heart and hand of an errant knight. Beneath Marianne's effusions on nature
and her passionate yearning for a hero lies the same "hunger of imagination"
that Mary Wollstonecraft tried and failed to analyze in *Maria*. But to take
Marianne's passions and longings seriously on their own terms would be to call
into question the basis of Christian moral authority, the social order that ideally
institutionalizes that authority, and, finally, the capacity of orthodox religion or
society to gratify imaginative desires.[23] Elinor's sense, despite its admirable capacity to discipline and protect the self, cannot begin to satisfy this appetite, and
no other social institution in the novel does any better. Instead of taking this
implicit criticism to its logical conclusion, as Wollstonecraft tried to do, Jane
Austen defuses its threat by directing our judgment away from bourgeois society and toward the self-indulgent individual. Austen caricatures just enough
of Marianne's responses to nature and love to make her seem intermittently
ridiculous, and, when her desires finally explode all social conventions, Austen
stifles her with an illness that is not only a result but also a purgation of her
passion. At the end of the novel, Austen ushers Marianne into Brandon's world
of diminished desires in such a way as to make Marianne herself negate everything she has previously wanted to have and to be.

> Marianne Dashwood was born to an extraordinary fate. She
> was born to discover the falsehood of her own opinions, and to
> counteract, by her conduct, her most favourite maxims. She was
> born to overcome an affection formed so late in life as at seventeen,
> and with no sentiment superior to strong esteem and lively
> friendship, voluntarily to give her hand to another! ... Marianne
> could never love by halves; and her whole heart became, in time, as
> much devoted to her husband, as it had once been to Willoughby.
> [pp. 378–79]

To further defuse the questions raised by Marianne's assertive subjectiv-
ity, Austen seconds the opinion of eighteenth-century moralists that women's

appetites are particularly dangerous and more akin to inexplicable natural forces than to socialized—hence socializable—responses. Except for Elinor, nearly all of the women in *Sense and Sensibility* are given to one kind of excess or another. Mrs. John Dashwood and her mother, Mrs. Ferrars, attempt to dominate the opinions, the professions, and even the emotions of the men who are closest to them; Willoughby's aunt, who is empowered by money and age, is even more tyrannical; and Sophia Grey, Willoughby's fiancée, enacts her passion and her will when she commands Willoughby to copy her cruel letter for Marianne. Austen implies that these women are exceptional only in the extent of their power, not in the force of their desires. The narrator describes a "fond mother," for example, as "the most rapacious of human beings" (p. 120)—a description borne out by the monomaniacal Lady Middleton—and she refers lightly to the "suffering" endured by every lady who has the "insatiable appetite of fifteen" (p. 33). Until her compassion is necessary to the plot, even Mrs. Jennings seems dominated by a single uncontrollable desire, the hunger to live vicariously through the romantic attachments of her young friends.

Austen's female characters certainly do not monopolize passion, nor are their little contrivances finally more destructive than Willoughby's deceit. But the implications of her characterizations of such women can be identified by contrasting them with her presentation of male characters. Austen consistently provides men's behavior with a realistic explanation by describing the social or psychological contexts that shaped it. Mr. Palmer's general contempt, Elinor concludes (without any narrative qualification), "was the desire of appearing superior to other people" (p. 112)—a desire that is an understandable compensation for Palmer's initial error: "his temper might perhaps be a little soured by finding, like many others of his sex, that through some unaccountable bias in favour of beauty, he was the husband of a very silly woman" (p. 112). Austen's comparable references to Mrs. Palmer's history are both cursory and curt: her mantelpiece, the narrator informs us, is adorned with "a landscape in coloured silks of her performance, in proof of her having spent seven years at a great school in town to some effect" (p. 160). Austen also more extensively explains the differences between the Ferrars brothers than between the oldest Dashwood sisters; she makes no attempt to account for the temperamental contrast between Elinor and Marianne but carefully attributes the differences between Robert and Edward to their education. The only female character Austen appears to explain is Lucy Steele. Initially, Lucy's "deficiency of all mental improvement" seems to be the effect of her neglected education: "Lucy was naturally clever; her remarks were often just and amusing . . . but her powers had received no aid from education, she was ignorant and illiterate, and her deficiency of mental improvement . . . could not be concealed from Miss Dashwood" (p. 127). Soon we discover,

however, that this "explanation" is really only Elinor's generous and erroneous
first impression. Austen explicitly ridicules the notion that Lucy's "want of
liberality" could be "due to her want of education" by having Edward cling to
this rationalization to the end. But in jilting Edward for his brother Robert,
Lucy conclusively proves herself inherently flawed. Like Shelley's 1831 characterization of Frankenstein, and like both portrayals of the monster, female
nature appears to be fated, fixed. Austen's final comments on Lucy are decisive: her behavior exposes "a wanton ill-nature" (p. 366), characterized by "an
earnest, an unceasing attention to self-interest" (p. 376).

The harshness with which Austen disposes of Lucy Steele exceeds the
necessities of the plot, but it is perfectly in keeping with her moral design.
For, like Shelley, Austen wants to convince the reader that female nature is
simply inexplicable and that propriety must restrain this natural, amoral force.
At least one other set of female characters also supports this argument, but,
paradoxically, the episode in which they appear alludes not to an innate female nature but to the constraints imposed on women by patriarchal society.
Because of this, the episode threatens to subvert the argument for propriety it
theoretically should support. The characters are the two Elizas, and their story
belongs to Colonel Brandon.

Colonel Brandon relates the story of the two Elizas to Elinor ostensibly
to persuade her to warn Marianne about Willoughby. But both the hesita-
tions with which he interrupts his narrative and the fact that he focuses not
on the second Eliza (Willoughby's victim) but on her mother ("his" Eliza)
suggest that Brandon does not fully recognize his own motives for telling the
story. As the tale unfolds, it becomes clear that Brandon's deepest intention
is to warn Marianne about the dangerous nature of her own passion; paradoxically, however, the overall effect of the episode is to reveal to the reader
the depth—and consequences—of *Brandon*'s sexual anxiety.[24] This anxiety,
initially aroused by the first Eliza, is now being reactivated by Marianne. But
there is one critical difference between the two situations: unlike the first Eliza, Marianne's passion is not for Brandon but for Willoughby. Thus Brandon's
anxiety is doubly displaced: it is a past fear of too much emotion *and* a present
fear of too little love. The first Eliza *did* love him, Brandon asserts, as if to en-
hance his own appeal, but she could not withstand her guardian's pressure to
marry Brandon's older brother, heir to the family's encumbered estate. As he
tells the story, Brandon stumbles over the details that wounded him most:

> "My brother did not deserve her; he did not even love her. I had
> hoped that her regard for me would support her under any difficulty,
> and for some time it did; but at last the misery of her situation, for
> she experienced great unkindness, overcame all her resolution, and
> though she had promised me that nothing—but how blindly I

relate! I have never told you how this was brought on. We were within a few hours of eloping together for Scotland. The treachery, or the folly, of my cousin's maid betrayed us. I was banished ... and she was allowed no liberty, no society, no amusement, till my father's point was gained. I had depended on her fortitude too far, ...—but had her marriage been happy, ... a few months must have reconciled me to it.... This however was not the case. My brother had no regard for her.... The consequence of this, upon a mind so young, so lively, so inexperienced as Mrs. Brandon's, was but too natural.... Can we wonder that with such a husband to provoke inconstancy, and without a friend to advise or restrain her ... she should fall? Had I remained in England, perhaps—but I meant to promote the happiness of both by removing from her for years.... The shock which her marriage had given me," he continued, in a voice of great agitation, "was of trifling weight—was nothing—to what I felt when I heard, about two years afterwards, of her divorce. It was *that* which threw this gloom,—even now the recollection of what I suffered—" ... [pp. 205–06; ellipses added]

The story begins and ends in Eliza's infidelity to Brandon; only as an extension of this does her infidelity to her husband matter, only as the origin of his pain does Eliza's unhappiness figure. The weakness of this woman—and her sexual abandon—are "natural," according to Brandon; only the presence of a male guardian could have protected her from herself. Once Eliza has fallen, her fate is so predictable (and disturbing) that it warrants only summary description—except in regard to Brandon's own misery:

So altered—so faded—worn down by acute suffering of every kind! hardly could I believe the melancholy and sickly figure before me, to be the remains of the lovely, blooming, healthful girl, on whom I had once doated. What I endured in so beholding her—but I have no right to wound your feelings by attempting to describe it—I have pained you too much already. [p. 207]

Given the fate of the mother, Brandon is not surprised at the fall of the second Eliza, the daughter, who has been bequeathed to his protection. At seventeen, her mother's fatal year and Marianne's current age, she too evaded her male guardian and ran away with Willoughby. Now pregnant, abandoned, poor, and miserable, this Eliza is a second monument to the passionate excesses of women.

The intense anxiety that Brandon betrays here is produced by his fear of female sexual appetite. If female sexuality had caused the first Eliza to betray him, how vulnerable might the excitable Marianne be to Willoughby, who had seduced the second Eliza? Yet Brandon expressly admires Marianne for the very passion that occasioned the downfall of the two Elizas. Brandon wants Marianne to be emotionally responsive, but he wants her sexuality to answer only to his command. When Elinor wishes that Marianne would renounce sentimental prejudices, Brandon's response is swift: "No, no, do not desire it,—for when the romantic refinements of a young mind are obliged to give way, how frequently are they succeeded by such opinions as are but too common, and too dangerous! I speak from experience" (pp. 56–57). The allusion is clearly to the first Eliza; Brandon fears that beneath the "romantic refinements" of the girl lurks a woman's sexual appetite, which is both "common" and "dangerous." Better far to keep women innocent, to protect them from themselves—and to protect men from their "natural" volatility.

The anxieties Brandon unwittingly reveals suggest that Austen at least intuits the twin imperatives that anchor patriarchal society: men want women to be passionate, but, because they fear the consequences of this appetite, they want to retain control over its expression. This anxiety explains why women in this society must experience so problematic a relation to their own desire. In order to win the husband necessary to their social position, women must gratify both of men's desires by concealing whatever genuine emotions they feel so as to allow men to believe that *they* have all the power. Women must use indirection, in other words, the allure of "romantic refinements," and the subterfuges of manners and modesty in order to arouse male desires and assuage male anxieties.

The implications of this passage are very close to those Mary Wollstonecraft specifically addresses in both *The Rights of Woman* and *Maria*. But in *Sense and Sensibility* Jane Austen will no more pursue the criticism of patriarchy that is inherent in this insight than she will pursue the grim reality that is implicit in the narrator's account of the Dashwood's economic situation. Despite its gestures toward realism, *Sense and Sensibility* repeatedly dismisses the analysis of society that realism might imply and instead embraces the idealism of romance. But Austen's idealism never completely banishes her realistic impulse either. Instead, Austen retains both "principles" and romance. Thus Marianne debunks her own youthful romance, and the novel as a whole endorses the "heroism" (the word itself appears on pp. 242 and 265) of Elinor's self-denial. Nevertheless, Austen rewards both characters at the conclusion of the novel precisely in terms of romantic love and of lives lived happily ever after.

Some of the tensions that we finally feel in *Sense and Sensibility* emerge, then, from the conflict between the realism in which the action is anchored and the romantic elements that Austen harnesses to this realism. Throughout, she attempts to use realism to control the imaginative excesses that romances both encourage and depict: not only does the point of view repress the romantic plot, but Austen also suggests that Elinor's self-denial—her refusal to reveal Lucy Steele's secret and her willingness to help Edward even to her own disadvantage—ultimately contributes to her own happiness as well as to the happiness of others. The prerogatives of society, Austen suggests, sometimes make secrecy and repression necessary; but if one submits to society, every dream will come true. The last part of this formulation reminds us, of course, that, just as Austen uses realism to control the irresponsible and morally anarchic imagination, she also enlists the power of the reader's wishes to buttress her moral design. Theoretically, if her readers will submit to a version of the frustration Elinor suffers or even the compromise to which Marianne grows accustomed, their wish for a happy ending will be legitimized and gratified. This fusion of realism and romance in the service of aesthetic closure decisively distinguishes between Wollstonecraft's *Maria* and Austen's early novels. For notwithstanding her imaginative engagement in "romantic expectations," Wollstonecraft's persistent goal is to criticize the social institutions that seem to her to thwart female feeling. Jane Austen, on the other hand, despite her recognition of the limitations of social institutions, is more concerned with correcting the dangerous excesses of female feeling than with liberating this anarchic energy. Her turn to aesthetic closure enables her to dismiss many of the problems her own divided sympathies have introduced. That the need for such closure grows out of society's inability to grant happiness to everyone in the terms it promises is a problem that can remain unexamined because it is, ideally, irrelevant to this fiction. The most troubling aspect of *Sense and Sensibility* is Austen's inability to establish narrative authority because she is ambivalent toward both realism and romance. Her inability to establish moral authority is clearly related to this ambivalence. But its complexities and implications are more clearly apparent in her next novel, *Pride and Prejudice*.

Pride and Prejudice

In *Pride and Prejudice* (1813) the challenge that feeling and imaginative energy offer to moral authority is particularly persistent and problematic, for it is posed by the heroine herself. As the outspoken champion of the prerogatives of individual desire, Elizabeth Bennet should jeopardize both the social order, which demands self-denial, and the moral order, which is based on absolute Christian principles. Yet, despite the dangers she seems to embody, Elizabeth Bennet was Jane Austen's special favorite. "I think her as delightful a creature as ever appeared in print," she wrote to Cassandra (*JAL*, 2:297; 29 January 1813). And, as a favorite, Elizabeth is handsomely rewarded: she marries the richest man in all of Jane Austen's novels and is established as mistress of Pemberley, one of those great country estates that superintend and stabilize patriarchal society. In fact, Elizabeth's triumph signals the achievement of the balance that characterizes Austen's mature novels, for it is the result, on the one hand, of the gradual transformation of social and psychological realism into romance and, on the other, of a redefinition of romance. Essentially, Austen legitimizes romance by making it seem the corrective—not the origin or the product—of individualism. By such narrative magic, Austen is able to defuse the thematic conflict between sense and sensibility—or reason and feeling, or realism and romance—that troubled her earlier works. What is more, by forcing her reader to participate in creating the moral order that governs the novel's conclusion, Austen is able to make this aesthetic "solution" seem, at least momentarily, both natural and right.

Pride and Prejudice depicts a world riven by ethical relativity, a fact that both mocks any pretense to absolute moral standards and enhances the quality of everyday life in a small country village. "The country," Darcy remarks, "can in general supply but few subjects for such a study. In a country neighbourhood you move in a very confined and unvarying society." "But people themselves alter so much," pert Elizabeth responds, "that there is something new to be observed in them for ever."[25] This principle of infinite variety within apparent unity extends from the object of study to the observer, of course; the fact that Elizabeth can praise Bingley for his compliance when he offers to remain at Netherfield and call that same trait weakness when he stays away (pp. 50, 135) tells us more about Elizabeth's desires than the principle of tractability. And the fact that Elizabeth can excuse Wickham for preferring a practical marriage when she will forever blame Charlotte for making the same choice reveals more about Elizabeth's personal investment in these two situations than Jane Austen's views on matrimony or money. Judgment is always inflected—modulated—by personal desire, Austen suggests, just as vision is always governed by perspective. "Principles" are often merely prejudices, and prejudices simply project one's own interests onto the shifting scene outside so as to defend and reinforce the self.

Ideally, in such a world, conventions of propriety and morality make living together possible by compensating for the competing desires of individuals and by stabilizing standards of judgment and value. But in *Pride and Prejudice*, as in Austen's other novels and, presumably, in her society as well, social conventions no longer necessarily serve this end; instead, as Wollstonecraft complained, social institutions have ossified until they threaten to crush the desire from which they theoretically grew and which they ought to accommodate. Beside the arrogant Miss Bingley, parading around the drawing room in hopes of catching Darcy's eye, or Mr. Collins, pompous embodiment of unyielding propriety itself, Elizabeth's impulsiveness, outspokenness, and generosity seem admirable and necessary correctives. When she bursts into

Netherfield to see her sick sister, for example, the mud on her skirts becomes completely irrelevant beside the healthiness of her unself-conscious concern for Jane. That Miss Bingley despises Elizabeth for what she calls "conceited independence" simply enhances our sympathy for conceit and independence, if these are the traits Elizabeth embodies. And when Elizabeth refuses to be subdued by Lady Catherine, whether on the subject of her music or her marriage, we feel nothing but admiration for her, "impertinence"—if this is what her energy really is.

Yet the juxtaposition of Elizabeth's lively wit with this pretentious and repressive society cuts both ways; for if the vacuity of her surroundings highlights her energy, it also encourages her to cultivate her natural vivacity beyond its legitimate bounds. As the novel unfolds, we begin to recognize that Elizabeth's charming wit is another incarnation of willful desire, which, by rendering judgment unstable, contributes to moral relativity. As Elizabeth embellishes her surroundings with imaginative flourishes, we begin to see that indulging the imagination can harm others and that it in fact serves as a defense against emotional involvement. Through this juxtaposition, then, Austen is able to enlist the reader's initial imaginative engagement with Elizabeth in the service of moral education—an education for the reader, which shadows (but does not correspond precisely to) Elizabeth's own education, and which schools the imagination by means of its own irrepressible energy.

One of the first indications that Elizabeth's quick wit and powerful feelings may be unreliable moral guides emerges in her initial conversation with George Wickham. Until this moment, Elizabeth's companions and the settings in which she has appeared have enhanced her charm and appeal. But as soon as Elizabeth enters into her intimate conversation with Wickham, Austen encourages us to recognize that something is wrong. The problem here is not that a responsive young woman is attracted to a handsome young militia man; instead, the problem is that Elizabeth is unconsciously using Wickham to reinforce her prejudice against Darcy and is, as a consequence, allowing herself to be used by Wickham to reinforce his own false position. There are no disinterested or straightforward emotions in this scene; what appears to be Elizabeth's simple response to Wickham's physical and emotional charm is actually being fed by the subterranean force of her anger at Darcy. Elizabeth is flattered by Wickham's particular attention to her, but she is equally aroused by the fact that his story justifies her anger at Darcy. As a consequence of this double flattery, Elizabeth is blinded to the impropriety of this stranger's intimacy, she is seduced into judging on the grounds of Wickham's "countenance" rather than some less arbitrary principle, and she is encouraged to credit her feelings instead of testing her perceptions against reality.

The action of *Pride and Prejudice* generally reveals that, despite what looks like a generous overflow of irrepressible energy, Elizabeth's "liveliness" is primarily defensive.[26] More specifically, her "impertinence" is a psychological defense against the vulnerability to which her situation as a dependent woman exposes her. Elizabeth's prejudice against Darcy is so quickly formed and so persistent because, at the first assembly, he unthinkingly confronts her with the very facts that it is most in her interest to deny. "She is tolerable," Darcy concedes, rejecting Bingley's overtures on Elizabeth's behalf, "but not handsome enough to tempt *me*; and I am in no humour at present to give consequence to young ladies who are slighted by other men" (p. 12).

Despite the fact that Elizabeth's "playful disposition" enables her to turn this "ridiculous" remark against Darcy, his cool observation continues to vex and haunt her for much of the novel and to govern not only her anger toward Darcy but also her "mortification" at the antics of her family. It has this effect for two closely related reasons. First of all, in spite of her professed unconcern, Elizabeth, like everyone else, is immediately attracted to this handsome, eminently eligible bachelor, and, if only for a short time, he engages her natural romantic fantasies. We discover this later, when Darcy offers to make her dream come true and Elizabeth retorts by acknowledging that, though she once considered him as a possible husband, she no longer does so: "I had not known you a month," she exults, inadvertently acknowledging the longevity of her fantasy, "before I felt that you were the last man in the world whom I could ever be prevailed on to marry" (p. 193). But, given Elizabeth's social position and economic situation, even to dream of marrying Darcy is an act of imaginative presumption. The second reason for her lingering pain, then, is that Darcy's rejection deflates not only her romantic fantasies of marriage to a handsome aristocrat but, more important, the image of herself upon which such fantasies are based.

Darcy's casual remark suggests that the fact that Elizabeth is momentarily without a partner indicates that she will always be so "slighted," that her "tolerable" beauty will never attract the permanent partner she desires. And this remark strikes very close to home. For the inevitable result of an entail in a household more blessed with daughters than frugality is, at best, a limited choice of suitors; at worst, the Bennet's shortage of money for dowries and their equivocal social position foretell spinsterhood, dependence on a generous relative, or, most ominous of all, work as a governess or lady's companion. Austen never lets the reader or Elizabeth forget how very likely such a future is. Darcy lays the groundwork for this scenario when, alluding to their uncles in trade and law, he remarks that such connections "must very materially lessen [the sisters'] chance of marrying men of any consideration in the world" (p. 37). Even closer to home, when Charlotte Lucas rejects romance, she does so for its opposite, the matter-of-fact assessment that a "comfortable home" is more substantial than romantic fantasies. Elizabeth's mother is even more brutally frank. "If you take it into your head," she warns Elizabeth, "to go on refusing every offer of marriage in this way, you will never get a husband at all—and I am sure I do not know who is to maintain you when your father is dead" (p. 113). In the context of such dark realism, even Mr. Collins's compensatory retaliation sounds ominously like a self-evident truth. "Your portion is unhappily so small," he smugly informs Elizabeth, "that it will in all likelihood undo the effects of your loveliness and amiable qualifications" (p. 108).

Elizabeth chooses to ignore all of these warnings, of course, because, with the arrogance born of youth, natural high spirits, and intellectual superiority, she believes herself too good for such a fate. But Darcy challenges her self-confidence, and, in the disappointment he indirectly inflicts on Jane, he proves himself capable of bringing the Bennet family face to face with undeniable reality. In the face of real dependence and practical powerlessness, Elizabeth grasps at any possible source of power or distinction. As she confides to Jane in a moment of telling self-awareness, wit and prejudice have been her two sources of power, two means of distinguishing herself:

> I meant to be uncommonly clever in taking so decided a dislike to him, without any reason. It is such a spur to one's genius, such an opening for wit to have a dislike of that kind. One may be continually abusive without saying any thing just; but one cannot be always laughing at a man without now and then stumbling on something witty. [pp. 225–26]

From this statement, Elizabeth's psychological economy is clear: she directs her intelligence toward defending herself against emotional vulnerability; she bases her moral judgments at least partially on her defensiveness; and she rationalizes both the romantic fantasies with which she consoles herself and the forays of wit with which she protects herself as spontaneous effusions of a lively and superior mind.

Such criticism of Elizabeth's "liveliness" is elaborated by Austen's characterizations of both Mr. Bennet and Lydia. Elizabeth is her father's favorite daughter, and Mr. Bennet's witty intelligence clearly reinforces and feeds off Elizabeth's superiority. But Mr. Bennet is finally a failure, for he is lax when it comes to the social duties that are most important to the Bennet family as a whole and to Elizabeth in particular. Like Elizabeth's society in general, Mr. Bennet's character is a moral vacuum; his "indolence and the little attention he has [given] to what was going forward in his family" (p. 283) finally permit, if they do not encourage, Lydia's rebellion. Mr. Bennet tries to make light of his moral irresponsibility by describing social relations as an amusing game. "For what do we live," he asks rhetorically, "but to make sport for our neighbours, and laugh at them in our turn?" (p. 364). But the pain that unthinking Lydia visits on the rest of the family proves conclusively how serious—and how selfish—his evasion really is.

Just as her father's defensive intelligence refracts and exaggerates Elizabeth's intellectual "liveliness," so Lydia's wild, noisy laughter helps clarify Elizabeth's "impertinence." But perhaps the most important function of Lydia's story derives from its placement. For Austen positions the announcement of Lydia's elopement so as to precipitate the second, and most important, stage of Elizabeth's education. Through Darcy's letter, Elizabeth has already learned that she was wrong about both Wickham and Darcy, but Darcy's proposal and her angry rejection have, if anything, increased, not lessened, her pride and sense of superiority. "Vanity, not love, has been my folly," Elizabeth exclaims at the moment of this first "humiliation" (p. 208); but, on second thought, she is deeply flattered by the great man's attentions, and, since she does not regret her decision, she is free to bask in the triumph his proposal gives her over his "pride," over his "prejudices," and over Lady Catherine and Miss Bingley as well. Thus, even though she feels that her own "past behaviour" constitutes "a constant source of vexation and regret" (p. 212), Elizabeth visits Pemberley with her vanity very much intact: "at that moment she felt, that to be mistress of Pemberley might be something!" (p. 245). This dream of what she might have been is jolted into the present and then into the future when Darcy suddenly appears, proves courteous to the very relatives he had previously slighted, and then invites Elizabeth back to Pemberley to meet his sister. At this moment, Elizabeth realizes that her "power" is even greater than she had dared imagine it to be.

> She respected, she esteemed, she was grateful to him, she felt a real interest in his welfare; and she only wanted to know how far she wished that welfare to depend upon herself, and how far it would be for the happiness of both that she should employ the power, which her fancy told her she still possessed, of bringing on the renewal of his addresses. [p. 266]

While this reflection is neither cool nor calculating, it does suggest that Elizabeth feels herself more superior than ever—not so much to Darcy as to love.

Jane's letter arrives when Elizabeth is basking in this self-confidence; its effect is to strip her of self-control, self-assurance, and her confident superiority over feeling. In Darcy's presence she bursts into tears and then, suddenly recognizing what she now believes she has lost, she realizes that true power belongs not to the imagination but to love: "Her power was sinking; every thing must sink under such a proof of family weakness. . . . The belief of his self-conquest . . . afforded no palliation of her distress. It was, on the contrary, exactly calculated to make her understand her own wishes; and never had she so honestly felt that she could have loved him, as now, when all love must be vain" (p. 278).

Elizabeth's fantasies no longer seem as wild or romantic as they once did, but, before her wish can be fulfilled, she must be "humbled" by her own sister—not only so that she (and the reader) will recognize the pernicious effects of Lydia's passionate self-indulgence, but so that Elizabeth herself will understand how intimately her own fate is bound up in the actions and characters of others. Individualism is not simply morally suspect, Austen suggests; it is also based on a naive overestimation of personal autonomy and power. To pretend that one can transcend social categories or refuse a social role (as Mr. Bennet does) is not only irresponsible; it also reveals a radical misunderstanding of the fact that, for an individual living in society, every action is automatically linked to the actions of others. And to believe that one can exercise free will, even when parents do not intercede, is to mistake the complex nature of desire and the way in which social situation affects psychology and self-knowledge.

Yet, despite its sobering implications, the "mortification" of Elizabeth's vanity does not constitute a rebuke to the premises or promises of romance, as Marianne's illness does in *Sense and Sensibility*. Instead, in order to convert the power of romance into a legitimate corrective for harsh realism, Austen redeems romance by purging it of all traces of egotism. As we have already seen, to believe that one's beauty and wit will captivate a powerful lord is really a form of vanity. But Elizabeth's actual romantic fantasies about Darcy are short-lived; the only dashing young man she fantasizes extensively about is Wickham. Elizabeth's response to her aunt's query about Wickham may be only half serious, but her confusion does reveal the extent of her susceptibility.

> At present I am not in love with Mr. Wickham; no, I certainly am not. But he is, beyond all comparison, the most agreeable man I ever saw—and if he becomes really attached to me—I believe it will be better that he should not. I see the imprudence of it.—Oh! that abominable Mr. Darcy!—My father's opinion of me does me the greatest honor, and I should be miserable to forfeit it. My father, however, is partial to Mr. Wickham. In short, my dear aunt, I should be very sorry to be the means of making any of you unhappy; but since we see every day that where there is affection, young people are seldom withheld by immediate want of fortune from entering into engagements with each other, how can

I promise to be wiser than so many of my fellow creatures if I am tempted, or how am I even to know that it would be wisdom to resist? All that I can promise you, therefore, is not to be in a hurry. I will not be in a hurry to believe myself his first object. When I am in company with him, I will not be wishing. In short, I will do my best. [pp. 144–45]

Just as Elizabeth's prejudice against Darcy originally fed her admiration for Wickham, now her attraction to the young soldier focuses her resentment against Darcy: if Wickham's story is true, after all, Darcy has been directly (although inadvertently) responsible for preventing a marriage between Elizabeth and Wickham. But Austen does not allow this or any other romance to develop or capture Elizabeth's imagination; indeed, when she dismisses this particular suitor, she does not ridicule either the claims or the attractions of romance. Instead, when Wickham declares for the wealthy Miss King, Elizabeth remains undisturbed, and the entire issue of romantic love is simply pushed to the periphery of the narrative. Wickham's decision to marry for money does, after all, leave Elizabeth's vanity intact. "His apparent partiality had subsided, his attentions were over, he was the admirer of some one else. Elizabeth was watchful enough to see it all, but she could see it and write of it without material pain. Her heart had been but slightly touched, and her vanity was satisfied with believing that *she* would have been his only choice, had fortune permitted it" (p. 149).

Elizabeth's eventual love for Darcy is legitimate because it springs not from the vanity we ordinarily associate with romantic expectations but precisely from the mortification of pride. Yet because Elizabeth only belatedly realizes that she loves Darcy, her humbling does not entail a rejection of romantic love. Indeed, unaccountable, uncontrollable romantic love continues to play a role in *Pride and Prejudice*—in Darcy's desire for Elizabeth. This passion, which Austen notes but does not dwell on, is the subtextual force behind much of the action. In response to love, Darcy overcomes his prejudices against Elizabeth's connections, proposes to her, returns to her even after hope seems gone, and eventually brings about the marriages of three of the Bennet daughters. The narrative does not focus on the development or pressures of this passion; even when Elizabeth playfully asks Darcy for an account of his love, her mocking celebration of "impertinence" deflects any explanation he might have given. Romantic love remains the unexamined and unaccountable source of power in a novel preoccupied with various forms of social and psychological power and powerlessness. It not only overcomes all obstacles; it brings about a perfect society at the end of the novel.

The romantic conclusion of *Pride and Prejudice* effectively dismisses the social and psychological realism with which the novel began. Elizabeth's "impertinence" may have originated in her need to dispel the vulnerability of her dependent situation, but when marriage with Darcy cancels all the gloomy forecasts about Elizabeth's future, Austen no longer suggests a possible relationship between social causes and psychological effects. Elizabeth's "liveliness" persists, of course, but it is purified of its defensiveness and its egotism. In essence, in awarding Elizabeth this handsome husband with ten thousand pounds a year, Austen is gratifying the reader's fantasy that such outspoken liveliness will be successful in material terms, but she earns the right to do so precisely because Elizabeth's first fantasy of personal power *is not* rewarded. *Pride and Prejudice*, in other words, legitimizes the reader's romantic wishes by humbling the heroine's vanity. At the level of the plot, power is taken from egotism and given to love; at the level of the reading experience, power seems miraculously both to emanate from and to reward individualistic desire.

Darcy and Elizabeth, then, learn complementary lessons: he recognizes that individual feelings outweigh conventional social distinctions; she realizes the nature of society's power. Their marriage purports to unite individual gratification with social responsibility, to overcome the class distinctions that elevated Lady Catherine over the worthy Gardiners, and to make of society one big happy family. The last pages of *Pride and Prejudice* describe family connections radiating throughout society, closing the gap between geographical locations, social classes, and temperamental differences. The union that concludes this novel reestablishes the ideal, paternalistic society that Mr. Bennet's irresponsibility and Wickham's insubordination once seemed to threaten. With Darcy at its head and Elizabeth at its heart, society will apparently be able to contain the anarchic impulses of individualism and humanize the rigidities of prejudice, and everyone—even Miss Bingley—will live more or less happily in the environs of Pemberley, the vast estate whose permanence, prominence, and unique and uniquely satisfying fusion of individual taste and utility, of nature and art, symbolize Jane Austen's ideal.[27]

Austen is able to effect an aesthetic resolution of what is essentially a moral dilemma partly because the realistic elements in her portrayal of the situation are so carefully contained. As in *Sense and Sensibility*, Austen simply does not explore to the full the social or psychological implications of her realism. Darcy, Charlotte Lucas, Mr. Collins, and Mrs. Bennet all warn Elizabeth that her impertinence will probably result in spinsterhood, but Austen does not imperil the integrity of the romantic ending by dramatizing the perils of such a future in a character like Jane Fairfax, Miss Bates, or Mrs. Smith. But even beyond curtailing the extent of her realism, Austen controls the response of her readers by drawing them into a system of values that seems, by the end of the novel, both "natural" and right. She can generate this system of common values because one of the fundamental principles of her art is to assume that the relationship between an author and an audience is ideally (if not automatically) a version of the relationship she knew best: the family.

The model of the family governs Jane Austen's art in at least three important ways. To begin with, her own personal family served as her first and most appreciative audience. Like the Brontës after her, Jane Austen wrote her first stories for the amusement of her family; most of her surviving juvenilia are dedicated to her siblings or cousins, and it is easy to imagine these stories and plays being read in the family circle, with various members contributing jokes from time to time. Austen's first longer works—*First Impressions* (later *Pride and Prejudice*) and *Elinor and Marianne* (later *Sense and Sensibility*)—were also apparently family entertainments, and, even after she became a published author, she continued to solicit and value the responses of her family as she composed and revised her novels.[28] For Austen, the entire enterprise of writing was associated with hospitality and familial bonds. Her letters reveal that she sometimes half jokingly talked of her novels as her "children" and of her characters as if they were family friends. She assured her sister, for instance, that she could "no more forget" *Sense and Sensibility* "than a mother can forget her sucking child" (*JAL*, 2:272; 25 April 1811); she referred to *Pride and Prejudice* as her "own child" (*JAL*, 2:297; 29 January 1813); and she pretended to find a portrait of Jane Bingley exhibited in Spring Gardens: "There never was a greater likeness," Austen playfully announced; "She is dressed in a white gown, with green ornaments, which convinces me of what I had always supposed, that green was a favourite colour with her" (*JAL*, 2:310; 24 May 1813).[29]

The fact that Austen's completed novels and the activity of writing itself were part of the fabric of her family relationships helps to explain why she was able to avoid both the aggressive polemicism that Mary Wollstonecraft employed and the enfeebling defensiveness to which Mary Shelley resorted. Austen actively wondered what her readers thought of her novels, and she regretted that her works did not receive adequate critical attention, but she never seems to have imagined an audience openly hostile to either her novels or herself, as both Wollstonecraft and Shelley did, for different reasons. But in addition to providing a hospitable transitional area between her private imagination and the public bookstall, Jane Austen's experience of a close and supportive family also provided models both for the way an individual's desires could be accommodated by social institutions and for the context of shared values that an author could ideally rely on to provide a moral basis for art.

The notion of the family that served Jane Austen as a model for the proper coexistence of the individual and society was essentially patriarchal, supportive of, and supported by, the allegiances and hierarchy that feminine propriety implied. Its smallest unit—the marriage—embodied for Austen the ideal union of individual desire and social responsibility; if a woman could legitimately express herself *only* by choosing to marry and then by *sustaining* her marriage, Austen suggests, she could, through her marriage, not only satisfy her own needs but also influence society. For the most part, the culminating marriages in Austen's novels lack the undercurrents of ambivalence that characterize Shelley's depictions of even happy marriages. This is true in part because the energies of Austen's heroines are not so rigorously channeled by propriety into self-denial either before or after marriage. As *Sense and Sensibility* suggests, however, Austen does discipline female energies, but, increasingly, she also suggests that the psychological toll exacted by patriarchal society from women is too high. The fact that almost all of the peripheral marriages in her novels are dissatisfying in one way or another seems to indicate that Austen recognized both the social liabilities that Wollstonecraft identified and the psychological complexities that Shelley intuited. Nevertheless, and especially in *Pride and Prejudice*, the most idealistic of all of her novels, marriage remains for Austen the ideal paradigm of the most perfect fission between the individual and society.

As the actual basis and ideal model of the contract between an author and an audience, the family also promised a context of shared experiences, assumptions, and values against which the writer could play and to which he or she could eventually return. And it is in this sense—and for this reason—that the moral relativism theoretically unleashed by individualism does not necessarily undermine Austen's conservative moral pattern or her didactic purpose. For if an author can assume a set of basic assumptions and values, such as family members share, then he or she can depend on the reader's returning with the narrator to that common ground, in spite of liberties to stray that have been permitted in the course of the fiction. In fact, given the common ground, these liberties often contribute to the didactic design of the novel, for they foster the illusion that challenges to ethical and aesthetic authority are actually being engaged and defeated in their own terms.

In *Pride and Prejudice* Austen tries to ensure that her readers will share a common ground by making them participate in constructing the value system that governs the novel. This participation is a necessary part of reading *Pride and Prejudice* because Austen combines a predominantly dramatic presentation of the action with an irony so persistent that it almost destroys narrative authority.[30] Even what looks like omniscient commentary often turns out, on closer inspection, to carry the accents of a single character. The famous first sentence of the novel, for example—"It is a truth universally acknowledged, that a single man in possession of a good fortune, must be in want of a wife"—points to the radical limitations of both "truth" and "universally."

Masquerading as a statement of fact—if not about all unmarried men, then certainly about a community that collectively assumes it to be true—this sentence actually tells us more about Mrs. Bennet than anyone else. In such local instances, irony allows us a certain freedom of interpretation even when it teases us to test our "first impressions" against our developing understanding of individual characters and the priorities of the novel as a whole.

As Wayne Booth has noted, irony forces the reader not only to participate in interpretation and evaluation but to choose one *system* of values over another.[31] And it is through the value system developed in the overall action of the novel that Austen hopes to counter the relativism that the localized ironies might permit.[32] We can see this principle at work in Charlotte Lucas's argument about marriage. The narrator, conveying Charlotte's thoughts indirectly, takes no explicit stand on her position: "Without thinking highly either of men or of matrimony, marriage had always been her object; it was the only honourable provision for well-educated young women of small fortune, and however uncertain of giving happiness, must be their pleasantest preservative from want" (pp. 122–23). Certainly this statement illuminates the limitations of Charlotte's romantic expectations, but is it meant to be an authoritative assessment of reality? Or is Elizabeth's indignant rejoinder more authoritative? "You must feel, as well as I do," she exclaims to Jane, "that the woman who marries him, cannot have a proper way of thinking" (p. 135). Elsewhere Elizabeth's "proper way of thinking" has proved self-interested. Is this case any different? And how are we, finally, to decide?

In such passages, Austen is both permitting momentary freedom of choice and demonstrating the vertigo that accompanies it. But through the unfolding action of the novel she seems to qualify this freedom by endorsing one option over the other: Mr. Bingley and Mr. Darcy *do* both want and need wives; the love matches Elizabeth believed in *do* come about, despite all the odds against them. And, most important, the paternal order established at the end of the novel both embodies an authoritative system of values and abolishes the apparent discrepancy between individual desire and social responsibility. Jane Austen's irony, then, enables her to reproduce—without exposing in any systematic way—some of the contradictions inherent in bourgeois ideology; for by simultaneously dramatizing and rewarding individual desire *and* establishing a critical distance from individualism, she endorses both the individualistic perspective inherent in the bourgeois value system *and* the authoritarian hierarchy retained from traditional, paternalistic society. Moreover, by allowing her reader to exercise freedom of judgment in individual instances while controlling the final value system through the action as a whole, Austen replicates, at the level of the reading experience, the marriage of romantic desire and realistic necessity that she believed was capable of containing individualism's challenge to traditional authority.

In *Pride and Prejudice* this strategy effectively focuses what had remained two distinct narrative parts in *Lady Susan* and two competing centers of authority in *Northanger Abbey* and *Sense and Sensibility*. The closure of *Pride and Prejudice* is thus aesthetically successful, but whether it insures a comparable ideological resolution is doubtful. For at the level of the plot Austen can grant moral authority to feeling by stripping desire of egotism, but she cannot guarantee that every reader will be as educable as Elizabeth or that all expressions of feeling will be as socially constructive as Elizabeth's desire for Darcy. This problem is raised specifically in *Pride and Prejudice* by Lydia, and Austen never really dismisses this character or the unruly energy she embodies:

> Lydia was Lydia still; untamed, unabashed, wild, noisy, and fearless. She turned from sister to sister, demanding their congratulations, and when at length they all sat down, looked eagerly round the room, took notice of some little alteration in it, and observed, with a laugh, that it was a great while since she had been there. [p. 315]

Even Austen's concluding comment on Lydia acknowledges that she finally finds a place within the same society that Elizabeth superintends. "In spite of her youth and her manners," the narrator informs us, Lydia "retained all the claims to reputation which her marriage had given her" (p. 387).

Austen's tacit assumption that her readers will renounce the moral anarchy epitomized in Lydia and generated by the pattern of localized ironies would be accurate only if her audience already shared her own experiences and values. For the purposes of her art, Austen makes this assumption because it allows her to contain not only individual interpretations but also the social criticisms implicitly raised in the course of *Pride and Prejudice*. In fact, this assumption enables her to bring the real experiences of her readers to bear on her narrative in such a way as to underscore the necessity of the aesthetic solution, which pushes aside social realism and criticism. Austen's contemporary readers would no doubt have been all too familiar with the facts and pressures that made Charlotte Lucas's cool assessment of marriage reasonable, and, merely by alluding to this shared experience, Austen enhances the gratification that Elizabeth's improbable success provides. Thus she introduces the specters of spinsterhood, dependence, and compromise less to explore the social strictures of Elizabeth's situation than to invoke the reality that makes her own consoling art necessary. The inadequacy of the aesthetic solution to the social problems it supposedly answers remains implicit but unproblematic; for it is precisely the gap between imaginative desire and social reality—a gap that still exists—that makes the escape into romance attractive to all readers and probably made Austen's contemporaries, in particular, anxious to believe that Elizabeth's happiness was available to every daughter of the middle class.

The special resonance and impact that her contemporaries sensed in the statements and situations of Austen's novels are dim or absent altogether for twentieth-century readers. But even the experiences Austen's contemporaries shared with her, merely by virtue of their historical, geographical, and class proximity, would not have guaranteed a common set of values. For, as we have seen, in this period of social turmoil even the dominant system of values was characterized by internal tensions and contradictions—stresses that reflected the competition between bourgeois individualism and old patterns of patronage and also the inevitable gap between the promises of individualism and the general inequalities and personal repressions that bourgeois society requires. Given the structure of bourgeois society, the system of absolute Christian principles that is the foundation of Austen's novels necessarily had to have its everyday, functional version, which allowed one to be "rather" selfish in pursuit of material prosperity as long as one practiced charity and thought good thoughts. It is precisely the latitude of interpretations permitted by this compromise of ethical and moral absolutes that finally imperils the didactic design of *Pride and Prejudice*. For the family of readers that Austen posited did not necessarily exist; even in her own day, the consensus of values she needed to assume was as wishful a fiction as Elizabeth Bennet's marriage to Darcy.

Because of the sophistication of her narrative skills, the romance Austen dramatizes at the end of *Pride and Prejudice* seems not only right but plausible. But it is plausible only because, in this novel, Austen separates the power to gratify and discipline desire from the conditions that generate and frustrate that desire. The power moves from society to the realm of art; in *Pride and Prejudice* Austen substitutes aesthetic gratification—the pleasures of the "light and bright and sparkling" plays of wit—for the practical solutions that neither her society nor her art could provide. That we do not more often feel shortchanged by this sleight-of-hand attests to the power of her artistry and to the magnitude of our own desire to deny the disturbing ideological contradictions that have made such imaginative compensation necessary.

NOTES

1. The most extensive discussion of Austen's treatment of propriety is Jane Nardin's *Those Elegant Decorums: The Concept of Propriety in Jane Austen's Novels* (Albany: State University of New York Press, 1973). Nardin's analysis is extremely perceptive and discriminating, but, finally, I cannot accept the degree of conscious intention she attributes to Austen (see pp. 10–11). The most telling recent analysis of the contradictions in Austen's novels, and thus a reading more in keeping with my own, is Igor

Webb's *From Custom to Capital: The English Novel and the Industrial Revolution* (Ithaca and London: Cornell University Press, 1981), pp. 49–70, 101–21, 158–61.

2. One example of Austen's apparent self-contradiction is evident in her opinions about Evangelicalism. On 24 January 1809 she told Cassandra: "You have by no means raised my curiosity after *Caleb* (Hannah More's *Coelebs in Search of a Wife*;—My disinclination for it before was affected, but now it is real; I do not like the Evangelicals." On 18 November 1814, however, she informed Fanny Knight that "I am by no means convinced that we ought not all to be Evangelicals, & am at least persuaded that they who are so from Reason and Feeling, must be happiest & safest" (*Jane Austen's Letters to Her Sister Cassandra and Others*, ed. R. W. Chapman, 2 vols. [Oxford: Clarendon Press, 1932], 1:256; 2:410; hereafter cited as *JAL*). Austen might simply have changed her opinion; on the other hand, she might have been making distinctions we can no longer confidently reconstruct.

3. The one extant copy of *Lady Susan* is a fair copy that bears the watermark 1805. Chapman acknowledges, however, that the transcription of the novel could easily have postdated its composition by a number of years. B. C. Southam, in *Jane Austen's Literary Manuscripts: A Study of the Novelist's Development through the Surviving Papers* (London: Oxford University Press, 1964), pp. 45–62, presents a strong case for the earlier date.

4. *Lady Susan*, vol. 6 of *The Works of Jane Austen*, ed. R. W. Chapman (London: Oxford University Press, 1954), p. 243. (Volumes 1–5 appeared in the second edition of the *Works*, published in 1926.)

5. See Lloyd W. Brown, "Jane Austen and the Feminist Tradition," *Nineteenth-Century Fiction* 28 (1973): 334, and Sandra M. Gilbert and Susan Gubar, *The Madwoman in the Attic: The Woman Writer and the Nineteenth-Century Literary Imagination* (New Haven: Yale University Press, 1979), p. 118.

6. See Lloyd W. Brown, *Bits of Ivory: Narrative Techniques in Jane Austen's Fiction* (Baton Rouge: Louisiana State University Press, 1973), pp. 147–48, 153.

7. Gilbert and Gubar point out that one way in which Austen attempts to control our sympathy for Lady Susan is by making her cruelty to Frederica exceed the demands of the plot. See *Madwoman*, pp. 155–56.

8. William Wordsworth, letter to Daniel Stuart, 1817, quoted by Alistair M. Duckworth, *The Improvement of the Estate: A Study of Jane Austen's Novels* (Baltimore: Johns Hopkins University Press, 1971), p. 81.

9. For a discussion of the spirit of "party" and the "contrary systems of thought" typical of the literature of this period, see L. J. Swingle, "The Poets, the Novelists, and the English Romantic Situation," *Wordsworth Circle* 3 (1979): 218–28, and David Simpson, *Irony and Authority in Romantic Poetry* (Totowa, N.J.: Rowman & Littlefield, 1979).

10. Donald J. Greene, "Jane Austen and the Peerage," *PMLA* 68 (1953): 1017–31; reprinted in *Jane Austen: A Collection of Critical Essays*, ed. Ian Watt (Englewood Cliffs, N.J.: Prentice-Hall, 1963), pp. 156–57.

11. See Marilyn Butler, *Jane Austen and the War of Ideas* (Oxford: Clarendon Press, 1975), pp. 161–67, 284–85, and Duckworth, *The Improvement*, pp. 2–80. For another discussion of Jane Austen's religion, see Warren Roberts, *Jane Austen and the French Revolution* (New York: St. Martin's Press, 1979), pp. 109–54.

12. See Terry Lovell, "Jane Austen and the Gentry: A Study in Literature and Ideology," *The Sociology of Literature: Applied Studies*, ed. Diana Laurenson (Hanley, Eng.: Wood Mitchell & Co., 1978), pp. 20–21.

13. See ibid., p. 21.

14. For an excellent discussion of the complexities of parody, see George Levine, "Translating the Monstrous: *Northanger Abbey*," *Nineteenth-Century Fiction* 30 (1975): 337.

15. Samuel Johnson, *Rambler* 4, in *The Yale Edition of the Works of Samuel Johnson*, ed. W. J. Bate and Albrecht B. Strauss, 14 vols. (New Haven: Yale University Press, 1969), 3:21, 22.

16. *Persuasion*, in *The Works of Jane Austen*, 5:101.

17. Johnson, *Rambler* 4, pp. 23, 21.

18. *Northanger Abbey*, in *The Works of Jane Austen*, 5:37, 38. Patricia Meyer Spacks also points out that education in an Austen novel requires imaginative engagement; see her "Muted Discord: Generational Conflict in Jane Austen," in *Jane Austen in a Social Context*, ed. David Monaghan (Totowa, N.J.: Barnes & Noble, 1981), pp. 170, 174, 177–78.

19. The precise order in which Austen composed her major works is unknown, but B. C. Southam, having consulted Cassandra's original memorandum and the surviving manuscripts, argues persuasively for the following chronology: *Elinor and Marianne*—completed before 1796; *First Impressions*—October 1796–August 1797; *Sense and Sensibility*, the revision of *Elinor and Marianne*—begun November 1797, revised again at Chawton 1809–10; *Northanger Abbey*, originally entitled *Susan*—c. 1798–99, never substantially revised; *Pride and Prejudice*, the revision of *First Impressions*—conducted in 1809–10 and 1812; *Mansfield Park*—February 1811 June 1813; *Emma*—21 January 1814–29 March 1815; *Persuasion*—8 August 1815–6 August 1816 (Southam, *Jane Austen's Literary Manuscripts*, pp. 52–58). The dates given in parentheses in my text are the publication dates.

20. For a discussion of Austen's "free, indirect speech," see Norman Page, *The Language of Jane Austen* (New York: Barnes & Noble, 1972), pp. 123 ff.

21. *Sense and Sensibility*, in *The Works of Jane Austen*, 1:8.

22. Tony Tanner, Introduction to the Penguin edition of *Sense and Sensibility* (Harmondsworth, Eng., 1969), p. 32.

23. See Tanner, ibid., p. 30.

24. I am indebted to Patricia Meyer Spacks and to her Yale College seminar on Jane Austen for many of the observations about this episode.

25. *Pride and Prejudice*, in *The Works of Jane Austen*, 2:42–43.

26. Bernard J. Paris makes this point in *Character and Conflict in Jane Austen's Novels: A Psychological Approach* (Detroit: Wayne State University Press, 1978), pp. 118–39. While many of my observations are consistent with Paris's reading, I disagree with his central thesis that Elizabeth can be treated as a "real" person throughout the novel. It is precisely Austen's aborting of psychological realism that interests me.

27. See Duckworth, *The Improvement of the Estate*, pp. 123–26 (see n. 8, above).

28. In 1799, for instance, Austen remarked to her sister Cassandra, "I do not wonder at your wanting to read 'First Impressions' again" (*JAL*, 1:52; 8 January 1799); her letters also show her sharing *Mansfield Park* with her brother Henry before its publication, and she kept a list of the responses her family and friends made to that novel and to *Emma*. See "Opinions of *Mansfield Park* and *Emma*" in *The Works of Jane Austen*, 6:431–39. For another discussion of the relationship between Austen's composition and her family, see Mary Lascelles, *Jane Austen and Her Art* (Oxford: Clarendon Press, 1939), pp. 4, 146.

29. Austen's niece Catherine Hubback commented that her aunt "always said her books were her children" (quoted by R. W. Chapman, *Jane Austen: Facts and Problems* [Oxford: Clarendon Press, 1948], p. 67), and from her nephews we learn that Austen supplied her family with information about her characters' "after-life": "In this tradition any way we learned that Miss Steele never succeeded in catching the Doctor; that Kitty Bennet was satisfactorily married to a clergyman near Pemberley, while Mary obtained nothing higher than one of her uncle Phillips' clerks, and was content to be considered a star in the society of Meriton; that the 'considerable sum' given by Mrs. Norris to William Price was one pound; that Mr. Woodhouse survived his daughter's marriage, and kept her and Mr. Knightley from settling at Donwell, about two years; and that the letters placed by Frank Churchill before Jane Fairfax, which she swept away unread, contained the word 'pardon'" (J. E. Austen-Leigh, *A Memoir of Jane Austen* [London: Macmillan, 1906], pp. 148–49). Julia Prewitt Brown also discusses the importance of the family for Austen; see her *Jane Austen's Novels: Social Change and Literary Form* (Cambridge, Mass.: Harvard University Press, 1979), p. 9.

30. One of the best discussions of this function of irony is in Nardin, *Those Elegant Decorums*, pp. 4–11.

31. See Wayne C. Booth, *A Rhetoric of Irony* (Chicago: University of Chicago Press, 1974), p. 44 and passim.

32. See A. Walton Litz, *Jane Austen: A Study of Her Artistic Development* (New York: Oxford University Press, 1965), p. 108.

E.B. MOON

"A Model of Female Excellence": Anne Elliot, Persuasion, and the Vindication of a Richardsonian Ideal of the Female Character

Some of the most interesting questions to vex the minds of critics about Jane Austen's *Persuasion* have been to do with the persuasion itself. What is its role in the novel? Is the question of whether or not Anne Elliot was right in allowing herself to be persuaded to reject Captain Wentworth ever convincingly resolved?[1]

Probably the most satisfactory readings of the work are those which see the issue of persuasion as important not so much for itself or in its working out as a theme, but in its relation to character.[2] The opening chapters serve to characterise Anne Elliot and to evaluate her against Sir Walter and Elizabeth in such a way that she immediately becomes a measure of proper behaviour. So, before we are presented with questions about persuasion, Anne's character has been established as not only gentle and self-effacing but also as morally strong and exemplary. When, in due course, we discover that some years earlier Anne had been persuaded to give up the man she deeply loved, we cannot then simply conclude, as Captain Wentworth had done, that hers must be a weak or shallow character. We are led, instead, to wonder what exactly those qualities are which render a character persuadable, and how we should regard them. It is in the building up of this implicit question—'What kind of character is a persuadable one?'—that Jane Austen gives us her directive to the novel's mode and structure. It is this question which the rest of the novel sets out to answer.[3]

From *AUMLA* 67 (May 1987): pp. 25–42. © 1987 by the Australasian Universities Language and Literature Association.

The question, 'What kind of character is a persuadable one?', becomes a means of scrutinizing a special kind of female character; the kind which, in exemplifying what are traditionally considered as 'feminine' characteristics, is both gentle and yielding, but which can only mistakenly be seen, as a consequence of this, as necessarily weak or excessively pliable. It is this character which Austen explores in its relation to 'being persuaded' and which she ultimately vindicates as 'a model of female excellence' (159).[4]

Jane Austen's treatment of the female character has been the subject of much recent criticism, a great deal of it feminist. Some of the latter critics see Austen as using her female characters to take up the issues, and the problems, of sexual stereotyping, demonstrating the undervaluing of women in the patriarchal society. For many of these critics, though, the marriages which end the novels embody an ultimate endorsement of conventional views about women as wives that undermines the basic critique.[5] An alternative view is that Austen uses irony and parody as 'subversive strategies', and that the conclusions of the novels are themselves parodic.[6] This present study, while agreeing that *Persuasion* does suggest that society underrates women, nonetheless would argue that the novel's conclusion postulates proper fulfilment for Anne Elliot as possible, within society, through marriage.

Margaret Kirkham, arguing for a feminist perspective (akin to Mary Wollstonecraft's) in Austen's novels,[7] makes the salient comment that, in *Persuasion*, 'Jane Austen comes close to completely reversing the role of the heroine as pupil-improver and of the hero as guardian-guide.'[8] And Kirkham's view that, although Anne's portrayal is close to the sentimental ideal, there is nonetheless careful discrimination between Anne's qualities and those of the ideal,[9] is similar to my own view. However, the particular feminist premises on which Kirkham's argument and conclusions are based do not seem to be self-evidently there. What does seem to be present, pointed to it as we are by Austen's other directives in the novel, is an invoking of an earlier ideal, one which, in Richardson's hands, had drawn the approval of the blue-stocking ladies of the 1750s: an ideal which had provided the basis for the sentimental heroine of the second half of the century but which itself differed, in certain important ways, from what the ideal popularly became.[10] Austen's directives to what is being invoked are embodied in allusion, and signalled through the use of the device of persuasion.

In choosing persuasion, and the ethical questions which attend it, Jane Austen has used an issue which has a well-established literary history, one which locates the problem surrounding Anne as deriving from that tradition of dilemmas of love and duty which confronted the exemplary heroines of an earlier age.[11] The employment of such a situation, with its own expectations and conventions, acts to place Anne Elliot within that tradition.[12] Arguably, then, the vindication of the character and nature of Anne Elliot as a realisable and recognisable ideal of woman is a major concern of *Persuasion*. I suggest that there is a quality of allusiveness to the literature of the past and a subtle, understated, but unmistakeable, reference to the characters and themes of Richardson's works, particularly *Sir Charles Grandison*.

I am not, of course, suggesting that Jane Austen is using *Grandison* as a specific model, nor that she is being directly emulative of that work. (It has become generally accepted, though, that she had a fondness for, and a debt to, Richardson; and although this view has not passed unchallenged, it seems fairly well proven.[13]) One of her very few specific allusions to an earlier work—in fact, not one of Richardson's—through its very specificity serves to illustrate the nature of her allusive method. This is the reference to Prior's *Henry and Emma*. In this work, the notes to the Penguin edition tell us, 'Emma expresses abject willingness to serve the nonexistent rival with whom her Henry pretends to be in love in order to test her' (Note 8, 394).[14] Jane Austen writes: 'Without emulating the feelings of an Emma towards her Henry, she [Anne] would have attended on Louisa with a zeal above the common claims of regard, for his sake . . .' (116). Jane Austen does not tell us the precise point of *Henry and Emma* to which she is referring, but her reference is obviously to something which is readily recognisable to her contemporary readers. By means of such recognition, the reader is given a sketched-in awareness of the particular tradition of the ideal woman that Jane Austen was drawing on. This, in turn, enlarges understanding of how the novel's question, 'What kind of character is a persuadable one?', might be approached. Anne's character is aligned to a tradition, but it does not simply reproduce the tradition. Through the novel an earlier ideal is reworked; and this, perhaps, is one of the most exciting things about *Persuasion* and part of its point.

* * *

Some support for the view that Austen in *Persuasion* was drawing on a Richardsonian ideal of feminine excellence, embodied most famously in his Clarissa but most readily emulative in his Harriet Byron—and that she was evoking a recognisable problem[15]—can be drawn from a (necessarily selective) comparison of *Persuasion* with *Sir Charles Grandison*, to suggest a degree of similarity between Anne Elliot and Richardson's two heroines, Harriet Byron and Clementina della Porretta.

All are, of course, sweet, gentle, delicate[16] and open, qualities shared with other exemplary heroines of the period. Harriet is initially more lively than Anne. She is younger, too, in years and experience, and her spiritedness diminishes as both increase—the years little, the experience much. A basic likeness between the two, however, is always there. Anne's loss of bloom, arising out of an enforced renunciation of love, is paralleled by Harriet's decline when it appears that Sir Charles is committed to Clementina. Both women, however, exhibit self-control, and each shows great fortitude under the duress of having to hide heartache. Moler sees this as aligning Austen to the views held by the 'conservative' novelists of the eighteenth century, views which had been challenged by those of the 'romantic-revolutionary' writers who followed Godwin and Rousseau.[17]

Neither Anne nor Harriet can stand cant or hypocrisy. Their comments about lack of openness being a fault are fairly similar. (See Anne on Mr Elliot [161] and Harriet on Sir Charles [I, 183]: a criticism which is later done away with.)[18]

Fairly, conventionally, both are motherless. Harriet, of course, has Mrs Shirley and Mrs Selby and the warmth and affection of family life which, suggestively, is what Anne envies the Musgroves (41). However, it is not surprising to note that Lady Russell, who stands in place of a mother for Anne during her childhood years, to some extent has her counterpart in *Sir Charles Grandison* in the Countess of D. The Countess, who would dearly like to have Harriet for a daughter-in-law, writes to her with 'the affectionate freedom of a mother' (II, 546). Both women would like their charges to marry, making it clear that a woman's potential remained generally unfulfilled if she did not. The Countess of D., indeed, urges Harriet to permit herself 'to be called out into active life' (II, 547), meaning marriage.

On another note, both heroines have a considerable degree of education and cultivation; and a superior level of accomplishment is indicated for each through a proficiency in Italian.[19] Anne, for example, translates the words of an Italian song for Mr Elliot and apologises for any deficiencies of meaning: 'I am a very poor Italian scholar' (186). Mr Elliot says:

> 'Yes, yes, I see you are. I see you know nothing of the matter. You have only knowledge enough of the language to translate at sight these inverted, transposed, curtailed Italian lines, into clear, comprehensible, elegant English. You need not say anything more of your ignorance.' (186)

Harriet was taught by her grandfather and although she, too, makes similarly modest disclaimers about her knowledge,[20] as with Anne this accomplishment distinguishes her from others around her.

Apart from parallels of nature and nurture, other suggestive links exist between Anne and Harriet as types. Both make similar moral judgements about the men who are their suitors. Harriet says she told Sir Hargrave: 'I had not the opinion of his morals that I must have of those of the man to whom I gave my hand in marriage' (I, 96). Anne knows that she could never accept Mr Elliot because her 'judgement' is 'against him'. She ponders it:

He certainly knew what was right, nor could she fix on any one article of moral duty evidently transgressed; but yet she would have been afraid to answer for his conduct. She distrusted the past, if not the present ... (160–161)

The authorial presentation of Mr Elliot, too, has certain similarities with Richardson's presentation of Sir Hargrave. Sir John Allestree gives Harriet Sir Hargreave's 'character':

... he is a very dangerous and enterprising man ... laughing and light as he is in company, he is malicious, ill-natured and designing; and sticks at nothing to carry a point on which he has once set his heart. (I, 63)

Mrs Smith gives Anne the 'character' of Mr Elliot:

'Mr Elliot is a man without heart or conscience; a designing, wary, cold-blooded being, who thinks only of himself; who, for his own interest or ease, would be guilty of any cruelty, or any treachery, that could be perpetrated without risk of his general character.' (199)

Sir John Allestree 'made no manner of doubt' that, despite Sir Hargrave's character, 'he was quite in earnest' in wanting to marry Harriet (I, 63). Mrs Smith assures Anne that Mr Elliot is 'no hypocrite now. He truly wants to marry you' (204). Each girl rejoices, later, in her escape from such a man and from the 'misery which must have followed' marriage (*Persuasion*, 211).[21]
    Jane Austen, then, sets her heroine within a well-established, Richardsonian framework. Significantly, in introducing Anne Elliot, she departs from the *Grandison* pattern in an important point. Harriet and Clementina are highly valued by their families. For Sir Walter Elliot, Anne's 'word had no weight; her convenience was always to give way;—she was only Anne' (5). By implicitly comparing and contrasting the responses which are part of this particular literary convention with the way Anne's family actually regards her, the author allows the expectation to be raised that, included in the novel's subject, will be the question of such a heroine's proper worth and how it should be assessed.
    When a group in Bath discuss Anne's prettiness they agree that they admire her more than Elizabeth, but add: 'But the men are all wild after Miss Elliot. Anne is too delicate for them' (178). 'Delicate' here refers to Anne's looks, of course, but these looks reflect her inner being; and Mr Elliot, who prefers Anne, joins the 'villains' in Richardson's and Jane Austen's novels (Lovelace in *Clarissa*, Sir Hargrave Pollexfen in *Grandison*, and Henry

Crawford in *Mansfield Park*) who are distinguished by having the penetration to discern and respond to such women, women of true female 'excellence'. That Anne is such a woman is Mr Elliot's expressed view (a view which delights Lady Russell):

> He thought her a most extraordinary young woman; in her temper, manners, mind, a model of female excellence. (159)[22]

And both Harriet and Clementina are frequently referred to as 'excellent creatures', even 'sister-excellencies' (III, 343).

In each novel, an ideal of female excellence forms part of the subject of the work. What, in fact, constitutes such excellence is canvassed and scrutinized, the novels themselves finally endorsing a clearly delineated ideal. In a sense, in both works, evaluation of the heroine/s becomes a test of character for others.

There are two main issues in *Persuasion* which might be held to derive in considerable part from Richardsonian models. One of these is evaluation of female character. The second is allied to it and is to do with problems of love and marriage for women. These are problems partly arising from the domestic, private and passive nature of women's lives but partly, also, from the way the behaviour of the mild and gentle woman can be misconstrued, her nature mistaken, and persuasion too often applied in the erroneous belief that such a nature will invariably yield because yielding is its natural response. It is in the working out of the great themes in *Persuasion*, of love and constancy, and of persuasion itself, that these issues are able to be explored.

* * *

Both *Persuasion* and *Sir Charles Grandison* deal with love and constancy and with the suffering which comes from love. Richardson is concerned to put forward the conservative position that 'first love' is not necessarily a one-and-only love; that if it should be overcome, then it can be. The novel argues the well-known romantic and anti-romantic views on this topic. The two heroines, Harriet and Clementina, both love Sir Charles Grandison, in each case a first love. Most of the material on the many aspects of love which are canvassed in Richardson's novel seems to prefigure the way such matters are looked at in *Persuasion*.[23] Again, Jane Austen seems not to borrow directly but to want to draw on a well-known area of debate and to arrive at her own conclusions, many of which in fact reinforce Richardson's. There are certain strong parallels between Clementina's case and Anne Elliot's (disregarding, for the moment, the acts of persuasion, which can also be paralleled). Each young woman gives up the man by her own act, motivated, at least in part, by the belief that it is for the man's own good. In both cases, the novels show that the renunciation of love, for however high a motive, can be blighting—in Clementina's case, almost catastrophic. She breaks under the strain and becomes deranged.

The results of the blighting of love are also felt through the story of Harriet, and felt the more strongly perhaps because portrayed in a more matter-of-fact manner and through a more ordinary character than Clementina, the 'noble enthusiast'. Overall, the parallels between Anne and Harriet are stronger than those between Anne and Clementina, although Jane Austen has, perhaps, drawn issues selectively from the combined stories of Richardson's two heroines. Harriet believes that, however hopeless her love for Sir Charles might be, she can now never seriously contemplate marriage with another man.[24] For Anne,

> ... be the conclusion of the present suspense good or bad, her affection would be his [Captain Wentworth's] for ever. Their union, she believed, could not divide her more from other men, than their final separation. (192)

In *Persuasion*, Jane Austen appears almost to be using Anne Elliot's position as a means of taking up and re-working particular issues about women and love as they are aired in *Sir Charles Grandison*, and taking them up in a manner that is like offering proof for the truth of what was, in the earlier novel, only an hypothesis. What I am suggesting is that, although *Sir Charles Grandison* uses the retrospective mode for the first part of Clementina's story, the novel is mostly written in the tense of the on-going present, and many of the issues debated are problematical. They concern what *may* happen in the future to Harriet and Clementina in relation to their love for Sir Charles and their belief in the certainty of their own constancy. The broad soundness of many of these projections is vindicated through the account of Anne Elliot's experiences in the eight years *after* she gave up Captain Wentworth.

The debate is very lively in *Sir Charles Grandison* as to whether or not constancy in hopeless cases is a selfish and unwise indulgence; as to whether or not romantic views of love stand up against the practical tests of what makes a happy marriage; about the almost inevitable loneliness and unhappiness of the unmarried woman in the 'solitary and unheeded' state which Harriet's grandmother, Mrs Shirley, argues that a woman moves into, if she remains single (III, 397). Much of what is said, on both sides, bears on Anne's situation as we are given it in *Persuasion*. And both novels probe the natures of men and women in order to differentiate between them in certain essential ways. Anne and Harriet each believes, for example, that, although men love deeply, they are more readily able than are women to turn their affections to another. Both women realize that, in part, this can be attributed to social role and to the more public lives which men generally lead. When Captain Harville says that it would not have been in his sister's nature to have forgotten Benwick as soon as Benwick appears to have forgotten her, Anne agrees, and pushes the point further: 'It would not be the nature of any woman who truly loved' (232). However, she qualifies this remark by relating women's constancy to the domestic nature of their lives:

> 'We certainly do not forget you, so soon as you forget us. It is perhaps, our fate rather than our merit. We cannot help ourselves. We live at home, quiet, confined, and our feelings prey upon us.' (232)

Men, Anne argues, 'have always a profession, pursuits, business of some sort or other, to take [them] back into the world immediately' (232). Certainly Sir Charles Grandison, deeply disturbed when, honour bound to Clementina, he finds that Harriet has made an impression on his heart, consciously turns to 'avocations in town.'[25]

Both the different kinds of life men's and women's roles force on them and the categorizing of 'man's nature' and 'woman's nature', with the different sex roles which rise from what is 'natural', are basic to the point of each novel, and there is some similarity in the way each author pursues these concerns. When Captain Harville, for example, points out that Benwick has not had the postulated diversions in the world to enable him to transfer his attachment from one woman to another, Anne takes the argument to the logical conclusion that, in that case, 'it must be nature, man's nature, which has done the business for Captain Benwick' (233). Harville will not allow this, arguing an analogy between men's 'bodily frames' and their 'mental':

> '... as our bodies are the strongest, so are our feelings: capable of bearing most rough usage, and riding out the heaviest weather.' (233)

But Anne, continuing the analogy, presses it further:

> 'Your feelings may be the strongest ... but the same spirit of analogy will authorise me to assert that ours are the most tender. Man is more robust than woman, but he is not longer-lived; which exactly explains my view of the nature of their attachments.' (233)

These comments, with certain differences made between masculine and feminine viewpoint, generally tally with those in *Sir Charles Grandison*. In Richardson's novel it is conceded that the differences between men and women are, frequently, those of opportunity and education (cf. Anne and the 'pen'—234), but Sir Charles, while allowing for individual exceptions, puts forward the novel's generally approved—though not unchallenged—point of view:

> 'There is a difference ... in the constitution, in the temperament of the two Sexes, that gives to the one advantage which it denies to the other ... Why has nature made a difference in the beauty, proportion, and symmetry, in the *persons* of the two Sexes? Why gave it delicacy, softness, grace, to that of the woman ... strength, firmness to men; a capacity to bear labour and fatigue; and courage, to protect the other?' (III, 247)

Persuasion, with some qualifications, accepts this view of differences as a *donnée*, and part of the book's point is to exemplify and justify Anne Elliot's character in its terms. Indeed, that Anne herself also holds such a view is demonstrated in what she goes on to say to Captain Harville, in defence of her opinion that men's feelings are not so tender as women's:

> 'Nay, it would be too hard upon you, if it were otherwise. You have difficulties, and privations, and dangers enough to struggle with. You are always labouring and toiling, exposed to every risk and hardship. Your home, country, friends, all quitted. Neither time, nor health, nor life, to be called your own. It would be too hard indeed' (with a faltering voice) 'if woman's feelings were to be added to all this.' (233)

This description of the sailor's lot is matched rather well by Sir Charles' (highly romantic) summing-up of man's lot in general, offered after his speech relating sex roles to constitution and temperament:

> I, for my part, would only contend, that we men should have power and right given us to protect and serve your Sex; that we should purchase and build for them; travel and toil for them; run through, at the call of Providence, or of our king and Country dangers and difficulties; and, at last, lay all our trophies, all our acquirements, at your feet; enough rewarded in the conscience of duty done, and your favourable acceptance. (III, 248, 249)

What Anne says bespeaks the feminine perspective on the male role; what Sir Charles says, the masculine. Anne has used her description to support her view of the different qualities of male and female *feeling*, rather than differences in simple natural capacity, but the same concepts underlie what each says. At Captain Harville's protests at what she has said, however, Anne is stricken:

> 'God forbid that I should undervalue the warm and faithful feelings of any of my fellow-creatures. I should deserve utter contempt if I dared to suppose that true attachment and constancy were known only by woman.' (235)

Full of remorse, she is forced into further explaining her own view. In doing this, she gets to what she sees as the nub of the difference between the way men and women love:

> 'No, I believe you capable of everything great and good in your married lives. I believe you equal to every important exertion and to every domestic forbearance, so long as—if I may be allowed the expression, so long as you have an object. I mean, while the woman you love lives, and lives for you. All the privilege I claim for my own sex (it is not a very enviable one, you need not covet it) is that of loving longest, when existence or when hope is gone.' (235)

In Anne's assertion that man's affection is deep and lasting, but that it essentially needs an object on which that affection can be focussed, Jane Austen has, I believe, adapted the sense of a crucial point in *Sir Charles Grandison*. This is the point which enables that novel's resolution of the dilemma of Sir Charles' 'double love' to be arrived at. Torn by duties and proprieties between Harriet and Clementina, loving both, Sir Charles finally, as a result of particular circumstances, marries Harriet. Richardson has to justify both Sir Charles' being able to love two women at once, and his eventual, fully acceptable marriage to one of them. What becomes apparent is that Sir Charles, despite difficulties, is *properly* able to turn all his love to the woman who can most *properly* be his object. This, finally, is Harriet. When Sir Charles is at last released from Clementina, and is seeking Harriet's hand, he declares to Mrs Shirley, Mrs Selby and Harriet:

> . . . had not Heaven given a Miss Byron for the object of my hope, I had hardly, after what had befallen me *abroad*, ever looked forward to a wedded love. (III, 79)

Such a declaration supports Anne's view that it is not that men are more fickle than women but that they are more readily able to conceive and maintain affection if they have an object for that affection towards which they can 'hope' and on which, thereafter, they can continue to focus.

Both Wentworth and Grandison rather manage to exemplify Anne's warm acknowledgement that 'true attachment and constancy' do exist among men. 'I have loved none but you,' (237) Wentworth writes. Lady G. says of Sir Charles: 'where he *once* loves, he *always* loves' (II, 660). In both books, however, it is the women who demonstrate the capacity 'of loving longest, when existence or when hope is gone'.

* * *

In each novel, the delicate, gentle, modest heroine is accorded her full worth. What gives credibility to the apportioning of high value to such a heroine is that the action enables the feminine character to reveal itself in its nature and to demonstrate its particular strengths. As we have seen, the theme of constancy in each novel works in just this way. It is, however, the theme of persuasion which is used, particularly in Jane Austen's novel, to raise the issues of what constitutes a morally weak character and what a strong, and of how the common notions about this in relation to women can often be mistaken ones.

Each novel looks at persuasion *out of*, and persuasion *into*, marriage. The stress in *Persuasion* is on the first kind, with the second looked at briefly with regard to Mr Elliot. The stress in *Sir Charles Grandison* is, overall, on the second kind, although the first part of Clementina's story has as a major aspect the role that the family disapproval of any marriage to Sir Charles plays in her mental breakdown. It is in the points that the novel raises about the feminine character, in relation to persuasion deployed through affection, that some most useful and illuminating parallels with Jane Austen's novel can be made. Clementina talks of 'cruel persuasion' (III, 60), cruel because exerted by those whom she loves, whose wishes she finds it very difficult to withstand. Anne Elliot once faced similar pressures, and we are told;

> Young and gentle as she was, it might yet have been possible to withstand her father's ill-will ... but Lady Russell, whom she had always loved and relied on, could not, with such steadiness of opinion, and such tenderness of manner, be continually advising her in vain. (27)

In both examples we get a sense of affection being used, not exactly manipulatively yet not entirely judiciously, and we feel the very real dangers of such usage.

Both Anne and Clementina have a strong sense of duty. It is the conflict between duty and love in Clementina's mind which has unhinged her reason. 'My duty calls upon me one way: My heart resists my duty, and tempts me not to perform it . . .' (II, 564). Anne Elliot says of herself in *Persuasion*:

> 'If I was wrong in yielding to persuasion once, remember that it was to persuasion exerted on the side of safety, not of risk. When I yielded, I thought it was to duty . . .' (244)

Richardson is concerned with both 'duty' and the moral rights and wrongs of the persuader. Austen has Anne, far from simply assigning blame to Lady Russell, very concerned to sort out the moral rights and wrongs of her own original decision. She relates this to what she still sees as having been her 'duty', Lady Russell being in the place of a parent to her:

> 'I am not saying that she did not err in her advice ... But I mean, that I was right in submitting to her, and that if I had done otherwise, I should have suffered more in continuing the engagement than I did even in giving it up, because I should have suffered in my conscience. I have now, as far as such a sentiment is allowable in human nature, nothing to reproach myself with; and if I mistake not, a strong sense of duty is no bad part of a woman's portion.' (246)[26]

Letting one's self be persuaded emerges under such a scrutiny, then, as being not *necessarily* a matter of feelings or of weakness. It can be a matter of fine and discriminating judgement. This point is brought explicitly into the novel by the overheard conversation between Louisa and Captain Wentworth about decision and firmness of mind,[27] and developed through the events at Lyme. It is Louisa's accident at Lyme when, against Wentworth's advice she has jumped a second time from the Cobb, that leads to Anne's wondering:

> whether it ever occurred to him [Captain Wentworth] now, to question the justness of his own previous opinion as to the universal felicity and advantage of firmness of character; and whether it might not strike him, that, like all other qualities of the mind, it should have its proportions and limits. (116)

It was at Lyme, Wentworth later admits, that he had finally understood 'the perfect excellence of the mind with which Louisa's could so ill bear a comparison' (242).

> There, he had learnt to distinguish between the steadiness of
> principle and the obstinacy of selfwill, between the darings of
> heedlessness and the resolution of a collected mind. (242)

Thus we are given a succinct expression of the morality of persuasion in
relation to character. For Wentworth her character 'was now fixed on his
mind as perfection itself, maintaining the loveliest medium of fortitude and
gentleness' (241). In this way, an ideal of feminine excellence is established.
This draws, it would seem, on certain conservative conventions and didactic
certainties but is modified by Anne's affirmation of the value of love (and by
the novel's strong sense of her eight wasted years), and endorses the moral
power of 'principled feeling'.[28] The whole of the novel, with the twin themes
of persuasion and constancy, is thus structured and designed to scrutinise
and demonstrate the true character of the ideally feminine woman. This is
why, at the conclusion of the novel, the sorting out of the issues of whether
persuasion is a good thing or a bad seems to be a little unsatisfactory. We
do not get a simple answer to any question on the matter because there is
not one question in the novel on this theme, but two: not only, was the persuasion right or wrong in itself, but also, does having allowed herself to be
persuaded make Anne Elliot strong or weak? Jane Austen has intertwined
her themes of the value of feeling and of woman's natural constancy with
the themes of the rights and wrongs of persuasion and the need for perception and judgement. Anne Elliot's suffering was caused, in large part, by
the world's not knowing how to value her, nor how to assess her motives
and conduct.

In endorsing gentle and reflective Anne as 'a model of female excellence'
Jane Austen has not, I believe, at all turned her back on wit and vivacity.
Anne is neither a stuffy, didactic exemplar nor a prig. She is capable of wry
amusement at herself and her own actions, and she assesses others shrewdly
and well. Her portrayal need not, in any way, negate the value of what Elizabeth Bennet and Emma Woodhouse are, nor what they represent in the Austen canon. Jane Austen (again like Richardson) has always used two distinct
female character types as heroines, one lively, one quiet. So Anne is not a
completely new kind of heroine in the novels, and she has certain things in
common with Elinor Dashwood and with Fanny Price.[29]

David Monaghan, in his essay, 'Jane Austen and the Position of Wom-
en,'[30] compares and contrasts the various forms of female excellence presented in Austen's novels (suggesting, for example, 'quickness of observation'
and 'judgement' as the qualities in Elizabeth Bennet which make her superior
to both her sister Jane and Miss Bingley [107]. He argues that 'by the standards established in the earlier novels Anne Elliot is perhaps the most perfect
of all Jane Austen's women' (119). He sees Austen in *Persuasion*, however, as

demonstrating that, in the changed social circumstances the novel depicts, Anne can 'no longer provide the model for womanhood' (120). Monaghan believes that, despite Austen's 'admiration' for Anne, it is Mrs Croft who is being put forward as possible new 'model', woman in 'a new arena of 'exertion', exemplifying 'some tentative proposals for a redefinition of the female role' (119).

This argument is tantalising and attractive, and Mrs Croft is certainly sympathetically drawn. However, I do not believe we need or, indeed, *may* read the novel's signals in this way. The final chapter leaves us with Anne happily, busily, fulfillingly married—'a sailor's wife' (252). She has proved herself completely adaptable to her new social circumstances and the novel in no way suggests that she is anachronistic or non-viable in her new role. It seems, if anything, that one of the things the novel is affirming is that the feminine ideal as exemplified in Anne Elliot is adaptable.[31]

The ideal's adaptability, too, is perhaps being demonstrated in the way that the 'indispensable characteristic' of 'tenderness of heart' (*Grandison*, II, 395) of Richardson's heroines moves acceptably in *Persuasion* into being an affirmation of the Romantic position of the goodness of true feeling and of the need for both men and women to acknowledge and express love in their lives. Against this, it would also seem that, in relation to the period's elevation of the value of feeling as an infallible moral guide, the novel is giving its own *caveat*: Do not under-estimate the worth of the woman who controls her feelings for the sake of duty and of others.

The novel is, in many ways, a vindication of a standard of moral excellence in women which derives, as we have seen, almost directly from Richardson. He has a didactic certainty, in his portrayals, of the intrinsic worth of the morally exemplary heroine. Jane Austen draws on this certainty, even as she airs Richardson's heroines' problems again, with variations, as part of her own scrutiny of the real value of such a heroine.

NOTES

1. Anne Molan ('Persuasion in *Persuasion*', *CR* [24, 1982], 16–29) believes that the problem for many critics is that Jane Austen 'has not explained how we should judge whether persuasion and persuadability are good or bad' (28). Critics generally, though, as Leroy W. Smith points out in *Jane Austen and the Drama of Women* (London and Basingstoke: Macmillan, 1983), differ on this issue as to whether Austen 'upholds eighteenth-century values or sympathizes with new values' (p. 156). Smith largely assigns the problem to misunderstanding due to sexual stereotyping; and sees the novel's 'movement towards a concept of androgynous being' (p. 171) as providing a resolution.

2. For example, R.S. Crane, '*Persuasion*' (*The Idea of the Humanities and Other Essays Critical and Historical*, 2 vols., Chicago: University of Chicago Press, 1966, II, 283–302). Mary Poovey, '*Persuasion* and the Promises of Love', in *The Representation*

of Women in Fiction (Baltimore and London: Johns Hopkins University Press, 1983), sees Austen as using two systems of values in the novel, one representing individualism, the other paternalistic values, each one used 'to correct the abuses of the other' (p. 155).

3. It must not be forgotten that Austen did not, herself give the title *Persuasion* !o the work, but the fact that her executors did see fit to use that title is in itself interesting; and the matter does not materially affect the argument of this article.

4. *Persuasion* (*Novels of Jane Austen*, Vol. 5, O.U.P., 3rd ed., 1933; 1954). All quotations from the novel are taken from this edition, ed. R. W. Chapman (1923).

5. See the discussion of this issue by Karen Newman in 'Can this Marriage be Saved': Jane Austen makes Sense of an Ending' (*ELH*, 1983 winter, 40 [4], 693–710). For a full and detailed summary of critical points raised by feminists, see Leroy W. Smith, *op. cit.*

6. Newman, *op. cit.*, p. 708.

7. *Jane Austen, Feminism and Fiction* (Sussex and Totowa, N.J.: The Harvester Press and Barnes and Noble, 1983), *Introduction*, p. xi *et passim*. See also Lloyd W. Brown, 'Jane Austen and the Feminist Tradition' (*Nineteenth-Century Fiction* [28] 1973–74).

8. Kirkham, *op. cit.*, pp. 145, 146.

9. *Ibid.*, pp. 159, 160.

10. Particularly in the belief that feeling, though recognized as a potent moral force, should not, alone, be used as a guide to conduct. It should be regulated by principle and reason.

11. See Kenneth L. Moler, *Jane Austen's Art of Allusion* (Lincoln: University of Nebraska Press, 1968) 192–195, and J.M.S. Tompkins, *The Popular Novel to England 1770–1800* (London: Methuen, 1961; 1969), 84 ff. for discussions of this issue. Moler points out that 'a parental attempt to influence a child's choice of a matrimonial partner was frequently described as "persuasion"' (1963).

12. For a discussion of the characteristics of the exemplary conservative heroine in the 1790s, and a comparison between the novels of Mrs West and those of Jane Austen, see Marilyn Butler, *Jane Austen and the War of Ideas* (Oxford: Clarendon Press, 1975), p. 98ff.

13. See discussions on the links between Richardson, or the Richardsonian tradition, and Austen in Henrietta Ten Harmsel, *Jane Austen: A Study in Fictional Conventions* (The Hague: Mouton, 1964), and E.W. Bradbrook, *Jane Austen and Her Predecessors* (Cambridge: Cambridge University Press, 1966). Alistair Duckworth, in *The Improvement of the Estate* (Baltimore: Johns Hopkins, 1971, pp. 14–20), agrees with Bradbrook that the conventions came to Jane Austen more immediately from Fanny Burney than from Richardson himself, but his use of *Clarissa* as a gloss for Jane Austen's fiction makes a strong case for at least indirect influence by that novel.

Margaret Kirkham (*op. cit.*) disputes Jane Austen's supposed affection for *Grandison*. She writes: 'The evidence of Austen's own writings suggests a highly critical attitude to *Grandison* and some antipathy to Richardson in general' (p. 30). Much of Kirkham's discussion is speculative (as to why we should 'take with a grain of salt' (p. 30) Jane Austen's brother's comment that she admired *Grandison* particularly). Her main argument rests on (doubtful) mocking references to *Grandison* in *Northanger Abbey* (and to Richardson in *Sanditon*), that the Juvenilia includes a number of parodies on *Grandison*, and that the 'dramatisation of "Sir

Charles Grandison" . . . mocks its parent-novel mercilessly' (p. 31). It seems an over-simplified view to take the mockery of a few absurdities in *Grandison* as evidence that Jane Austen did not like the novel. With regard to the critical reference to Richardson in *Sanditon*, it is not difficult to understand why Jane Austen should disapprove of glamourised depictions of the rake, in Richardson or anyone else, and this is the substance of her satiric description of Sir Edward Denham, who models himself on Lovelace. It should, however, be noted that Richardson, too, was alarmed by the favourable reception Lovelace received from readers, and that Sir Hargrave Pollexfen, the rake in *Grandison*, is portrayed as unlikeable. Kirkham sees both *Persuasion* and *Sanditon*, too, as anti-Grandisonian in that they depict baronets as faulty human beings (pp. 144–5). It is worth recalling that Sir Charles' father, Sir Thomas Grandison, is also portrayed as faulty. In both novels, *Persuasion* and *Grandison*, the need to accept moral and social responsibility along with position and privilege is strongly advocated, so any anti-baronet comment as such seems somewhat misdirected. Finally, it is probably worth noting the comments of another critic, who makes a strong case for Austen's links with Richardson. Jocelyn Harris, in '"As if they had been living friends": *Sir Charles Grandison* into *Mansfield Park*' (*Bulletin of Research in the Humanities*, Vol. 83, No. 3, Autumn 1980), writes: 'Given such lively affection, such imaginative and professional involvement with Richardson's novel, it need surprise no-one that Jane Austen mined *Grandison* directly and substantially' (pp. 360–61).

14. *Persuasion* (ed. D.W. Harding, Harmondsworth: Penguin, 1975).

15. I am partly indebted to the discussions of this point in Moler, Ch. 6, *op. cit.*, and in Ten Harmsel, *op. cit.*, p. 166 ff.

16. Tomkins, *op. cit.*, discuss the difficulty of defining delicacy (p. 93) but, drawing on descriptions from the novels of her period (1770–1800), terms it 'spontaneous moral taste, embracing but transcending propriety or decorum' (p. 144).

17. See both Moler and Butler for discussions of the division between the conservative novelists of the late-eighteenth century and those who followed the 'modern philosophers' and who admired 'strength of mind and strength of feeling'. The conservative writers consisted 'true fortitude' consisted for women in 'self-control rather than in self-assertion, in the ability to restrain one's emotions rather than in the determination to indulge them at all costs' (Moler, *op. cit.*, p. 204).

18. *Sir Charles Grandison*, edited and with an Introduction by Jocelyn Harris (London: O.U.P., 1972). All quotations from the novel are taken from this edition.

19. This was regarded as a suitable accomplishment for all young women of the period but few, if any, of their peers seem to share it with them.

20. 'Lady Maffei . . . often directed herself to me in Italian. I answered her in it as well as I could. I do not talk it well: . . . But Lady Olivia made me a compliment on my faulty accent, when I acknowledged it to be so' (II, 369).

21. Marilyn Butler regards the portrayal of Mr Elliot as one of Jane Austen's failures because he 'never represents any kind of real temptation' to Anne (*op. cit.*, p. 280). Mr Elliot's presence, however, is to do with the issues of persuasion and the choice of marriage partner on worldly grounds; and the tempter-figure is not Mr Elliot but Lady Russell!

22. The term 'female excellence' was obviously much used to refer to the ennobling qualities of women. Tompkins quotes from one of Fordyce's sermons to the effect that the 'best guardian of the soul of man against vice was "the near and frequent view of Female Excellence"' (*op. cit.*, p. 150).

23. Cf. Duckworth '. . . in some interesting ways the dilemma and response of Richardson's heroine [Clarissa] looks forward to, and comments upon, the dilemmas and responses of Jane Austen's heroines' (*op. cit.*, p. 14).

24. See Harriet's letter to Lady G. (III, 31).

25. See *Grandison* III, 54.

26. Margaret Kirkham points out that this behaviour of Anne's conforms to what Wollstonecraft had laid down as 'proper in a dutiful child of a "solicitous" and affectionate, even though mistaken, parent' (*op. cit.*, p. 149). Richardson, of course, does make similar points in *Clarissa* and *Grandison*.

27. See Marilyn Butler's discussion of the image of the 'nut' in this scene, *op. cit.*, p. 278.

28. Cf. Mary Poovey who sees Austen dramatising the *'power* of principled feeling' in the novel (*op. cit.*, p. 162).

29. Nina Auerbach, in 'O Brave New World: Evolution and Revolution in *Persuasion*' (*ELH* [39] 1972, 112–128), sees Anne Elliot as a descendant of Marianne Dashwood (p. 115).

30. In *Jane Austen in a Social Context* (Totowa, N.J.: Macmillan, and Barnes and Noble, 1981), pp. 105–121.

31. Indeed see the men in the novel, too, adapting to changed social circumstances. And Wentworth's helpfulness to Mrs Smith in her affairs reads remarkably like Sir Charles Grandison's helpfulness to all and sundry.

ANNE K. MELLOR

Why Women Didn't Like Romanticism:
The Views of Jane Austen and Mary Shelley

For many years scholars and critics have been speaking in one way or another of what we might call the romantic "spirit of the age." But the spirit we have been describing animated at best but a small portion of the people living in England at the time. Among those it did *not* animate were the leading women intellectuals and writers of the day. In order to understand their antipathy to the "spirit of the age," I must first offer a working definition of romanticism. I will not renumerate A. O. Lovejoy's multiple "romanticisms." Rather I wish to emphasize a few fundamental and shared beliefs of the major English romantic poets, beliefs which were profoundly disturbing to the women who encountered them.

When we try to define romanticism as a set of cultural ideas and values, we usually turn first to the beliefs that developed out of the eighteenth-century Enlightenment and that inspired both the American and the French Revolutions. Remembering Rousseau and Thomas Paine, we identify romanticism with the political doctrines of democracy and the rights of the common man, the assumption that every individual is born with an inalienable right to life, liberty, and the pursuit of happiness. This doctrine also assumes that human beings are born free of sin, whether we are seen as empty vessels which experience will fill, as noble savages, or as children of innocence trailing clouds of glory. Fundamental to romanticism, then, is a conviction in the

From *The Romantics and Us: Essays on Literature and Culture*, edited by Gene W. Ruoff, pp. 274–287. © 1990 by Rutgers, The State University.

value of the individual and a belief in an ethic of justice which treats every person equally under the law.

For the romantic poets, the assumption that the individual, rather than the state or society as a whole, was of fundamental significance meant that their poetry was concerned above all with describing the nature and growth of the individual. Wordsworth in *The Prelude; or, Growth of a Poet's Mind* implicitly claimed that his own autobiography, the development of his own mind and character, was of epic importance. And the stages of the growth of consciousness which all of Wordsworth's poetry traced was fundamentally an exploration of the nature of perception: how does the human mind come to know the external world? What is the relationship between the perceiving subject and the perceived object? For Wordsworth, as for Coleridge, Blake, and the later romantic poets who had been inspired by the philosophy of Immanuel Kant, the human mind actively shapes and transforms the sense-data it receives from nature into the "language of the sense." As Percy Shelley put it in "Mont Blanc":

> The everlasting universe of things
> Flows through the mind and rolls its rapid waves,
> Now dark—now glittering—now reflecting gloom—
> Now lending splendour, where from secret springs
> The source of human thought its tribute brings
> Of waters,—with a sound but half its own . . .

As the innocent child becomes a man, he comes to know the creative powers of his own mind, a mighty mind whose capacity to use language to transform, build up, and renew is as great as nature's own life-giving power. If the human mind creates the myths or meanings by which we live, then its powers can be compared to a god's. As William Blake repeatedly proclaimed, "All deities reside in the human breast," the "human form" is "divine," and "God becomes as we are, that we may be as he is." For the romantic poets, the creative powers of the human imagination are identical with the creative powers of the Infinite I AM; when inspired, the poet can imitate the works of God and create, as does the poet of Coleridge's "Kubla Khan," "a miracle of rare device." Without the transforming and myth-making work of the imagination, nature is but a vacancy, for as Coleridge insisted in "Dejection: An Ode," "we receive but what we give, / And in our life alone does Nature live."

If one celebrates the human imagination as divine and locates the source of all cultural meaning and value in the mythopoeic powers of the creative mind, then one must also celebrate those emotions that arouse and inspire the imagination, emotions above all of desire and love. As opposed to their

Enlightenment forebears, the romantic poets insisted on the value of bodily sensations and emotions: in the moment of creation, not analytical reason but rather the uninhibited flow of powerful feeling is at work. The romantic poets therefore rebelled against the domination of reason, common sense, and rigorous logic, insisting like Wordsworth that "we murder to dissect." Or as Keats put it in *Lamia*,

> There was an awful rainbow once in heaven;
> We know her woof, her texture; she is given
> In the dull catalogue of common things.
> Philosophy will clip an Angel's wings,
> Conquer all mysteries by rule and line,
>
> . . . .
>
> Unweave a rainbow.

Turning against "cold" philosophy and abstract reason, the romantic poets insisted instead on the ultimate value of passionate love, that love which is embodied in Percy Shelley's *Prometheus Unbound* as Asia and which alone can overcome the evil of Jupiter and bring about the mystic marriage of man and nature, heaven and earth, that climaxes Shelley's epic poem.

Modern critics of romantic poetry, responding to these concepts, have offered various paradigms for organizing romantic thought. M. H. Abrams in his masterful *Natural Supernaturalism* argued that the greatest romantic poems traced what he called a "circuitous journey" from innocence to experience to a higher innocence, a quest that begins with the child's unconscious conviction of a primal oneness between himself and mother nature and his fall away from that communion into an experience of alienated self-consciousness and isolation. But this fall, like Milton's, proves finally fortunate, for it enables the poet to spiral upward to a higher state of consciousness, even a sublime transcendence, in which he consciously understands the ultimate harmony between the workings of nature and his own mind and consummates a marriage with nature through his "spousal verse." More attentive to the scepticism inherent in much romantic poetry, especially the writings of Byron and Keats, I suggested in my book on *English Romantic Irony* an alternative paradigm to Abrams's, the model of a poet's participation in an ongoing, chaotic life that is simultaneously creative and destructive. If nature is constantly in flux, as Byron, Shelley, and Keats believed, then all the structures designed by the human imagination, including the myths of the poets, are false, simply because they impose a static order upon a chaotic and constantly changing world. To represent such an abundant chaos, I argued, some romantic poets devised linguistic strategies which were simultaneously creative and de-creative—poems like *Don Juan* and "Ode on a Grecian Urn" which put forth symbols and ideals only to undercut them, as when Byron tells us that the snake is in the eyes of Juan's beloved and innocent Haidée, or Keats reminds us that the Urn's image of a love that can never change is but a "cold pastoral."

Commenting on both these paradigms of romanticism, Jerome McGann has subsequently called them "the romantic ideology," a description of romanticism as a creative process. McGann insists that we must critically detach ourselves from the values of romanticism when we interpret it and acknowledge the despair expressed in much romantic thought, the moments when Byron and Coleridge, Wordsworth and Keats, confronted the limitations of mortality and recognized the failure of their creative powers. McGann's emphasis on what Mario Praz first called "romantic agony" is entirely appropriate, but it is only half the story. I still believe that the English romanticism of which we have been speaking is best understood as an ongoing, enthusiastic engagement with the creative energy of both nature and the human mind, an engagement that acknowledges human limitations—as Byron said, man is "half dust, half deity"—but nonetheless continues in a dialectical, perhaps ever-to-be-frustrated, yearning for transcendence and enduring meaning.[1]

How did the women writers of the age respond to romanticism's celebration of the creative process and of passionate feeling? On both counts, they responded negatively, very negatively. But why? To answer that, I will take as representative Jane Austen and Mary Shelley, two of the best-known women writers of the day.

To understand Austen's and Shelley's hostility to the romantic imagination and to romantic love, we must think back to the book that perhaps more than any other influenced them both, Mary Wollstonecraft's *A Vindication of the Rights of Woman*, published in 1792. Wollstonecraft was Mary Shelley's mother and died giving birth to her; perhaps as an act of compensation, or simply in filial love, Mary Shelley throughout her youth obsessively read and reread her mother's books. It is less well known that Jane Austen was also a committed disciple of Wollstonecraft's teaching. Austen frequently quotes *A Vindication* in her novels, even though she never dared to acknowledge openly her debt to Wollstonecraft, mainly because the publication of Godwin's loving but injudicious *Memoirs* of the life, opinions, love affairs, and suicide attempts of his dead wife had led the British press to denounce Wollstonecraft as a whore and an atheist. In Jane Austen's circle, no respectable woman could publically avow her agreement with Wollstonecraft's opinions. Even today, the extent of Jane Austen's debt to Wollstonecraft has only begun to be documented.[2]

In *A Vindication of the Rights of Woman*, Mary Wollstonecraft attacked her society's ideological definition of the female as innately emotional, intuitive, illogical, capable of moral sentiment but not of rational understanding. Pointing out that women are assumed to have souls and to be capable of sinning or becoming virtuous, Mary Wollstonecraft argued that if women are to be held ethically responsible for their actions, then it must follow that they are capable of ethical thinking. And if women are capable of thinking, they must have a rational faculty. And if they have a rational faculty which is capable of guiding and improving their character and actions, then that rational faculty should be developed and exercised to its greatest capacity. From this rigorously logical argument, Wollstonecraft launched a passionate plea for the education of women, for only if women were educated as fully as men would they be able to realize their innate capacities for moral virtue. Appealing to her male readers, Wollstonecraft further argued that more highly educated women will not only be more virtuous, but they will also be better mothers, more interesting wives and "companions," and more responsible citizens. In contrast, Wollstonecraft observed, her society's practice of teaching females only "accomplishments"—singing, dancing, needlework, a smattering of foreign languages—produced women who were obsessed with their personal appearance and fashion, who devoted all their energies to arousing a man's sexual appetites while duplicitously appearing "modest" and chaste in order to capture the husband upon whom their financial welfare depended, and who became "slaves" to their masters but petty tyrants to their children and servants. "Created to feel, not to think," the women of her time were kept in "a state of perpetual childhood" and necessarily became "cunning, mean and selfish."[3]

Inspired by Wollstonecraft's attempt to develop women's ability to think rationally, Jane Austen portrayed the heroines of her novels, not as the women of sensibility celebrated by the romantic poets and the prevailing ideological doctrine of the separate spheres which consigned women to the role of promoting the domestic affections. Instead her heroines are women of sense, women like Elinor Dashwood who refuse to succumb to erotic passion. Even those heroines who are seduced by Gothic romances and fairy tales of romantic love, like Catherine Morland in *Northanger Abbey*, are capable of recognizing the errors of their youthful delusions.

Indeed, all of Austen's novels are novels of female education, novels in which an intelligent but ignorant girl learns to perceive the world more correctly and to understand more fully the workings of human nature and society. Emma Woodhouse must recognize her own cruelty to Miss Bates, must understand how wrongly she has perceived both Jane Fairfax and Harriet Smith, before she can equal the intelligence and benevolence of a Mr. Knightley. Elizabeth Bennet must overcome both her proud confidence in her own ability to distinguish simple and intricate human characters and her prejudiced and inaccurate reading of Mr. Darcy, through a process of painful mortification, self analysis, and learning, before she can recognize that Mr. Darcy is the man best suited to be her husband. Elizabeth

Bennet's marriage to Fitzwilliam Darcy in *Pride and Prejudice* exemplifies Mary Wollstonecraft's ideal marriage, a marriage based on rational love, mutual understanding, and respect. It is a further sign of Elizabeth's intelligence that the overriding emotion she feels for Darcy, as Jane Austen repeatedly states, is "gratitude." For in a society where every woman is in want of a husband with a good fortune, where marriage is, as Charlotte Lucas reminds us, "a woman's pleasantest preservative from want," a woman must above all be grateful to the man who rescues her from the financial deprivations of spinsterhood.

Jane Austen's conviction that women must above all be rational is perhaps clearest in *Mansfield Park*, where we are asked to endorse the cautious, chaste modesty of a Fanny Price rather than the energetic imagination of a Mary Crawford. Fanny is the voice of prudence in the novel, of good moral and intellectual sense, a voice that sustains the organic growth of the family within a clean, well-lighted home, a voice that is finally beyond price. In contrast, the women of *Mansfield Park* who are badly educated, like the Bertram sisters who can recite by rote but cannot recognize the insincerity of a Henry Crawford, or who rebel against the discipline of logic and morality, like Mary Crawford, whose wit and charm identify her as the romantic revolutionary in the novel, all end badly. Seduced by erotic desire, Maria Bertram Rushford must end her days in banishment from both the husband she abandoned and her family home at Mansfield Park, condemned to the foolish, selfish, and manipulative company of Aunt Norris. And Mary Crawford, despite her cleverness and capacity for genuine affection, cannot have the stable, enduring affection of an Edmund Bertram and must settle instead for the company of her restless, self-indulgent, and irresponsible brother.

Jane Austen's fierce commitment to hard, calculating good sense is most apparent in *Mansfield Park*, her least likeable novel. Its title was carefully chosen—Lord Mansfield's famous legal judgment in the case of Somerset versus Stewart in 1772 proclaimed that while the slave trade was appropriate for the colonies (we must remember that Sir Thomas Bertram owns a slave plantation in Antigua, which has been badly managed), nonetheless England "is a soil whose air is deemed too pure for slaves to breathe in."[4] But Jane Austen recognized that the English women of her day were little better than domestic slaves, bought and sold on the marriage market, and kept at home by fathers and husbands under "restraint."[5] The best that her countrywomen could attain was a generous master, one who must be cautiously and wisely chosen, one who would allow his wife, as Darcy allows Elizabeth, "to take liberties" with him.[6] In such a situation, women cannot follow the impulses and dictates of their feelings alone. For sexual desire and passionate love can too easily lead women into unhappy marriages, as we see when Lydia Bennet is punished for her "high animal spirits" and promiscuous desire by the indifferent contempt of Wickham. Or worse, it can lead women into the perpetual disgrace and ostracism endured by Maria Bertram and the two Elizas in *Sense and Sensibility*.

In direct opposition to the romantic poets' celebration of love, the leading woman writers of the day urged their female readers to foreswear passion—which too often left women seduced, abandoned, disgraced ... and pregnant, with only the career of prostitution remaining to them—and to embrace instead reason, virtue, and caution. The overflow of passionate feeling in a female mind that has *not* thought long and deeply can be disastrous for the welfare of women. Whether we read Wollstonecraft or Austen, Susan Ferrier's *Marriage* or Hannah More's *Strictures on the Modern System of Female Education*, Eliza Haywood's *Miss Betsy Thoughtless*, or Mary Brunton's *Self-Control*, we hear a call, not for sensibility but for sense, not for erotic passion but for rational love, a love based on understanding, compatibility, equality, and mutual respect.

The second reason why women didn't like romanticism was voiced most powerfully by a woman who knew the romantic ideology as well as it could be known, by a woman who had lived it at home, first as the daughter of the radical philosopher William Godwin and then as the mistress and wife of the poet Percy Shelley. Mary Wollstonecraft Godwin Shelley articulated her profound disillusion with the central philosophical, poetic, and political tenets of romanticism in her mythic novel, *Frankenstein, or The Modern Prometheus*, written two years after her elopement at the age of sixteen with Percy Shelley. *Frankenstein* is a direct attack on the romantic celebration of the creative process. It is, first and foremost, the story of what happens when a man tries to have a baby without a woman. Victor Frankenstein, who shares Percy Shelley's first pen-name "Victor", his "sister" Elizabeth, his education and his favorite reading, also shares Percy Shelley's romantic desire to transcend mortality by participating directly in the divine creative energy of the universe. Frankenstein's goal, to discover "whence ... did the principle of life proceed" (46), specifically echoes the goal of Percy Shelley's narrator in "Alastor" (whom Mary Shelley saw as his spokesman[7]), who addresses Mother Nature thus:

> I have made my bed
> In charnels and on coffins, where black death
> Keeps record of the trophies won from thee,
> Hoping to still these obstinate questionings
> Of thee and thine, by forcing some lone ghost,
> Thy messenger, to render up the tale
> Of what we are.

Percy Shelley's desire to participate continuously in the creative power of the universe and thus to become the equivalent of God is even more directly articulated in his "Ode to the West Wind." Here Shelley pleads with the Power that creates, preserves, and destroys the universe to lift him "as a wave, a leaf, a cloud" and make him its lyre or linguistic voice. "Be thou, Spirit fierce, / My spirit!" Shelley prays, and then moves to the triumphant rhetorical question that climaxes the poem:

> Drive my dead thoughts over the universe
> Like withered leaves to quicken a new birth!
> And, by the incantation of this verse,
>
> Scatter, as from an unextinguished hearth
> Ashes and sparks, my words among mankind!
> Be through my lips to unawakened earth
> The trumpet of a prophecy! O, Wind,
> If Winter comes, can Spring be far behind?

Shelley's words are "dead thoughts" because, once spoken, they become part of a static, fixed language-system which cannot represent the ever-changing flux of the universe of things which flows through the mind. As Shelley put it in A *Defence of Poetry*: "The mind in creation is as a fading coal which some invisible influence, like an inconstant wind, awakens to transitory brightness."[8] If the poem is at best a faded coal, mere ashes, then the most the poet can hope is that his words will arouse other minds to other creative actions, that his thoughts—dead in themselves—will nonetheless prophesy future revolutions and transformations.

But as Mary Shelley pointed out in *Frankenstein*, a romantic poetic ideology that celebrated the creative process over its created products, that dismissed the composed poem as but a "fading coal" of its originary inspiration, and that ironically insisted upon the inability of language to capture the infinite power, beauty, and goodness for which the poet yearned—such an ideology can be seen as profoundly immoral. For Victor Frankenstein, having stolen a "spark of being" from mother nature in order to animate the reconstructed corpse lying at his feet, looks with horror at his wretched composition and flees from the room. Victor Frankenstein thus abandons the child to whom he has given birth, and by failing to provide his creature with the mothering it requires, he creates—to use a modern idiom—a battered child who becomes a battering adult, a monster who subsequently murders his brother, his best friend, and his wife.

Mary Shelley clearly believed that a poet must take responsibility not only for the creative process but also for the created product. He must take

responsibility for the predictable consequences of his poems and for the probable realizations of the utopian ideals he propounds. If Percy Shelley in *Prometheus Unbound* urges his readers "To defy Power, which seems omnipotent,"
and in the "Ode to the West Wind" invokes a political revolution that will
bring down "black rain, and fire, and hail" upon the vaulted sepulchre of Europe, then he must also take responsibility for the deeds of those to whom the
incantations of his verse become a clarion call to revolutionary political action. Mary Shelley was particularly sensitive to the suffering and cruelty that
a romantic idealization of radical political change could cause. She had seen
at first hand the devastations wrought in France by the fifteen years of war
initiated by the French Revolution, the Terror, and the subsequent Napoleonic campaigns when she travelled through France on her elopement journey in
1814. She had then found the French village of Echemine "a wretched place
. . . [which] had been once large and populous, but now the houses were roof-
less, and the ruins that lay scattered about, the gardens covered with the white
dust of the torn cottages, the black burnt beams, and squalid looks of the inhabitants, present in every direction the melancholy aspect of devastation."[9]
In her novel, she represented the havoc wrought by the French Revolution
in the gigantic and misshapen body of Frankenstein's creature. As I have argued at length in my book on Mary Shelley, Frankenstein's creature—like
the French Revolution—originated in the idealistic desire to liberate all men
from the oppressions of tyranny and mortality.[10] But the Girondist Revolution, like the monster, failed to find the parental guidance, control, and nur-
turance it required to develop into a rational and benevolent state.

    As a mother, Mary Shelley understood that all one's created progeny,
however hideous, must be well cared for. One cannot simply ignore one's
compositions because one has ceased to be inspired by them. Mary Shelley
was profoundly disturbed by what she saw to be a powerful egotism at the
core of the romantic ideology: an affirmation of the human imagination as
divine defined the mission of the poet as not only the destroyer of "mind-
forged manacles" and political tyranny but also as the savior of mankind, the
"unacknowledged legislators of the world." She had seen at first hand how
self-indulgent this self-image of the poet-savior could be. Her father had
withdrawn from his children in order to pursue an increasingly unsuccessful
writing career and had remorselessly scrounged money from every passing acquaintance in order to pay his growing debts; Coleridge had become a parasite
on his admirers, unable to complete his Magnum Opus; Byron had callously
compromised numerous women, including her stepsister Claire Clairmont;
Leigh Hunt tormented his wife—and her best friend—Marianne Hunt with
his obvious preference for her more intellectual sister Bessy Kent; and her
own lover Percy Shelley had coldly abandoned his first wife and daughter in
his quest for intellectual beauty and the perfect soulmate and might easily

do the same again to Mary. Mary Shelley clearly perceived that the romantic ideology, grounded as it is on a never-ending, perhaps never-successful, effort to marry contraries, to unite the finite and the infinite, through the agency of the poetic imagination and its "spousal verse," too often entailed a sublime indifference to the children of that marriage.

In contrast to a revolutionary politics and a poetics grounded on the self-consuming artifact of romanticism, Mary Shelley posed an alternative ideology grounded on the trope of the family-politic and its gradual evolution and rational reform. Turning to Edmund Burke, she invoked his concept of the organic development of both human minds and nation-states under benevolent parental guidance as her model of a successful human community. Her credo is based on what Carol Gilligan has taught us to call an "ethic of care," the moral principle that in whatever actions we undertake, we must insure that no one shall be hurt, an ethical vision that Gilligan has found most often articulated by women.[11] Mary Shelley voiced this belief in a passage in *Frankenstein* that functions both as moral touchstone and as a statement of her commitment to the preservation of the domestic affections and the family unit:

> A human being in perfection ought always to preserve a calm and peaceful mind, and never to allow passion or a transitory desire to disturb his tranquillity. I do not think that the pursuit of knowledge is an exception to this rule. If the study to which you apply yourself has a tendency to weaken your affections, and to destroy your taste for those simple pleasures in which no alloy can possibly mix, then that study is certainly unlawful, that is to say, not befitting the human mind. If this rule were always observed; if no man allowed any pursuit whatsoever to interfere with the tranquillity of his domestic affections, Greece had not been enslaved; Caesar would have spared his country; America would have been discovered more gradually; and the empires of Mexico and Peru had not been destroyed.[12]

If we take seriously the views of Mary Shelley and Jane Austen, in the future when we speak of romanticism, we will have to speak of at least *two* romanticisms, the men's and the women's. The male writers promoted an ideology that celebrated revolutionary change, the divinity of the poetic creative process, the development of the man of feeling, and the "acquisition of the philosophic mind." In opposition, the female writers heralded an equally revolutionary ideology, what Mary Wollstonecraft called "a REVOLUTION in female manners."[13] This feminist ideology celebrated the education of the rational woman and an ethic of care that required one to take full responsibility for the predictable consequences of one's thoughts and actions, for all the children of one's mind and body. The failure of the masculine romantic ideology to care for the created product as much as for the creative process, together with its implicit assumption that the ends can justify the means, can produce a romanticism that, as Mary Shelley showed, is truly monstrous. In his quest to participate in a divine creative energy, the English romantic poet—whether we think of Percy Shelley, Wordsworth, Coleridge, Blake, or Byron—acts out an egotistical desire for omnipotence and immortality that is the prototype of the modern scientist who seeks to penetrate nature in order to control and harness her powers to serve his own selfish interests. Mary Shelley's vision of Victor Frankenstein as the poet-scientist who creates a monster he can't control resonates ever more powerfully for us today, as we wrestle with the fallout of America's romantic desire to save the world for democracy, the nuclear age initiated by the Manhattan Project's creation of the atomic bomb, an age in which we are capable of destroying—not merely the enemy—but human civilization itself. As Frankenstein's abandoned and unloved monster tells him: "Remember that I have power; . . . I can make you so wretched that the light of day will be hateful to you. You are my creator, but I am your master;—obey!"[14]

The self-indulgent egotism of the romantic poets was painfully apparent to the women writers who knew them best. The valid insights these poets have given us have been many, especially into the philosophic debates we still continue concerning the relation of the perceiving mind to the object of perception, the role of feeling in shaping our mental processes, and the ways in which language determines human consciousness. But we must balance these insights with an understanding of the ways in which they encode a masculine-gendered and thus limited view of human experience. In dialogue with these powerful male romantic voices we must now hear other, female voices, voices that remind us that calm reason and the domestic affections may be necessary to preserve human society from a romantic idealism that might otherwise unleash, however unintentionally, a revolution with truly monstrous consequences.

Notes

1. See M. H. Abrams, *Natural Supernaturalism: Tradition and Revolution in Romantic Literature* (New York: W. W. Norton & Co., 1971); Anne K. Mellor, *English Romantic Irony* (Cambridge, Mass: Harvard University Press, 1980); and Jerome J. McGann, *The Romantic Ideology—A Critical Investigation* (Chicago: University of Chicago Press, 1983). This view of romanticism was also promulgated in the exhibition on William Wordsworth and the Age of English Romanticism which appeared in New York, Bloomington, and Chicago in 1987–88; see the catalogue by Jonathan Wordsworth, Michael C. Jaye, and Robert Woof (New Brunswick: Rutgers University Press, 1987).

2. See Margaret Kirkham, *Jane Austen, Feminism and Fiction* (Totowa, NJ.: Barnes and Noble, 1983), 33–52; Claudia L. Johnson, *Jane Austen—Women, Politics, and the Novel* (Chicago: University of Chicago Press, 1988), xxii.

3. Mary Wollstonecraft, *A Vindication of the Rights of Woman*, ed. Carol H. Poston (New York: W. W. Norton, 1975), 167, 62, 9, 141.

4. "Somerset v. Stewart," *The English Reports* 98 (King's Bench Division 27) Lofft I (London: Stevens and Sons, Ltd; Edinburgh: William Green and Sons, 1909), 500.

5. Jane Austen, *Mansfield Park*, chap. 21: "She was less and less able to endure the restraint which her father imposed" (London: Penguin, 1966; repr. 1980), 216.

6. Jane Austen, *Pride and Prejudice*, 3:19: "by Elizabeth's instructions she began to comprehend that a woman may take liberties with her husband, which a brother will not always allow in a sister more than ten years younger than himself" (New York: Norton, 1966), 268.

7. That Mary Shelley regarded the narrator of "Alastor" as a spokesman for Percy Shelley is evident from her "Note on Alastor" in which she describes the poem as "the outpouring of his [Percy Shelley's] own emotions." See *The Complete Poetical Works of Percy Bysshe Shelley*, ed. Thomas Hutchinson (London: Oxford University Press, 1905; repr. 1960), 31.

8. Percy Shelley, "A Defence of Poetry," in *Shelley's Prose*, ed. David Lee Clark (Albuquerque: University of New Mexico Press, 1954), 294.

9. Mary Wollstonecraft Shelley, *History of A Six Weeks Tour through a part of France, Switzerland, Germany, and Holland, with Letters descriptive of a Sail round the Lake of Geneva, and of the Glaciers of Chamouni* (London: T. Hookham, Jr., and C. and J. Ollier, 1817), 22–23.

10. Anne K. Mellor, *Mary Shelley: Her Life, Her Fiction, Her Monsters* (New York and London: Methuen, 1988), chapter 4.

11. Carol Gilligan, *In A Different Voice—Psychological Theory and Women's Development* (Cambridge, Mass.: Harvard University Press, 1982), see esp. 173–174.

12. Mary Wollstonecraft Shelley, *Frankenstein, or The Modern Prometheus* (The 1818 Text), ed. James Rieger (Chicago: University of Chicago Press, 1974; repr. 1982), 51.

13. Wollstonecraft, *Vindication*, 192.

14. Shelley, *Frankenstein*, 165.

CYNTHIA WALL

Gendering Rooms:
Domestic Architecture and Literary Acts

Every person of rank here is either a member of the legislation, or
entitled by his condition to take part in the political arrangements
of his country, and to enter with ardour into those discussions to
which they give rise; these circumstances lead men to live more
with one another, and more detached from the society of ladies.
The eating rooms are considered as the apartments of conversation,
in which we are to pass a great part of our time. This renders it
desireable to have them fitted up with elegance and splendour, but
in a style different from that of other apartments. . . .

Next to the great eating-room, lies a splendid with-drawing
room, for the ladies . . . [1]

In the last quarter of the eighteenth century, the fashionable architects
Robert and James Adam articulated and affirmed a social as well as structural change in the interiors of upper- and middle-class English houses.
The dining-room had become the explicit territory of men, the space for
political and other kinds of discourse; the drawing-room came under the
supervision of women. But where the dining-room had dominated the
floorplan in the late seventeenth and early eighteenth centuries, when men
and women tended to co-occupy its space in shared entertainment, by the
end of the eighteenth century the division into gendered space between the

From *Eighteenth-Century Fiction* 5, no. 4 (July 1993): 349–372. © 1993 by McMaster
University.

dining and drawing-rooms corresponded to altered proportions: the drawing-room became the usually symmetrical counterpart to the dining-room,
both architecturally and socially.[2] It would appear that a bargain of sorts
had been struck, consciously or unconsciously: in exchange for increasing
exclusion from formerly shared space, women were given or (assumed) a
separate (but equal?) space of their own.

The changing significance of and relationship between drawing-room
and dining-room mark new patterns of behaviour between women and men,
and these changes surface in a diachronic sampling of eighteenth-century
novels through characters acting both within and against the evolving patterns of domestic interiors.[3] In *Roxana* (1724), *Clarissa* (1747–48), and *Pride
and Prejudice* (1813),[4] the central characters all work to define, protect, or
resist the boundaries of inhabited space, although the actions and reactions
of each are shaped by the changing dimensions and significations of her domestic interiors. Roxana, in the first quarter of the century, enacts a more general—less specifically or architecturally gendered—struggle to understand,
possess, and control the rooms she inhabits. At her famous ball she seems to
command the centre of her rooms, carefully arranging them to announce and
confirm her social and sexual power, although the rest of the novel charts the
disintegration of her spatial and psychological control. In mid-century, in ac-
cord with increasing popular awareness of architectural issues, Richardson fits
the massive story of *Clarissa* into smaller and smaller spaces, each carefully
described and circumscribed. At the narrative centre of the novel, Clarissa
tries to define and defend a sanctuary of private space in which the dining-room becomes as psychologically significant as the bedroom. And Elizabeth Bennet, like so many of Austen's heroines, begins to push against the
now-codified boundaries of masculine and feminine spaces: although much
of the sustained dialogue takes place within drawing or dining-rooms, some
of the most significant moments occur in more ambiguous, liminal spaces,
both physical and social—from windows, through doorways, on staircases;
the character as wallflower, eavesdropper, or tourist. Changes in eighteenth-
century interior design would obviously influence social behaviour, but they
also provided literary (and presumably real) spaces for resistance as well as
accommodation.

* * *

The connection between architectural change and literary expression in
the eighteenth century is neither arbitrary nor artificial. The publication
in 1715 of *Vitruvius Britannicus* and of Giacomo Leoni's English transla-
tion of Palladio caught the public imagination, and a general awareness
and appreciation of architectural matters increased significantly throughout

the century.[5] Nor was that appreciation limited to the upper-class patrons and practitioners of art, to Burlington, Kent, and Pope. Craftsmen as well as architects published a wide selection of books devoted to the theory and practice of architectural design.[6] These manuals, together with the new standardization of middle-class townhouse design, meant that almost anyone who could afford a house at all could afford one that conformed to the current notions of Palladian taste and proportion.[7] Attention to architectural structure and detail, both interior and exterior, was not simply a matter for the designer and builder, but an issue of great excitement and some knowledge to the occupant and observer. Defoe, Richardson, and Austen were themselves each knowledgeable occupants and acute observers of architectural space.[8]

The distribution and the gendering of interior domestic space also excited popular interest, but neither so early nor (at first) so explicitly. Robert Adam notes in the preface to *Works in Architecture* that "within these few years [there has been] a remarkable improvement in the form, convenience, arrangement, and relief of apartments" (1:1). He credits this latter-day awakening to the growing influence of French architectural theory, for it had been in the "proper arrangement and relief of apartments . . . [that] the French have excelled all other nations" (1:8). The idea of gendered space may have been imported with the French influence: earlier in the century Jacques-François Blondel had insisted upon a sober character for the dining-room, designed with an "*architecture mâle*"—a masculine decor, deliberately and distinctly different from rooms designed for other forms of receiving and entertaining.[9] But unlike the French, the English architects began to take the figurative characterization of a masculine style quite literally, to create a space not simply "masculine" in design or decor (a trope long known in classical architecture),[10] but a space designed explicitly for men—"in which 'we' are to pass a great part of 'our' time."

In the late-seventeenth century, entertainment in the formal house, whether town or country, meant that by and large the guests followed each other through a pattern of room-centred activities: dining in the saloon (the architecturally and linguistically anglicized counterpart of the French *salon*) or dining-parlour, withdrawing to an antechamber for tea or dessert, cards or music, and then returning to the dining-room for dancing and supper. A handsome dining-room was socially and architecturally prominent, usually one of the largest and grandest rooms in the house. By the middle of the century, however, fashionable entertaining required a series of rooms offering diverse but simultaneous activities. Although the mid-century assembly was defined as "a stated and general meeting of the polite persons of both sexes, for the sake of conversation, gallantry, news, and play,"[11] entertainment was decentralized and divided: "Dancing, tea-drinking, and cards went on at the

same time, [but] usually in different rooms. . . . On occasions a running supper was provided, and the guests went in and out of the supper room as they
felt like it" (Girouard, p. 193).

At the same time that the general social space of the upper-class house
splintered into a series of smaller rooms of synchronic activity, some of those
fragments assumed gendered identities.[12] The physical contours and the implicit functions of the different rooms—their form and their content—also
changed. Girouard shows that, while in the seventeenth century the drawing-
room had been invariably smaller than the dining-room, by the middle of the
eighteenth century the two rooms were more or less the same size (pp. 205,
233).[13] Women often seemed to determine the position and size as well as
the decoration of the drawing-room:

> At Hagley [Hall in Worcestershire] the drawing room is separated
> from the dining room by the gallery. In 1752, when the plan was
> still being worked out, Lyttelton wrote to the architect that "Lady
> Lyttelton wishes for a room of separation between the eating room
> and the drawing room, to hinder the ladies from the noise and
> talk of the men when left to their bottle, which must sometimes
> happen, even at Hagley."[14]

In the novels to be discussed here, Roxana and Clarissa, like Lady Lyttelton,
are (or become) overtly interested in determining spatial boundaries, in
claiming or reclaiming rooms; although Elizabeth Bennet's dramas are
enacted within socially presupposed spaces, she approves her friend Charlotte
Collins's quietly aggressive redistribution of space at Hunsford Parsonage.
The interior spaces of each of these novels plot the gradual redefinitions of
space, but they also suggest forms of resistance to those redefinitions, forms
which themselves change in response not only to individual circumstance or
narrative demands, but also to the changing cultural pressures and possibilities in terms of controlled, defended, or integrated space.

* * *

As popular awareness and knowledge of architectural matters gathered
energy and sophistication throughout the eighteenth century, it is not surprising that literary attention to architectural detail should become more
concentrated and precise.[15] But many of these concerns about the significance of interior domestic space are to be found in Defoe's novels. *Roxana*,
published in 1724 and allegedly set in the Restoration, differs strikingly
from *Clarissa* and *Pride and Prejudice*, since Roxana's interest in defining
and controlling formal interior space is aggressively self-conscious. At a

time when such space had no specifically gendered contours or prescriptions, Roxana quite literally draws *all* her rooms around her to generate and consolidate forms of power. Her story enacts a prelude to the gendering of rooms: she dramatizes the larger, constant, generally human desire to define and control space (and, implicitly, its occupants). Yet in the end she forfeits that power by misdefining and misoccupying that space. Her story pivots on the most socially powerful arrangement and employment of London lodgings, but it begins in an empty house and ends in a haunted one. The first and final spaces of the novel invalidate her command of its centre and punish her for the attempt. In the end, all her inhabited space—psychological as well as architectural—becomes haunted space.

Roxana regards all rooms not as general or gendered spaces for men and women, but as the potential property or extension of herself. Her psychological story begins when her first husband abandons her and she confronts the poverty of a naked room:

> I was in a Parlour, sitting on the Ground, with a great Heap of old Rags, Linnen, and other things about me, looking them over, to see if I had anything among them that would Sell or Pawn for a little Money, and had been crying ready to burst myself, to think what I should do next. . . . [I was] in Rags and Dirt, who was but a little before riding in my Coach; thin, and looking almost like one Starv'd, who was before fat and beautiful: The House, that was before handsomely furnish'd with Pictures and Ornaments, Cabinets, Peir-Glasses, and every thing suitable, was now stripp'd, and naked . . . in a word, all was Misery and Distress, the Face of Ruin was every where to be seen. (pp. 17–18)

Roxana's body and her house are bound together by parallel clauses in an identity that she will learn to exploit. Within this chilling interior emptiness she begins a series of invisible occupancies, secretly inhabiting (and learning to control) spaces that appear closed and empty to the rest of the world. Her maid Amy thrusts the five children onto their unwilling paternal relatives and spreads the story that Roxana has been turned out of doors and the house shut up, although she actually continues to live there for several years (pp. 21–22). The landlord, who had before seized her goods and stripped her house, now discovers she is beautiful, and replenishes her domestic interiors in the hope of exploring her sexual interior. Roxana quickly manipulates his desire and assumes control of the actual and symbolic function of the rooms, of the whole house, by *appearing* to transfer spatial control: "after Dinner he took me by the Hand, Come, now Madam, says he, you must show me your House, (for he had a-Mind to see every thing over again) No,

Sir, said I, but I'll go show you *your* House, if you please; so we went up thro' all the Rooms, and into the Room which was appointed for himself" (p. 33, emphasis added). She presses the landlord to stay the night (in the room *she* appoints), and then with a great show of reluctance sleeps with him—after he has legally endowed her with a good share of his wealth. Through it all Roxana appears grateful, submissive, and flattered, but she manages to acquire a deeper possession, a finer control, a steely dominance that occasionally surfaces in startlingly brutal ways: one night she strips Amy, throws open the landlord's bed, thrusts her in, then stands aside to watch (p. 46). The landlord may pay the bills and give orders to the staff, but Roxana orders the space itself, determining and controlling social and sexual boundaries.

Roxana repeats this pattern of secret occupation and invisible control during her long affair with the prince in Paris. The prince is so taken with her lodgings ("having a Way out into Three Streets, and not overlook'd by any Neighbours, so that he could pass and repass, without Observation," p. 66), as well as with her person, that she offers: "I would be wholly within-Doors, and have it given out, that I was oblig'd to go to *England*. . . . I made no Scruple of the Confinement . . . so I made the House be, as it were, shut up" (p. 67). She again collapses generic living space into powerful sexual space, manipulating its apparent master by exaggerating the forms of obeisance within the contours of her room: "When he came into my Room, I fell down at his Feet, *before* he could come to salute me . . . and *refus'd* to rise till he would allow me the Honour to kiss his Hand" (p. 61, emphasis added). The apparent acts of homage implicitly forestall and disobey the prince's commands.[16] Such manoeuvres prove so successful that by the time the affair is ended Roxana is an exceedingly wealthy and increasingly confident woman, almost ready to occupy private space publicly.

The central scene of the novel, in terms of narrative, psychological, and architectural control, is Roxana's ball in London, where she dons her Turkish dress and dances for the assembled company. She seems to understand and take full advantage of the sexual power implicit in social space (which implicit power hints at some of the cultural incentives for breaking that space apart later in the century). After acquiring impressive lodgings in Pall Mall, and marketing a dazzlingly remote self-image, she gives a ball for her admirers in which her attention to physical space and dramatic timing is exquisitely controlled. She not only anticipates what will become the most fashionable arrangements for upper-class entertainment, she also plots out one possible evolutionary track of the drawing-room:

> I had a large Dining-Room in my Apartments, with five other
> Rooms on the same Floor, all which I made Drawing-Rooms for

> the Occasion, having all the Beds taken down for the Day; in three
> of these I had Tables plac'd, cover'd with Wine and Sweet-Meats;
> the fourth had a green Table for Play, and the fifth was my own
> Room, where I sat, and where I receiv'd all the Company that came
> to pay their Compliments to me. (p. 173)

Roxana entertains in truly magnificent apartments: most town houses in
London, even those of the aristocracy, could rarely boast so many rooms
on one floor.[17] Although those rooms most probably follow the kind of
floor plan introduced by Inigo Jones in the mid-seventeenth century, which
continued to dominate upper-class town and country houses through the
first quarter of the eighteenth century, Roxana's method of occupying them
anticipates the social changes of the middle of the eighteenth century. Her
series of rooms, each with its separate activity, breaks away from the tradition that guided all the guests together through the various events of the
evening, moving instead towards social diversity and independence. All
rooms are equally theirs (hers). Yet as her own description testifies, though
the dining-room is structurally prominent, her arrangement and occupation
of the rooms for the ball pointedly emphasize her own drawing-room as the
socially (sexually) powerful centre.

When Roxana learns that the king might appear at her ball in masquer-
ade, she decides to publicize her absolute ability to empower interior space.
She slips upstairs to change into the Turkish costume, and then reappears in
the drawing-room:

> I order'd the Folding-Doors to be shut for a Minute or two, till I
> had receiv'd the Compliments of the Ladies that were in the Room,
> and had given them a full View of my Dress. . . . The Folding-Doors
> were flung open, and [my dancing partner] led me into the Room:
> The Company were under the greatest Surprize imaginable; the very
> Musick stopp'd a-while to gaze. . . . [And when my partner] led me
> to the Drawing-Room Door ... I did not go in, as he thought I
> would have done, but turn'd about, and show'd myself to the whole
> Rooms, and calling my Woman to me, gave her some Directions
> to the Musick, by which the Company presently understood that I
> would give them a Dance by myself. (pp. 174–75)

No longer does Roxana invisibly inhabit the secret centre of a house,
manipulating its spaces from behind a screen of gratitude; she has now
moved firmly into the centre of fashionable London society, demanding
public admiration and ordering domestic obedience. At a period when
social space was architecturally ungendered and therefore theoretically

permissive, Roxana has apparently succeeded in her wish of becoming a *"Man-Woman"* (p. 171), assuming full control of the social and spatial centres of her life.

But the end of the novel subverts its middle, and undermines the faith we can put here in the extent of Roxana's control of her interior spaces. Unknown to Roxana (as well as to the reader), one of her domestics, watching from the margins of this scene, turns out to be her daughter Susan, one of the children whom Amy had pushed onto the unenthusiastic aunt (p. 266). Susan does not put the pieces together until much later in the novel, but the retroactive shadow of her presence in this scene suggests that Roxana's past habits of invisible occupancy breed the very ghosts that come to haunt her.

Roxana begins to disintegrate even before Susan actually appears. She slips back suddenly into invisible darkness, sacrificing something of what she had wanted and achieved as a "Man-Woman" to become the courtesan, she hints, perhaps of the King himself. After a three-year retirement, compressed for the purpose of secrecy into a short paragraph ("with a Person, which Duty, and private Vows, obliges her not to reveal, at least, not yet" [p. 181]), Roxana emerges again into the public eye, but notes: "I did not come Abroad again with the same Lustre, or shine with so much Advantage as before. . . . It began to be publick, that *Roxana* was . . . not that Woman of Honour and Virtue that was at first suppos'd" (pp. 181–82). After her personal and social triumph in Pall Mall, she retreats into old patterns of secret habitations, but begins to find that its darkness clings: "I seem'd like an old Piece of Plate that had been hoarded up some Years, and comes out tarnish'd and discolour'd" (p. 182). The consequences of self-hoarding are psychologically disfiguring.

Roxana tries to repolish her image, to make herself publicly presentable, but she never acquires more than the *appearance* of respectability and wholesomeness.[18] Even that appearance is soon shaken by the need for secrecy, which induces a sort of psychological homelessness, a paralysis of agency. She never really learns to live in her rooms; she occupies interiors in various roles, never truly comfortable when psychologically naked in a private space, until finally *no* rooms are hers. With Amy's help, she can "transform [herself] into a new Shape, all in a Moment" (p. 209). She lodges with a Quaker lady in the Minories, and gradually adopts her style, dress, and apparent security, claiming triumphantly: "I was now in a perfect Retreat indeed; remote from the Eyes of all that ever had seen me" (p. 211). At precisely this point of complete disguise and protected enclosure, she begins to lose control of space more rapidly and to recover less easily. In some sense she has reverted to invisible occupancy, but this time without the sense of invisible agency. The success of the Dutch merchant's resumed courtship depends more on the discreet choreography of Roxana's landlady than on Roxana's own efforts:

It was one Afternoon, about four a-Clock, my Friendly QUAKER
and I sitting in her Chamber up-stairs ... when somebody ringing
hastily at the Door, and no Servant just then in the way, she ran
down *herself*, to the Door.... She [brought the merchant] into
a very handsome Parlour below-stairs.... I cou'd not speak one
Word to her, nor stir off of my Chair, but sat as motionless as a
Statue. (pp. 221–22)

For Roxana, the parlour seems suddenly inaccessible—architecturally,
physically, psychologically. "Parlour," at this time, could refer either to a
drawing-room (i.e., a smallish, private room for conversation), or to a dining-room (*OED*). The room obviously functions here as a place in which
temporarily to deposit the merchant, not to feed him. Yet in any context,
whether as drawing-room or dining-room, whether gendered or neutral, the
room has moved beyond Roxana's reach.

Though Roxana does in time marry the merchant and become a countess, the habits of secret occupation and dark retreat stealthily undermine her
foundations of security. More and more often she finds herself paralysed,
trapped in a room, terrified by doors and windows and wide open streets,
conflating psychological and structural dangers: "*In a word*, it never Lightn'd
or Thunder'd, but I expected the next Flash wou'd penetrate my Vitals ...
it never blew a Storm of Wind, but I expected the Fall of some Stack of
Chimneys, or some Part of the House wou'd bury me in its Ruins" (p. 260).
As a sort of darkly logical consequence of her earlier identification of building with body, Roxana now anticipates her psychological collapse in terms of
structural disintegration.

In the end, no room, no arrangement of rooms, no prestigious or incon-
spicuous address, offers Roxana interior security or admits her spatial control. Her daughter Susan relentlessly tracks her down, invading her lodgings,
demanding acknowledgment, haunting her daily thoughts, and eroding her
self-control until all her series of houses seem to entrap rather than empower
her. Amy, so often the extreme manifestation of Roxana's most secret spaces,[19] acts out their shared sense of walled-in panic: thinking about Susan, she
"starts up, runs about the Room like a distracted body; I'll put an End to it,
that I will; I can't bear it; I must murther her ... and then repeated it over
three or four times, walking to-and-again in the Room" (pp. 272–73). Interior
space crackles with frenetic, hostile, frustrated energy; the walls enclose and
confine without protecting; the threat from without is met by a worse within.
Finally Roxana loses even the semblance of spatial control, and her friend
the Quaker has to determine her actions, monitor her house, and direct her
escape:

> I was so confounded, I knew not what to do, or to say.
>
> My happy Visitor had more Presence of Mind than I; and ask'd me . . . but hast thou no Way out backward to go to her? . . . Now it happen'd there was a Back-Door in the Garden, by which we usually went and came to and from the House; so I told her of it: Well, well, says she, Go out and make a Visit then, and leave the rest to me. (pp. 318–19)

Susan has challenged Roxana's ability to control the spaces she inhabits, and her alleged murder destroys it altogether: "As for the poor Girl herself, she was ever before my Eyes; I saw her by-Night, and by-Day; she haunted my Imagination, if she did not haunt the House; my Fancy show'd her me in a hundred Shapes and Postures; sleeping or waking, she was with me" (p. 325). All Roxana's inhabited space is now haunted space. But in a sense Susan's invisible presence had *already* haunted the apartments of Pall Mall, repeating Roxana's own habits of invisible occupancy, infiltrating spaces that seemed most securely subordinated.[20] Roxana has lost whatever control she might have had over her interior spaces, both architectural and psychological. All her manipulations of space—her tricks with folding-doors and drawing-room entrances—prove only an illusion of control. She has inhabited her houses on false pretences, and as such she is punished for presuming to command the centres of rooms.

* * *

In perhaps surprising contrast, *Clarissa*, read architecturally, suggests a triumph of spatial control. Clarissa's difficulties, more overtly than Roxana's, arise in opposition to masculine usurpation of her domestic as well as sexual interiors. Not coincidentally, Clarissa's struggles with Lovelace in London are centred as much on the dining-room as on the bedroom, at a time when the dining-room was becoming emblematically male. But though Lovelace penetrates both her bedroom and her body, his command of interior space—whether private or public, sexual or social, gendered or general—is no more authentic or durable than Roxana's. Clarissa never aspires to the kinds of spatial control that dominate Roxana's imagination—on the contrary, she continually offers to confine herself, to relinquish her dairy house—but unlike Roxana, she never loses control within any space she occupies. She fills them, utterly, with herself. Although she is raped and dies, she has (at least) the literary victory of escaping into an eternally inviolable space and occupying—even commanding, dominating, haunting—everyone else's psychological space.

The novel in some ways begins and ends in Clarissa's parlour (and a parlour, "when more spacious and handsomely furnished, is usually called the drawing room," *OED*). Clarissa explains: "There are two doors to my parlour, as I used to call it . . . a wainscot partition only parting [it from the next parlour]. I remember them both in one: but they were separated in favour of us girls, for each to receive her visitors in at her pleasure" (p. 303; 78). As a loved and admired child, she was granted, along with her less remarkable sister Arabella, the social and architectural anomaly of a public room of her own. In this room she learns the art of bringing larger spaces into small. She decks its walls with drawings of her favourite view: the wooded, hilly countryside seen from "her" ivy summerhouse (p. 351n; 86). The large prospect in the small, personal room prefigures Clarissa's ability, in the words of Gaston Bachelard, to transcend the limits of geometrical space.[21] She discovers the ability to open up a psychological—and to some extent even a physical—freedom within her closest confinement.

But it is Clarissa's public ownership of space—her parlour, her ivy summerhouse, her dairy house—that, in flagrant disregard of her brother's ideas of patriarchal possession, in part originates and fuels the family effort to dispossess and displace her. Her brother, her father, her uncles, and her lovers each demand the right (the power) to say: Only I can grant you, a woman, a room of your own. (So go to your room.) Clarissa's family revenges itself upon her by dismantling her parlour and denying her presence. Understanding all too well—and envying all too much—the power conferred by personal space, Arabella nastily sends Clarissa the details of its destruction:

> Your drawings and your pieces are all taken down; as is also your
> own whole-length picture in the Vandyke taste, from your late
> parlour: they are taken down and thrown into your closet, which
> will be nailed up as if it were not a part of the house; there to perish
> together: for who can bear to see them? (p. 509; 147)

The family's spitefully nailing up the closet feebly prefigures Clarissa's far more definitive self-enclosure in her coffin. The family dreads Clarissa's power of presence, her command of interior space, and they struggle mightily to compress her spaces into their own; but as she becomes their unmentionable secret, the idea of her becomes proportionately larger, until, like Roxana's daughter Susan, she penetrates the whole house in death.

Lovelace is equally interested in colonizing Clarissa's domestic spaces. Although Clarissa begins and ends her story within the space of her private parlour, the house where Lovelace first entraps and finally rapes her occupies the strategic centre of the book. He baits her with a disingenuous description of Mrs Sinclair's house:

> She rents two good houses, distant from each other, only joined by a large handsome passage. The inner house is the genteelest, and is very elegantly furnished; but you may have the use of a very handsome parlour in the outer house, if you choose to look into the street. . . . The apartments she has to let are in the inner house: they are a dining-room, two neat parlours, a withdrawing-room, two or three handsome bedchambers (one with a pretty light closet in it, which looks into the little garden); all furnished in taste. (p. 470; 130.1)

Clarissa writes with some small satisfaction to Anna Howe: "I am to have the dining-room, the bedchamber with the light closet (of which, if I stay any time at the widow's, I shall make great use), and a servant's room" (p. 471; 130). It is this dining-room as much as this bedchamber that becomes the focal point for psychological domination, and its increasing cultural significance as a masculine territory increases the significance of Clarissa's spatial triumph.[22]

Until the actual rape, much of the dramatic conflict between Lovelace and Clarissa is centred on the control of "her" dining-room.[23] Unable to penetrate her bedroom, Lovelace badgers her into meeting him in the presumably safe public space of the dining-room, where he usually plans, attempts, and fails to overpower her. In his accounts to Belford, Clarissa seems to acquire a psychological and even a physical superiority in the dining-room, as if the nature of the space itself confers power:

> She flew to the door. I threw myself in her way, shut it, and in the humblest manner besought her to forgive me . . . but pushing me rudely from the door, as if I had been nothing . . . she gaining that force through passion, which I had lost *through* fear; and out she shot to her own apartment (thank my stars she could fly no further!); and as soon as she entered it, in a passion still, she double-locked and double-bolted herself in. (p. 573; 175)

The "fear" that Lovelace confesses to in fact determines the outcome of every direct confrontation between them. He later corners her again in the dining-room, and, although her apparent fear makes him release her, he admits: "till she had actually withdrawn (which I permitted under promise of a speedy return . . .), all the motions of my heart were as pure as her own" (p. 646; 201). In the most dramatic dining-room scene of all, she confronts, outwits, and firmly subdues the combined forces of Lovelace, Sinclair, and the servants with the threat of suicide:

> Now, Belford, see us all sitting in judgement [in the dining-room], resolved to punish the fair briberess ... and hear her *unbolt, unlock, unbar*, the door; ... then *hear* her step towards us, and instantly *see* her enter among us, confiding in her own innocence; and with a majesty in her person and manner that is *natural* to her; but which then shone out in all its glory! ... looking down my guilt into confusion.... She withdrew to the door, and set her back against it, holding the pointed knife to her heaving bosom ... from the moment she entered the dining-room with so much intrepidity, it was absolutely impossible to think of prosecuting my villainous designs against her. (pp. 948–52; 281)

It is her presence—in particular, her presence in that room of social and architectural dominance—that "unmans" him, so to speak, and he realizes that she must not be present at her own rape. He is able to penetrate her sexual space only when he has drugged her, dislodging her from her body and therefore transforming sexual space into merely genital area. After Clarissa has established psychological possession of the dining-room, Lovelace makes his ultimate stab at sexual possession in the bedroom—but only when that room is essentially empty.

Lovelace's empty rape typifies the larger fissures in his spatial and psychological dominance. He insists that he controls every space he occupies and even some that he does not. But the nature of his possession is reduced to a simple, ineffectual gesture, either physical or linguistic. When he first learns of Clarissa's escape to Hampstead, he runs frantically to her room: "I have been traversing her room, meditating, or taking up everything she but touched or used.... From her room to my own; in the dining-room, and in and out of every place where I have seen the beloved of my heart, do I hurry; in none can I tarry; her lovely image in every one" (p. 740; 228). He tries to recapture the sense of her presence by reclaiming her space, by folding up her smallest habitation in his arms. His servant Will tries to accommodate that fierce desire to repossess Clarissa by helping to usurp her space: "They showed her up to the very room where I now am. She sat at the very table I now write upon; and I believe the chair I sit in was hers" (p. 762; 232). Yet the possessive pronoun is hers; her image stamps each room; absent as well as present, Clarissa dominates the dining-room, her bedroom, and Lovelace's own room. Like the spatially dysfunctional Roxana, Lovelace in the end defines *no* rooms, commands *no* space. When he returns in disgrace to his own family, he boasts:

I have one half of the house to myself; and that the best; for the great enjoy that least, which costs them most: *grandeur* and use are two things: the common part is theirs; the state part is mine: and here I lord it, and *will* lord it, as long as I please; while the two pursy sisters, the old gouty brother, and the two musty nieces, are stived up in the other half, and dare not stir for fear of meeting me: whom (that's the jest of it) they have forbidden coming into their apartments, as I have them into mine. And so I have them all prisoners while I range about as I please. (p. 1182; 395)

But Lovelace's lordship, as he inadvertently admits, is a puppet monarchy. The state rooms, of such prominence in the seventeenth century, were becoming socially and architecturally obsolete. He occupies the rooms of show rather than those of real and daily life: rooms of archaic ceremony and no living value. He reigns undisputed over unwanted, untenanted space.[24]

Though Lovelace does recapture and rape Clarissa, the rest of the novel relentlessly records the way that she finally and comprehensively eludes his possession, retreating into her own ultimately inviolable space. The bounding walls of drawing-room and dining-room and bedroom gradually recede before the abstract interiority of mind and soul. Clarissa's spatial as well as spiritual defeat of Lovelace also signifies a spatial and spiritual triumph over her father and brother, the original delimiters of her domestic—and, they hoped, psychological—interior space. She deludes Lovelace into believing she has returned to her family, when she implies her own death, yet her words become devastatingly literal as well: "I HAVE good news to tell you. I am setting out with all diligence for my father's house" (p. 1233; 421.1). She talks repeatedly and cheerfully to those with whom she lodges about buying a house of her own (pp. 1250; 426, 1273; 440). Within that last and most confining habitation—her coffin—she returns to occupy, dominate, and overflow, with poetic finality, the centre of her old parlour, in the centre of her father's house:

When the corpse was carried into the lesser parlour adjoining to the hall, which she used to call *her* parlour, and put on a table in the middle of the room, and the father and mother, the two uncles, her Aunt Hervey, and her sister came in (joining her brother and [Colonel Morden] ...), the scene was still more affecting. Their sorrow was heightened no doubt by the remembrance of their unforgiving severity: and now seeing before them the receptacle that contained the glory of their family, who so lately was driven thence by their indiscreet violence (never, never more to be restored

to them!), no wonder that their grief was more than common grief.
(p. 1398; 500)

Clarissa herself becomes an example of something conceptually enormous only nominally contained in a small space.[25] Unforgiven in life, but forgiving in death, she exquisitely, magnificently tortures her family and Lovelace: she has conquered all space, and she cannot be reached. She repossesses for all time (haunting her family and, through her letters, her readers) inviolable and unalterable space.

* * *

Austen's female characters, like Richardson's, seem initially confined as well as defined by the spaces they inhabit, and are concerned both to locate and to test the strength of their boundaries. Clarissa, at first distinguished by that gift of space, her parlour, then equally marked by her immurement, works successfully to inhabit and reclaim for herself the centre of her limited spaces, and finally the centre of all her spaces—domestic, social, psychological, architectural, and narrative. Her final triumph is prefigured by her psychological possession of the dining-room at a time when the dining-room was becoming literally and manifestly masculine. By the time of Austen's novels, the separation of masculine and feminine interior space was complete, explicit, and (as with Adam's claim) ideologically self-justified. Austen's reader almost always knows exactly in which room any scene takes place; and those scenes are set primarily in the drawing-rooms. Her heroines seldom have any apparent quarrel with where they are placed: they await the gentlemen in the drawing-room, and then proceed with their story. But those drawing-room scenes tend to obscure the more subtle activity on their perimeters: opinions are formed, prejudices confirmed, and dramatic twists enacted in the more ambiguous spaces of stairs, vestibules, doorways, windows, and outside the houses altogether—quietly pressing against the boundaries of the drawing-room as the sphere for feminine activity.[26]

In *Pride and Prejudice* Elizabeth discovers throughout the novel the disadvantages that attend the strict codification of social space. At the first dinner at Rosings, "when the ladies returned to the drawing room, there was little to be done but to hear Lady Catherine talk, which she did without any intermission till coffee came in" (p. 146). Implicitly different from the dining-room (dominated by or at least tempered with men), the drawing-room victimizes the women by allowing Lady Catherine to exploit her social precedence and verbally tyrannize them. An earlier drawing-room scene between Elizabeth and Bingley's sisters shows how the importance of the men's entrance becomes absurdly exaggerated by the after-dinner separation, and how the women's response to that entrance can undercut whatever of value might have emerged in the private female circle:

> When the ladies removed after dinner, Elizabeth ... attended her [sister] into the drawing-room. ... Elizabeth had never seen [Miss Bingley and Mrs Hurst] so agreeable as they were during the hour which passed before the gentlemen appeared. Their powers of conversation were considerable. They could describe an entertainment with accuracy, relate an anecdote with humour, and laugh at their acquaintance with spirit. But when the gentlemen entered, Jane was no longer the first object. (p. 47)

Miss Bingley's foremost interest now is to attract Darcy's attention. The drawing-room, which would seem to provide the space for intelligent conversation between women, more often functions as itself a liminal space, a place in which to wait for men.

But not always. The characterization above is complicated by the example of that stoic woman, Charlotte Lucas Collins, who, in a strategy rather like that of the early Roxana, appears to sacrifice superior space in order to control personal space:

> The room in which the ladies sat was backwards. Elizabeth at first had rather wondered that Charlotte should not prefer the dining parlour for common use; it was a better sized room, and had a pleasanter aspect; but she soon saw that her friend had an excellent reason for what she did, for Mr. Collins would undoubtedly have been much less in his own apartment, had they sat in one equally lively; and she gave Charlotte credit for the arrangement. (p. 150)

The act of defining spatial boundaries is displaced onto the character who, from one point of view in the novel, made the wrong choice and delimited her own sphere of action. But from Charlotte's point of view, of course, it is precisely this obvious chance to govern and redistribute interior space that legitimates her decision to marry. Escaping Mr Collins validates almost any deviation in domestic arrangements. Mr Collins is free to contemplate with endless satisfaction the neighbouring estate of Rosings; Charlotte's backward room forwards her freedom from embarrassment.

Many of the most important misunderstandings and misinterpretations of the novel occur in the *centre* of such socially sanctioned areas of discourse as the drawing room.[27] Elizabeth and Wickham share their ill-judged opinions about Darcy in the drawing-room of Mrs Philips. The entire Bennet family catalogues Darcy's shortcomings in their family gatherings after dinner.

Bingley's sisters vent their spite against Elizabeth in their brother's drawing-room. And Darcy first (and unsuccessfully) proposes marriage to Elizabeth in the visual (if not spatial) centre of the drawing-room at Hunsford—by the mantlepiece (p. 169). This central scene occupies the narrative centre of the novel, and throws the centres themselves into doubt.

Yet many of the negative moments in the novel also seem initiated at entrances, which might seem to discredit liminal spaces as well. Darcy enters the drawing-room at Hunsford Parsonage several times to overturn Elizabeth's peace (pp. 157, 168). After Elizabeth returns to Longbourn at the news of Lydia's scandalous elopement, Jane meets Elizabeth in the vestibule and whispers the latest news (p. 252). When Lady Catherine arrives at Longbourn to demand Elizabeth's intentions regarding Darcy, she "entered the room with an air more than usually ungracious" (p. 311), promising unpleasantness before delivering it. But all these cornered moments of discomfort, distress, or displeasure contain or herald some form of knowledge, some piece of truth, or some moment of self-understanding, and so become the true psychological, moral, and narrative centres of the novel.[28]

The principal resolutions of the novel retreat beyond the sanctioned drawing-rooms into these slippery spaces, and the architectural margins are emphasized by social and psychological parallels. At the opening dance of the novel, Elizabeth first attracts the notice of Darcy as she sits in the uncomfortably liminal position of wallflower and eavesdropper:

> Elizabeth Bennet had been obliged, by the scarcity of gentlemen, to sit down for two dances; and during part of that time, Mr. Darcy had been standing near enough for her to overhear a conversation between him and Mr. Bingley. . . . [Darcy] turning round, . . . looked for a moment at Elizabeth, till catching her eye, he withdrew his own and coldly said, "She is tolerable, but not handsome enough to tempt *me*; and I am in no humour at present to give consequence to young ladies who are slighted by other men." (pp. 8–9)

Darcy seems determined to keep Elizabeth as well as himself well within their respective, apparently non-tangential, spheres of interested and emphatically uninterested observers. But Elizabeth of course overhears him, and thus their first important connection is inadvertently established in that awkward space outside the dance.

Darcy gives his haughty explanatory letter to Elizabeth as she wanders outside the perimeters of Rosings:

> She was proceeding directly to her favourite walk, when the recollection of Mr. Darcy's sometimes coming there stopped her,

and instead of entering the park, she turned up the lane, which led her farther from the turnpike road. The park paling was still the boundary on one side, and she soon passed one of the gates into the ground.

　　After walking two or three times along that part of the lane, she was tempted . . . to stop at the gates and look into the park. . . . She was on the point of continuing her walk, when she caught a glimpse of a gentleman within the sort of grove which edged the park; he was moving that way; and fearful of its being Mr. Darcy, she was directly retreating. (p. 173)

Before she can enter the centre space of the park, Mr Darcy, himself hovering in a "sort of grove," gives her his momentous letter.[29] The spatial margins of the novel—not its drawing-rooms—are where things have room to change.

　　Elizabeth and Darcy learn to understand and respond to each other in the spaces between rooms, on the edges of estates. Elizabeth's change of heart begins in the between-spaces of Pemberley, which she visits from the liminal position of a tourist with her aunt and uncle Gardiner. She begins to discover Darcy's sterling qualities from the housekeeper—herself a marginal but useful character—who, we are told, "dwelt with energy on his many merits, as they proceeded together up the great staircase" (p. 219). Eventually the tour-group returns outside, where Darcy himself appears from behind the house: "As they walked across the lawn towards the river, Elizabeth turned back to look again; her uncle and aunt stopped also, and while the former was conjecturing as to the date of the building, the owner of it himself suddenly came forward from the road, which led behind it to the stables" (p. 221). Elizabeth is just leaving, Darcy returning; Elizabeth is the tourist, the apparent eavesdropper, Darcy the unexpectedly materializing presence-assumed-absent; in a fortuitous intersection of time and space, they meet again upon psychologically neutral ground, and bend over backwards to demonstrate their respective new attitudes. When after a walk they arrive ahead of the Gardiners at the house, Elizabeth declines Darcy's invitation to reenter the house, as if she prefers to keep them on this threshold (p. 226). Later, at the inn at Lambton, when Elizabeth first gets the shocking news of Lydia's elopement, Darcy appears in the doorway and forgets his manners so far as to cry out in naked concern, "Good God! what is the matter?" (p. 243). (She later misunderstands his subsequent gravity as distaste when he more conventionally occupies the room as he listens to her story.) And finally, Darcy's second and successful proposal occurs on a spontaneous walk towards town (p. 324).

　　The importance of temporal and psychological margins reinforces the prominence of spatial margins. Elizabeth's admission of and pleasure in her own happiness occurs within the liminal edges of time. She derives most comfort and satisfaction in recollection and anticipation. After Darcy and his sister paid their visit to Elizabeth and the Gardiners at the inn at Lambton, "Elizabeth ... found herself, when their visitors left them, capable of considering the last half hour with some satisfaction, though while it was passing, the enjoyment of it had been little" (p. 232). When they return the visit at Pemberley, and she is trapped with Bingley's sisters in the drawing room, "she expected every moment that some of the gentlemen would enter the room. She wished, she feared that the master of the house might be amongst them" (p. 236). When she later talks over the visit with her aunt Gardiner, she will only speak over or around its centre: "they talked of his sister, his friends, his house, his fruit, of everything but himself" (p. 239). When Darcy appears with Bingley at Longbourn, "she looked forward to their entrance, as the point on which all her chance of pleasure for the evening must depend" (p. 302). And when all is understood, and Darcy and Elizabeth have declared their love for each other (in the garden), later that evening in the Longbourn drawing-room "Elizabeth, agitated and confused, rather *knew* that she was happy, than *felt* herself to be so" (p. 331). Although the resolution of the novel returns Elizabeth to the centre of the drawing-room, she still pushes beyond its limits. The happy ending of the novel, its appearance of traditional closure, still resists the implications of that closure. Elizabeth returns to the drawing-room with a more complete understanding of herself and of Darcy, but emotionally and psychologically she reserves the right to cross boundaries.

The fracturing of social interiors into masculine and feminine spaces in the eighteenth century generated changing patterns of resistance within differently accommodating walls. The evolving contours of the drawing-room were on the one hand cultural and ideological constructions shaping the female character. As Simon Varey argues, "the spaces created (in theory or in practice) by architects and those created by the novelists—whether or not they are the same spaces—express specific ideology. . . . For one who resists the pressure to conform as for one who does not, the self is defined, to a remarkable degree, by space" (p. 4). The drawing-room, in which women were to pass a great deal of *their* time (as implied by Adam's separate claim for men), would contribute to shaping the social and intellectual habits, manners, and assumptions of upper and middle-class Englishwomen, and to the increasing sense of division and difference between men and women, between public and private, between the political and the domestic.

On the other hand, Heidegger defines space as "something that has been made room for, something that is cleared and free, namely, within a boundary, Greek *peras*. A boundary is not that at which something stops but, as the Greeks recognized, the boundary is that from which something *begins its essential unfolding*."[30] Walls as boundaries in Heidegger's sense do more

108   Cynthia Wall

than define and enclose: they imply and even generate alternate space; they establish individual as well as cultural relationships between interiors and exteriors; they suggest ways to resist as well as accommodate their own limits. Women such as Lady Lyttelton actively worked to create the institution of the drawing-room, determining its size, its position, its significance. The female characters discussed here do more than simply inhabit their domestic spaces: they transgress, transform, and sometimes even transcend them. Roxana forges and then forfeits control of formal architectural space; Clarissa achieves control of psychological space by transcending her confined domestic space; and Elizabeth pushes through the codified walls of the feminine sphere to find some room to breathe. As the drawing-room changed, along with its implicit possibilities or restrictions, so did narrative patterns of imaginative opposition.

NOTES

1. Robert and James Adam, *Works in Architecture, 1773–79*, 3 vols (reprinted Dourdan: E. Thézard Fils, 1900), 1:9. References are to this edition.

2. See Mark Girouard, *Life in the English Country House* (New Haven: Yale University Press, 1978), pp. 203–6, 232–34.

3. The boundaries of my project here—the fictional habitation of culturally and sexually determined interior space within otherwise widely dispersed canonical works—naturally suggest what will be left outside. I reserve for future work the inspection of architectural spaces in marginal texts, where I suspect that, as in Sarah Scott's *Millenium Hall* (1762), different and perhaps more harmonious configurations of interior space may be imagined and enacted. Another line of questioning—which also belongs in a different essay—is the position of canonical novels that do *not* fit in the literary or ideological contexts I am establishing here. The novels of Fielding and Smollett, for example, pay a distinctly different kind of attention to architectural structures (both interior and exterior) from those of Defoe, Richardson, and Austen. I see Fielding's and Smollett's architectural imagery emerging from but loyal to a prior literary tradition, more akin to Pope's *Epistle to Burlington* and the tradition of the country-house poem, where the houses function emblematically, as reliable signs in themselves rather than as structures that define or influence spheres of human action.

4. References are to the following editions: Daniel Defoe, *Roxana; The Fortunate Mistress*, ed. Jane Jack (Oxford: Oxford University Press, 1964); Samuel Richardson, *Clarissa; or, The History of a Young Lady*, ed. Angus Ross (New York: Penguin, 1985), with page number followed by letter number; Jane Austen, *Pride and Prejudice*, ed. James Kinsley, based on R.W. Chapman's text (Oxford: Oxford University Press, 1990).

5. For a more detailed account of the popularization and professionalization of architecture, see Sir John Summerson, *Architecture in Britain 1530–1830* (7th ed., Harmondsworth: Penguin, 1983), pp. 269, 320–21; Summerson, *Georgian London* (Harmondsworth: Penguin, 1945, 1978), pp. 17–83; Simon Varey, *Space and the Eighteenth-Century English Novel* (Cambridge: Cambridge University Press, 1990), pp. 1–2, 10–23.

6. See Summerson, *Georgian London*, pp. 72–75, 145; Reginald Tumor, *The Smaller English House 1500–1939* (London: B.T. Batsford, 1952), p. 75. Derek Jarrett points out that "within a short time [after the publication of Thomas Chippendale's *Gentleman's and Cabinet-Maker's Directory* in 1754] even the most conservative local cabinet-maker was forced to buy books of design for himself and keep abreast of standards of elegance." *England in the Age of Hogarth* (New Haven: Yale University Press, 1986), p. 141.

7. See Summerson, *Georgian London*, pp. 38–51; A.E. Richardson and C. Lovett Gill, *London Houses from 1660 to 1820* (London: B.T. Batsford, 1911), pp. 2–4, 9–13, 25–27. The labouring classes in the country were also affected—particularly by the end of the century—since their houses on estates were frequently remodelled, usually for reasons of health as well as taste. See Maurice Barley, *Houses and History* (London: Faber and Faber, 1962), pp. 259–61. The living quarters of the poorest classes in London itself, of course, were not terribly affected by questions of taste.

8. Richardson's and Austen's interest in architecture is well known through their letters. Defoe's equal interest is less well documented and frequently discounted by his biographers and critics. In my doctoral dissertation, "Housing Defoe's Projects: The Rebuilding of London and 'Modern' Literary Space" (University of Chicago, 1992), I have argued that in fact much of Defoe's life and most of his important works are centrally concerned with the psychological and social implications of architectural structures.

9. Peter Thornton, *Authentic Decor: The Domestic Interior 1620–1920* (New York: Viking Press, 1984), p. 93. Thornton cites Blondel's *Maisons de Plaisance* (1737–38) and *Architecture Françoise* (1752). Summerson agrees that French influence was always important to British architecture, but emphasizes that French styles were rarely directly imported, particularly in the first half of the century (*Architecture in Britain*, pp. 267–68). Thornton also points out a striking difference between the gendered spaces of the French and English upper classes: in France, husbands and wives occupied separate apartments, but by mid-century the wife held her court in the larger suites, while her husband retired to the smaller and more private rooms.

10. Vitruvius, for example, explains that when the Athenians erected temples to Apollo and Diana, they invented two kinds of columns in which "they borrowed manly beauty, naked and unadorned, for the one [Doric], and for the other [Ionic and later Corinthian] the delicacy, adornment, and proportions characteristic of women." *The Ten Books on Architecture*, trans. Morris Hicky Morgan (Cambridge: Harvard University Press, 1914; reprinted New York: Dover, 1960), pp. 103–4.

11. *OED* citing Chambers's *Cyclopaedia* (1751), quoted in Girouard, p. 191.

12. Girouard argues that the separation and change probably evolved out of the practice of tea-drinking: the ladies would retire a short while before the gentlemen in order to prepare the tea or coffee, while the men gradually became more enamoured of their waiting period for its own sake. The lag time evolved from minutes into (sometimes) hours. (One hour appears to be standard in Austen's novels.) Ralph Fastnedge suggests, on the other hand, that the habit of withdrawing to a smaller "tea-room" contributed to the "softening" of manners and in fact replaced the heavy drinking of the seventeenth century. See Fastnedge, *English Furniture Styles from 1500 to 1830* (Harmondsworth: Penguin, 1955, 1967), p. 115. Neither explanation necessarily affects the social consequences of increasingly gendered space.

13. See also Barley, pp. 202–12; Hugh Braun, *Old English Houses* (London: Faber and Faber, 1962), pp. 129–30; Richardson and Gill, pp. 25–35; Summerson, *Georgian London*, pp. 143–44.

14. Girouard, p. 204.

15. Although Nikolaus Pevsner, among others, remarked upon the surprising lack of architectural detail in Austen's works, given her well-known interest in houses (see "The Architectural Setting of Jane Austen's Novels," *Journal of the Warburg and Courtauld Institutes* 31 [1968], 404–22), Austen's highly charged attention to the distribution and occupation (if not the appearance) of interior domestic space not only reveals her own interest in architectural significance, but also matches the larger public interest in the definitions and implications of structural space.

16. For additional examples of Roxana manipulating the prince through and within interior space, see pp. 62, 63, 71, 77, 78–79, 96–97, 100.

17. See Barley, pp. 264–80; Braun, pp. 129–30; Richardson and Gill, pp. 25–35; Summerson, *Georgian London*, pp. 65–83; Tumor, p. 56.

18. As I argue elsewhere, some of Defoe's other characters, in contrast, do seem to achieve in the end an untroubled occupation of space. Moll Flanders in some sense earns the full measure of security and gentility she had long wanted: in declaring and sharing her full wealth with Jemy in the end, she finally fortifies her original (deceptive) appearance of wealth with its reality. Crusoe's redemption appears in his ultimate ability to share his real estate with the mutineers.

19. See Terry J. Castle, "'Amy, who Knew My Disease': A Psychosexual Pattern in Defoe's *Roxana*," *ELH* 46 (1979), 81–96.

20. In a sense, Roxana's problems with Susan dramatize the threat for the socially powerful that is always dimly implicit in their dependence upon a servant class, and her efforts to expunge the presence of Susan from her life and mind indirectly anticipate a larger social and architectural change. During the late-seventeenth and eighteenth centuries, and culminating in the nineteenth, the upper classes became in general increasingly uneasy at the visible presence of servants, and mazes of passages and back staircases began to riddle the plans of the great houses in both town and country, so that all the functions of service could be performed without the owners of the house encountering those who performed those functions. Confrontation—personal and political—seemed to be architecturally occluded. (See Girouard, pp. 138, 285.)

21. Gaston Bachelard, *The Poetics of Space*, trans. Maria Jolas (1958; Boston: Beacon Press, 1969), p. 47.

22. Mrs Sinclair's putative address (see p. 744) in Dover Street would have been in the relatively new and overwhelmingly Palladian area near Burlington House and Berkeley Square (see John Rocque's map of London, 1747, I0Ab). The fashionable architectural uniformity of this area supports the idea that this particular dining-room shares the architectural and social significance of Palladian pressures, which increasingly promoted the separation as well as symmetry of dining-room and drawing-room (Summerson, *Architecture in Britain*, pp. 387–88).

23. Pamela also wages battle in the dining-room. Pamela, of course, as a servant has no title to *any* space of her own, and she experiences more immediately than women of more protected classes (with the obvious Richardsonian exception) the peculiar tenuousness of walls, the sense of domestic space as trap as well as refuge. But she also utterly understands the gradations of social significance in rooms, and the niceties of properly inhabiting them, particularly after she has married Mr B

and must stand up to Lady Davers. See Samuel Richardson, *Pamela* (1740), ed. M. Kinkead-Weekes, 2 vols (London: Dent, 1926, 1976), especially 1:349, 386.

24. See Girouard, pp. 203–206, 230; Philippa Tristram, *Living Space in Fact and Fiction* (London: Routledge, 1989), p. 256.

25. For an excellent discussion of closets, confinement, and freedom in *Clarissa* see Tristram, pp. 255–56.

26. This argument does not work the same way in all of Austen's novels, although the level of attention to the configuration and signification of interior space remains consistent. In *Mansfield Park*, for instance, Fanny hovers too much on the edges of interiors—in her attic, on the stairway with Edmund, in window recesses. Fanny finds the closed feminine circle of the drawing room a release, where "she was able to think as she would." She must learn to occupy the centres—as her return to Portsmouth reveals. In *Sense and Sensibility* Marianne Dashwood must learn to control and contain herself within public space, rather as Fanny Price must learn to enter it; Elinor, on the other hand, suffers like Elizabeth Bennet from the insipidity of drawing rooms. In *Persuasion*, Sir Walter, Elizabeth, and Mary all place undue emphasis on the size and appearance and number of drawing rooms, while Anne captures attention, regains confidence, and reclaims Wentworth all in passageways or staircases or corners of drawing rooms. The novel that significantly does not fit into this pattern of plotted space is *Emma*—but Emma, of course, already commands a house and by the end of the novel Mr Knightley moves into it *with* her.

27. Another socially gendered and architecturally central room at this time, of course, is the library. In *Pride and Prejudice* until the very end Mr Bennet consistently retreats into his library to protect and prolong his patriarchal inadequacy and inaction.

28. One possible exception to this theory is Wickham: when he enters the room at Elizabeth's aunt Philips's, his dashing appearance confirms her initial prejudice in his favour (p. 67). But even here, Wickham is seen in the company of "a very creditable, gentlemanlike set," which he excels as much as "*they* were superior to the broad-faced stuffy uncle Philips, breathing port wine, who followed them into the room." Knowledge of sorts, perhaps.

29. Tristram notes: "Austen's gardens always mediate between the house and the world around it" (p. 243).

30. Martin Heidegger, "Building Dwelling Thinking" (1951), *Basic Writings*, ed. David Farrell Krell (New York: Harper and Row, 1977), p. 332.

WILLIAM DERESIEWICZ

Community and Cognition
in Pride and Prejudice

The opening of *Pride and Prejudice* vies with "Call me Ishmael" as the most famous first sentence in English-language fiction, yet that which makes it memorable also makes it anomalous within its author's corpus. Each of Jane Austen's other novels begins by introducing one of its principal characters.[1] Only *Pride and Prejudice* begins with an aphorism: "It is a truth universally acknowledged, that a single man in possession of a good fortune, must be in want of a wife." An aphorism, or rather a mock aphorism, for it is immediately intimated that this "truth universally acknowledged" is in fact nothing more than one of the fixed opinions of the "neighborhood" of "surrounding families" amidst which the novel's action is to take place.[2] The introduction of individual characters is delayed until the third paragraph (even then withholding the usual Austenian fanfare of station, condition, and history), and the community turns out to be the novel's true point of departure. Indeed, the note on which this opening ends, that our bachelor of property will himself become the property of "some one or other" of the local young ladies, lends, if only for a moment, a teasingly arbitrary air to the identity of the specific family the narrator finally does introduce. In other words, *Pride and Prejudice* can also be seen as beginning with the introduction of one of its principal figures, only here that figure is a community. One might think this a strange choice given the protagonist with whom we

From *ELH* 64, no. 2 (1997): 503–535. © 1997 by the Johns Hopkins University Press.

are to be concerned; of all of Austen's heroines, surely the brilliant, exuberant Elizabeth Bennett deserves star billing. But as one tends to forget in retrospect—so thoroughly does her presence dominate the novel as a whole, so large does her energy and brilliance bulk in one's imagination—Elizabeth is very far from being the center of attention in the early chapters, scarcely mentioned at all until the third, not clearly emerging as the heroine until the sixth. What is presented in these first scenes is more than anything the story of a community: of communal expectations, communal conventions, communal activities. These pressures drive Mrs. Bennet, and consequently the rest of her family, into the actions that occupy the novel's first chapters. And in the most important of the early episodes, the assembly at which Mr. Bingley and his friends make their debut in the neighborhood of Meryton gentry, the community itself steps forward, through a kind of disembodied collective consciousness, to engage in acts of observation and judgment that set the course of the rest of the narrative. Elizabeth cannot appear until well into this initial story because it is that story—the story of how a community thinks, talks, exerts influence—that produces her plot, that produces her.

These considerations suggest a relationship between Elizabeth and her community very different from that generally depicted in the critical literature. A host of readers have emphasized her individuality and imaginative freedom, but in crucial ways she is not free and very little of an individualist, ways in which her story must be seen, not as an exercise of freedom, but as an effort to achieve freedom, not as a light-footed dance away from a community that cannot contain her, but as a struggle to wake herself out of a community in which she is all too comfortably embedded.[3] From this point of view, *Pride and Prejudice* can be seen as Austen's most deliberate and sustained critique of community—a constructive critique, since the novel ends by sketching an alternative vision of communal life that corrects what has been shown to be vicious and preserves what has been shown to cherishable in it. To trace these processes through the narrative we should take Austen's hint and look at the community first, Elizabeth's place within it only afterwards.

Cognition and the Single Woman

The essential respect in which the community of the novel shapes the lives and characters of its members turns out to be the least obvious. The community, as one might expect, functions as a set of social activities and behavioral norms, but it also functions as a set of cognitive processes, or in other words, mental habits.[4] Consider the content of the collective consciousness implicitly present in the early chapters: "He was discovered to be proud," "His character was decided," "'Every body says that.'" Judgments such as these reflect common values, but they first of all require the gathering and transmitting of specific information: "a report soon followed," "the report

which was in general circulation," "Mrs. Long says that," "Lady Lucas quieted [Mrs. Bennet's] fears a little by starting the idea of," and on and on.
Only then comes the application: "the gentlemen pronounced," "the ladies
declared." Such informal circulation of information and opinion is the focus
of communal life. Even dancing seems a mere pretext; what matters is what
is assumed, learned, known, believed, communicated. "It is a truth universally acknowledged": that is, it is a belief ensconced in "the minds of the
surrounding families." The novel takes as its point of departure, not customs
or conventions, but cognitive processes. In particular, it begins by setting out
the kind of cognitive process that crucially characterizes the community's
thinking, the deductive logic of the syllogism. As we might reformulate it:

> All single men in possession of a good fortune must be in want
>   of a wife.
> *Mr. Bingley is a single man in possession of a good fortune*
> Mr. Bingley must be in want of a wife.

Our "universal truth," "well fixed" as it is in the minds of the surrounding families, serves as the major premise, the starting-point of deduction. "The
feelings or views" of the single man in question—empirical evidence that may
be thought to bear on the issue—have no place in the process and are therefore discounted. And because they are discounted, there is no possibility that
they will modify the major premise. Without the countercheck of induction,
of fresh observation and reconsideration, conjecture crowns itself as certainty
("must be"), and beliefs once accepted harden into "universal truths."

A host of distortions, mainly rather comic, follows from this basic
blindness:

> A report soon followed that Mr. Bingley was to bring twelve
> ladies and seven gentlemen with him to the assembly. The girls
> were grieved at such a large number of ladies, but were comforted
> the day before the ball by hearing, that instead of twelve, he had
> brought only six with him from London, his five sisters and a
> cousin. And when the party entered the assembly room, it con-
> sisted of only five altogether. (10)

The funniest thing about this passage is that Austen manages to write
"twelve ladies and seven gentlemen" with a straight face. But it is no surprise
that the initial report was so wildly off. The whole idea that Bingley had gone
to London to get a large party was simply invented by Lady Lucas on the
spot, this being the idea she "starts" in order to "quiet" Mrs. Bennet. Scrupu-
lousness of report is not a great concern in this community, nor is scrupulous-

ness of observation. Darcy's ten thousand a year leads the ladies to declare that "he was much handsomer than Mr. Bingley," but after the discovery of his pride, "not all his estate in Derbyshire could . . . save him from having a most forbidding, disagreeable countenance." The few occasions upon which the collective consciousness returns late in the novel show that the community's confidence in its judgment remains unshaken even when its conclusions have been discredited. After Wickham elopes with Lydia, we learn that

> All Meryton seemed striving to blacken the man, who, but three months before, had been almost an angel of light. . . . Every body declared that he was the wickedest young man in the world; and every body began to find out, that they had always distrusted the appearance of his goodness. (294)

Revisionism saves the community from an admission of error and what seems an even greater threat, of uncertainty, but at the cost of subordinating perception and reason to expediency, desire, and self-conceit.

These observations might seem fairly unimportant until one recognizes how powerful are the community's cognitive patterns to compel individual action. Induction is a slow and uncertain process; no wealth of observation suffices to prove a general truth. But deduction is certain and swift; it springs like a mousetrap. Given a certain belief about single men in possession of good fortunes, the syllogistic mechanism need only be baited with the proper morsel of cheese, a Charles Bingley, for it to slam down on Mrs. Bennet and thus on her whole family. Syllogistic mousetraps of this kind are scattered throughout the novel, mental reflexes waiting to be triggered, waiting in turn to trigger reflexive behavior. The most important concerns the age at which young women are eligible to be married. That, after all, is the really fundamental "truth" underlying the action of the first scenes, so anxiety-producing that it cannot even be spoken aloud. Thus Mrs. Bennet:

> "Mrs. Long says that Netherfield is taken by a young man of large fortune from the north of England; that he came down on Monday in a chaise and four to see the place, and was so much delighted with it that he agreed with Mr. Morris immediately that he is to take possession before Michaelmas, and some of his servants are to be in the house by the end of next week." (3)

"Monday . . . immediately . . . Michaelmas . . . the end of next week": there's a clock ticking in Mrs. Bennet's head, and it's ticking very loudly. Time to get the girls married. Mechanical thought produces mechanical behavior, and communal life, like the universal truths of communal thought, remains forever "well-fixed."

Surely Elizabeth comes, when she comes, as the exception to all this. A stile-jumper by conviction as well as instinct, she not only flouts convention, she holds it up for deliberate mockery. But does she exhibit the same relationship to her community's patterns of thought as she does to its norms of behavior? She makes terrible blunders of judgment, yet don't these also proceed from her energy, freedom, and brilliance—her desire either to laugh at everyone, as she would have it, or "willfully to misunderstand them" (58), as Darcy believes? If anyone is unlikely to have her opinions dictated to her, one would think, it is Elizabeth Bennet. Yet this is precisely what happens, and in the most important of all instances. There is no more crucial judgment in the novel than the one she makes about Darcy at the very start of their acquaintance. Pride, she decides: inexcusable, insufferable pride. The word becomes the tonic note of the book, and the whole course of the heroes' relationship can be charted through the reorchestrations its meaning undergoes.[5] Some three hundred pages later, Elizabeth finds herself telling her father that Darcy "has no improper pride" (376), and the novel is ready to come to rest on its final, glorious harmony.

But how does Elizabeth come to make that pivotal judgment in the first place? Quite simply, it is handed to her by her community. The movement of the word "pride" through the narrative and into Elizabeth's voice and mind follows the course I just traced: from community to family to individual. It begins as one of the judgments made by the collective consciousness at the first assembly, the very first negative judgment rendered against Darcy: "His manners gave a disgust which turned the tide of his popularity; for he was discovered to be proud, to be above his company, and above being pleased" (10). By the end of the evening, the opinion has hardened: "His character was decided. He was the proudest, most disagreeable man in the world." Mrs. Bennet, we are given to understand, participates in the formation of this opinion, but her feelings are couched in words such as "dislike" and "resentment," with no characterological judgment made. By the next morning, however, she has ceded both authority and articulation to the voice of her community: "'every body says that he is ate up with pride'" (19). She is talking here (chapter 5) to her daughters and the Miss Lucases, and the word proceeds to circulate within this inlet of the communal lake. Charlotte accepts the characterization, dissenting only as to its moral valence: "'His pride,' said Miss Lucas, 'does not offend *me* so much as pride often does, because there is an excuse for it . . . he has a right to be proud.'" Now and only now is the word taken up by Elizabeth: "'That is very true . . . and I could easily forgive *his* pride if he had not mortified *mine*.'" Playing on Charlotte's emphasis of the personal pronoun, she reverses the moral direction of her friend's analysis with typical irony, but assimilates the characterological assessment without a thought. Mary affirms the consensus in her own way ("'Pride ... is a very common failing, I believe'"), but her remarks serve mainly as a device to end the conversation, and the point of the episode seems precisely to have been the introduction of the word "pride" into Elizabeth's head. Had Austen simply wished to show her making the judgment herself, either at the moment of Darcy's snub or afterwards, she could have done so with a great deal less effort.

Even the feeling of "mortification" connected with the snub—at least as important to Elizabeth's subsequent behavior as is the judg-ment it-self—is urged on her by her community. Elizabeth was certainly not pleased with Darcy's behavior at first, but neither was she much affected by it: "Elizabeth remained with no cordial feelings towards him. She told the story however with great spirit among her friends; for she had a lively, playful disposition, which delighted in any thing ridiculous" (12). There is a wide space between thinking something "ridiculous" and being "morti-fied" by it, and if Elizabeth had been mortified at the time, as she certainly is later, she would hardly have "told the story with great spirit among her friends." Indeed, when she and Jane discuss the ball that same night, Darcy isn't so much as mentioned, not even when the snobbery of Bingley's sisters is explicitly canvassed. As Mrs. Bennet perceives ("I beg you not to put it into Lizzy's head to be vexed by his ill treatment" [19]), Elizabeth's resentment arises in the course of that next morning's conversation, when she finds that her friends take the incident as a more serious affront than she was at first inclined to do. In short, while Elizabeth herself sends the story of Darcy's snub out into the community, she gets her opinion and feeling about it handed back to her.[6]

Elizabeth's second important judgment in the early stages of the novel, her delighted approval of George Wickham, is no less an act of unconscious mental conformity. Here the conformity is not to an opinion, but to the very way the community makes and maintains its opinions, that is, to the logical pattern I analyzed above. Another syllogistic mousetrap snaps shut, and it stays shut for twenty chapters. Elizabeth's response to Wickham is encap-sulated in a silent thought that occurs during their long conversation about Darcy's perfidy and pride. The subject has already rendered her indistinguish-able from her mother ("'He is not at all liked in Hertfordshire. Every body is disgusted with his pride'" [78]), and at one point she exclaims:

> "To treat in such a manner, the godson, the friend, the favourite
> of his father!"—She could have added, "A young man too, like *you*,
> whose very countenance may vouch for your being amiable."
> In other words:

All men of good countenance are amiable.
Wickham is a man of good countenance.
Wickham is amiable.

Not only is the logic the same, so is its grounding in desire. Elizabeth, like her community, won't let the facts stand in the way of what she wants to believe. This is, of course, a well-attested observation in the critical literature; the modification I am making concerns the origin of Elizabeth's "prejudice." It may well be that most everyone in the world thinks this way—excessively syllogistic, insufficiently self-critical, blinded by desire—but had Austen wished to make that point, she would have done so. The point she does make is much more specific; Elizabeth is presented not as a typical person, but as a typical member of her community. She assents to and helps propagate collective judgments; she takes her opinions for universal truths; witty as she is, she risks the same mental gridlock as those around her. Darcy, the product of a different community, displays different shortcomings. His errors are ones of behavior, not of thought.[7] But Elizabeth, in one of her least admirable moments, blurts out what could be the motto of all the "good people of Meryton": "'I beg your pardon;—one knows exactly what to think'" (86).

The intellectual fault that Elizabeth shares with her community can be understood at its most basic level as an inability to deal with contradiction. Much of Mrs. Bennet's foolishness, and the humor of that foolishness, consists of an inability to see the contradictions in her own thinking: "'Well, Lizzy ... what is your opinion of this sad business of Jane's? For my part, I am determined never to speak of it again to anybody. I told my sister Philips so the other day'" (227). Mr. Bennet's moral indolence is made possible through the equivocations of irony: "'I admire all three of my sons-in-law highly ... Wickham, perhaps, is my favorite, but I think I shall like *your* husband quite as well as Jane's'" (379). The tension between his disgust for Wickham and the recognition that he is responsible for Wickham's presence in his family is resolved by the use of a single word, "admire," to name both itself and its opposite. But the leading exemplar of the desire to evade contradiction is Elizabeth herself. The most telling examples occur in dialogues with Jane and Charlotte, her two intimates. In one, Jane tries to suggest that Darcy may not be as bad as Elizabeth has concluded (86). In another, Charlotte simply wants her to understand that she, Charlotte, believes that "happiness in marriage is entirely a matter of chance" and that "it is better to know as little as possible of the defects of the person with whom you are to pass your life" (23). In neither case does Elizabeth alter her opinion even slightly, and in both she closes the exchange with an arrogantly self-affirming gesture. The first we have already seen: "one knows exactly what to think." The other is deaf even to the possibility of contradiction: "You make me laugh Charlotte; but it is not sound. You know it is not sound, and that you would never act in this way yourself." It is no wonder that she spends so much of the novel being surprised.

Finally, even for Elizabeth, cognitive inertia becomes behavioral and emotional stasis. On the fundamental question that confronts her she is, for all her rapid motion, as jammed stuck as her mother ever is. Replying to Charlotte's suggestion that a young woman should secure a man first and then worry about falling in love, she says: "Your plan is a good one ... where nothing is in question but the desire of being well married; and if I were determined to get a rich husband, or any husband, I dare say I should adopt it" (22). "Or any husband": like Richardson's Clarissa, Elizabeth has forsworn marriage. But though the gesture may have been conventional by this point, Austen does not use it casually. Essentially reflexive, it carries for that very reason a tone of utter finality. And although one may see it as nothing more than a prop that allows Elizabeth to maintain her self-esteem until the right man comes along, that observation points to the essential problem: the right man comes along, yet Elizabeth remains stuck in her old pattern. A complacent consciousness is at war with unsettled feelings, but complacency is winning. The process of breaking this pattern constitutes the burden of the plot: the positive outcome is a foregone conclusion only in retrospect. At this point, certain of what she knows and of what she wants, Elizabeth has stopped questioning herself. She knows exactly what to think, and she knows exactly how to act. She is, like her community, "well-fixed."

The Pleasures of Density

I have so far been discussing the community as a homogenous totality, but as illustrated by the group conversation of chapter 5, it also possesses a complex internal environment that looks different to each character. Elizabeth's experience of the community is in large measure her experience within the subgroup of Bennets and Lucases. The importance of such groups is suggested by the remark that introduces that very conversation: "That the Miss Lucases and the Miss Bennets should meet to talk over a ball was absolutely necessary; and the morning after the assembly brought the former to Longbourn to hear and to communicate" (18). While "absolutely necessary" may exhibit, in its extravagance, a rainbow edge of irony, the very fact that the characters think it absolutely necessary makes it at least quite important. In fact, it is clear from the outset that something more is happening than the mere exercise of sociability. The young women get together not, as Lydia and Kitty do, to go out and hunt up officers, but to "talk over"—to discuss and analyze. We may note, as the scene unfolds, the game of one-upsmanship that Mrs. Bennet and Charlotte

Lucas play with each other, but even as this tussle progresses to its inevitably inconclusive end, more fundamental purposes are being accomplished. A consensus, as we saw above, is being formed about Darcy's character; whatever the individual women had thought about him going into the conversation, each leaves knowing that he suffers from "pride." But it is also clear that none of them (except Mrs. Bennet) had much known what she thought of him. The conversation serves to evoke, shape, and strengthen their opinions. What is more, the clarification that takes place involves both homogenization and differentiation: the characters disagree, now that they come to think of it, over the significance of Darcy's pride. Yet if we examine the structure of the conversation more closely, we discover, not a series of flat contradictions (we already know how poorly the community deals with those), but the gradual shaping of a collective understanding. It is less a debate than a kind of game, a game in which one pivots one's interlocutor's statements in an unintended direction even while seeming to agree with them. Mrs. Bennet's contest with Charlotte Lucas displays this pattern:

> [Mrs. Bennet:] "If [Darcy] had been so very agreeable he would have talked to Mrs. Long . . . I dare say he had heard somehow that Mrs. Long does not keep a carriage, and had come to the ball in a hack chaise."

> "I do not mind his not talking to Mrs. Long," said Miss Lucas, "but I wish he had danced with Eliza." [In other words, "Yes, he snubbed Mrs. Long as well, but that doesn't make his treatment of your daughter any less humiliating."]

The group maintains cohesion through the manner in which it manages conflict, allowing it expression within conventionalized bounds. A more important example, for it embodies real differences of opinion, is the exchange we looked at above:

> "His pride," said Miss Lucas, "does not offend *me* so much as pride often does, because there is an excuse for it . . . he has a right to be proud."

> "That is very true," replied Elizabeth, "and I could easily forgive *his* pride if he had not mortified *mine*."

It is a bit like the parlor game, sometimes used with adolescents to teach positive social skills, in which participants collectively create a sentence by taking turns adding one word at a time. The sense of the conversation here (like the sense of the sentence in the game) takes a new direction with each contribution, but is at every point the sum of all previous contributions. Individual expression occurs within collective expression; individual expressions together create collective expression. At bottom, the implicit meaning of this mode of conversation, as it is the implicit lesson of the game, is that every voice is valid.[8] The exceptions underscore the rule. Mrs. Bennet can flatly contradict Jane when Jane quotes Miss Bingley ("I do not believe a word of it, my dear"), not because Miss Bingley isn't present (Mrs. Long's testimony is also introduced), but because she is outside of the community (at this point in the novel) and thus merits no voice in shaping the discussion. Mary's utterance, as always, makes no attempt to play off or play with anything that has already been said and thus has no effect on the conversation whatsoever, except indeed to end it by breaking its momentum. What is going forward is not about the kind of general truths Mary tries to enunciate, but about the play of opinions—valued as opinions—around specific, local truths. That is why the ultimate consensus is only partial and only implicit. What is achieved is not unanimity and is not supposed to be, but a delicate interplay of conflict and agreement.

One finds, then, that values differ within the group, albeit within limits, and differ over what may be presumed to be an important matter. What does not differ—what is actively made to be the same—is the perception of the events upon which those values operate. The conversation has served to mark the circle of common judgment and the permissible limits of difference, but it has also performed a more basic cognitive function, for it has constituted what will henceforth be in this group the official version of the events of that night: what Mr. Darcy said to Mrs. Long, what Mr. Bingley said to Mr. Robinson, and also, since this will undoubtedly become part of the story for Mrs. Bennet and Charlotte Lucas (and Lady Lucas and Mrs. Long and so forth), what Elizabeth thinks about what Mr. Darcy did. And even more simply, the conversation has determined that "what happened" at the assembly will mean those points and not others.[9] (Compare the exhaustive account that Mrs. Bennet had tried to give her husband the previous night [12–13].) Elizabeth's personal history is being made here, but in this community the making is collective. That is why it is "absolutely necessary"—one may not want to take the characterization quite so ironically any more—that the previous evening be "talked over." The phrase has a certain resonance: the assembly happens over again, in talk.

The application of this episode to the whole of Elizabeth's relationship to her community is quite suggestive. We see, first of all, the great extent to which her participation in that community helps constitute her sense of reality. We see further how the community gives her a framework within which to work out her responses to that reality. Most importantly for what is to follow in the novel, we see how Elizabeth tends to place herself in relation to that community. That she is a mocker of convention is central to the image she projects—such mockery is her main mode of discourse in group situations—but what we find in this scene we find everywhere her ironic detachment makes itself felt: she could not stand apart from the group were she not standing firmly within it. She mocks convention in just such a way as to affirm its necessity. Probably the most complex and interesting example occurs at a decisive moment in her relationship with Darcy. Wickham has already turned her against him, but she also already recognizes the possibility of finding him attractive. The two are dancing together in silence when Elizabeth decides to begin conversation in a way so conventional that Austen doesn't even bother to report it directly:

> She made some slight observation on the dance. He replied, and was again silent. After a pause of some minutes she addressed him a second time with "It is *your* turn to say something now, Mr. Darcy.— I talked about the dance, and *you* ought to make some kind of remark on the size of the room, or the number of couples." (91)

Having attempted to use a convention for its proper purpose—to open conversation during a dance—Elizabeth turns to a mocking exposure of both convention and purpose in order to accomplish the exact same purpose. (It works.) In this unusual case, where normal and "unconventional" use occur in quick succession, we are able to see how similar they really are. Elizabeth's unconventional behavior is a way of including herself within the circle of convention while still marking what she believes to be her superior imaginative freedom. The fine structure of her wit tells the same story: playing with other people's language as she does means necessarily locating herself within that language.[10] In this light it is wholly unsurprising that she accepts the word "pride" as her own; modification, not rejection, is her typical mode of response. In a community that includes everyone by allowing each a slightly different role, the role it allows her—but it is only a role—is that of the person who is not fully included.

For all that can be discerned about the community in *Pride and Prejudice* through the examination of specific situations and interactions, there remains a certain ambient quality, a texture, that eludes such analysis and yet ought to figure prominently in this or any account. This quality can be characterized, I believe, as the sense of a saturated social environment, an environment in which no space exists that is not social: a sense that at every point towards which a character might turn she will encounter someone she recognizes and with whom she shares all requisite codes of communication; that her every utterance will be met with substantial interest, as immediately touching upon the concerns of the person to whom it is addressed; and most importantly, that her every action will bear consequences for people to whom she feels, and feels she ought to feel, significant responsibility. I will call this quality "density," in part to denote that it is an aesthetic, not a sociological artifact, a feature not of the community as such but of its narrative representation.[11] A narrative is made dense, first of all, by the elimination of everything extraneous to socially significant interaction. Austen's novels were revolutionary in this respect, and *Pride and Prejudice* the most extreme case among them.[12] Both scenic description and general reflection--two of the major types of material the novel's capaciousness had allowed it to develop--are completely absent from its pages. What is even more striking, privacy and introspection are almost completely absent until Elizabeth departs for Hunsford. Within the community, every act and utterance, every moment, is social, and Elizabeth, for all the force and color of her personality, possesses only an implicit interiority. But density is not only a matter of what is left out. It also involves the existence of "multiplex" social relationships--relationships in which individuals are connected in a plurality of ways.[13] That is why we are able to find it in a novel that takes place within a small and relatively stable community. Charlotte Lucas is Elizabeth's friend, but she is also her mother's friend's daughter, and to a certain extent also her mother's friend. Miss Bingley, while she is part of the community, is Elizabeth's friend, at least in theory, but she is also her sister's friend, as well as her sister's love-interest's sister. With multiplexity, the array of relationships within a community becomes something more than a family tree or set of family trees, more than a single large circle, more even than a network or web. It is not just that there are several short paths that connect Elizabeth and Charlotte through other people, but that when Elizabeth and Charlotte encounter each other directly they do so in and through a multiplicity of relationships. They are tied together by multiple strands. And because custom dictates that all these relationships carry the right and indeed the responsibility of comment and interference, what we find, in sum, is a large group of people all minding each other's business and all passing each other's secrets back and forth all the time. Everywhere a member of the community looks, someone is related to her somehow and has something to say to her about everyone else in her life.

Density involves communication—utterance and response—but it also involves causation—action and consequence. In other words, density provides the matrix of the novel's plot. Two striking examples occur at crucial moments in the interweaving of the action, both in the ball scene of chapter 18, the long episode in which Darcy is turned against the courtship of Jane and Bingley, and Elizabeth, at a time when she seems to be softening towards him, is turned ever more decidedly against Darcy. The first occurs when Sir

William Lucas happens to walk past Elizabeth and Darcy on his way through the dancing set. Because he has already formed a connection to Darcy (disown it though the latter might wish), he stops and bows. And because he has always had connections to Elizabeth, he permits himself to make a reference, in front of both of them, to the time after which "a certain desirable event, my dear Miss Eliza, (glancing at her sister and Bingley,) shall take place" (92). That is how Darcy is put on guard about the danger of his friend marrying into a family of vulgarians, and that is how Sir William sets the fibers of his community vibrating just by walking across the room.

A short time later, Miss Bingley more deliberately plays a disruptive role: "So Miss Eliza, I hear you are quite delighted with George Wickham!—Your sister has been talking to me about him . . . and I find that the young man forgot to tell you" (94) and so on for a long paragraph of vituperative snobbery about "old Wickham" and "the late Mr. Darcy" that turns Elizabeth decisively against the whole Netherfield crowd. Even given Miss Bingley's disposition, only density—the possibility and expectation of communication—could have allowed Jane to speak with her about Elizabeth's interest in Wickham in the first place, and only density—the right of interference—could have justified her presumption in speaking to Elizabeth about Darcy and Wickham's relationship. If, as I noted above, the novel is structured so as to suggest that its plot emerges from the threshing of communal mechanisms more than from the movements of individual will, here is one of the ways in which that emergence takes place. Chapter 18, which began with Jane and Bingley in the fairest way to happiness and Elizabeth and Darcy in a pretty steady way to indifference, ends with the first pair taking their last looks at each other for a long while, and the latter, as a direct result, careening towards their decisive confrontations. What has ultimately wrought these changes is not the acts of any individual or individuals, but the fact of a dense interconnectivity among individuals.

Now all this may be well and good, but there are more important things one can do in a conversation than communicate information. For instance, one can flirt. Or at least, one can in an Austen novel, for what passes as the talk of eligible young people in earlier works could hardly be dignified by that name. Consider the case of *Evelina*, one of the novels often cited as a precursor of Austen's work. Sir Clement has such a tough time of it with the object of his desires because he has no legitimate excuse for talking to her, as well as nothing to talk to her about once he has obtruded himself on her attention. The density of Austenian communities solves both of these problems at a stroke, providing a young gentleman and a young lady both with many topics of conversation—all the concerns of all the people they know in common—and with many pretexts for conversation—all the ways they are already connected other than as potential mates. Conversation may be serious or light-hearted, sententious or witty, but it need not be overtly personal, and so can be easy and abundant. Under the cover of such talk, potential lovers can share the sustained physical and social proximity that leads to familiarity and, possibly, to intimacy. As one might put it, the first parts of their bodies that touch are their voices. Examples pervade the Austenian corpus: Emma and Frank, Edmund and Mary, Anne and Captain Benwick, and in *Pride and Prejudice*, Elizabeth and both Wickham and Colonel Fitzwilliam, the Darcy cousin she meets at Rosings. For all the surface brilliance of so many of the conversations these young people have, more important things get exchanged than words. Because feelings need not be declared, they can be communicated.

The density of the communal environment also makes possible another essential aspect of Austenian courtship. Not only does Austen show young ladies talking freely with their young gentlemen, she shows them passing judgment on them as well, and not only on their breeding or income, but also on their character, intelligence, and education. This is a possibility that Fanny Burney did not seem to have imagined. Of course, the making of such judgments is central to Austen's conception of the proper conduct of life—central to her plots, central to her authorial stance—but how are they to get made in the first place? Whether a Sir Clement negotiates the conventions of love-talk well or ill, Evelina will learn nothing about him other than his ability to negotiate the conventions of love-talk; they carry not even the pretense of meaningful external reference. Though the plot of *Evelina* confirms Lord Orville's goodness, the heroine renders her rapturous approval immediately, and on the exclusive basis of his breeding. True, we are intended to take breeding as an index of character, but so facile and dubious a substitution is very far from the mature and considered judgment Austen advances as essential. For the Austenian heroine, flirtatious conversation provides the material upon which such judgment can operate. In listening to a Wickham or a Frank or a Wentworth speak about what is most important in their world—the conduct of the people around them—a young lady has the opportunity to assess intelligence, character, and judgment.[14] The opportunity only: as these examples indicate, several of Austen's novels hinge on the fact that the heroine does not always do so properly. But that she can do so at all is a function of the communal environment in which she lives.

Judgment would be of little use to an Austenian heroine, however, did she not have a genuine choice in marriage. It is a third remarkable feature of Austenian courtship that young ladies do have such a choice, whatever pressure they are sometimes placed under by the parental generation. In order to exercise choice, however, a young lady needs room to maneuver. Again the density of the communal context makes this possible. By creating non-romantic premises for young men and women to develop familiar relationships with one another—the many non-romantic forms of connection that also and already exist between potential mates—the communal environment enables those relationships to develop non-romantic dimensions. In other words, the multiplexity of relationships in Austenian communities creates the conditions for friendship between women and men. The point is not that romantic interest is dissimulated—friendship is achieved between potential mates not in spite of erotic energy, but because of it—but that a great deal of space is opened up within relationships that is not marked as romantic. An emotional investment can be made before a decision is required. A young lady can feel affection for a young gentleman, and feel what it feels like, and even discover whether it is requited, without taking irrevocable or potentially embarrassing steps. Many other fictional heroines and heroes, before Austen and after, do not have such freedom. Because romantic feeling is the only form of affection their worlds make available between young men and women, to indicate affection is already to declare romantic interest and, very quickly, to commit oneself to a choice.[15] (Tertius Lydgate learns this lesson in *Middlemarch*.) I mentioned Colonel Fitzwilliam before because he provides so unusual a case in fiction: a man who turns out to be neither Mr. Right nor Mr. Wrong, neither Darcy nor Wickham, Lord Orville nor Sir Clement. He is simply an appealing young man who walks briefly through the heroine's life, but not so briefly that she does not consider him as a serious romantic possibility. He is interested in her, and Charlotte is interested for her; that Elizabeth herself had been interested we learn only later, after the upheaval of Darcy's proposal (209). But before that proposal we see her coming to know this Colonel Fitzwilliam, and coming to be friends with him, in a way that enables her to test her feelings for him, judge him, and then consider what she wants to do about him. What seems to happen between them, on both sides, is a spreading of affectionate feelings along a continuum from eros to amity. The exact status of the relationship is meanwhile held in suspension in a way that would be unthinkable in other novels, where "maybe" simply doesn't exist, and where the only possible delay—rather poor in both narrative and human interest—is the lag between a lady's ritual "no" and her inevitable "yes." I am not suggesting that this is a situation without peril—Elizabeth has to manage her conversation with Colonel Fitzwilliam rather skillfully at several points—but it is one that enables them to advance to either form of resolution with relatively little pain and a relatively great degree of freedom. It is also quite a lot of fun, and it is exactly the way in which courtship is managed throughout Austen's work.

By situating her novels within communities, then, Austen transforms the process of courtship as she found it in her novelistic predecessors, making it both more conscious and more emotionally profound and fitting it more naturally into an array of other relationships. It is not too much to say that she also transforms love as it was understood in the novel. No longer an ecstasy antithetical or at least unrelated to friendship, it becomes instead a form of friendship.[16] Indeed, it arises in the context of friendship, in the situations I discussed as creating the opportunity for friendship. To Tobin Siebers's insight that Austen's novels are about "the philosophical and conversational play in which men and women engage in order to test and choose each other" I am adding the observation that men and women in Austen's novels develop the affection that leads them to choose each other through that very philosophical and conversational play.[17] Affection (Austen's preferred word) rises on the wings of what I have been somewhat clumsily calling cognition. But in Austen, of course, this kind of friendship—the friendship of playful, opinionated conversation—is not confined to lovers. We have already watched it in action in the group conversation of chapter 5, where cognition and affection (albeit somewhat strained) are intertwined in playful, opinionated conversation. Such friendship might indeed be called "communal friendship," for it becomes possible when proximity and density act as the structural underpinnings of familiarity, ease, and common interest. It could thus hardly be more different from the friendship idealized in the sentimental novels of Austen's day, with their conventions of instantaneous intimacy and, upon the young heroines' separation, a correspondence of sufficient avidity and detail to engross three volumes. Austen made it abundantly clear what she thought of such stuff. The ridicule of that kind of intimacy is prominent in the juvenilia and continues into the published work.[18] As for the convention of girlish correspondence, what we find instead in Austen are false friendships exposed by the neglect or mendacity of such correspondence: Catherine Morland and Isabella Thorpe, Elinor Dashwood and Lucy Steele, Jane Bennet and Caroline Bingley, Fanny Price and Mary Crawford. For Austen, "closeness" necessitates closeness. In her conception, the energies of friendship and romance are not mutually exclusive, but deeply interfused.

Although I began by speaking of the ways in which *Pride and Prejudice* criticizes the community it represents, it should be clear by now how powerful were the reasons for Austen's evident attachment to communal life, how rich in her conception were its satisfactions, embracing not only the social connections one normally thinks of as communal, but also the stronger and more intimate ones of friendship and love. With this in mind it becomes clear that the social process I have been describing, the process of flirtation, courtship, and betrothal, contains a rather bitter contradiction: that which is depicted as sweetest about life within a community—friendship—and that which is depicted as most glorious about it for a young woman—flirtation and courtship—are the vehicles for removing her from it. Austen herself may be presumed to have felt this contradiction with particular sharpness. Though as a young woman she was "the prettiest, silliest, most affected, husband-hunting butterfly" Mrs. Mitford ever remembered, she finally chose not to complete the logic of flirtation, not to allow marriage to remove her from what we know to have been a large and loving family, a family that seems to have possessed many of the qualities of an Austenian community.[19] Instead, she chose to write novel after novel in which this fate was imaginatively averted, the contradiction that necessitated it, reconciled.[20]

Friendly Fire

It is the task and privilege of the Austenian heroine to make a new home for herself in the world. In no case is this process more carefully elaborated than in that of Elizabeth Bennet; in Pride and Prejudice, the story of maturation and the story of the creation of a new community are one story. The terms in which Elizabeth's original community are presented—cognition and courtship (in other words, reason and love)—turn out to be central to her maturation. It is in her dealings with eligible men that Elizabeth is tripped up by and finally fights herself free from the cognitive constraints of her community, and it is through her love for one of those men that she begins to establish a new and better community. I noted before that Austen's narrative structures give her young women the opportunity to exercise careful judgment in the evaluation of a potential husband. Fanny Price exercises such judgment relative to Henry Crawford, and we can infer that Anne Eliot did so relative to Frederick Wentworth when they first courted. Emma Woodhouse, however, is blinded by her egotism. What Elizabeth is blinded by we already know: the cognitive faults of her community. Her encounter with Wickham enables her to indulge those faults; her encounter with Darcy at first frustrates and finally forces her to break free of them.

Elizabeth's judgment is never worse than in her long flirtatious conversation with Wickham in chapter 16, the conversation in which he charms her and reinforces her opinions about Darcy. For all that she can play the gadfly, let it once become clear that she will hear only what confirms her own judgments, and she settles into a steady rhythm of assent. Nearly every one of her utterances during the main part of the conversation begins with (and often includes little more than) such affirmations as, "Indeed!", "Good heavens!", "This is quite shocking!", and "How strange! How abominable!", matched on Wickham's side by such replies as "Yes—", "Probably not" and "It *is* wonderful" (79–81). Beyond this, her remarks mainly consist of questions or interjections designed to cue further explanation and affirmation. The exchange becomes a kind of a positive feedback loop, a conversational form of circular reasoning ("Darcy is wicked, therefore he does wicked things, therefore he is wicked"). It could hardly have been otherwise; two identical positions are not likely to force each other to change. No wonder we are told, after the passages reported directly, that Elizabeth and Wickham "continued talking together with mutual satisfaction" (84). Austen quite clearly wishes us to understand that "mutual satisfaction" is not the feeling people ought to have in a conversation, mutual agreement not the logical structure a conversation ought to have. Once again, Elizabeth is avoiding contradiction; though Wickham doesn't undermine her position, he does undermine his own, a fact she will allow herself to recognize only many pages later:

> She perfectly remembered everything that had passed in conversation between Wickham and herself, in their first evening at Mr. Philip's . . . She was *now* struck with the impropriety of such communications to a stranger, and wondered it had escaped her before. (206–7)

But we do not wonder. Elizabeth's intellectual complacency does not incline her to question what flatters her own opinion. The communal environment, moreover, while it creates a familiarity that makes searching judgment possible, also creates an intimacy that makes it undesirable. (Like Fanny Price maintaining her resistance to Henry Crawford, an Austenian heroine must be willing to ruffle a few feathers in order to win her creator's approval.) Recall how the "rule" of the group conversation in chapter 5 managed conflict by smoothing it into a semblance of concord, as well as the manner in which Charlotte allowed Elizabeth to mislead herself about her feelings towards marriage. The more Elizabeth welcomes Wickham into her social circle, the less likely is she to want to question what he says.

The causes of Elizabeth's failure with Wickham help explain some of the most significant elements of her encounter with Darcy in a fresh way. It is necessary first of all that the man who disrupts the patterns of Elizabeth's life be unpleasant to the point of cussedness. No affability, and no concern for social harmony, will prevent their conversations from being unrestrainedly oppositional. More important than Darcy's arrogance, however, even more important than his intelligence, is his insistence on searching out the truth of a situation. At times, in fact, he seems to mistake the drawing-room for a very different setting:

> "Allowing the case, however, to stand according to your representation, you must remember, Miss Bennet, that the friend who is supposed to require [Bingley's] return to the house, and the delay of his plan, has merely desired it, asked it without offering one argument in favour of its propriety." (50)

Austen seems to be deliberately evoking and affirming the epistemological procedures of a courtroom, where contradictory positions are debated and adjudicated rather than mitigated or dissembled. For Darcy, quite unlike the good people of Meryton, there is no such thing as compromise and no such thing as dropping the subject. His conversations with Elizabeth, particularly those in which they engage during her stay at Netherfield, are fundamentally different from the others we have seen. They are, in a word, arguments, as Darcy readily admits when his host disrupts the longest of them with some good-humored nonsense: "'I see your design, Bingley,' said his friend.—'You dislike an argument, and want to silence this'" (51). Bingley does indeed dislike them, and he knows why he does, as well: "'Arguments are too much like disputes.'" The distinction that Bingley is having difficulty maintaining has by our time almost completely disappeared, but the context (as well as the *OED*) suggests that in the usage of the day the difference between an "argument" and a "dispute" turned on the presence or absence of rancor. Bingley dislikes arguments because he can't distinguish between rational disagreement and personal enmity.[21] Elizabeth has the identical problem. It is she who loses her poise, with italicized flagrancy, at the conclusion of the final conversation at Netherfield. Darcy has been reflecting on his own character:

> "My temper would perhaps be called resentful—My good opinion once lost is lost for ever."

> "*That* is a failing indeed!"—cried Elizabeth. "Implacable resentment *is* a shade in a character. But you have chosen your fault well. I really cannot *laugh* at it. You are safe from me."
>
> "There is, I believe, in every disposition a tendency to some particular evil, a natural defect, which not even the best education can overcome."
>
> "And *your* defect is a propensity to hate every body."
>
> "And yours," he replied with a smile, "is willfully to misunderstand them." (58)

The contrast with Elizabeth and Wickham's "mutual satisfaction" could hardly be more sharply drawn.

No wonder Elizabeth recoils. Neither social niceties nor the conventions of intimacy nor her own wit or intellect enable her to eliminate the contradictions Darcy presents. We see now why it takes his letter to break through her resistance. First of all, there is the location of its delivery. Elizabeth, physically outside of her community, is thus outside of it symbolically as well, beyond the confines of its long bourn. But the symbolic dimension is grounded in the social. Had Elizabeth been at home, we know by now how she would have responded both to the letter and to the conversations that surround it. She would have "talked them over": squared her position on them with her like-minded intimates, resolving them into nothing threatening. But we don't need to guess about this, because Elizabeth says as much once she is back at home with her sister, pretending to lament how unhappy she had been "with no one to speak to of what I felt, no Jane to comfort me and say that I had not been so very weak and vain and nonsensical as I knew I had!" (226). Talking-over is replaced by introspection when Elizabeth finds herself alone, which is also to say that when she had not found herself alone it had forestalled introspection.

It is also essential that Darcy put his apologia in written form. Elizabeth is forced to take its antithetical positions seriously. No longer can they remain externalized, embodied in the person of an interlocutor whose rebuff can be made to stand for their refutation. No longer can the words that express them be driven back on themselves, turned, toyed with, punned into a new meaning, pooh-poohed, or subjected to any of the countless other tactics permitted by the fluidity and impalpability of conversation and by the demand that conversation places on any position to continue generating verbiage for itself. The only way Elizabeth can defend herself against a written text is to choose not to think about it, which is at first precisely what she does. But she cannot be satisfied with this evasion, and when she examines the letter again, this time with care, she must at last admit a contradictory voice into her own mind. Yet while the setting deprives her of the social resources with which she has heretofore resisted such voices, so too does it remove the social context that made an intolerable humiliation the price of the failure of such resistance. Even so, she begins her reconsideration with what is for her the least sensitive question, Wickham's reputation. But because her judgments on these matters constitute a single fabric, they all unravel once she takes up Darcy's arguments at any point. Searching for evidence to refute his claims of Wickham's malevolence, she recognizes the nature of the observations on which she had built her good opinion: "His countenance, voice, and manner, had established him at once in possession of every virtue" (206). In other words, "all men of good countenance are amiable." Beyond that, "she could remember no more substantial good about him than the general approbation of the neighborhood"—that is, the approval of the voices of her community. The inductive reexamination of deductive conclusions now enters its next phase. New observations having overthrown the major premise that was used to evaluate the original ones (men of good countenance are clearly not all amiable), those original ones are recalled for reevaluation: "She perfectly remembered everything that had passed in conversation between Wickham and herself, in their first evening at Mr. Philip's ... She was *now* struck with the impropriety of such communications." So begins a page-long bill of particulars, until: "Of neither Darcy nor Wickham could she think, without feeling that she had been blind, partial, prejudiced, absurd." Having thus turned against herself, against what already begins to feel like her old self ("Till this moment, I never knew myself"), she can return to those issues—Jane and Bingley's courtship,

Darcy's proposal—in which she has a far greater personal stake. "Widely different was the effect of a second perusal.—How could she deny that credit to his assertions, in one instance, which she had been obliged to give in the other?" Darcy's credibility, the conclusion of one line of reasoning, becomes the major premise that governs these others. Elizabeth acknowledges "the justice" both of his description of Jane as not apparently in love with Bingley and of his "charge" of impropriety against the Bennet family, and the scene ends as quickly as Austen can get the job done.[22]

The crisis has been reached and passed. Elizabeth returns twice more to Longbourn, but no longer does she participate in those communal activities in which we had seen her so deeply and happily embedded: no dancing, no visiting, no gossip. Ultimately this will be the result of a sense that she is soon to relocate to Pemberley (where the reconciling movement begins, again outside the confines of her community), but for a long time it simply marks a profound alienation from her surroundings. The feeling is already there in her first conversation with Jane. Evoking the name of her characteristic error (and this time it is her name, her word), she indicates the communal origin of that error, takes responsibility for having fostered it in herself, and finally distances herself from both error and community:

> "The misfortune of speaking with bitterness, is a most natural consequence of the prejudices I have been encouraging . . . The general prejudice against Mr. Darcy is so violent, that it would be the death of half the good people in Meryton, to attempt to place him in an amiable light." (226)

A subtle instance of Elizabeth's desire for separation, and of the community's resistance to it, occurs late in the novel. Darcy has returned to the neighborhood but is remaining frustratingly out of reach. When he accompanies Bingley to a party at Longbourn, Elizabeth hopes that the tea table will finally provide a pretext for contact. But the ladies crowd too closely:

> And on the gentlemen's approaching, one of the girls moved closer to her than ever, and said, in a whisper,
>
> "The men shan't come and part us, I am determined. We want none of them; do we?" (341)

The girl's anonymity is particularly striking (she is the only unnamed speaker in the novel); it is as if the voice of the communal consciousness heard so strongly at the beginning of the novel had assumed bodily form and were whispering in Elizabeth's ear.

Elizabeth has had to step outside of her community in order to mature and fall in love, but the manner in which these processes take place remains true to the principles elaborated in the novel's presentation of communal life. Once again, affection rises on the wings of cognition. Elizabeth learns a new way of feeling just where she has learned a new way of seeing and thinking and knowing. A biological metaphor is useful here: a new life, Elizabeth's new life, forms within her only after she has opened her mind to Darcy's antithetical voice. The neighborhood of Meryton, despite its dullness, is not a sexless place; reproduction in the strictest sense of the term (as represented, for example, by the courtship of Charlotte and Collins) is perfectly capable of taking place there. What that community lacks is something that we might call "sexiness": that in sex which is exhilarating and risky because it threatens uncontrollable change, the disruption or even destruction of existing cognitive, psychological, and social structures. Left to itself, the community will reproduce—itself. The creation of a Lydia by a Mrs. Bennet—or an Elizabeth by a Mr. Bennet, for that matter—is a kind of parthenogenesis, reproduction without variation. What is needed, in the biological sphere, is a seed of difference; in the logical sphere, an antithetical proposition; in the sphere of individual psychology and social relations, a challenge to frozen patterns of thinking and feeling. "Growth through contradictions"—the principle Richard Simpson found to be central to Austen's artistic development—is also central to the stories she tells.[23]

In this novel, at least, contradiction can arrive only from outside the community. There is a tendency in literary criticism, prominent especially in discussions of the genre of comedy or the category of the comic, to think of community as the place where divergent voices can encounter one another.[24] We have seen at least one sense, embodied in chapter 5, in which this idea is borne out by the novel, but we have also seen how the community acts to shut out voices that diverge too much. Even so, that community is in other ways indispensable to Elizabeth and Darcy's courtship. Their conversations at Netherfield, though by no means affectionate or even cordial, follow the pattern of communal flirtation and ultimately accomplish its purpose. They give Elizabeth a knowledge of Darcy's intellect and probity that remains in memory until such time as love calls it forth. They also create a degree of intimacy even in the absence of affection. The word "closeness" is again apt as a description of communal feelings; when proximity is unavoidable, intimacy and enmity cease to be incompatible. Finally, Elizabeth's love for Darcy crystallizes only after he has symbolically identified himself as a member of her community. The man who lost his first chance for Elizabeth's love by disdaining her "connections" now welcomes her uncle and aunt to his estate and then, in an outright act of self-humiliation, becomes the agent for connecting himself to those very connections.

These acts and symbols, however, have more to do with the novel's second community than with its first. Darcy is already helping to create, hoping to create, that which he cannot yet know will come into being. The new community quickens in the last chapter, Elizabeth and Darcy's marriage at its center, but the narrative swings towards that configuration throughout the whole last third of the book. What resemblance does this new community bear to the one already presented? If the first community is inadequate, what does a good community look like? We are not given the chance to observe the new community in anything like the detail in which we have observed the old, but its character may be inferred from two sources: the last chapter, which gives a *précis* of the new arrangements; and, because the lovers stand at the center of the new community, what Elizabeth and Darcy do together over the course of the last three chapters but one. What they do together, not surprisingly, is talk. But how do their conversations compare to those that took place in Meryton? Do the lovers find a medium between "mutual satisfaction" and rancorous "dispute"? In fact, these conversations are arguments—albeit mainly over which of the lovers has the right to claim the greater share of blame in their past conflict—yet they are able to remain both incisive and amicable through a complementary interplay between the very qualities of character—Darcy's insistence, Elizabeth's wit—that once clashed so irremediably:

> [Darcy:] "I knew enough of your disposition to be certain, that, had you been absolutely, irrevocably decided against me, you would have acknowledged it to Lady Catherine, frankly and openly."

> Elizabeth coloured and laughed as she replied, "Yes, you know enough of my frankness to believe me capable of that. After abusing you so abominably to your face, I could have no scruple in abusing you to all your relations."

> "What did you say of me, that I did not deserve? For, though your accusations were ill-founded, formed on mistaken premises, my behavior to you at that time, had merited the severest reproof." (367)

The difference between this and Netherfield lies not in the weapons used, but in their targets. Both Darcy and Elizabeth are even tougher on themselves than they are on each other. Darcy's protestations of guilt are not merely attempts to win additional approval from his fiancée. They persist throughout a long exchange, culminating in his rejection of Elizabeth's dictum that one should "think only of the past as its remembrance gives

you pleasure." As for Elizabeth, she may not believe quite all her self-
mockery, but with it she accomplishes several important things: she gives
Darcy the rhetorical and emotional space he needs to criticize her himself,
she enables herself to receive his criticism without humiliation, and she
enables Darcy to continue listening when he does again become the target
of her mockery:

> "I must ask whether you were surprised [at Jane and Bingley's
> engagement]?" said Elizabeth.
>
> "Not at all. When I went away, I felt that it would soon
> happen."
>
> "That is to say, you had given your permission. I guessed as
> much." And though he exclaimed at the term, she found that it
> had been pretty much the case. (370)

Even Darcy, for all his strenuous self-examination, cannot see himself
clearly without the help of Elizabeth's eyes. He can recognize his errors, but
not his absurdities. Elizabeth is in even greater need of a loving critic; without Darcy's integrity, she might easily slip back into self-satisfaction ("think
only of the past as its remembrance gives you pleasure"). Neither can see
themselves without the other, and only together—in the back and forth of
critical conversation—can either progress towards greater understanding.
Love is pedagogic in all of Austen's novels, Platonic in that sense, but only
in *Pride and Prejudice* do the lovers lead each other towards truth.[25]
     There is some question, however, as to the nature of this truth and the
manner in which Elizabeth and Darcy progress towards it. Is it, in Austen's
conception, a state of definitive knowledge—a right answer—or is it rather a
path along which one can progress but at whose terminus one never arrives? I
have already said enough to indicate that I share the second view.[26] My belief
rests in part on the course of Elizabeth's thinking during and after her great
recognition. She does not pass in an instant from total blindness to total insight. There is self-deception even in her immediate response ("Till this moment, I never knew myself"), a compensatory gesture that ought to be taken
in the same spirit as the end of Joyce's "Araby": too good an epiphany to be
true. What is more, the last chapters of the novel are replete both with fresh
errors on Elizabeth's part and with the narrator's ironic jibes at her supposed
self-knowledge:

> Elizabeth walked out to recover her spirits; or in other words, to
> dwell without interruption on those subjects that must deaden

them more. Mr. Darcy's behavior astonished and vexed her. "Teazing, teazing, man! I will think no more about him."

Her resolution was for a short time involuntarily kept by the approach of her sister. (339)

Austen sketches an arc of error and correction and error, an upward curve of self-knowledge and maturation that we are meant to see as extending beyond the end of the novel. The work of thought is never done: second impressions are only slightly better than first. One moves from a state of ignorance to a state of slightly lesser ignorance. The only difference between the later parts of the novel and the "afterwards" (385) it projects in its last chapter is that Elizabeth will no longer have to do this work on her own. But though she and Darcy educate each other, neither has access to any source of certainty. I do not question that Austen believed that "variability is a function of human perception and not a characteristic of truth itself," but in this novel, and indeed in all her novels, human perception is all we have.[27] The best her characters can do is to combine their individual perspectives. By the lovers' second conversation, Elizabeth herself recognizes the incipient dynamic: "'My good qualities are under your protection, and you are to exaggerate them as much as possible; and, in return, it belongs to me to find occasions for teazing and quarreling with you as often as may be'" (381). Deciphering the inevitable irony, one reads Elizabeth's recognition that she will receive no empty flattery from her husband and her announcement that she will return the favor in her own way. An ongoing "conversation" will avert the mental inertia of the novel's first community, averting too the mechanical behavior that is the evil extreme of social order.[28] One may read the crowning declaration of Elizabeth's final letter to her Aunt Gardiner in this light: "'I am happier even than Jane; she only smiles, I laugh'" (383). Laughter signifies many things in this novel, but bliss is not one of them. Bliss belongs to Jane; to Elizabeth belongs the blessing of awakened consciousness.

As we saw, the group conversation in chapter 5—the novel's most concentrated picture of communal interaction—accomplished several purposes: it shaped perceptions, elicited judgments of value, and established a collective sense of reality. I have just noted how Elizabeth and Darcy's conversations accomplish the first of these purposes. As for the second, while the cognitive component of judgment becomes more vigorously debated, more open, than in Meryton, the evaluative component--the standards by which what is known is judged--becomes less so. Pemberley is far less tolerant of vice and stupidity than Meryton is (Mrs. Bennet is made to feel unwelcome; Wickham is excluded), and thus far less tolerant of differences in values. The lovers' conversations contain nothing equivalent to Elizabeth and Charlotte's unresolved disagreement over the excusability of Darcy's pride or the proper attitude towards marriage. In this sense, the boundaries of permissible dissent are far narrower than in Meryton, and it is not the business of conversation to draw them. As for the third and most important purpose enumerated above, by spending so much of their time discussing the past, ascertaining its content and meaning, Elizabeth and Darcy together create the foundational myth of their marriage. The very fact that they have two conversations in the final chapters helps to emphasize this: in the first they write the basic plot of their common story, in the second they begin to discuss it as an established thing. In Siebers's terms, "recounting a story does not necessarily bring an end to . . . conflict," but it "may at least give us a chance to find a place in the world."[29]

But I have been avoiding what is the essential question about the novel's final configuration. What community? Is the novel's final community Elizabeth and Darcy's marriage (in which case it isn't really a community at all) or is it the larger group that includes that marriage? The only answer that makes sense of all the available evidence is that it is both. To say so is already to indicate that this final community has significant structural differences from the one with which the novel began. It is not a community of people all living in the same place. Austen has granted her heroine the privilege of no longer having to live as a social equal among her intellectual (and now, moral) inferiors. The group laid out in the final chapter is thus something of an imagined community, while the marriage assumes many of the functions of a community in the strict sense. As we have just seen, Elizabeth and Darcy do properly what the community of Meryton could not do properly. But a marriage can't do everything. In particular, it cannot provide the multiplexity of relationships so essential to the value of the novel's first community. The narrator's envoi delineates such multiplexity with respect to the second. Jane, Bingley, Georgiana Darcy, Kitty, Mr. Bennet, the Gardiners: all help to form the array of relationships within which Elizabeth and Darcy will live. Where, indeed, does the marriage end and this larger web begin? As the phrase that concludes the penultimate chapter suggests—"their family party at Pemberley"—the distinction finally cannot be made. Elizabeth will be married to her sister's husband's best friend, her surrogate daughter's surrogate father, her uncle's shooting partner, and so forth. I return to the observation that love in Austen is a form of friendship, and that friendship is an essentially communal relation. It is often said that comic plots involve the reconciliation of communal and erotic energies, the implication being that the two are necessarily in tension. Austen goes beyond this; for her, the two are one. Friendship steps in as the essential middle term, mediating between marriage and community both as a social form and as a type of feeling, permitting the flow of energy between all three, a single elemental energy that infuses all human bonding.

Notes

1. Two begin with the heroine: *Northanger Abbey* and *Emma*, in each of which she is the exclusive center of action. Two begin with the *paterfamilias: Mansfield Park* and *Persuasion*, in each of which he is a dominating presence. *Sense and Sensibility*, a partial exception, begins by naming a family, but the Dashwoods can be considered as constituting a kind of collective protagonist.

2. Jane Austen, *The Novels of Jane Austen*, 3rd ed., ed. R. W. Chapman, 6 vols.(Oxford: Oxford Univ. Press, 1932), 2:3. Volume 2 is hereafter cited parenthetically in the text by page.

3. Marvin Mudrick, for example, sees Elizabeth as the novel's chief exemplar of "people with individuality and will" as against those "who are simply reproductions of their social type" (*Irony as Defense and Discovery* [Princeton: Princeton Univ. Press, 1952], 125). For Alastair Duckworth, Elizabeth represents "individualism" as opposed to Darcy's "tradition" (*The Improvement of the Estate* [Baltimore: Johns Hopkins Univ. Press, 1971], 117). A more recent form of the same position replaces the dichotomization of embodied abstractions (Elizabeth at one pole) with the counterposition of Elizabeth to her community. For Tony Tanner, "it is not at first clear that Elizabeth will consent to be contained within the highly structured social space available to her" (*Jane Austen* [Houndmills: Macmillan, 1986], 135). To Rachel M. Brownstein, Elizabeth "scrutinizes the world so as to assess it and to keep herself at a distance from it" (*Becoming a Heroine: Reading About Women in Novels* [New York: Viking, 1982], 124). This view has found its most magniloquent exponent in Harold Bloom, who sees Elizabeth as "a heroine of the Protestant will" and as "incarnat[ing] the standard of measurement in her cosmos" (introduction to *Jane Austen*, ed. Harold Bloom [New York: Chelsea House, 1986], 11 and 5).

For other critics Elizabeth's freedom is more intellectual than existential. Appropriately, there has been much celebration of her intelligence and wit, but often without sufficient attention to its limitations. And again, the terms of that celebration have commonly been such as to draw the strongest possible contrast between Elizabeth's mind and those that surround it. Dorothy van Ghent sets Elizabeth's "emotional intelligence and quickness of moral perception" against an "all-environing imbecility" (*The English Novel: Form and Function* [New York: Holt, Rinehart and Winston, 1953], 107). To D. W. Harding, Elizabeth, like Catherine Morland and Elinor Dashwood, is a type of Cinderella, "isolated from those around her by being more sensitive or of finer moral insight or sounder judgment" ("Regulated Hatred: An Aspect of the Work of Jane Austen," in *Jane Austen: A Collection of Critical Essays*, ed. Ian Watt [Englewood Cliffs: Prentice-Hall, 1963], 173). More recent critics have turned to the other side of the question, exploring the initial limitations of thought and feeling that make Elizabeth's story one of growth rather than of simple triumph, but persist in seeing the heroine, even with those limitations, as sharply distinguished from those around her. Susan Morgan, while critiquing Elizabeth's freedom, still perforce asserts it and indeed characterizes it as "the freedom to think for [one]self" ("Intelligence in *Pride and Prejudice*," in *Pride and Prejudice*, ed. Harold Bloom [New York: Chelsea House, 1987], 85). My purpose here is not to replace one form of unbalance with its opposite, to reinvent Elizabeth as a fool or automaton, but to show that her apparent freedom and mental agility exist within more subtle and more powerful structures of habit and conformity.

4. Questions of knowledge and judgment in *Pride and Prejudice* have been ably discussed by a number of critics using different approaches from the one I follow here. Such discussion is sometimes couched in terms of the epistemology embodied by the novel as a whole (for example, see Tanner), sometimes, as I have indicated, in terms of Elizabeth's own mental growth (see Morgan).

5. See Robert B. Heilman, "*E pluribus unum*: Parts and Whole in *Pride and Prejudice*," in *Jane Austen: Bicentenary Essays*, ed. John Halperin (Cambridge: Cambridge Univ. Press, 1975), 127-33.

6. The point touches upon one of the basic questions that arise in the reading of the novel: does Darcy's snub make Elizabeth genuinely hate him, or does it provoke a kind of hating love, a burning need to win his esteem? Are Elizabeth's provocations at Netherfield and Rosings expressions of simple malice or of unwitting desire? (For the latter position, see for example David Monaghan, "*Pride and Prejudice*: Structure and Total Vision," in Bloom, *Pride and Prejudice*, 61; and Brownstein, 119. For the former, see for example Joseph Wiesenfarth, *The Errand of Form: An Assay of Jane Austen's Art* [New York: Fordham Univ. Press, 1967], 63; and Morgan, 88.) To a great extent these questions can never be put to rest--nor would one want them to be, since they are of the type that tests a reader's own conceptions. If one sees banter, even fairly hostile banter, as a sign of desire, one will need no additional proof in this case. But it is at least worth noting that the novel does not afford such proof. In my view, Elizabeth does not love Darcy as long as she is under misconceptions about him. Only when those are removed does she begin to realize that "he was exactly the man, who, in disposition and talents, would most suit her." Before she can modify her feelings, in other words, she must correct the cognitions upon which those feelings are based. Austen has not forgotten the deeper impulses to which consciousness is tied, but neither does she believe that the line of determination runs in a single direction. Indeed, one of her highest and most persistent themes is the conditioning of deeper impulses by consciousness. The point is worth emphasizing precisely because the course of intellectual history since her time has led to so strong a perception of the opposite process.

7. That is why the word "prejudice" appears so much less than its titular partner. Because the narrative looks mainly through Elizabeth's eyes, it sees Darcy's leading flaw much more than it does hers. "Prejudice" does crop up precisely when Elizabeth examines her own character (Heilman, 126-27).

8. This does not mean, however, that every voice is equal, since verbal skill counts. What also counts in this conversation, though not in the simpler and more formalized game, are such non-verbal factors as age, decidedness, and the ability to speak in the name of an outside authority, three factors that give Mrs. Bennet the largest voice, the voice that introduces the word "pride."

9. For a discussion of the ways in which novelists have portrayed gossip as helping to create communal myth (more massively than in the episode discussed here), see Patricia Meyers Spacks, *Gossip* (Chicago: Univ. of Chicago Press, 1985), 229-57. Spacks has illuminating things to say about the relationship of gossip and communities throughout the later chapters of the book. For a discussion of the functions of gossip in another of Jane Austen's novels, see Casey Finch and Peter Bowen, "'The Tittle-Tattle of Highbury': Gossip and the Free Indirect Style in *Emma*," *Representations* 31 (1990): 1-18. Finch and Bowen insist on gossip as an exclusively repressive force, as if the community constituted in and through it always existed separate from and, as it were, above the individual upon which it fastened its gaze.

But as my descriptions indicate in the case of this community, at least, individuals also gossip about *themselves*, thus participating in the formation of the narrative that constitutes them. The Austenian community is typically small enough to permit a dialectical interplay between individual and collective power.

10. The already-cited utterance from the end of chapter 5 is one example ("I could easily forgive *his* pride if he had not mortified *mine*"), improving upon the other moves in that "game" by exhibiting linguistic as well as logical concurrence. Here as elsewhere, such banter involves a brilliant probing of the layers of social feeling by means of language. In the space of a few words, Elizabeth allows Darcy his pride, disallows it for its mortification of her feelings, then rounds on her own criticism by admitting that those mortified feelings are the very ones that, in Darcy, commit the mortification. Pride can injure only pride; to inveigh against pride is thus to own the very vice one condemns. And yet it stings.

11. The danger with Austen is that one will confuse density with what might be called "snugness," or as Virginia Woolf put it, "that sense of security which gradually, delightfully, and completely overcomes us" as we read her ("How It Strikes a Contemporary," in *The Common Reader* [New York: Harcourt Brace Jovanovich, 1925], 238). This snug sense of security is a feeling that I believe many readers of Austen (including this one) perceive and delight in, but that ultimately strikes me as little more than nostalgic projection.

12. The difference between artistic representation and sociological description is worth emphasizing. Emile Durkheim, in a perception analogous to the one I am developing here, uses the phrase "dynamic or moral density" to describe the outcome of the "drawing together" of individuals into "sufficient . . . contact with one another to be able mutually to act and react on one another" (*The Division of Labor in Society*, tr. W. D. Halls [New York: Macmillan, 1984], 201). But though the real-world equivalent of a town such as Meryton was far less dense in Durkheim's sense than was the city of London in Fielding's day, the social environment of *Pride and Prejudice* is far more dense in my terms than is that of the last third of *Tom Jones*.

13. The term comes from C. J. Calhoun, ("Community: Toward a Variable Conceptualization for Comparative Research," *Social History* 5 [1980], 118-19) who proposes it as a constitutive feature of all real-world communities. Calhoun also notes the moral implication I touched upon above: "The responsibility for meeting the claims of one relationship is enforced by the other strands which also tie its parties together. . . . Such 'moral import' forces people to look beyond the immediate instrumental considerations which might otherwise determine their actions."

14. My discussion here is indebted to Tobin Siebers, "Jane Austen and Comic Virtue," in *Morals and Stories* (New York: Columbia Univ. Press, 1992). In Siebers's words, "it is tempting to coin the term 'courtship novels' for [Austen's] works because they are about the philosophical and conversational play in which men and women engage in order to test and choose each other" (138).

15. My discussion here is indebted to D. A. Miller's analysis of flirtation in *Narrative and its Discontents* (Princeton: Princeton Univ. Press, 1981), 21.

16. This observation appears in two of Austen's most important nineteenth-century critics, Walter Scott and Richard Simpson. Scott wrote, of *Emma*, that "Cupid walks decorously, and with good discretion, bearing his torch under a lanthorn, instead of flourishing it around to set the house on fire" (*Jane Austen: The Critical Heritage*, ed. B. C. Southam, [London: Routledge & Kegan Paul, 1968], 67). His review concludes with an appeal to the novel-writers of Britain to restore

to some of his ancient rights "that once powerful divinity, Cupid, king of gods and men." For Simpson, apparently more at home with Austen's sensibility, "in her ideal love was only an accident of friendship, friendship being the true light of life, while love was often only a troublesome and flickering blaze which interrupted its equable and soothing influence" (Southam, 246).

17. Siebers, 138.

18. See Marvin Mudrick's discussion of the juvenilia, 1-36. In the novels, with the shift from burlesque to irony, the ridicule becomes more subtle. The sentimental position is undermined indirectly, by being placed in the mouth of a discreditable character: in *Sense and Sensibility*, Marianne, in *Pride and Prejudice*, Lydia.

19. Quoted in Woolf, 137.

20. The solutions take a number of forms: multiple marriages that create a community where none had been before (*Northanger Abbey* and *Sense and Sensibility*); an incest plot, in which marriage takes place within the original community (*Mansfield Park* and *Emma*); or the establishment of a new community in place of an unsatisfactory one (*Pride and Prejudice* and *Persuasion*).

It is worth noting that Jane Austen's favorite activity--and the communal activity that appears most frequently in her work--also constitutes a symbolic resolution of the contradiction between the community and the romantic couple. In English country dancing, individuals dance simultaneously as part of a couple and as part of a larger group, the row of couples referred to as a "set." Each couple makes its way down the set dancing the same four-person pattern, in turn, with each other couple. These quartets thus resemble the groups that carry on so many of the conversations we find in Austen's novels. The iterated pattern often has the two women of the quartet switching partners temporarily, a woman's relationship with each of the two men thereby suggesting, in different ways, the spreading of erotic and amicable energies I discussed above. Indeed, it is sometimes the case that the two women take hands during the iteration of the pattern, and likewise the two men, just as one sometimes detects the presence of erotic energies in Austen's same-sex friendships. Finally, the practice of changing partners every two dances, indicated several times in Austen's novels (see, for example, *Pride and Prejudice*, 13), parallels the process of courtship, providing the women intimate and easy--though regulated and restrained--engagement with a series of young men. (See Kate Van Winkle Keller and Genevieve Shimer, *The Playford Ball: 103 Early English Country Dances* [Chicago: A Cappella-Chicago Review Press and Northampton, MA: The Country Dance and Song Society, 1990].) One begins to understand where Austen got her ideas.

21. The contrast between Darcy and Bingley thus typifies what a number of thinkers have identified as the transition from the "public man" of the Enlightenment, who kept his feelings removed from the realm of civic discourse, to the private, emotive individual of modernity, for whom every issue is personal. (See for example Hannah Arendt, *The Human Condition* [Chicago: Univ. Chicago Press, 1958]; Lionel Trilling, *Sincerity and Authenticity* [New York: Harcourt Brace Jovanovich, 1974]; and Richard Sennett, *The Fall of Public Man* [New York: Knopf, 1977.]) In other words, though Austen may have been on Darcy's side, history turned out to be on his friend's.

22. The quoted words indicate that Elizabeth's language has picked up traces of Darcy's legalisms. The presence of such a discourse at this point in the text is no idiosyncrasy. Northrop Frye, in a passage that helped guide my analysis here,

notes that "the action of comedy . . . is not unlike the action of a lawsuit" and that the "resemblance of the rhetoric of comedy to the rhetoric of jurisprudence has been recognized from earliest times" (*Anatomy of Criticism* [Princeton: Princeton Univ. Press, 1957], 166).

23. Southam, 243.

24. I am referring among other things to C. L. Barber's work on Shakespearean comedy as well as to M. M. Bakhtin's ideas about heteroglossia, laughter, folk literature, and much else.

25. The point, that love in Austen may be understood as Platonic, made first by Simpson, 244, is revisited by Trilling, 76-77, and Tanner, 24.

26. For the first, see, for example, Duckworth and Stuart M. Tave, *Some Words of Jane Austen* (Chicago: Univ. of Chicago Press, 1973).

27. The quotation is from Duckworth, 125.

28. "Conversation" is Siebers's word, 156.

29. Siebers, 157. My thinking on these points is also indebted to Karl Kroeber, *Retelling/Rereading: The Fate of Storytelling in Modern Times* (New Brunswick: Rutgers Univ. Press, 1992).

JO ALYSON PARKER

Mansfield Park:
Dismantling Pemberley

The heroine's friendship to be sought after by a young Woman in the same Neighbourhood, of Talents & Shrewdness, with light eyes & a fair skin, but having a considerable degree of Wit, Heroine shall shrink from the acquaintance.

—Jane Austen, "Plan of a Novel" (*MW* 429)

The woman who has only been taught to please will soon find that her charms are oblique sunbeams, and that they cannot have much effect on her husband's heart when they are seen every day, when the summer is passed and gone. Will she then have sufficient native energy to look into herself for comfort, and cultivate her dormant faculties? or is it not more rational to expect that she will try to please other men, and, in the emotions raised by the experience of new conquests, endeavour to forget the mortifications her love or pride has received?

—Mary Wollstonecraft, *Vindication of the Rights of Woman*

If, indeed, women were mere outside form and face only, and if mind made up no part of her composition, it would follow that a ballroom was quite as appropriate a place for choosing a wife, as an exhibition room for choosing a picture....

—Hannah More, *Stricture on the Modern System of Female Education*

From *The Author's Inheritance: Henry Fielding, Jane Austen, and the Establishment of the Novel*, pp. 155–180, 217–220. © 1998 by Northern Illinois University Press.

145

In *The Opposing Self,* Lionel Trilling points out that "Fielding's *Amelia* . . . may be said to bear the same relation to *Tom Jones* that *Mansfield Park* bears to *Pride and Prejudice.*"[1] Trilling's statement anticipates the intra-canonic, trans-gendered, trans-generational connections that I have been making throughout. I would add that *Mansfield Park* not only serves as the dark counterpoint to *Pride and Prejudice* but also revises many of the themes and motifs of *Amelia.* It explores the implications of the conduct-book heroine ideal that Fielding's final novel helped promulgate, addresses the issue of adultery from a woman's perspective, and problematizes the issue of moral and literary authority in a patriarchal society.

Tom Jones and *Amelia*, its contrapuntal sequel, test various ways of reviving a moribund social structure, each with varying degrees of success. Seemingly subversive in both content and presentation, *Tom Jones* comes to argue for the recuperability of traditional forms through the incorporation of something new—the bastard Tom or the novel form. With its exemplary heroine and its didactic tone, *Amelia* ostensibly puts forth a conservative agenda, but this conservatism is straining at the seams.

Pride and Prejudice and *Mansfield Park* have a similar obverse relationship. Like *Tom Jones, Pride and Prejudice* attempts to solve the problem of societal decline through seemingly subversive means—the insertion of a woman into the patriarchal plot of the reconstitution of the estate. But, as with Fielding's novel, Austen's also falls back on the old verities; traditional forms may require the introduction of a new element but they are intrinsically good. To a certain extent, just as *Amelia* appears at first as a sort of sequel to *Tom Jones*, the opening setup in *Mansfield Park* speaks back to the conclusion of *Pride and Prejudice*. Claudia Johnson notes that "The Bertrams end where Darcy begins—with the family circle which Austen's more attractive patricians learn to outgrow."[2] But we might also say that the Bertrams begin where Darcy ends—with the marriage of a proud and wealthy gentleman to a woman of inferior social standing. Lady Bertram may not be an older avatar of Elizabeth Bennet; but Sir Thomas Bertram, like Darcy, is the quintessential patriarch—sober, authoritative, responsible—and Mansfield Park, like Pemberley, is the repository of traditional values. The manor, in fact, provides the model for proper social behavior, as Fanny Price's wistful assessment makes clear: "At Mansfield, no sounds of contention, no raised voices, no abrupt bursts, no tread of violence was ever heard; all proceeded in a regular course of cheerful orderliness; every body had their due importance; every body's feelings were consulted" (*MP* 391–92). The "cheerful orderliness," the "due importance" of everyone, the consultation of everyone's feelings—such a description suggests that this is a well-regulated world, its hierarchical structure balanced with an almost democratic consideration of the wishes of all its members. But Fanny deludes herself, seemingly forgetting the miserable experiences she has so recently undergone there. As we see, the inhabitants of Mansfield Park often pervert or ignore such values. Whereas *Pride and Prejudice* holds forth hope for a renewal—an improvement—of the estate, Mansfield Park implicitly qualifies such hope, calling such values into question even as it attempts to assert their soundness.

The predominant features of *Mansfield Park* explicitly support traditional values. Fanny Price is an exemplary heroine, faithful to a hero who is momentarily deflected from her steadfast love but finally cognizant of her perfections. The resolution of the plot—wherein the constant Fanny gets her man and the instigators of change are banished from Mansfield—validates the argument for supporting the status quo.

However, the surface polemic of Austen's novel is disturbed by an underlying countercurrent of skepticism. Austen may explicitly sanction Fanny's good behavior, but as Fanny's story shows, female exemplarity is an insidious notion. The attributes of the exemplary woman—obedience to authority, self-effacement, and silence—actually disable her from fulfilling her function of providing proper moral guidance. The plot may resolve itself in a conventionally happy ending, but such happiness is built upon an underlying foundation of misery. The very things that promise social reformation highlight the fissures in society, fissures that have an implicit connection with the overarching values of Austen's time. Like *Amelia*, *Mansfield Park* reworks, recontextualizes, and refutes the easy solutions of an earlier text.[3]

Yet *Mansfield Park* also calls into question several of the assumptions underlying *Amelia*. Drawing on the motif of the beleaguered heroine, each text attempts to revise the status quo and testifies to the difficulty of so doing. Yet although *Amelia* demonstrates Fielding's increasing doubt that society can return to traditional values, it never questions the appropriateness of such a return. By reworking Fielding's material Austen calls such values into question, however. She shows us the underside of Amelia-like exemplarity and faults the overarching patriarchal structure that implicitly encourages behavior leading to social breakdown.

Excellent Woman

From the outset, nobody has known what to make of Fanny Price. Austen's earliest readers were divided on the subject; one of her nieces, for example, was "delighted with Fanny" while another "could not bear" her ("Opinions of *Mansfield Park*," *MW* 431, 432). Our own assessments of *Mansfield Park* are, in fact, integrally related to our assessments of Fanny. Her perverse integrity and her unprepossessing virtues prompt the ambivalence and dissatisfaction we feel in regard to the text as a whole. Nina Auerbach subtitles an essay on *Mansfield Park* "Feeling as One Ought about Fanny Price"—a title suggestive of the quandary in which we find ourselves when confronted with Austen's least engaging heroine.[4] Fanny's sickliness, her voicelessness, her rectitude put us off, especially in that she is wedged between Austen's two most lively heroines, Elizabeth Bennet and Emma Woodhouse. Although Tony Tanner notes that "nobody falls in love with Fanny Price," he joins with Lionel Trilling in defending her, arguing that she is a typical Christian heroine, thus subject to unwarranted antipathy on the part of the more secular modern-day reader.[5] Auerbach, on the other hand, seems to regard Fanny's connection with otherworldly realms as tending toward the demonic rather than the angelic: Fanny is "a blighter of ceremonies and a divider of families," a vampire figure who "feasts secretly upon human vitality in the dark."[6] Yet the problem lies not so much with Fanny's conduct-book character, off-putting as that may sometimes be. Rather, it lies with the fact that Fanny's story shows us how little is to be gained by maintaining such a character.

Although the conduct-book heroine had thrived in the half-century since Richardson and Fielding put forward their paragons, Jane Austen generally mocked it. Austen's most memorable protagonists are not of the conduct-book type but instead are lively, somewhat wrong-headed characters capable of change and growth. They consistently transgress, or at least stretch, the bounds of what is considered proper behavior for women. The texts we have tended to favor, such as *Pride and Prejudice*, follow a *bildungsroman* structure; the protagonist errs, faces up to her faults (generally at the instigation of the male mentor), and undergoes a certain amount of development. Violations of what is strictly proper lead in part to chastisement and self-recognition, certainly, but such violations also bring about positive outcomes—for example, Elizabeth's sassing of Lady Catherine makes Darcy aware of her love for him. Furthermore, although each heroine may renounce a propensity toward imaginative flights, none evidences a newfound desire to become a model woman.[7] Elizabeth Bennet persists in "her lively, sportive manner" of talking to Darcy (*PP* 387–88); and Mr. Knightly marries Emma in part, we are to assume, because she is "faultless in spite of her faults" (*Em* 433), that is, because her very faults make her attractive in his eyes.

Fanny may not be Austen's only conduct-book protagonist, but she is the most insistently so. With her strict adherence to duty Elinor Dashwood has affinities to the model, but she also has an acerbic, domineering quality that keeps her out of the ranks of exemplary womanhood; her sister, Marianne, has gotten all the allotment of tenderness that is essential for ideality. Anne Eliot, although she has often been regarded as an older version of Fanny, explicitly questions the implications and consequences of her own dutifulness, which thus enables Austen to engage in a deliberate self-conscious assessment of conduct-book behavior.

Fanny, however, is consistently exemplary, the text validating her as the epitome of womanhood. She just about fulfills Edmund Bertram's prescription for "the perfect model of a woman" (*MP* 347)—and he only holds back his full praise because he lacks the insight that has been granted his gentle cousin. Henry Crawford describes her in terms that elevate her above the common run of womankind: "She is exactly the woman to do away every prejudice of such a man as the Admiral, for she is exactly such a woman as he thinks does not exist in the world. She is the very impossibility he would describe" (293). Such panegyrics come not only from Edmund and Henry but also from the Austen narrator, the narrative voice thus lending authority to a definition of womanhood that, because of our prior acquaintance with Austen, we might otherwise suspect. The narrator continually sings Fanny's praises; she has "heroism of principle" (265) and a "delicacy of taste, of mind, of feeling" (81) that we are told Mary Crawford lacks. Despite Mary's attractiveness to readers, in the contest between her and Fanny the narrator always weighs in on Fanny's side, encouraging us to champion her, as is evidenced by the epithet "my Fanny" (461), the phrase marking a brief, uncharacteristic return to the overtly authorial stance. Constant in her affections and her principles, combining a melting tenderness with an adherence to what is right, Fanny is represented as the most gendered of her gender according to contemporary notions of femininity.

Fanny comes from a long line of model heroines, and by comparing her with some of these we can begin to see how Austen attenuates the tradition. Fanny's forebears include not only Fielding's happy homemaker Amelia, but also the angelic martyr Clarissa and the noble-minded name-dropper Cecilia. Like them Fanny is gentle and pious; she is the only one of Austen's heroines for whom a place of worship clearly means more than a gathering place for village society, although Anne Eliot's concern for her cousin's traveling on Sunday might indicate that she is equally pious. It is likely that when we picture Fanny, we think of her in her virginal white dress—"A woman can never be too fine while she is all in white," says Edmund (*MP* 222)—and her amber cross, as if she were a little nun.

With regard to the piety of conduct-book heroines, we might reverse the old cliché and say that behind every great woman is a great man. Often, the exemplary heroine owes her moral authority to a male mentor who is a man of the cloth. Amelia has her Dr. Harrison, Clarissa has her Dr. Lewen, Cecilia her Dean, and Matilda (the heroine of the second half of Elizabeth Inchbald's *A Simple Story*) her priest Sandford. This configuration of church-sanctioned female exemplarity is suggestive of what Jacques Donzelot calls the "ancient complicity" operating "between the system of matrimonial exchanges—the key to the old familial order—and the religious apparatus."[8] In effect, by having the female exemplar authorized/authored by the clergy, the novels can provide a transcendental imperative for her behavior and thus mask how well it serves secular interests. And Fanny is no exception. As with her sister heroines, her mind has been "formed" by a clergyman (in this case, an aspiring one): Edmund "recommended the books which charmed her leisure hours, he encouraged her taste, and corrected her judgment; he made reading useful by talking to her of what she had read, and heightened its attraction by judicious praise" (*MP* 22). Fanny indeed outdoes her mentor, standing firm against Henry Crawford while Edmund succumbs to the temptation of Crawford's sister.[9] Overall, Austen locates the source of Fanny's moral authority firmly in a patriarchal structure.

To a certain extent, Fanny outdoes her sister heroines in exemplarity. Lionel Trilling points out that, in creating her frail heroine, Austen was following "the tradition which affirmed the peculiar sanctity of the sick, the weak, and the dying."[10] Fanny must be on her way to sainthood—we hear a litany of her ills, from headache to exhaustion to excessive sensitivity to noise. Clarissa, after all, is fairly robust up until the time of the rape, and Amelia seems to bounce back from her fainting fits with renewed vigor. We should bear in mind that, as Mary Wollstonecraft had pointed out fifteen years earlier, conduct books advise a woman to hide the fact that "she can take more exercise than another" and that "she has a sound constitution."[11] Fanny's illness thus goes hand in hand with ultra-femininity. Whereas Amelia and Cecilia properly disdain putting themselves forward, Fanny effaces herself to the point of disappearing altogether. She is not just quiet-spoken ("an excellent thing in woman"), she is practically voiceless—the sentence "Fanny coloured, and said nothing" (*MP* 225) epitomizes her behavior. When Sir Thomas attempts to gauge Fanny's feelings toward Henry Crawford, he realizes that she is a cipher to him: "She was always so gentle and retiring, that her emotions were beyond his discrimination" (366). Pamela, Clarissa, Amelia, and Cecilia make a few missteps, Clarissa indeed stepping fatally outside her father's walls and into the arms of her ravisher. But Fanny makes no false moves. She understands the pernicious nature of the theatricals, she correctly assesses the true character of the Crawfords, and so forth. Overall, she is hyper-exemplary.

Yet, as the text demonstrates, pushed to its logical conclusion the notion of the exemplary woman will show signs of strain, on the levels of both symbol and plot. Clarissa's physical disintegration after the rape symbolizes her gradual transcendence to a higher plane where she will leave earthly woes behind and, presumably, take her place among the angels. Fanny's illness, on the other hand, tends toward no heavenly elevation; it leaves us instead with an idea of chronic enervation, suggestive of the enervation of exemplars. If Fanny represents enduring values, such values are sickened.

The implicit connection between Fanny and Lady Bertram bears out this notion. I would not go so far as Gilbert and Gubar, who argue that Fanny is "destined to become the next Lady Bertram, following the example of Sir Thomas's corpselike wife."[12] But there certainly are similarities between the two. Fanny prefers Lady Bertram for female companionship: "She talked to her, listened to her, read to her; and the tranquillity of such evenings, her perfect security in such a *tête-à-tête* from any sounds of unkindness, was unspeakably welcome to a mind which had seldom known a pause in its alarms or embarrassments" (*MP* 35). Both Fanny and Lady Bertram depend on others to articulate for them, although Fanny (unlike her indolent aunt) actually has a thought or two to articulate. Both are fixed—Lady Bertram on her couch, Fanny in her opinions. Fanny, of course, has a core of moral fiber that Lady Bertram lacks, but the outward appearance is the same. Rather than considering Fanny as the replacement for Lady Bertram, we might consider Lady Bertram as the replacement for Fanny, a bloodless doppelgänger with the form—though not substance—of the proper lady. This connection is suggestive of the fact that hyper-exemplarity and hyper-insipidity can be easily confused.

Fanny's gentleness points to another area of strain in the notion of exemplary womanhood. She cannot make herself understood. Henry Crawford persists in his suit in part because Fanny is too ladylike in her refusals: "Her manner was incurably gentle, and she was not aware of how much it concealed the sternness of her purpose. Her diffidence, gratitude, and softness, made every expression of indifference seem almost an effort of self-denial; seem at least, to be giving nearly as much pain to herself as to him" (*MP* 327). The very sweetness "which makes so essential a part of every woman's worth in the judgment of man" (294) renders her own judgment incapable of being considered.

We have one anomalous instance of Fanny's voicing opposition to the match between herself and Crawford. In *Pride and Prejudice* Elizabeth's rejection of Mr. Collins's proposal provided Austen with an opportunity to expose the plight of women forced to hear out the addresses of men they do not like. Yet Austen leaves it to the generally taciturn Fanny rather than the loquacious Elizabeth to articulate most fervently this plight. Fanny's speech to Edmund to this effect is, in fact, her longest speech in the text. Herein she protests against the assumption that a woman must find a man acceptable because he has found her so: "Let him have all the perfections in the world, I think it ought not to he set down as certain, that a man must be acceptable to every woman he may happen to like himself" (*MP* 353). She questions a code of sexual conduct that both prohibits a woman from having feelings for a man until he has made clear he has feelings for her and then requires that the woman reciprocate in kind: "How then was I to be—to be in love with him the moment he said he was with me?" (353). Fanny may generally conform to conduct-book behavior, but she herein voices a sharp critique of the behavioral absurdities to which women are expected to accede, a critique Austen seems to agree with.[13] It is significant that Edmund just does not get it: "My dear, dear Fanny," he tells her, "now I have the truth ... the very circumstance of the novelty of Crawford's addresses was against him" (353–54). He lays claim to "the truth"—but by seizing on the notion of novelty he ignores Fanny's truth, that she does not and cannot love Henry. Fanny's statement that "we think very different of the nature of women" points to a rift between female and male assessments of woman's nature that even the seemingly enlightened Edmund cannot bridge and that the text brings to the fore with its portrait of the conflicted Fanny.

Generally, however, Fanny "properly" lacks assertion and rhetorical force, and as a consequence she is unacknowledged. When paragons undergo trials, they usually have the dubious satisfaction of having their perfections recognized. As Anna Howe writes Clarissa, in the first letter of the novel, "Every eye, in short, is upon you with the expectation of an example."[14] Cecilia's excellencies are known far and wide, prompting the male paragon Delvile to seek her out. Even the rivalrous Miss Mathews acknowledges that Amelia is "a much better Woman" than herself, and Amelia's husband, Booth, talks of "the general Admiration which ... pursued her, the Respect paid her by Persons of the highest Rank" (*Am* 38, 66). Few sing Fanny's praises, however. Edmund and (later) Henry Crawford recognize her virtues, certainly, and by the end of the novel her importance to the Mansfield residents has been acknowledged. But no one says of her, as Anna Howe says of Clarissa, "She was a wonderful creature from her infancy."[15] People are much more likely to point out, as Mrs. Norris does, that her behavior "is very stupid indeed, and shows a great want of genius and emulation" (*MP* 19). And although Edmund discovers her virtues early on, not until he has undergone disappointment and heartbreak does he "learn to prefer soft light eyes to sparkling dark ones" (470). Sir Thomas eventually realizes that she is "the daughter that he wanted" (472), but it is only his actual daughters' transgressions that throw his niece's virtues into relief. Henry's love is an odd one, spurred perhaps as much by his desire for the unattainable as his recognition of Fanny's excellencies. Neither Mrs. Norris nor the Bertram daughters nor Fanny's parents ever recognize that they have a little paragon in their midst, and in the concluding pages Lady Bertram, after some initial resistance, soon comes to substitute Susan for Fanny, even coming to find her "the most beloved of the two" (472–73). So much for Fanny's importance to Lady Bertram!

Readers themselves may have a hard time recognizing Fanny's importance. Like Amelia, Fanny is somewhat of a hidden heroine. Granted, we are in her mind pretty much from the outset of the novel. But, as the other characters are active rather than passive, they take over the action and thus the interest of the story. They often take over the narrative focus as well. In each of her novels Austen shifts the focalization at times from her main character to various subsidiary ones. In no other, however, does she so consistently explore the motives and feelings of the other characters or give us so much access to the minds of her villains. We receive vivid, emotionally charged accounts of Mary Crawford's fondness for Edmund and her disappointed hopes, of Julia's jealousy of her sister, of Maria's humiliation at Henry's defection. We end up feeling that the other stories have potential. Mary certainly threatens to supplant Fanny in the readers' affections just as she supplants her in Edmund's. As has often been noted, she has the liveliness that makes Elizabeth Bennet so endearing; "with her lively dark eye, clear brown complexion, and general prettiness" (*MP* 44), Mary bears more than a passing resemblance to Elizabeth, whose "fine eyes" first attract Darcy and whose tanned complexion later prompts his defense of her to Caroline Bingley. Fanny's closest analogues in Austen's novels (besides Anne Eliot, who is a deepened, matured, more self-aware version) are the shadowy secondary characters that occur in the texts written before and after *Mansfield Park*—the two Janes, Bennet and Fairfax. Both are sweet girls, forced to bear in silence a lover's apparent defection. With Fanny it is as if Austen tries to bring forward the kind of character she is generally content to leave in the background—and then runs up against the problem that a Rosencrantz can never have the impact of a Hamlet.

Ignored and unrecognized for what she is, Fanny virtually has no impact. Richardson's Pamela almost single-handedly reforms a corrupt squirarchy; Clarissa is highly influential in life and death; Cecilia's noble example prompts noble action on the part of others. Although Amelia cannot single-handedly reform the corrupt society that surrounds her (Fielding also acknowledging the fading power of exemplars, though for different purposes), she does manage to provide important instruction to her children and, ultimately, to inspire Booth and a small circle of friends. Moreover, throughout the text that bears her name, Amelia functions consistently as the emblem for good to which Booth must aspire. But Fanny is granted little or no capacity for influence. She is unable to stop Maria Bertram from slipping around the iron gate with Mr. Crawford, to bring order to the Portsmouth house, or to dissuade Edmund from participating in the play and falling in love with the improper Mary. The only significant influence she has is over her sister, Susan, and rather than attempting to reform the Portsmouth residents the two sisters retreat up the stairs to avoid "a great deal of the disturbance of the house" (*MP* 398), just as the Mansfield residents retreat from the rest of society at the end of the novel.

Fanny's most significant failure is with Henry Crawford. Austen clearly sets up a story that is meant to remind us of the "rake reformed" theme of

Pamela. Henry sets out a net for Fanny, but he is caught in it himself. He seems to be on the road to reformation—he recognizes her superiority to other women, and he takes on the squirarchical duties he had previously neglected. But, as Frank Bradbrook suggests, there is more than a little of a Laclos influence in *Mansfield Park*, and Henry may be more of a Valmont than a Mr. B., mouthing a reformation that has only partially taken hold.[16] If Fanny is indeed "the woman whom he had rationally, as well as passionately loved" (*MP* 469), we must wonder at a passion that can be deflected by seeming whim, and all the narrator's explanations as to the faultiness of Henry's education do little to satisfy us. To a certain extent Henry's love for Fanny seems to have less to do with his growing appreciation of her virtues than with her indifference to his suit: "it was a love which . . . made her affection appear of greater consequence because it was withheld, and determined him to have the glory, as well as the felicity, of forcing her to love him" (326). Henry thus regards Fanny not so much as a person to be valued than as an object to be conquered, and he pursues a course similar to that of the Noble Lord in *Amelia*, who abandons a woman once he has seduced her. It is significant that Henry turns his attention to the less-than-exemplary Maria when she seems to offer greater resistance: "He must exert himself to subdue so proud a display of resentment" (468). By thwarting our expectations that Fanny will reform Henry and become his bride, Austen drives home the inadequacy of the exemplary woman/reformed rake paradigm.

She seems here to have borrowed a leaf from Hannah More's book. Fifteen years prior More had scoffed at "that fatal and most indelicate, nay gross maxim, that a reformed rake makes the best husband," arguing that it goes on the "preposterous supposition . . . that habitual vice creates rectitude of character, and that sin produces happiness."[17] In undermining the maxim herself, Austen reinforces our sense of Fanny's negligible capacity for influence.

Indeed, whatever reformation occurs in *Mansfield Park* results not from Fanny's influence but from the bad experiences the characters undergo. Fanny essentially wins Edmund's affections by default, Mary's weaknesses rather than Fanny's virtues leading him to transfer his affections to his gentle cousin. Sir Thomas recognizes his folly only after Maria's elopement. And it takes a brush with death to make Tom Bertram a better man.

Not only is Fanny incapable of influencing the characters within the text, but the representation of her is probably incapable of influencing those who read the text. As Nancy Armstrong argues in *Desire and Domestic Fiction*, the rising novel enabled a social agenda whereby "the female relinquishes political control to the male in order to acquire exclusive authority over domestic life, emotions, taste, and morality."[18] In effect, the versions of female exemplarity that novels put forth were intended to provide a model for feminine authority and to carve out its particular realm of influence—the inculcation of values within the domestic sphere. Samuel Richardson, for instance, made no bones about his didactic purposes. After listing Pamela's manifold virtues at the conclusion of the novel, he points out that they "Are all so many signal instances of the excellency of her mind, which may make her character worthy of the *imitation* of her sex" (*Pam* 509, emphasis mine). More grandly, in his postscript to *Clarissa*, he explains that he intended the novel to "inculcate upon the human mind, under the guise of an amusement, the great lessons of Christianity," specifically through making the reader desire to emulate his saintly-heroine: "And who that are in earnest in their profession of Christianity but will rather envy than regret the triumphant death of CLARISSA, whose piety from her early childhood, whose diffusive charity; whose steady virtue; whose Christian humility; whose forgiving spirit; whose meekness, whose resignation, HEAVEN only could reward?"[19] Fielding's and Burney's heroines are also put forth as worthy of emulation. How worthwhile can it be to emulate Fanny, however, if such emulation leads to naught? Imitating Fanny would not give one the capacity to lead others to virtue, or so *Mansfield Park* implies.

Moreover, imitating Fanny would mean resigning oneself to a painful existence. Stories such as those of Pamela, Clarissa, Amelia, Miss Sidney Biddulph, and Cecilia show us that the lot of the model woman is to suffer. After all, if the protagonist's exemplary character is fixed, the novel's action cannot depend upon self-revelation and internal growth but must instead depend upon the external events that beset the heroine—preferably, events that enable her exemplarity to shine forth. Fanny ostensibly goes through no more than her sisters in ideality.

Or does she? Her sister heroines at least can pride themselves on their consciousness of their own virtue, but Fanny has no such salve. Pamela and Clarissa, for example, know that they are right to resist the importunities of their would-be seducers. Cecilia, in renouncing a secret marriage with Delvile, takes consolation in her own virtue, as the following passage indicates:

> notwithstanding the sorrow she felt in apparently injuring the man whom, in the whole world, she most wished to oblige, she yet found a satisfaction in the sacrifice she had made, that recompensed her for much of her sufferings and soothed her into something like tranquillity; the true power of virtue she had scarce experienced before, for she found it a resource against the cruelest dejection, and a supporter in the bitterest disappointment.[20]

Compare the above with Austen's description of Fanny's feelings after she has told Sir Thomas she cannot marry Henry Crawford:

> Her mind was all disorder. The past, present, future, every thing was terrible. But her uncle's anger gave her the severest pain of all. Selfish and ungrateful! to have appeared so to him! She was miserable for ever. She had no one to take her part, to counsel, or speak for her. Her only friend was absent. He might have softened his father; but all, perhaps all, would think her selfish and ungrateful. She might have to endure the reproach again and again; she might hear it, or see it, or know it to exist for ever in every connection about her. She could not but feel some resentment against Mr. Crawford; yet, if he really loved her, and were unhappy too!—it was all wretchedness together. (*MP* 321)

Fanny is damned if she does and damned if she does not. She cannot act without violating some prescription of proper feminine behavior. She may see more clearly than Sir Thomas, but she may not derive consolation from this fact.

The changes Austen rings on the term "duty" underscore the double bind in which the model woman finds herself. For Fanny, duty consists of sticking to her principles, as she acknowledges resignedly after that dreadful interview with Sir Thomas: "she believed she had no right to wonder at the line of conduct he pursued. He who had married a daughter to Mr. Rushworth. Romantic delicacy was certainly not to be expected from him. She must do her duty, and trust that time might make her duty easier than it now was" (*MP* 331). But only a few pages later Lady Bertram puts forward a different definition of duty with her reiteration of Sir Thomas's view that Fanny has an obligation to accept Henry: "And you must be aware, Fanny, that it is every young woman's duty to accept such a very unexceptionable offer" (333). We have, of course, encountered a similar notion of female duty in an earlier passage—and we might recall what fatal results attend it:

> Being now in her twenty-first year, Maria Bertram was beginning to think matrimony a duty; and as a marriage with Mr. Rushworth would give her the enjoyment of a larger income than her father's, as well as ensure her the house in town, which was now a prime object, it became, by the same rile of moral obligation, her evident duty to marry Mr. Rushworth if she could. (38–39)

The contested meanings of "duty" underscore Austen's point that the model woman often must attempt to align what may be mutually exclusive aims—the preservation of moral integrity and the attainment of wealth and standing. Here we have no happy resolution as in *Pride and Prejudice*, wherein Elizabeth manages to preserve her integrity and marry a man with ten thousand pounds a year. (Charlotte Lucas's situation, of course, hints at the dilemma faced by Fanny.) Fanny's conception of her "moral obligation" is directly at odds with the Bertrams'.

By the end of the text the Bertrams will come to redefine duty, learning that Fanny's conception of it really serves the family's interests after all, but in the meantime we are made privy to Fanny's suffering as she struggles with impossible demands. Indeed, she is unable to find a Cecilia-like tranquillity until the end of the volume. Overall, few moments of pleasure relieve the long scenes of torture that Fanny undergoes. Even her pleasures are riddled with painful sensations: as she prepares for the ball given in her honor she worries about whether to wear Mary's or Edmund's necklace and sighs over Edmund's profession of love for Mary; the welcome news of William's promotion is followed by Henry's unwelcome proposal. Austen makes clear the connection between Fanny's feelings of oppression and her conduct-book behavior. After refusing Henry's proposal, Fanny dreads an encounter with Mary, rightly fearing that Mary will bring up distressing issues. But Mary need only appeal to Fanny's notion of proper behavior:

> She was determined to see Fanny alone, and therefore said to her tolerably soon, in a low voice, "I must speak to you for a few minutes somewhere;" words that Fanny felt all over her, in all her pulses, and all her nerves. Denial was impossible. Her habits of ready submission, on the contrary, made her almost instantly rise and lead the way out of the room. She did it with wretched feelings, but it was inevitable. (*MP* 357)

The intensity of Fanny's emotions is played off against her almost automaton-like behavior. As in the scene after her interview with Sir Thomas, Fanny's sense of propriety renders her miserable. No wonder that the text gives us such oxymorons as "painful gratitude" (322); to be an exemplary woman means to be beset with contradictory impulses.

Austen's final disposition of her conduct-book protagonist is ambivalent. Fanny does get the requisite happy ending that would seem to validate her "womanly" behavior: she is married to Edmund; William is on his way to naval glory; and Susan has supplanted her as Lady Bertram's companion, thus freeing Fanny of the guilt she might feel at not being able to make all of the people happy all of the time. But we might bear in mind that Austen rewards all her protagonists with a happy ending, and she gives us no indication that Elizabeth will stop teasing Darcy or that the imperious Emma will be satisfied with any but "the best treatment." Austen's improper ladies may briefly pay penance for their sins. The scene wherein Emma reproaches herself after insulting Miss Bates, for example, may be one of the most emotionally charged in the Austen canon. The proper Fanny, however, continually pays penance for sins she does not commit, essentially serving as a scapegoat for society's failures to regulate itself correctly. At one time, she evokes a Griselda-figure, willing to humble herself for the sins of others: "Sir Thomas's look implied, 'On your judgment, Edmund, I depended; what have you been about?'—She knelt in spirit to her uncle, and her bosom swelled to utter, 'Oh! not to him. Look so to all the others, but not to him'" (*MP* 185). We must assume that only Fanny's habitual self-effacement keeps her from kneeling in actuality. And, despite the uncharacteristic emphasis on religion, Austen offers us no more suggestion that a heavenly reward awaits Fanny than she does in regard to her other protagonists.

When Mrs. Norris—that mouthpiece for all that is awry in the social structure—tells Fanny that she "must be the lowest and the last" (*MP* 221), she may indeed be voicing the implicit agenda of a society that depends on female submission. For the behavior that it prescribes for rendering women "womanly" is that which calls for their obedience, their dependence, their sense of their own inferiority. We might consider Fanny as exemplary to the second power—as the exemplary case of the exemplary woman, allowing us to see the consequences of the concept. The character of Fanny may stem from Austen's internalizations of society's "should-be's," but the plot in which she is inscribed may stem from Austen's concurrent resistance to the plot of feminizing women.

The Fall of the House of Mansfield

As in *Amelia*, the resolution of the plot overtly champions conservative values but simultaneously problematizes them by the evidence put forward in their support. Maria's adulterous liaison with Henry flies in the face of such values, but it also is the inevitable offshoot of an extreme version of them. The reestablishment of spiritual principles in Mansfield, represented by Fanny's new role there, serves as an ostensible solution to the problems besetting the estate, but Austen implicitly demonstrates that the solution works on only a limited scale.[21]

Soon after the Crawfords arrive in the Mansfield neighborhood, Mrs. Grant optimistically predicts that "Mansfield shall cure you both—and without any taking in. Stay with us and we will cure you" (*MP* 47). In a world wherein Mansfield had maintained its emblematic significance as a center of moral authority, such an outcome might be possible. Henry would marry Fanny, renouncing his libertine ways and taking his squirarchical duties seriously. Mary would marry Edmund, learning like Elizabeth Bennet to use her wit as a corrective rather than destructive force. Maria Bertram would console herself with high society. Aunt Norris, after her initial resentment had passed, would take credit for Fanny's match, becoming as obnoxious in her attentions to Fanny as she had been in her snubs. Henry himself offers a view of an ideal community that might, in other circumstances, have served Austen as a final line for the novel: "'Mansfield, Sotherton, Thornton Lacey,' he continued, 'what a society will be comprised in those houses! And at Michaelmas, perhaps, a fourth may be added, some small hunting-box in the vicinity of every thing so dear'" (405). Such an outcome does not occur, of course, and the contrast between Henry's vision and the actual conclusion throws into relief the fissures running through the seemingly solid edifice of Mansfield Park.

Rather than finding a cure at Mansfield, the Crawfords infect—or at least lower—the Bertrams' resistance to disease. Although the taint of city living may give the Crawfords a certain outsider status, essentially they are insiders, members of the same class as the Bertrams and certainly more acceptable socially than the child of a lieutenant of Marines. Henry is, after all, a landowner, responsible for the well-being of his tenants. In effect, the threat to the gentry comes from within the gentry.

Such a threat has all the more force in that it cannot be easily discerned. Despite Henry's fears of being "taken in," it is the Bertrams who are taken in, blinded to the Crawfords' moral bankruptcy by their attractiveness. Sir Thomas regards both Crawfords as suitable matches for his own children; the connection he envisions ends up, ironically, an illicit one. We might expect Edmund—the only one of Austen's clergymen with an actual vocation (with the possible exception of Edward Ferrars)—to have the surest sense of the threat posed by the Crawfords, but he becomes the particular friend of both. Only Fanny, the silent observer, can assess the true implications of their apparently innocent high-spirited behavior, and she has no voice with which to alert the others.

The characterization of the Crawfords also blinds us—or at least destabilizes our expectations. In *Amelia* Fielding eschews his usual practice of succinctly summing up the characters when he introduces them, thus often leaving us uncertain as to characters' motives and dependent on further revelations. Austen similarly keeps us off-balance. The Crawfords are initially attractive to us as well as to the characters within the novel, and for the most part Austen forgoes the sort of commentary that might give us clear indications as to how we are to read them.[22] If, as Q. D. Leavis has argued, *Mansfield Park* is a revised version of Austen's epistolary "Lady Susan," it subtilizes the blatant character revelations of the earlier work, in which Lady Susan's letters to Mrs. Johnson provide a clear illustration of her character, and Mrs. Vernon's suspicions of her seem fairly disinterested.[23] In *Mansfield Park*, however, our main clues come from the Crawfords' speech and actions and Fanny's unvoiced assessments. But we may be inclined to read the Crawfords' speech and actions as evidence of a proper

lack of control rather than of villainy, and we may consider Fanny's assessments, when unseconded by the narrator's validation, as somewhat skewed,
especially in light of her evident jealousy of Mary. Furthermore, the Crawfords' genuinely kind acts mitigate their improprieties. Mary pays marked
attention to Fanny after one of Mrs. Norris's particularly virulent barbs, and
Henry envisions that in making Fanny his wife he can elevate her from her
"dependent, helpless, friendless, neglected, forgotten" condition (*MP* 297).
Granted, their behavior (particularly Henry's) often verges on the improper,
but the Crawfords appear redeemable.

After giving us an instance of misbehavior on the Crawfords' part, Austen generally juxtaposes an instance of kindness. It is only in the very last
chapters of the novel that the scales tip irrevocably toward the bad. Mary's
mercenary desire for Tom Bertram's death, expressed in a self-serving letter
to Fanny, reveals a cold-bloodedness that is inexcusable according to Austen's
worldview. Henry's elopement with Maria Bertram is an egregious social
transgression, indicative of his overweening selfishness and heartless lack of
concern for consequences. But it may be that up until these particular occurrences, we expect—perhaps even hope—that Austen will allow each Crawford an epiphanic moment of self-revelation and a subsequent reformation.
Unlike Austen's other novels, wherein we can predict the eventual partners if
not what will bring them together, *Mansfield Park* offers several possible plot
paths, and the hypothetical resolution envisioned by Henry does not seem to
be completely out of the question.

The elopement of Henry and Maria marks the point at which characters
in the novel and readers of the novel must have done with the Crawfords.
The man who "so requited hospitality, so injured family peace" (*MP* 469) no
longer has a place in the Mansfield world. Despite Edmund's high-minded-
ness, we might expect (as Fanny does) that his feelings for Mary would win
out over his elevated sense of propriety and that she at least would not have
the gates of Mansfield forever barred to her. But her plan to persuade Henry
to marry Maria implicates her in Henry's crime, at least in Edmund's eyes, as
he makes clear to Fanny:

> but the manner in which she spoke of the crime itself, giving it
> every reproach but the right, considering its ill consequences only as
> they were to be braved or overborne by a deficiency of decency and
> impudence in wrong; and, last of all, and above all, recommending
> to us a compliance, a compromise, an acquiescence, in the
> continuance of a sin, on the chance of a marriage which, thinking
> as I now thought of her brother, should rather be prevented than
> sought—all this together most grievously convinced me that I had
> never understood her before. (458)

Mary's attempt to unite the two transgressors in marriage might seem to have a certain affinity to Darcy's engineering of the wedding of Lydia and Wickham. But an adulterous liaison is not recuperable, and there is no grateful Elizabeth Bennet to thank Mary for her pains. Instead, Edmund regards the suggestion as evidence of Mary's duplicity: "How have I been deceived! Equally in brother and sister deceived!" (495). To Edmund the woman who can speak lightly of adultery is as culpable as the adulterer. Clearly, a proper lady must condemn adultery, and Fanny's "shudderings of horror" (41) mark the correct response.

The Henry-and-Maria elopement marks both the point beyond which the Crawfords can no longer be part of the Mansfield world and the point beyond which the Mansfield family unit cannot survive as a whole. In *Pride and Prejudice* Mr. Bennet receives the unrepentant Lydia Wickham back into the family circle. Sir Thomas, however, refuses to receive the abandoned Maria, offering the following justification: "Maria had destroyed her own character, and he would not by a vain attempt to restore what never could be restored, be affording his sanction to vice, or in seeking to lessen its disgrace, be anywise accessary to introducing such misery in another man's family, as he had known himself" (*MP* 465). No one, except the silly Mr. Collins, frets that Lydia's bad example may cause others to emulate her. Maria's dissimilar fate enables Austen to demonstrate that adultery signals an unassimilable infraction of the social code.

Although almost all of Austen's novels touch on some sort of illicit sexuality, none of these situations has the disruptive force—both within the story and as a symbolic element—of the Henry-and-Maria elopement. Maria's marriage to Rushworth links the grand estate of Mansfield with one of the largest estates and finest places in the country" (*MP* 38); it is "a connection exactly of the right sort; in the same country, and the same interest" (40). If it does not have the symbolic resonance of, say, Tom Jones's marriage to Sophia Western, the Bertram–Rushworth marriage nonetheless signifies a consolidation of squirarchical power, property, and wealth, and it reaffirms the continuation of the status quo through propagation. Maria and Henry's transgression flies directly in the face of such values, for it essentially disregards Rushworth's rights to his own "property." The potential threat of bastardy lies at the margins of the text, symbolically reinforced by the fact that Maria plays an unwed mother in *Lover's Vows*. As in *Amelia* adultery undermines the values that preserve the status quo, and adulterers cannot be reabsorbed into the society that they threaten.[24]

By drawing on the adultery motif Austen introduces an undermining element not only into Mansfield Park but into *Mansfield Park*. Once adultery has entered the world of the text, there can be no return to prior assumptions about the appropriateness of the status quo, despite the text's effort to establish this very point. As Tony Tanner suggests in *Adultery in the Novel*, adultery is a disruptive force for the novel genre itself: "In confronting the problems of marriage and adultery, the bourgeois novel finally has to confront not only the provisionality of social laws and rules and structures but the provisionality of its own procedures and assumptions."[25] This text's focus on adultery is much more limited than that of the bourgeois novels Tanner discusses or even that of *Amelia*, wherein adultery serves as the central problem addressed. After all, the Henry-and-Maria elopement takes place only within the last three chapters. Yet it is the crucial action of the novel, effecting the final disposition of all the major characters. Too, as with the bourgeois novels Tanner studies, the adultery motif in Mansfield implicitly undermines the surety of the values the text expresses.

As in *Amelia* adultery serves as both cause and effect of social breakdown, a positive feedback loop dismantling traditional values. Sir Thomas is the archetypal patriarch, perhaps the most formidable authority figure in the Austen canon. In a novel ostensibly pushing traditional values, we might expect that he would be their most staunch supporter. After all, despite his overabundance of pride, Darcy fulfills his patriarchal duties: he saves both Georgiana and Lydia from ruin, essentially preserving two households. Sir Thomas, however, enables or encourages the tendencies that lead to the destruction of the household. Sir Thomas errs throughout in valuing appearance over essence. Because his daughters have been educated in the surface accomplishments he is satisfied: "the Miss Bertrams continued to exercise their memories, practise their duets, and grow tall and womanly; and their father saw them becoming in person, manner, and accomplishments, every thing that could satisfy his anxiety" (*MP* 20). However, as Sir Thomas discovers too late, "with all the cost and care of an anxious and expensive education, he had brought up his daughters, without their understanding their first duties, or his being acquainted with their character and temper" (464–65). Making no attempt to delve below appearance, Sir Thomas is willing to accept Maria's feigned professions of respect for Rushworth. Prizing a blind obedience to the dictates of authority over a considered attempt to formulate right values, he browbeats Fanny in order to make her accept Henry Crawford. His manner authoritarian rather than authoritative, he prompts both Maria and Julia to flee from the restrictions he imposes.[26]

Granted, by the final chapter, Sir Thomas realizes his errors, and we must assume that he will be a better baronet in the future. But what is significant is that, unlike Darcy, the highest representative of social order in the novel facilitates, rather than quells, disorder. Nor do we have a sense that his children can do much better. Sir Thomas's heir has become, by the close of the novel, "useful to his father, steady and quiet" (*MP* 462), but we are given no instances of model behavior on Tom Bertram's part. Edmund, the guardian of Mansfield's spiritual values, gets no opportunity actively to enforce them. We have here no Darcy or Knightley to reassure us that, though flawed, the patriarch will ultimately put things to rights.

The critique of patriarchal values in *Mansfield Park* at times echoes Mary Wollstonecraft's radical *Vindication*. In the following passage, Wollstonecraft might as well be discussing Sir Thomas's confusion of external accomplishments with internal virtues, epitomized in the education he provides his daughters: "Manners and morals are so nearly allied that they have often been confounded; but, although the former should only be the natural reflection of the latter, yet when various causes have produced factitious and corrupt manners, which are very early caught, morality becomes an empty name."[27] When Wollstonecraft describes how woman's lack of real power "gives birth to cunning," we may recall how the Bertram daughters learn "to repress their spirits in [Sir Thomas's] presence" (*MP* 463), their powerlessness before their authoritarian father occasioning duplicity.[28] Even Fanny, exemplary in her powerlessness as well as in her virtue, may possess some share of this quality; we can certainly see in her some evidence of the contemporary manifestation of cunning—passive aggressive behavior. When things are not going as she would like, she tends to fall ill or assume a martyr role, as in the following passage wherein Fanny sulks at Edmund's absence: "she thought it a very bad exchange, and if Edmund were not there to mix the wine and water for her, would rather go without it than not" (66). Finally, as the epigraph at the outset of this chapter indicates, Wollstonecraft suggests that adultery itself results from a system of female education that teaches women their only object is to render themselves pleasing to men. Once trained in the art of attracting men, women will continue to do so even after they are married, a hypothesis confirmed by Maria's actions. In *Mansfield Park* Austen gives concrete representation to some of the arguments that Wollstonecraft makes in *Vindication*.

But Austen is not here subjecting patriarchal values to a radical critique à la Wollstonecraft. Some of the same sorts of concerns that Wollstonecraft addresses are addressed by Hannah More in her *Strictures* on female education. She too deals with the matrimonial difficulties of a woman who has been taught only to attract and please: she will "escape to the exhibition room" and put herself on display once more; she will be "exposed to the two-fold temptation of being at once neglected by her husband, and exhibited as an object of attraction to other men."[29] Thus, although Austen's text has affinities to Wollstonecraft's, it has affinities to More's as well, and although it is tempting to regard Austen as putting forward a feminist agenda, we can just as likely regard her as putting forward a *feminine* one—one wherein women's improvement is put in service of patriarchal values. The elevation of morals over manners would sustain, rather than undermine, the authority of the Sir

Thomas Bertrams of the land. Overall, Austen advocates not that traditional values be overthrown but that they be strengthened or revived—thus seemingly taking the same sort of conservative stance that we saw Fielding take in *Amelia*.

For all its conservatism, however, *Mansfield Park* unlike *Amelia* implicitly links societal breakdown to an overarching patriarchal structure. Through the fates meted out to its female characters, the text exposes the underside of a system that constrains and undermines women. Fielding gives us the exemplary Amelia, cheerful and supportive in the face of her husband's adultery, unfounded accusations, and improvidence. He also gives us transgressive female characters, such as Miss Mathews and Mrs. Atkinson, who are subject to ridicule and shown as deserving the fates they get. Austen, on the other hand, shows us that the fate of the exemplary woman is to suffer silently as she experiences the defection of the man she loves and faces conflicting demands. Even Austen's transgressive women are presented sympathetically. We are made aware that, however misguided they are, Mary Crawford, Maria Bertram, and Julia Bertram have feelings that may be wounded and manipulated. Mary does indeed care for Edmund, and when all intercourse has come to an end between them she finds herself "in need of the true kindness of her sister's heart" (*MP* 469). Maria succumbs to Henry's "animated perseverance" (468) of her, and although his pursuit of her is prompted by mere vanity, she is in love with him, hoping that he will marry her. Maria's act of adultery irrevocably destroys her reputation, necessitating her banishment from England, but Henry's will be forgiven, as Austen dryly acknowledges: "That punishment, the public punishment of disgrace, should in a just measure attend his share of the offence, is, we know, not one of the barriers, which society gives to virtue" (468). The text demonstrates the psychic toll that a patriarchal structure takes on women even as it overtly argues in favor of its soundness.

In order for traditional values to be revived and sustained, Austen—like Fielding in *Amelia*—emphasizes the important role played by religion. We might recall that one of the first acts performed by the reformed Mr. B. in *Pamela* is the reconsecration of the family chapel—a reconsecration symbolic of Pamela's accession to spiritual authority in Mr. B.'s household. Austen, too, gives symbolic resonance to the motif of the family chapel, making an implicit connection between the degeneration of the Rushworth family and the unused chapel at Sotherton. Fanny considers the custom of family prayers a vital part of the regulation of a great estate: "It was a valuable part of former times. There is something in a chapel and chaplain so much in character with a great house, with one's ideas of what such a household should be!" (*MP* 85). We are left with the sense that the continuance of such a custom may have made Rushworth less foolish and his mother less vain. We are told too that paying attention to religion might have saved the Bertram daughters from disgrace: "they had never been properly taught to govern their inclinations and tempers by that sense of duty which alone can suffice. They had been instructed theoretically in their religion, but never required to bring it into daily practice" (463). Religion it seems might provide the missing element that would keep society on track.

As the clergyman son of a noble family Edmund would appear to provide a hope for the future. Attempting to justify his choice of profession to Mary Crawford he prescribes the proper function of a clergyman, a prescription to which he will no doubt adhere:

> And with regard to their influencing public manners, Miss Crawford must not misunderstand me, or suppose I mean to call them the arbiters of good breeding, the regulators of refinement and courtesy, the masters of the ceremonies of life. The manners I speak of might rather be called conduct, perhaps, the result of good principles; the effect, in short, of those doctrines which it is their duty to teach and recommend; and it will, I believe, be every where found, that as the clergy are, or are not what they ought to be, so are the rest of the nation. (*MP* 93)

The proper clergyman as Edmund defines him could supply what is wanting in the Bertram daughters, in the Crawfords, in the household at Sotherton, in society at large.

Although the text gives us an optimistic glimpse of what that revitalized society might be, it concurrently undermines the likelihood of such a society occurring. In the world of Mansfield, Mary's succinct comment that "A clergyman is nothing" (*MP* 92) seems more apt. During the discussion of the Sotherton chapel, Mary offers an astute—if tactless—rejoinder to Fanny's notion about the importance and efficacy of family prayers: "It must do the heads of the family a great deal of good to force all the poor housemaids and footmen to leave business and pleasure, and say their prayers here twice a day, while they are inventing excuses themselves for staying away" (86–87). Fanny and Edmund take umbrage at Mary's remarks, Austen nudging us to identify with their values. Yet the dialogic interchange undermines our surety that religion ever did or could have the sort of regulatory power with which Edmund and Fanny invest it. Mary's high-spirited comment that "The young Mrs. Eleanors and Mrs. Bridgers" had their "heads full of something very different—especially if the poor chaplain were not worth looking at" compels us to consider that reinstituting family prayers may simply lead to false piety (87).

Rather than influencing others to do well, Edmund tends to be influenced by others to go against his principles. Granted, when he gives in to the others over the play, he is not yet ordained, but he clearly knows it is his duty to dissuade, not succumb. Although by the close of the novel Edmund has presumably become a proper shepherd to his flock, the only instance we have of his pastoral influence is the guidance he gives Fanny during her youth—and by the time of the actual story, teacher and pupil seem to have changed places. The only other clergyman in the novel is Dr. Grant, who, as Mary indecorously but accurately says, is "an indolent selfish bon vivant, who must have his palate consulted in every thing, who will not stir a finger for the convenience of any one, and who, moreover, if the cook makes a blunder, is out of humour with his excellent wife" (*MP* 111). With Dr. Grant, Austen gives us a picture of a bad clergyman in the tradition of Mr. Collins and Mr. Elton, and we are compelled to wonder whether this picture is not more apt than the one she gives us of Edmund Bertram. In any case, Austen does not reassure us as to the corrective influence of the clergy.

Because Austen gives neither Crawford an internal moment of self-revelation, we are left with the feeling that they will continue their thoughtless ways. Certainly, we are told that they regret their past actions. Mary, after all, is "long in finding" someone who can "put Edmund Bertram sufficiently out of her head" (*MP* 469). But she nonetheless is "perfectly resolved against ever attaching herself to a younger brother again"—a sign that she has not renounced the mercenary interests that made her wish for Tom Bertram's death. Henry, we are told, ends up with "no small portion of vexation and regret" (468). But as we get this information only in summary, we are divorced from any emotional involvement; we do not get a sense of the potency of Henry's pain as we get, for example, from Willoughby's anguished confession to Elinor in *Sense and Sensibility*. In forgiving Henry, society will enable if not encourage him to follow the course he has always followed.

Mansfield Park ends on an apparently happy note, like *Amelia*, but this conclusion—similar to that of Fielding's text—offers us little hope of societal reformation. In the final pages we are told that Tom Bertram has become "useful" and "steady"; Lady Bertram has found Susan to be an indispensable companion; Sir Thomas has discovered "the daughter he wanted"; and most important, Fanny and Edmund have been united in marriage. Tanner regards this marriage as a positive outcome: "a marriage it is, and a celebratory one, symbolising or suggesting more far-reaching reconciliations and restorations; a paradigmatic marriage for society in a larger sense, which transcends personal gratifications."[30] But the conclusion of *Mansfield Park* is suggestive of alienation and exclusion rather than of celebration and reconciliation. The effects of adultery, like those of a stone thrown in a pond, spread beyond the original incident, leaving havoc in their wake. Henry and Maria must be expelled from the world of Mansfield because their action threatens social breakdown. Despite their expulsion, however, social breakdown nevertheless occurs. The adultery divides Edmund from Mary, the Grants and the Rush-worths from the Bertrams, and the Bertrams from one another. Whereas the ending of *Pride and Prejudice* allows all to join in the final celebration, this is not the case with *Mansfield Park*. Even Lady Catherine, with all her arrogance and bossiness, can finally be readmitted to Pemberley; Aunt Norris, on the other hand, must die in exile.

Too, although clearly put forward as a happy event, the marriage of Edmund and Fanny is nevertheless suggestive of social regression. Several recent discussions of *Mansfield Park* have dealt with the troubling "incest" motif in the novel, and I think that we cannot ignore its symbolic import.[31] Cousin marriage, though legally sanctioned, still manages to invoke the old incest taboo. By continually referring to the consanguineous connection between Fanny and Edmund, Austen ensures that we keep this thought before us. At the end of the novel Fanny and Edmund are not "the married couple" but "the married cousins" (*MP* 473), their kinship relationship seemingly more important than their marital one. In his study of the connection between the incest taboo and social structure, Talcott Parsons suggests that the taboo enables the proper functioning of society: "it is essential that persons should be capable of assuming roles which contribute to functions which no nuclear family is able to perform, which involve the assumption of non-familial roles. Only if such non-familial roles can be adequately staffed can a society function." Without the incest taboo there can be no "formation and maintenance of supra-famil-ial bonds on which major economic, political and religious functions of the society are dependent."[32] The happy ending for Fanny and Edmund is para-digmatic of the ending of social intercourse. Mansfield may have its emblem-atic function restored, but this function will not extend beyond its grounds. We might playfully extend Austen's story and envision a marriage between Susan—"the stationary niece"—and the other Bertram son.[33]

What happens with the triangular romantic configurations in the nov-el reinforces the motif of *Mansfield Park* closing in on itself. In Volume I (wherein Fanny is not "out") we have Mary Crawford and the two Bertram brothers and Henry Crawford and the two Bertram sisters. Once Fanny has entered the game the configurations shift, and their elements are reduced; the triangles now consist of Mary-Edmund-Fanny and Edmund-Fanny-Henry. By the novel's conclusion only the two elements both triangles have in com-mon—the cousins Fanny and Edmund—remain.

The final centering of Edmund and Fanny within the household does indeed make clear that moral values have been restored to Mansfield Park. As Tony Tanner points out, Fanny is "the true inheritor of Mansfield Park."[34] Although Tom Bertram is the actual heir, Fanny and Edmund—installed in the living on the estate—presumably inherit Sir Thomas's moral authority and hold out the promise that Mansfield Park may attain the ideal that Fanny envisioned while exiled to Portsmouth.[35] As a good conduct-book heroine, of course, Fanny will work behind the scenes in her domestic realm, leaving to clergyman Edmund the active enforcement and modeling of morality.

But such moral revitalization is achieved at what cost? The first line of the final chapter has often been marked as signaling Austen's desire to hurry through the process of tying things up. What has not often been marked is the statement's irony. When Austen proclaims, "Let other pens dwell on guilt and misery" (*MP* 461), we expect that she intends to have done with such subjects. But rather than abandoning them she revels in them. The happy ending is offset by language hammering us with reminders of the unhappy events that have taken place, as the following somber litany, culled from the final chapter, demonstrates:

> guilt misery odious melancholy suffering disappointment regret sorry sorrow misery self-reproach anguish evil grievous bitterly wretchedly disappointment wretchedness hatred punishment misery despised disappointments punishment punishment guilt mortified unhappy reproach melancholy destroyed misery punishment evil bitter danger evil irritation tormenting hurtful disappointment bitterness dread horrors selfish guilt folly ruined cold-blooded coldness repulsive mortified anger regretting punishment punishment vexation regret vexation self-reproach regret wretchedness wound alienate distressing regret disappointment apoplexy death regretting anxious doubting sick poor hardship struggle death painful alarm.

No wonder we have trouble with Austen's claim that "the happiness of the married cousins must appear as secure as earthly happiness can be" (473). Such a positive statement lays but a thin veneer over the negative terms embedded within the chapter. In order "to complete the picture of good" (the accession of Fanny and Edmund to the Mansfield living), "the death of Dr. Grant" must occur, the happiness of the principles thus dependent upon the misfortune of others (473).

This is not to say that we can ignore the strong argument in favor of traditional values that is presented in the novel. The happy ending that rewards Fanny and Edmund ratifies the values they espouse. Although the Mansfield community ends up reorganized in part, it nevertheless revolves around most of its original members, the return to the status quo confirming the soundness of things as they are. Moreover, the argument of *Mansfield* is quite in keeping with views Austen expresses in a letter, which appeared soon after the publication of the text, in which she gives her niece Fanny Knight advice about a suitor:

> And as to there being any objection from his *Goodness*, from the
> danger of his becoming even Evangelical, I cannot admit that. I am
> by no means convinced that we ought not all to be Evangelicals,
> & am at least persuaded that they who are so from Reason and
> Feeling, must be happiest & safest.—Do not be frightened from
> the connection by your Brothers having most wit. Wisdom is better
> than Wit, & in the long run will certainly have the laugh on her
> side; & don't be frightened by the idea of his acting more strictly
> up to the precepts of the New Testament than others. (Letter 103,
> *LSC* 410)

Wisdom does indeed seem to have the laugh on her side as Austen banishes
the Crawfords from the sacrosanct grounds of Mansfield and installs Fanny
and Edmund as guardians of the Old World order.

We, on the other hand, do not laugh. Not (as sometimes has been argued) because we are uncomfortable with an Austen who validates the status
quo. After all, she does pretty much the same thing in the beloved *Pride and
Prejudice* when she lets super-patriarch Darcy save the day. We are uncomfortable with an Austen who puts forward an argument in favor of tradition
but who presents evidence that makes another case entirely.

Mansfield Park (as does *Amelia*) poses a problem to its readers in that
the ideological conflicts are never satisfactorily resolved. Austen here embraces the traditional conduct-book heroine, a figure she had earlier ridiculed;
in doing so she ostensibly embraces the conduct-book novel. There is not,
as in the first inheritance plot in *Pride and Prejudice*, a direct confrontation
with the patriarchal system of estate settlement, not is there any sense that
the nontraditional woman may revitalize the estate. Whatever revitalization
Mansfield Park undergoes occurs because Fanny adheres to tradition, seeing more clearly than the patriarch how she can best serve him. If we regard
Mansfield Park simply as an exemplary conduct-book novel, then we can say
that Austen puts her authorial vocation in the service of a patriarchal literary
tradition, creating a model version of feminine behavior.

Like *Amelia*, however, *Mansfield Park* works against its own ostensible
aims. Austen speaks with a double voice, as she does in *Pride and Prejudice*,
and she subtly interweaves her championing of traditional values with her
critique of patriarchal institutions that define and deny women. Like Fanny,
Austen generally is eminently ladylike and proper in expressing her sentiments here. Yet, also like Fanny, she draws our attention to the vexed position in which the exemplary woman finds herself. When Fanny, discussing
Henry's proposal with Edmund, attempts to articulate the truth of a woman's
experience she mirrors her creator, turning a perceptive eye to the ambiguities
of lived experience for women in her society. Austen may try her hand at the

conduct-book novel of her predecessors, but she problematizes its didactic tendencies and reveals, perhaps unwittingly, that this particular literary lineage has come to an end.

NOTES

1. Lionel Trilling, *The Opposing Self: New Essays in Criticism*, 214.

2. Johnson, *Women, Politics, and the Novel*, 119.

3. Austen's "problem novel" has, not surprisingly, received a good deal of critical attention over the last few decades—perhaps because it mitigates against any facile assumption of a coherent political stance on Austen's part. *Mansfield Park* has divided the critics as to whether it espouses conservative or subversive values. Duckworth has argued for its status as the paradigm text in the Austen canon—a Burkean affirmation of "improvement" over "innovation" (*Improvement of the Estate*). His chapter on *Mansfield Park* is the first chapter in a study that is otherwise ordered chronologically. Butler, in *War of Ideas*, similarly argues for Austen's essential conservatism, regarding *Sense and Sensibility* and *Mansfield Park* as exemplary. Said makes a case for the text's complicity in "imperialist expansion," arguing that it is "the most explicit in its ideological and moral affirmations of Austen's novels" (*Culture and Imperialism*, 84). Johnson in *Women, Politics, and the Novel* makes her case for a subversive Austen, arguing that *Mansfield Park* parodies conservative fiction and puts forth a consistent argument about the hollowness of the gentry's moral pretensions. I might point out that to an earlier generation of Austen readers the conservatism of Mansfield Park was taken as a given (and regarded as off-putting). One of the most recent debates over the novel occurs in Whit Stillman's witty film *Metropolitan*, wherein the Fanny-like heroine defends the novel to the hero, who, citing Lionel Trilling, calls it "notoriously bad" (Whit Stillman, writer and director, Westerly Films, 1991).

4. Nina Auerbach, *Romantic Imprisonment: Women and Other Glorified Outcasts*, 22–37.

5. Tanner, *Jane Austen*, 143, 156. See Trilling's comments on Fanny as a Christian heroine (*The Opposing Self*, 129). Andrew Wright defends Fanny on similar grounds in *Jane Austen's Novels: A Study in Structure* (New York: Oxford University Press, 1961), 124.

6. Auerbach, *Romantic Imprisonment*, 25, 27.

7. Gilbert and Gubar in *Madwoman in the Attic* argue that Austen's heroines are punished for their flights of imagination. None, however, end up adhering to a standard of proper female behavior that the notion of punishment implies.

8 .See Jacques Donzelot, *The Policing of Families*, 171.

9. In his biography of Austen, Park Honan implies that the private theatricals the Austen family enjoyed in 1787—wherein they were joined by their glamorous cousin Eliza de Feuillide—may have provided a real-life instance of morally upright young men succumbing to the charms of a worldly young woman: "it is probably true that before the rehearsals of *The Wonder* were over, both James and Henry were in love with [Eliza]. . . . [Henry's] feeling for Eliza might have been predictable, but his behavior was as unusual as James's neglect of clerical decorum. Jane Austen's attitude to theatricals was not that of Fanny Price in *Mansfield Park*, but she did have a chance to see how rehearsals mix with seduction" (*Her Life*, 50).

10. Trilling, *The Opposing Self*, 129.

11. Wollstonecraft, *Vindication*, 111–12.

12. Gilbert and Gubar, *Madwoman in the Attic*, 165.

13. This situation may be akin to the one Austen faced when Harris Wither proposed—a proposal she initially accepted but then turned down. Honan suggests that Austen probably had no idea she was the object of Wither's affections until he actually proposed: "nothing obviously had induced her to view him as a lover before he spoke. Initial attraction, flirtation and a deep, particular concern develop within a social world subject to intense social scrutiny, but neither she nor Cassandra nor anyone else could have seen that happening in her relations with poor Harris" (*Her Life*, 194).

14. Richardson, *Clarissa*, 40.

15. Ibid., 1466.

16. Bradbrook, *Jane Austen and Her Predecessors*, 123.

17. More, *Strictures*, 2:119. Spencer argues that "Jane Austen is deliberately undercutting the complacent belief in the power of love to reform" (*Rise of the Woman Novelist*, 174). Samuel Richardson himself turned the rake-reformed model on its head with Lovelace in *Clarissa*, but his purpose was not to show the receding power of the exemplary woman but the extraordinary fortitude with which she was possessed.

18. Armstrong, *Desire and Domestic Fiction*, 41.

19. Richardson, *Clarissa*, 1495, 1498.

20. Frances Burney, *Cecilia, or Memoirs of an Heiress*, 585.

21. David Spring argues that "the theme of landed decay and crisis has been taken to extremes" in interpretations of *Mansfield Park*: "It needs therefore to be said again that the world of the rural elite was neither going bankrupt in the early nineteenth century nor disintegrating spiritually and socially." Although he acknowledges that Austen might have "read the nature of her society differently from the way we might," he does not give that notion much credit ("Interpreters of Jane Austen's Social World," 66–67). I would, however, argue that even if there were no actual crisis, Austen perceived one, as the novels indicate.

22. In a letter to Cassandra, Austen noted that their brother Henry, who was then reading *Mansfield Park*, "admires H. Crawford: I mean properly as a clever, pleasant man" (Letter 92, *LSC* 377–78).

23. See Q. D. Leavis, "Jane Austen," *A Selection from "Scrutiny,"* 2:1–80.

24. For Copeland it is not adultery but runaway consumption that poses the greatest threat to the values of *Mansfield Park* (*Women Writing about Money*, 102–6). Copeland notes, however, the connection between runaway consumption and sexual transgression: "Consumer desire fuels the moral action of *Mansfield Park*, and sexual desire is inextricably intertwined in the struggle" (102).

25. Tanner, *Adultery in the Novel*, 15.

26. Johnson provides a thorough account of the failures of Sir Thomas: "He quiets but he does not quell lawlessness; his children tremble at the detection, rather than the commission of wrongs" (*Women, Politics, and the Novel*, 97). Unlike Johnson, however, I do not find in Austen an overall rejection of the values for which Sir Thomas stands.

27. Wollstonecraft, *Vindication*, 86. For an extended argument about Wollstonecraft's influence on Austen, see Kirkham, *Feminism and Fiction*. Although I think Kirkham exaggerates Austen's feminist tendencies, the connections she makes are provocative. For a discussion of Austen's and Wollstonecraft's methods of dealing with constructions of femininity, see Poovey, *The Proper Lady*.

28. Wollstonecraft, *Vindication*, 83.

29. More, *Strictures*, 2:163. Guest discusses the affinities between the conservative More and the radical Wollstonecraft in "The Dream of a Common Language." As Guest implies, women who were politically opposed could find a common ground as they considered means for female improvement. Yet, as I suggest, although the means may be the same, the ends are different.

30. Tanner, *Jane Austen*, 173.

31. Johnson regards the incest motif as reinforcing Austen's critique of patriarchy. See also Johanna M. Smith's argument that the motif "demonstrate[s] the constrictions of sister–brother love," in "'My Only Sister Now': Incest in *Mansfield Park*" (13). For an argument on the positive nature of the incestuous marriage see Glenda A. Hudson, "Incestuous Relationships: *Mansfield Park* Revisited."

32. Talcott Parsons, "The Incest Taboo in Relation to Social Structure," 21, 19.

33. Marilyn Sachs notes that Mrs. Francis Brown's 1930 *Susan Price, or Resolution*, a sequel to *Mansfield Park*, features such a cousin marriage. See her essay "The Sequels to Jane Austen's Novels," 375.

34. Tanner, *Jane Austen*, 157. Tanner discusses the main characters in *Mansfield Park* in terms of "guardians," "inheritors," and "interlopers" (142–75).

35. Greene argues that in *Mansfield Park*, "Jane Austen comes as close as she ever does to a thoroughgoing presentation of a Tory democracy" ("Jane Austen and the Peerage," 163). It is a Tory democracy that Fanny envisions.

IVOR MORRIS

Colloquy

When Charlotte waylays Mr Collins in the lane by Lucas Lodge, she is agreeably surprised by the amount of love and eloquence which awaits her there. Everything is settled between them in as short a time as his long speeches will permit. One assumes long-windedness, which is tiresome on any occasion, to be specially inopportune in a proposal of marriage; but Mr Darcy is scarcely brief as he sets about making his own declaration. Elizabeth goes through a variety of emotions while he is speaking, and upon anger supervening tries to 'compose herself to answer him with patience, when he should have done'. He seems to take a fair time.

If there was ever an excuse for prolixity, it belongs to the world of formal manners and ostentatious display which Jane Austen knew. For hers was an age of society's predominance, when man was viewed primarily as a social creature, and individuals were to be assessed in relation to their fellows, and according to widely accepted notions of decorum. Conversation being an acknowledged art, the judging of a person from the quality of his talk was if anything more pertinent then than it is today. And the speeches of someone like Mr Collins may be better appreciated in the light of other characteristic utterances.

Human nature not having changed, there can be no surprise that vanity is the chief motive in much of what is spoken. The choice examples in this

---

From *Jane Austen and the Interplay of Character*, pp. 68–87, 165. © 1987, 1999 by Ivor Morris.

respect are provided by Robert Ferrars, whose conversation is simply a series of harangues upon his own ability, knowledge and good taste. To impress Elinor Dashwood with his excessive fondness for a cottage as a residence, he tells her how he threw on the fire three plans of Bonomi which Lord Cartland had brought to show him, in the act of advising that peer that a cottage was the thing; or how the distraught Lady Elliot implored him to tell her how a dance could be managed in such confined space, failing to discern what was immediately obvious to him. The vaunt direct, in his hands, becomes a vehicle of detraction. Having been diverted beyond measure by the thought of his brother Edward living as an impecunious clergyman in a cramped parsonage, he turns more seriously to causes. 'Poor Edward!—His manners are certainly not the happiest in nature.—But we are not all born, you know, with the same powers—the same address.' Even more felicitous is his accounting to his mother for Edward's gaucherie: '"My dear Madam," I always say to her, "you must make yourself easy. The evil is now irremediable, and it has been entirely your own doing."' She should have sent him to Westminster, with himself, instead of to Mr Pratt's—and Mrs Ferrars, on hearing this, is 'perfectly convinced of her error'.

For such flights as these Mr Collins is too ponderous, and John Thorpe too shallow. The latter's vanity is capable only of the crude boast, for the exercise of which any subject is fitting. His equipage is the most complete of its kind in England, his carriage the neatest, his horse the best goer and himself the best coachman, holding the reins in peculiarly judicious style, and directing the whip with singular discernment and dexterity. His skills in selling horses, racing, shooting and hunting are legendary; and he is able to discompose General Tilney at billiards with what in all modesty he must confess to Catherine was 'one of the cleanest strokes that perhaps ever was made in this world'. Here also, self-praise propagates disparagement. James Morland's gig is a little tittuppy thing without a sound piece of iron about it, the most devilish little ricketty business ever beheld, able to be shaken to pieces at a touch—though in the hands of a good driver like himself capable of being driven to York and back without losing a nail. But the very worst of carriages is, by Jane Austen's invention, revealed as superior to almost any novel in existence. 'Udolpho!' Thorpe cries, upon Catherine's asking him if he has read it. 'Oh, Lord! not I; I never read novels; I have something else to do.' With the exception of *Tom Jones*, Lewis's *Monk* and the writings of Mrs Radcliffe, he affirms, they are 'the stupidest things in creation'.

Less braggart in tone, naturally, and more dexterously applied, are the speeches employed by more intelligent minds in the self-laudatory task. Isabella Thorpe uses to advantage Catherine's surprise at anything that is exorbitant or questionable in her remarks. Scolding a man for not admiring the angelically beautiful yet amazingly insipid Miss Andrews is thus the enactment of a principle of not loving people by halves, and being ready to do anything for a friend; determination to dress so as to be noticed devolves from the most maidenly rule of never minding what men say. And Catherine's report of Henry Tilney's subdued behaviour in his father's presence during her visit to Milsom-street provides opportunity for her friend's grandiloquent, 'How contemptible! Of all things in the world inconstancy is my aversion.' This concern to cut a figure is what we might expect in Isabella—but not in someone like General Tilney. Yet his purpose, and his method, are the same when he advises Catherine that he cannot pay Henry a visit at Woodston on the Tuesday. It is his club-day; his not attending would be taken amiss; 'and it is a rule with me, Miss Morland, never to give offence to any of my neighbours, if a small sacrifice of time and attention can prevent it.'

Less subtle, but just as efficacious at the right moment, is the direct laying of claim to a particular quality. Mrs Norris's declaring herself a woman of few words and professions, as she begins persuading Sir Thomas to take Fanny into his house, is the more awesome in its prognosticating a plethora of both. Lady Catherine's stated belief, at the diminished table at Rosings, that no one feels the loss of friends as much as she does, is as commanding in its way as her advising Elizabeth in the hermitage at Longbourn House that her character has been celebrated for a sincerity and frankness from which, at such a moment, she will not depart. No less impressive is her telling the assembled company in her drawing room that she supposes few people in England have more enjoyment of music or better taste than she, and that she would have been a great proficient if she had ever learnt.

But a greater proficient even than Lady Catherine at establishing a persona by boastful speech is Mrs Elton. She even outdoes her where music is concerned in being dotingly fond of it and absolutely unable to do without it as a necessity of life. It is one of the resources she is blessed with. Another is her unfailing discernment of what is admirable: she has noted Jane Fairfax's shyness and reserve, and likes her the better for it, being 'a great advocate for timidity' and also sure that one does not often meet with it. The quaint, old-fashioned politeness of Mr Woodhouse delights her; she is often disgusted by modern ease—and has, to boot, 'a vast dislike to puppies', and 'quite a horror of upstarts'. Sound as these views are, moreover, she has not rushed into them. Mrs Elton is as concerned to affect a deliberating independence of opinion as she is to publish the opinions themselves. Since she is one of those who always make their own decisions, she tells Mr Weston, she will judge his son as she finds him; and in announcing to the proud father her pleasure at meeting Frank, adds for his further edification, 'You may believe me. I never compliment.' Jane Fairfax's accomplished performance at the pianoforte thus will provoke, not enchantment, but instead the superbly meditative, 'I do not scruple to say that she plays extremely well.'

However, cogitation quickly fades when other means are called for. Emma learns that adding Jane to the Elton household would not in the least inconvenience its mistress, since her greatest danger perhaps in housekeeping lies in doing too much and being careless of expense; finding Jane a situation will likewise present no difficulty to one of her extensive circle of acquaintance. And the ladies whom Mr Weston bustles off to greet on their arrival at the Crown are certain to be Miss Bates and Jane, because the Elton's coachman and horses are so extremely expeditious: 'I believe we drive faster than anybody.' The confidential boast can do much; but should it falter, a vicarious distinction is to be gained through allusion to Maple Grove, the residence of Mrs Elton's brother Mr Suckling, who flies about amazingly to and from London with four horses and his friend Mr Bragge. If Enscombe, the abode of the Churchills, is the retired place Mr Weston says it is, then it must be like Maple Grove, than which nothing can stand more retired from the road; nor can it be the size of the room at Hartfield which impresses her so much upon her first visit, but its astonishing likeness to the Maple Grove morning room. However, any remaining pretence of discreetness or scruple is at an end when the moment comes for adopting the tones of authority—at a point, for example, where Mrs Weston can be told it will no longer be necessary for her carriage to convey Jane and her aunt, or Emma is silenced with the smiling assurance that only Surrey has ever been called the garden of England; or with the abruptness of an, 'Oh no; the meeting is certainly today'; or with the claim of equality coolly implied in a, 'My dear Miss Woodhouse, a vast deal may be done by those who dare to act. You and I need not be afraid.'

Mrs Elton is supreme through the whole gamut of self-magnification, including the use of the sententious to cover a weakness or inconsistency, or camouflage a purpose. Her never playing despite her passion for music is the result of a married woman having many things to demand her attention; and the natural taste for simplicity which gives her 'quite a horror of finery' springs into existence upon the alarming thought that her dress may be too plain and require a trimming. But she has a close rival in Isabella Thorpe. What could be more affecting than this young lady's plaint—which she makes at finding Catherine Morland determined to keep her appointment with the Tilneys—upon the painfulness of being slighted for strangers when one's own affections are beyond the power of any thing to change? Or her sentiment while Mr Morland's consent to her engagement to James, and his financial assistance, is awaited: 'Had I command of millions, were I mistress of the whole world, your brother would be my only choice'? Mrs Norris, too, must here not be overlooked. Her professions, while more homely, have charming appositeness. To shame Sir Thomas Bertram as he hesitates over bringing Fanny into his household, she discovers that, though far from faultless, she would rather deny herself life's necessities than do an ungenerous thing. Upon the plan being announced later that she should take Fanny at the White house, she becomes a poor, desolate, frail, low-spirited widow; and Lady Bertram's surprise at her resignation to living quite alone cannot move someone who, by further rapid transformation, is fit for nothing but solitude. This pitiable being is just able to live within her income, though she would dearly like to lay a little by the end of the year; but her sister's (for her) energetic, 'I dare say you will. You always do, don't you?' brings the pained and saintly remonstrance, 'My object, Lady Bertram, is to be of use to those that come after me.' *De mortuis nil nisi bonum.*

* * *

However much or little Mr Collins may be seen to indulge in these self-glorifying arts and wiles, he will in any case clearly be outdone by other adepts. There is, however, a class of conversation in which he is able to take but small, if any, part, because of the lack of a questioning intelligence—or, as some would doubtless have it, of intelligence itself. This is the variety of lively talk among acquaintances which Mr Bingley's circle would approvingly term an 'argument', and which, if opinion threatened to be too strongly urged, might develop into the kind of 'dispute' for which he had no inclination. Of this nature are the many interesting and amusing discussions which have endeared the novels through their analysis of motives and their commentary on human ways and pleasures—like that in which Elinor Dashwood confesses the many times she has mistaken people's characters by incautiously accepting what is said by others or themselves. These words, seized upon by Marianne as disproving her sister's tenet of subservience to society's judgments, are shown instead to clarify a position upon which the novel itself is founded: 'No, Marianne, never. My doctrine has never aimed at subjection of the understanding. All I have ever attempted to influence has been the behaviour.' In her quiet way Elinor is as redoubtable as Eliza Bennet. Edward Ferrars's airy announcement next morning after his walk to the village that he knows nothing of the picturesque brings upon him her charge of having reacted against the affectations of would-be connoisseurs by a personal affectation of indifference. He is rescued by Marianne's deploring the artistic jargon which has become so common; but he unrepentantly holds his own, and confounds his deliverer, by stating a simple dislike of 'crooked, twisted, blasted trees', ruined cottages, flourishing weeds and rampant banditti—to Elinor's great amusement.

This is his liveliest moment; and one is reminded by it of the somewhat warmer interchange at Netherfield Park when Bingley modestly seeks to account for his bad handwriting by saying his ideas flow so rapidly that he has not time to express them. Elizabeth's sardonic riposte that his humility must disarm reproof brings into deployment the heavy artillery of Darcy's acumen: nothing is more deceitful, he declares, than that appearance of humility, which is often mere carelessness of opinion, and sometimes the indirect boast—which Bingley's evident pride in his defects of writing shows to be in question. The marshalling of forces proceeds with the inclusion of Bingley's professed likelihood, if he ever quitted Netherfield, of being away within five minutes, and his readiness in principle to jump off his horse the instant a friend requested that he stay another week. Hostilities commence in earnest with a sharp skirmish between Elizabeth and Darcy on whether it is admirable or culpable to yield easily to persuasion. The master of the house is at pains to put a quick stop to the impending battle royal, and does so by comically insisting that the hypothetical friend's size and disposition be taken into account.

Just as much as these sprightly and diverting colloquies, one enjoys the gentler reasonings occasioned by the decencies of friendship and family life. 'That is the happiest conversation,' says Dr Johnson, 'where there is no competition, no vanity, but a calm quiet interchange of sentiments.'[1] Of this kind is the discussion that follows Jane Bennet's engagement to Bingley, when, on Jane's happiness bursting forth in wishes for her sister, Elizabeth replies with a profundity which takes the reader beyond the confines of the novel, 'Till I have your disposition, your goodness, I can never have your happiness'—and then brings him back with her plea to be allowed to shift for herself until another Mr Collins should come along. Or one recalls Mr Knightley and Mrs Weston in conference upon their shared concern for Emma, and anxiously wondering what will happen to her; or the youthful Catherine on the top of Beechen Cliff, so full of love for Henry Tilney and of knowledge, newly acquired in conversing with him, of foregrounds, second distances, sidescreens and perspectives, as voluntarily to reject the whole city of Bath as unworthy to make part of a landscape.

A variety of observation and sentiment arises with the communion of minds. Some critics are little impressed with Fanny Price's enthusiasms; but we would not be without her regret at the absence of anything awful in the chapel at Sotherton, and the discontinuance of the practice of regular prayers in a great house. Memorable, too, is her pleasure when, finding Edmund continuing at the window with her, she speaks her feelings in gazing with him at the stars: 'Here's harmony! Here's repose! Here's what may leave all painting and all music behind, and what poetry can only attempt to describe.' The same emotion, and proximity to a loved one, moves Henry Crawford to discourse on that something in the eloquence of the pulpit which is entitled to the highest respect. And it is the dawning of tenderness for both Louisa and Henrietta Musgrove that inspires Captain Wentworth to record, in rather different style displaying markedly less of reverence, the Admiralty's entertaining themselves now and then with sending a few hundred men to sea in an unseaworthy ship, and his own refined gallantry toward women which is characterised by a refusal to have them aboard.

* * *

Romantic attachment is the cause, naturally enough, of a great deal of conversation in the novels, the course of true love leading from instances of positive acrimony to as near the endearments of the betrothed as Jane Austen cares to take us. Some of the most entertaining, as well as informative, speeches come in the series of embroilments which breaks out as Mary Crawford, walking with Edmund and Fanny, pictures the Mrs Eleanors and Mrs Bridgets of former days starched up in seeming piety in Sotherton's chapel, their thoughts certainly not occupied with the chaplain who would have been inferior even to the parsons of the present. Her comment provokes discussion as to whether private prayer, being easier, is preferable to prayer in public. Edmund's dictum that a mind which will not struggle against itself under one set of circumstances is unlikely to prevail in others goes for the moment unchallenged; but he is soon to be assailed by the scorn for parsonical motive implied in Mary's sudden, 'There is a very good living kept for you, I understand, hereabouts.' He admits inevitable bias through the knowledge that provision has been made for him, but argues that this is no pointer to insincerity in a profession offering small worldly advantage. For his pains he is accused of preferring an income ready-made to the trouble of working for one, and of joining a body of men universally looked down upon. Debate of Mary's thesis that 'where an opinion is general, it is usually correct' is cut short by Fanny's exclaiming at the kindness William has met with from the chaplain of the *Antwerp*, but the conflict is to be renewed later; for it not only arises out of strong mutual feelings of attraction, but is charged with romantic meaning for the contenders.

It is only to be expected, amongst cultured and intelligent beings living beneath the precise regulations which their society decreed for the conduct of the sexes, that a diplomacy as to romance will be one of the arts of conversation. Someone as apparently staid as Edmund proves he can use it in this purpose as ably as the flirtatious Henry Crawford himself. As talk at the Parsonage comes round to matters of economy, Mary Crawford makes her assertion that a large income is the best recipe for happiness she has ever heard of, and goes on to declare her contempt for honest poverty and preference for honest wealth and distinction. Edmund answers her, in serious tone, that there are distinctions he desires and would be miserable at not attaining, but that they are of a different character. Fanny sees with a pang some reflection on Miss Crawford's side of his 'look of consciousness as he spoke'; but

Mary's response does not come until the dinner party Dr Grant gives the Bertrams, when discussion during the game of Speculation centres upon possible improvements to Thornton Lacey. Edmund rejects Henry's plans, saying he intends to make the house comfortable and attractive without any heavy expense: 'that must suffice me; and I hope may suffice all who care about me.' The sentiment, and the tone of voice and half-look with which it is uttered, move Mary hastily to secure William Price's knave at an exorbitant rate, and to exclaim, 'There, I will stake my last like a woman of spirit. No cold prudence for me.' The game resumes, the resolve conveyed in her words lost on all but Edmund and Fanny.

Henry Crawford's very considerable powers are enlivened with humour. In the drawing room at Mansfield Park, where he has been reading Shakespeare aloud, he catches at the suggestion Lady Bertram makes in complimenting him that he should fit up a theatre at his house in Norfolk:

> 'Do you, Ma'am?' cried he with quickness. 'No, no, that will never be. Your Ladyship is quite mistaken. No theatre at Everingham! Oh! no.'—And he looked at Fanny with an expressive smile, which evidently meant, 'that lady will never allow a theatre at Everingham.'

Edmund sees both what is meant and Fanny's determination not to see it, and decides that 'such a ready comprehension of a hint' is favourable to Henry's hopes. With far less aplomb does Mr Elton try the same thing, as Emma tells how Isabella's reluctant approval of her portrait of John Knightley caused her to make the resolution against portraiture which she will now break on Harriet's account, there being 'no husbands and wives in the case at present'. Elton seizes upon the phrase with an 'Exactly so—no husbands and wives', and with a consciousness so interesting that Emma begins to consider whether she had not better leave him and Harriet together at once.

There is here none of the finesse observable on that hot summer day at Sotherton Court when Henry Crawford pays his addresses to the bespoken Maria Bertram with circuitous eloquence. He has made an admirable preface in the chapel by stating, in the lady's hearing, a dislike of seeing Miss Bertram so near the altar—and, upon her inquiring as soon as she has regained composure if he will give her away, a conviction that he should do so very awkwardly. Before the locked iron gate in the pleasure grounds, having contrived to get Mr Rushworth sent off to find the key, he tells her that he thinks he will never see Sotherton with as much pleasure as he does now; and on being assured, after a moment's embarrassment on the lady's part, that a man of the world will see it improved, as others do, he claims feelings too little evanescent, and a memory rather too ungovernable for him to merit the category.

Soon, his reference to the smiling prospect before her eyes draws from Maria a confession of the 'feeling of restraint and hardship' the gate and the ha-ha cause; and Crawford's judicious reminder of Mr Rushworth's 'authority and protection', coupled with the assertion that she can get out easily with his own assistance if this is not prohibited, leads her to commitment with the words, 'Prohibited! nonsense! I certainly can get out that way, and I will.' Though the nature of the subject, perfectly understood by Fanny, arouses a flushed protest from her and disapproval in ourselves, the parley's sophistication, and indeed delicacy, cannot fail to impress.

A Louisa Musgrove is not to be compared with a Maria Bertram; but she must be to some extent aware, as she strolls with Captain Wentworth at Winthrop, that in discussing herself and her sentiments with a man to whom she is becoming increasingly attached, she is making an appeal to his heart: for this, in Jane Austen's terms, is an 'interesting' conversation that by its nature can but hint at romance. Yet Louisa is not really acting by design when she takes up Captain Wentworth's jest at his sister's indifference to being overturned by Admiral Croft's gigmanship, and professes eagerly a like bruising devotion to the man she should love. She speaks here with naturalness and on impulse; one must wonder, though, whether there might not be something more purposive in her condemning Henrietta's readiness to yield to Mary's haughty persuasions and give up her visit to Winthrop, and to Charles Hayter. Certainly what she has to say brings Wentworth's approval of the decision and firmness of character it denotes—such warmth of congratulation and advice, indeed, as can leave the attendant Anne Elliot in no doubt as to what Louisa must be feeling. The reappearance of Henrietta with the happy Charles Hayter is not the only thing that marks out Louisa for Captain Wentworth from then onwards.

It is from the heart—though it be a troubled heart—that Wentworth has spoken: true feeling must find expression. But, at certain times and in certain places, love cannot directly declare itself, and is compelled to suggest and insinuate. Even when Wentworth, sure now of his wishes, is standing beside Anne Elliot in the freedom which the Octagon Room's space and bustle of public thoroughfare affords, he can only glance at his own thoughts by speaking of his surprise that Captain Benwick should turn to someone like Louisa after having loved 'a very superior creature' like Fanny Harville. 'A man does not recover from such a devotion of the heart to such a woman!' he exclaims. '—He ought not—he does not.' Anne cannot speak; and he, uncertain as to her attitude and affections, can say no more—but he has said much. No less meaningful, or fraught with emotion, are the few words Anne exchanges later on with Mrs Musgrove at the White Hart on the subject of putting off the play till Tuesday so that they can all attend the party Sir Walter and Elizabeth are giving in Camden-place. She states her small inclination for the party and readiness to go to the theatre in Mrs Musgrove's company, while acknowledging the difficulty they would find in the proceeding. The remark is inconsequential in itself—'but she trembled when it was done, conscious that her words were listened to, and daring not even to try to observe their effect.' The effect is immediate: Captain Wentworth is at her side, speaking with new decision, and only Henrietta's hurrying in to interrupt the group can prevent his avowal.

In the end it is Anne who declares her love, through a masterly hinting during the course of conversation in the same apartment, where she has arrived to find Mrs Musgrove talking to Mrs Croft, and Captain Harville to Captain Wentworth, and Mary and Henrietta expected to join the party at any moment. She can only sit, outwardly composed but plunged in agitation, listening to the talk of others until she is herself beckoned into conversation by Captain Harville as he takes from its parcel the miniature of Captain Benwick, first drawn for his sister, and now destined for Louisa Musgrove. The trembling words, 'Poor Fanny! she would not have forgotten him so soon!' are the beginning of a discussion—of an 'argument'—upon love and devotion in men and women which takes increasing significance from the well-defined social situation—and the motionless figure of Captain Wentworth as he sits poised, pen in hand, striving to catch sounds which Anne thinks for a moment might not be reaching him. She has started smilingly with an assured, 'We certainly do not forget you, so soon as you forget us,' justifying it by a kindly contrasting of the confined lives of women with the exertions which men face in their careers; soon she and Harville are engaged in the deepest analysis of human feelings, each claiming for their sex strength and endurance in affection upon the analogy of the bodily frames of men and women, and by the verdict of literature, until the impossibility of proof confronts them. It is when Harville tries to describe the love of a sailor for his wife and family ashore—speaking 'only of such men as have hearts!' as he presses his own with emotion—that Anne is driven by the logic of debate and of her love for Wentworth to concede the point and to make, while composure lasts, an assertion of love undying:

> 'Oh!' cried Anne eagerly, 'I hope I do justice to all that is felt by you, and those who resemble you. God forbid that I should undervalue the warm and faithful feelings of any of my fellow-creatures. I should deserve utter contempt if I dared to suppose that true attachment and constancy were known only by woman. No, I believe you capable of every thing great and good in your married lives. I believe you equal to every important exertion, and to every domestic forbearance, so long as—if I may be allowed the expression, so long as you have an object. I mean, while the woman

you love lives, and lives for you. All the privilege I claim for my own sex (it is not a very enviable one, you need not covet it) is that of loving longest, when existence or when hope is gone.'

The speeches of Juliet herself are not more frank, tender or affecting than this of Anne Elliot, considered in its setting: for, with proper respect to decorum, she must woo her man through the screen of social circumstance by the skills of eloquence and simplicity of truth, without directing an overt word to him.

* * *

The ability to hint with delicacy at romantic attachment is not to be expected in Mr Collins. He has, one would think, neither the mental nor the emotional accomplishment for nurturing the art—though he does possess a command of words which might otherwise have stood him in good stead. What he manages to intimate to Charlotte Lucas at the dinner party the Bennets give her family to make her almost certain by the time it breaks up that her plan will succeed, we shall unfortunately never know. But there can, surely, be little room for hinting in association with so massive a self-regard. Mr Collins's wish, upon his arrival at Longbourn, to avoid appearing forward and precipitate on the subject of making amends to his fair cousins takes the alarming form of an assurance to the young ladies that he comes prepared to admire them. 'At present I will not say more,' he continues with thunderous caution, 'but perhaps when we are better acquainted—' A fortunate summons to dinner saves the family from the full revelation of his discretionary powers.

What Mr Collins in fact excels at is the address indiscreet and confessional. This distinction of being able to make common property of his inmost thoughts he shares with Miss Bates; but whereas actual ideas have to be searched for in her speeches amidst the welter of irrelevant material, Mr Collins's thinking is presented to his hearers in a manner engagingly pointed and precise. Thus when Mr Bennet receives an olive branch through the post, or when his daughter is favoured by a proposal of marriage, neither is left to guess at the motive. A wealth of personal information is laid at Elizabeth's feet: she is not only told of her suitor's having come with the intention of selecting a wife, and of his reasons for wishing to marry—among them being the expectation that it will add greatly to his happiness—but is made familiar with the exact terms and tones of Lady Catherine's prompting: 'Chuse properly, chuse a gentlewoman for *my* sake; and for your own, let her be an active, useful sort of person, not brought up high, but able to make a small income go a good way.' That what is at work here is not some rare genus of an otherwise exemplary candour, but an insensibility almost as rare, is clear from Mr Collins's ascribing Elizabeth's refusal, at the end of the interview, to her wish of increasing his love by suspense, 'according to the usual practice of elegant females'. She and her father have been under no illusion from the moment of their visitor's grave disclosure of his method of composing and delivering compliments to ladies.

Other people's feelings do not enter into Mr Collins's calculations—and scarcely into his consciousness. His near-perfect self-involvement is apparent not only when he holds the centre of the stage, but even in his exits and his entrances. It is announced in his letter telling Mr Bennet that the week's visit he proposes therein can be made 'without any inconvenience' since his patroness has no objection to his occasional absence from Hunsford. He enlivens his departure by accepting as renewed invitation Mrs Bennet's polite expression of happiness in seeing him at some future time, and sending in his letter of thanks the comforting explanation that he has done so merely with the view of enjoying the company of Charlotte Lucas. Aware of what she is dealing with, Elizabeth has come near to discouraging Mr Collins's amatory pursuit by suggesting that Lady Catherine will be displeased at her lack of qualification for the honour. Mrs Bennet, by ignorance, attains greater success in her outburst at her daughter's perversity. 'Pardon me for interrupting you, Madam,' the suitor cries, 'but if she is really headstrong and foolish, I know not whether she would altogether be a very desirable wife to a man in my situation, who naturally looks for happiness in the marriage state.' It is thus to be foreseen that in welcoming Elizabeth to Hunsford Mr Collins should speak to her as if wishing to make her feel what she has lost in refusing him; or that he should presume, in writing to Mr Bennet after Lydia's elopement, 'to reflect with augmented satisfaction on a certain event of last November, for had it been otherwise, I must have been involved in all your sorrow and disgrace.' Lack of discretion in this degree must be set down as pure folly. There is something curiously engaging, though, in the trust it implies in the value of every notion, and in the almost regal freedom through which these firstlings of the brain are scattered for others' edification.

If his achievements in self-revelation are set on one side, Mr Collins's speeches are seen to be limited in their range and uninspired in their quality when viewed beside typical modes of utterance in the novels. They show him to be, in sophistication, intelligence and moral quality, far removed from the best of the characters, though by no means so bad as the worst. Whatever social blunders he may commit, a complaisant manner ensures that many of the excesses of arrogance to be found in the pronouncements of others are avoided. His assumption of excellence, oddly enough, also helps to chasten his remarks. The crude boast is absent. If he is inclined to talk without ceasing of his house and garden at Hunsford, or to invite Elizabeth to admire everything within them, it is with a sense of wonder at his fortunate lot and an evident wish that such contentment might be spread abroad. There is no seeking for status in one whose dearest aspirations seem to be satisfied. He may name Rosings as frequently as Mrs Elton calls to aid Maple Grove, but his comparisons, unlike hers, are not odious: when he declares upon entering Mrs Philips's house that he might almost have supposed himself in Lady Catherine's small summer breakfast parlour, his aim is chiefly to flatter his hostess. And when that good lady learns that the chimneypiece alone in one of the drawing rooms at Rosings had cost eight hundred pounds, she feels the full force of the compliment, 'and would hardly have resented a comparison with the housekeeper's room.'

Similarly, there is in Mr Collins no such pressing desire to lay claim to perfections as can motivate persons as different as General Tilney and Isabella Thorpe. He does, it is true, assert his skill in the art of compliment—but the subject is mentioned in passing and pursued only through Mr Bennet's persistent questioning. Much the same applies to his boasting himself better qualified by education and habitual study to decide upon social niceties than his cousin Elizabeth: the claim only comes after she has implied the contrary in trying to stop him introducing himself to Mr Darcy. That he can be deficient in any way does not admit of question; his speeches are almost quite free of protestations designed to hide a weakness. The exceptions are those assurances of bearing Lydia no ill-will for interrupting his reading of Fordyce's Sermons, or of not resenting the behaviour of Elizabeth in turning down his proposal, or of not in the least regarding his losses at whist—all which, made in a manner or with a tone of voice indicating the contrary, are Mr Collins's way of reining in those impulses that might cause him to swerve from the path of rectitude.

* * *

But there is a tendency to be found in Mr Collins's statements which has no place in those of most of the other characters: a touch, not of steel, certainly, but of a stringency which entices him towards the captious. The truth, which he records with a certain sternness, that young ladies are little interested in books of a serious stamp despite there being nothing so advantageous to them as instruction, is made the means of mild rebuke. So is the more painful fact of Elizabeth's indifference to him, in leading him to reflect with some contentment upon unattained benefits found to be illusory. These less than civil reflections Mr Collins presents with his usual guileless candour, but they are followed by others more forcefully frank; and deepening acquaintance reveals in him a censoriousness which is the more trenchant (and diverting) in being divorced from discretion.

Thus, in condoling by letter with his cousin upon the grievous affliction of Lydia's elopement, he comments on the reason there is to think that
the girl's licentious conduct 'has proceeded from a faulty degree of indulgence'—adding, however, for the consolation of Mr Bennet and his wife, that
Lydia's own disposition must be naturally bad, as she could not otherwise be
guilty of such an enormity at so early an age. He ends by coupling pity for
the distressed parents with the certainty that this false step in one daughter
'will be injurious to the fortunes of all the others, for who, as lady Catherine
herself condescendingly says, will connect themselves to such a family'. This
is as round as need be, but the masterstroke of reprobation in the next letter
is reserved for Lydia's father: it is nothing less than a set-down, to which Mr
Bennet's own is a retort.

> 'I must not, however, neglect the duties of my station, or refrain
> from declaring my amazement, at hearing that you received the
> young couple into your house as soon as they were married. It was
> an encouragement of vice; and had I been the rector of Longbourn,
> I should very strenuously have opposed it.'

This indignation is of the righteous kind. The discarding of meekness in
favour of the posture militant is brought about in Mr Collins by what he feels
to be pastoral obligation. It was this which, if he is to be believed, first sent
him on his way to the Bennets to spread the blessing of peace, and, indeed,
which forms the basis of his estimate of himself. As he assures the perplexed
Elizabeth, he considers the clerical office 'as equal in point of dignity with
the highest rank in the kingdom—provided that a proper humility of behaviour is at the same time maintained'. The only vaunt that he is prepared to
make—one bemusing in its effect—is about his status as a clergyman.

The two most prominent aspects of his personality are united in the
address which, to Elizabeth's embarrassment and her father's delight, Mr
Collins declaims in a loud voice to the entire company in the ballroom at
Netherfield after Mr Darcy has rebuffed his attempt to introduce himself.
It is a masterpiece of presumptuous lowliness. Choosing the moment after
Mary's debacle at the pianoforte when others are being asked for a musical
contribution, he begins in his patroness's mode by declaring that an air would
certainly be forthcoming from him if he were so fortunate as to be able to
sing. This light introduction makes way for the august theme of a clergyman's
manifold responsibilities, the dominant motif of obtaining an advantageous
agreement on tithes ushering in the lesser refrains of sermon-writing, parish preoccupations, and improvements to the parsonage. But the profounder
statement is yet to come. The necessity of conciliatory manners towards every
body, especially those to whom the cleric owes preferment, is set forth with a

commanding resonance which makes all the more affecting the diminuendo of the concluding passage: 'I cannot acquit him of that duty; nor could I think well of the man who should omit an occasion of testifying his respect towards any body connected with the family.' The performer's bow brings by way of applause stares, smiles, and Mrs Bennet's commendations on the sensibleness of the remarks and the cleverness of the speaker.

Her judgment in the latter comment might be defended. Mr Collins has replied to Darcy's rudeness by an admirably impersonal allusion to his clerical responsibilities. It is thus unexceptionable in being perfectly polite; but as a retort and a self-vindication it is also emphatic. For not only does it justify his earlier conduct, but it infers a claim to social recognition and to station which, though of a kind subordinate to Darcy's own, ought nevertheless to command his respect.

Is the claim spurious? Darcy reacts to Mr Collins's social intrusion as one imagines Sir Walter Elliot would have responded to any familiarity from Mr Wentworth, the curate of Monkford. The term gentleman is hardly to be applied to such persons: Edmund Bertram's intention to make one of their number induces in Mary Crawford the near-horror implicit in her assertion, 'A clergyman is nothing.' Whatever he may urge on behalf of those who have charge of all that is of first importance to both the individual and society, temporally and eternally, Edmund cannot alter Mary's conviction that what makes men clergymen is a love of ease, an absence of ambition, and a deplorable manner. In her confidence that she is speaking the general opinion she is on firm ground. Only the rare mortal in the society presented in Jane Austen's novels appreciates the dignity of the clerical calling and function. Edmund's father is thus distinguished. When Henry Crawford makes known his wish to become the tenant of Thornton Lacey, on the assumption that Edmund will as a matter of course be an absentee parson, he receives a crushing rejoinder. Sir Thomas will be 'deeply mortified' if his son does not live in his own parish. Human nature, he tells Crawford, needs, more than weekly sermons, the friendship of the pastor: if he does not live amongst his people, 'he does very little either for their good or his own.' And he concludes with a deliberating courtesy that is eloquent of the clergyman's true status: 'Thornton Lacey is the only house in the neighbourhood in which I should *not* be happy to wait on Mr Crawford as occupier.'

Much as Mr Collins might be despised in the minds of his hearers at Netherfield, he is not at fault in affirming the parson's right to consideration. From many points of view the stand he takes is as defensible as that of Elizabeth Bennet in vindicating the right of younger daughters not to be socially handicapped by the custom of coming out. Perhaps like her own, though, his choice of time and place is not beyond criticism.

There is thus something original, and even vivacious, in the readiness which he reveals by word and action to break with the conventions—though always, be it understood, where his own interests are involved. It is not solely in escaping out of Longbourn House with admirable slyness in order to hasten to Lucas Lodge and there throw himself at Charlotte's feet that the 'fire and independence of his character' is apparent. But his speeches as a whole demonstrate a quality which must be creditable, and may be deemed admirable, in any human being, even if it will not normally lead to advancement and fortune. In Mr Collins's statements, be they civil or ceremonious, trivial or platitudinous, laughably presumptuous or stupidly contentious, there is almost a complete absence of pretence. Amidst his many shortcomings he is sincere, and, happily, nearly always transparently so. There is an element of the paradisal in its scarcely ever occurring to him that a covering is requisite for the nakedness of his thoughts. In this not insignificant respect Mr Collins appears as an innocent—though, doubtless, he is one of those who will not 'scape the thunderbolt of the reader's derision.

Note

1. J. Boswell, *Life of Johnson*, 3rd edn (ed. J.D. Fleeman), London, Oxford University Press, 1970, p. 623: Friday 14 April 1775.

PAULA BYRNE

Emma

The *Lovers' Vows* debacle reveals that for Jane Austen acting is not so much an aberration as an inevitability. The great lesson she took from the drama, that social life requires a strong element of role-playing, is also one of the guiding principles of her next novel. In addition, *Emma* returns to the territory of *Pride and Prejudice*: the interplay of different social classes and the quest to discover a language truthful to emotional experience.

The depiction in *Pride and Prejudice* of a fine lady who is also an unregenerate snob is brilliantly reworked in *Emma*. This time, however, rather than the heroine being the victim of the cruelty and injustice of social snobbery, she is its perpetrator. Like Lady Catherine de Bourgh, Emma is concerned with preserving 'the distinctions of rank', and, in spite of the novel's deep engagement with the concept of social mobility, she is initially resistant to social change, unless upon her own terms.

The most traditional method of movement between the classes was through marriage and in *Emma* there are a number of intermarriages. The novel begins with the marriage between a former governess, Miss Taylor, and a highly respected, albeit self-made, gentleman, Mr Weston.[1] This union finds its correlation towards the close of the novel with the marriage between a woman on the brink of becoming a governess and a wealthy gentleman, who is the son of Mr Weston. Furthermore, the novel ends with the promise

From *Jane Austen and the Theatre*, pp. 211–224, 256–258. © 2002 by Paula Byrne.

189

of future marriages (and matchmaking) between the daughter of the Westons and the offspring of the most genteel characters, the Knightleys.[2]

The assimilation of the social classes through marriage was one of the great themes of the drama, and alliances between 'blood' and 'money', or 'old' money and 'new', were the focuses of many successful comedies of the period.[3] In the novel tradition, Richardson's *Pamela* was the prime exemplar of an unlikely but successful union between a lowly servant girl and her master. In *Emma*, the theme of intermarriage comes full circle when Emma is faced with what she thinks is the probability, not merely the possibility, of a union between illegitimate Harriet and the well-born Mr Knightley: 'Mr Knightley and Harriet Smith!—Such an elevation on her side! Such a debasement on his! . . . Could it be?—No; it was impossible. And yet it was far, very far, from impossible' (*E*, p. 413). When Emma finally accepts that Harriet could well be 'the chosen, the first, the dearest, the friend, the wife to whom he looked for all the best blessings of existence', her wretchedness is increased by the reflection that 'it had been all her own work' (*E*, pp. 422–23).

Whilst Harriet Smith is no Pamela or Evelina, resembling more the simple country girl of David Garrick's popular comedy, she does possess the capacity for improvement. Eventually, Mr Knightley is forced to reconsider his opinion of her character, and admit her to be Mr Elton's equal: 'An unpretending, single-minded, artless girl—infinitely to be preferred by any man of sense and taste to such a woman as Mrs Elton' (*E*, p. 331).

Austen's comedy of errors between Emma, Elton and Harriet in the first volume of the novel is, however, dependent on the finely nuanced renderings of rank and station so beloved of eighteenth-century comedy. The comic misunderstandings between the three characters are made possible by their tenuous grasp of social realities. Harriet believes (or is made to believe) that she is worthy of Mr Elton, whilst he, in turn, believes that he is worthy of Emma. Emma's concurrence in the misunderstandings is in no small part due to the fact that she is unable to conceive that Mr Elton could aspire to her own lofty level.

The misunderstandings within the Emma/Harriet/Elton love triangle are very much in the tradition of stage comedy. In Hannah Cowley's *The Runaway* a similar set of comic misunderstandings (known in the period as equivoques) occur between a father and son. The son (George Hargrave) mistakenly believes that the elderly Lady Dinah is intended for his father, and duly shows his happiness and approval of the match as he unwittingly courts the lady. The situation allows for many opportunities for comic misunderstandings until the son is suitably enlightened and horrified to learn that he, not his father, is the true object of desire. Likewise, Emma woos on behalf of Harriet until the comic epiphany of Mr Elton's proposal. Though aware of his drunken state, Emma foolishly believes that she can restrain his advances by talking of the weather, and is astonished to find her efforts repulsed: 'It really was so. Without scruple—without apology—without much apparent diffidence, Mr Elton, the lover of Harriet, was professing himself *her* lover' (*E*, p. 129).

In *Pride and Prejudice*, Austen had displayed the range of her comic skills in the great proposal scene between Elizabeth Bennet and Mr Collins, and in *Emma* she reworks the idea to depict the discrepancy between male and female behaviour in the courtship process. The high comedy of Elton's proposal is greatly enhanced by Emma's unknowing compliance in the mistake, yet the scene is also charged with the archetypal male arrogance which little expects anything but grateful acceptance from the female:

> 'I have thought only of you. I protest against having paid the smallest attention to any one else. Every thing that I have said or done, for many weeks past, has been with the sole view of marking my adoration of yourself. You cannot really, seriously, doubt it. No!—(in an accent meant to be insinuating)—I am sure you have seen and understood me.' (*E* p. 131)

As with that other obtuse clergyman, Mr Collins, Elton interprets the lady's stunned silence as consent: 'allow me to interpret this interesting silence. It confesses that you have long understood me' (*E*, p. 131). Emma's incredulity at finding herself the object of Elton's desire is paralleled with his disdain at the discovery that the illegitimate Harriet is intended for himself. 'I think seriously of Miss Smith! . . . no doubt, there are men who might not object to—Every body has their level' (*E*, pp. 131–32).

The narrative of *Emma* moves with great speed and skill between external events and the inner consciousness of the heroine. Dramatic dialogue is thus often followed by 'free indirect discourse' in which the third-person narratorial voice follows the unfolding of Emma's thoughts.[4] The carriage scene is mainly rendered in dialogue, but it is immediately followed by Emma's ruminations on Elton. She quickly realises that 'there had been no real affection either in his language or manners', though 'sighs and fine words had been given in abundance' (*E*, p. 135). Furthermore, she understands that he is a social climber who 'only wanted to aggrandize and enrich himself' (*E*, p. 135). The great comic paradox is that Emma is angry with Elton for looking down on Harriet, but is equally furious that he looks up to her level: 'that he should suppose himself her equal in connection or mind!—look down upon her friend, so well understanding the gradations of rank below him, and be so blind to what rose above' (*E*, p. 136). Having shown the worst effects of social snobbery in Elton's dismissal of Harriet, the authorial irony re-establishes its attack on Emma, whose snobbishness has yet to be purged: 'He must know that the Woodhouses had been settled for several generations at Hartfield, the younger branch of a very ancient family—and that the Eltons were no-body' (*E*, p. 136).

Eighteenth-century drama's obsession with the comic interplay of rank and manners depended upon discrepancies between outward appearance and inner reality. Plays such as *She Stoops to Conquer*, *The Heir at Law*, *The Belle's Stratagem* and *The Clandestine Marriage* all exploited the comic possibilities of mistaken identity and social displacement. Emma's lack of judgement is most apparent in her opinions of Mr Elton and Robert Martin. Her conviction that the handsome and gallant Mr Elton is a 'model' of good manners is as wrong-headed as her observation of Robert Martin's 'clownish' manners. Her comments are restricted to Martin's lack of outward lack of polish, his 'un-modulated voice', and she duly condemns him as 'a completely gross, vulgar farmer—inattentive to appearances, and thinking of nothing but profit and loss' (*E*, p. 33). Emma's absurd remark that Robert Martin is 'not Harriet's equal' is angrily quashed by Mr Knightley: 'No, he is not her equal indeed, for he is as much her superior in sense as in situation' (*E*, p. 61).

The intricacies of social class are clearly understood by Robert Martin, who fears that Harriet is now 'considered (especially since *your* making so much of her) as in a line of society above him' (*E*, p. 59). Both Robert Martin and Mr Knightley know that Emma is to blame for her friend's recent social elevation. Yet again, there are distinctions made between different social lev-els. Emma thinks Robert Martin is unworthy of Harriet, and Mr Knightley considers Harriet unworthy of Robert Martin: 'my only scruple in advising the match was on his account, as being beneath his deserts, and a bad connex-ion for him' (*E*, p. 61). Emma, sounding dangerously like Lady Catherine de Bourgh, stoutly refuses to concede: 'The sphere in which she moves is much above his.—It would be a degradation' (*E*, p. 62).

Whilst Emma initially thinks of compatibility in terms of rank and station, Mr Knightley puts equal emphasis on compatibility of mind and disposition: 'A degradation to illegitimacy and ignorance, to be married to a respectable, intelligent gentleman-farmer'. Knightley approves of Robert Martin for being all that is 'open' and 'straightforward': 'Robert Martin's man-ners have sense, sincerity and good humour to recommend them; and his mind has more true gentility than Harriet Smith could understand' (*E*, p. 65). Mr Knightley perceives that Harriet's obscure origins are the insuper-able social barrier to her making a good marriage (and Mr Elton's comments confirm this truth). Nevertheless, Emma is caught up in the romantic idea that the natural child is of noble birth: 'That she is a gentleman's daughter, is indubitable to me' (*E*, p. 62). Such is her faith in Harriet's true gentility that she fires a parting shot that will later rebound upon her: 'Were you, yourself, ever to marry, she is the very woman for you' (*E*, p. 64).

Social mobility achieved either through intermarriage between the classes or by means of trade and commerce provided stage comedy and fiction with the perfect vehicle for comparing and contrasting different social types. Austen's own fascination with social mobility, explored in *Pride and Prejudice*, is given fuller emphasis in *Emma*, where there is a greater depiction of the assimilation of the trading classes into gentility. Whilst Miss Bates and Jane Fairfax are seen to be downwardly mobile, Mr Perry and the Coles are on the rise.[5] The Cole family, who are described as 'of low origin, in trade, and only moderately genteel', have risen to be 'in fortune and style of living, second only to the family at Hartfield', yet they still struggle to rise above the stigma of trade.

Emma initially sets herself against social mobility, for she has the common prejudice against trade and commerce, 'I have no doubt that he *will* thrive and be a very rich man in time—and his being illiterate and coarse need not disturb *us*' (*E*, p. 34). She dislikes visiting the Bateses at their humble home for fear of 'falling in with the second and third rate of Highbury, who were calling on them for ever'. Like Lady Catherine De Bourgh, Emma wishes to preserve the distinctions of rank, and is therefore rendered uncomfortable by events that dissolve social distinctions, such as the Coles's dinner party and the ball at the Crown Inn. Emma needs to be reassured that there will be no difficulty, 'in everybody's returning into their proper place the next morning' (*E*, p. 198).

But to her own astonishment, she discovers how much she enjoys the Coles's party (in contrast to the two more exclusive social gatherings at Donwell and Box Hill), finding the Coles to be 'worthy people', capable of giving 'real attention' (*E*, p. 208). This is in contrast to the vulgar Mrs Elton, who confirms Emma's worst prejudices about trade, with her airs and pretensions. Mrs Elton is a wonderful comic creation—in the mould of Fanny Burney's *nouveau riche* characters—with her incessant boasting of the Sucklings of Maple Grove and her horror of upstarts such as the Tupmans, 'encumbered with many low connections, but giving themselves immense airs' (*E*, p. 310). Her idiosyncratic speech captures her own particular brand of vulgarity: 'A cousin of Mr Suckling, Mrs Bragge, had such an infinity of applications; every body was anxious to be in her family, for she moves in the first circle. Wax-candles in the school-room! You may imagine how desirable!' (*E*, pp. 299–300). As with Burney's comic monsters, however, her moral inferiority is suggested in her treatment of her servants.[6] Whereas Emma and her father talk of James and Hannah with easy familiarity, Mrs Elton barely remembers the names of her servants: 'The man who fetches our letters every morning (one of our men, I forget his name)' (*E*, p. 295).[7]

Mrs Elton also uses her position of 'Lady Patroness' to bully Jane Fairfax and, together with her husband, to humiliate Harriet Smith: 'the enmity

which they dared not shew in open disrespect to [Emma], found a broader
vent in contemptuous treatment of Harriet' (*E*, p. 282). Mrs Elton takes up
Jane Fairfax because timidity is prepossessing in those 'who are at all inferior'
(*E*, p. 283). But, in an important speech, Mr Knightley conveys his understanding of the 'littleness' of her character:

> Mrs Elton does not talk to Miss Fairfax as she speaks of her.
> We all know the difference between the pronouns he or she and
> thou, the plainest-spoken amongst us; we all feel the influence of
> a something beyond common civility in our personal intercourse
> with each other—a something more early implanted. We cannot
> give any body the disagreeable hints that we may have been very
> full of the hour before. We feel things differently. (*E*, p. 286)

This elusive 'something' that Knightley speaks of is crucial to an understanding of the relationship between outward behaviour and inner feeling
that permeates Austen's moral vision. The 'something beyond common
civility' is of course precisely what Emma transgresses on Box Hill, but
this must be understood as an uncharacteristic act, otherwise it would have
no effect.

* * *

Jane Austen's interest in the disparity between what characters think and
what they say and do is an essential part of her dramatic inheritance. We
have seen how, from the juvenilia onwards, her works were in various ways
shaped by the comic drama of the period. But more than this, her very
vision of human beings in society is profoundly tied to her thinking about
acting and role-playing. Throughout the novels, she resorts to a lexicon of
theatre to explore the notion of the performed self. *Mansfield Park* explicitly
revealed the theatricality of the self, above all in the great scene between
Sir Thomas and Mr Yates; now in *Emma*, Austen explores this idea more
implicitly, through social structure and the interplay of character more than
in any particular incident.

Emma, though an 'imaginist', possesses a realistic grasp of the importance of social performance. She duly enacts her disappointment on behalf
of the Westons when Frank Churchill fails to appear at Randalls: 'She was
the first to announce it to Mr Knightley; and exclaimed quite as much as was
necessary (or, being acting a part, perhaps rather more) at the conduct of the
Churchills, in keeping him away' (*E*, p. 145).

When Frank himself dissembles on the subject of his prolonged absence
from Highbury, she accepts his duplicity with equilibrium: 'still if it were a

falsehood, it was a pleasant one, and pleasantly handled' (*E*, p. 191). At the same time, she observes him closely to ascertain 'that he had not been acting a part, or making a parade of insincere professions' (*E*, p. 197). Emma comprehends that, whilst she must act a part, she must also be on her guard to recognise acting in others. When sharing the news of her engagement to Mr Knightley, she is happy that 'Mrs Weston was acting no part, feigning no feelings in all that she said to him in favour of the event' (*E*, p. 467).

Whilst Emma accepts that 'acting a part', playing a social role, is sometimes 'necessary', she draws the line at the sort of affectation and disingenuousness that disclaims the practice. On hearing Frank profess, 'I am the wretchedest being at the world at a civil falsehood'. Emma cannot help but retort: 'I do not believe any such thing . . . I am persuaded that you can be as insincere as your neighbours, when necessary' (*E*, p. 234).

The disparity between outward conduct and inner feeling is also a source of endless amusement. Emma's impatience at having to observe right social form is sometimes mocked, as, for example, when decorum demands that she ask after Miss Fairfax, even though she doesn't want to:

'Have you heard from Miss Fairfax so lately? I am extremely happy. I hope she is well?'

'Thank you. You are so kind!' replied the happily deceived aunt. (*E*, p. 157)

Miss Bates and even Jane Fairfax demand Emma's polite forbearance, but most trying of all is Mrs Elton. Emma's solitary outbursts are all the more comic, as they contrast so vividly with her repressed politeness:

'Knightley!—I could not have believed it. Knightley!—never seen him in her life before, and call him Knightley!—and discover that he is a gentleman! A little upstart, vulgar being, with her Mr E., and her *caro sposo*, and her resources, and all her airs of pert pretension and under-bred finery. Actually to discover that Mr Knightley is a gentleman! I doubt whether he will return the compliment, and discover her to be a lady.' (*E*, p. 279)

Though Emma heartily dislikes Mrs Elton, and finds that on occasion 'the forbearance of her outward submission' is put to the test, she (crucially) keeps her disgruntled feelings to herself.[8]

Austen's most discerning heroines, such as Elinor Dashwood and Elizabeth Bennet, possess the skill of appearing courteous in public without sacrificing their personal integrity. Emma also well understands the discrepancy between what Elinor describes as the 'behaviour' and the 'understanding'.

Thus when Mr Weston claims that Mrs Elton 'is a good-natured woman after all', she finds the appropriate response: 'Emma denied none of it aloud, and agreed to none of it in private' (*E*, p. 353). Similarly, when Mr Elton's romantic attentions become annoyingly clear, Emma finds refuge in her ability to act a part but remain true to herself 'she had the comfort of appearing very polite, while feeling very cross' (*E*, p. 119). Even when her forbearance is most sorely tested, by Harriet's disclosure of her love for Mr Knightley, Emma's response is magnanimous: 'She listened with much inward suffering, but with great outward patience' (*E*, p. 409). In each case, the phrasing is weighted by the opposites—denied/agreed, appearing/feeling, inward/outward—to express the conflict between social and private expression.

Even when dealing with extremely difficult family members, such as John Knightley and Mr Woodhouse, Emma shows her capacity for 'uniting civility with truth'. Thus, when John Knightley begins a typically anti-social rant concerning a dinner party at Randalls, Emma is unable to give him the 'pleased assent, which no doubt he was in the habit of receiving'. Rather, we are told, 'she could not be complying, she dreaded being quarrelsome; her heroism reached only to silence' (*E*, p. 114).

Throughout the novel, Austen explores the importance of silence, plain-speaking and non-verbal communication, offset against verbal ambiguities, equivocations, comic misunderstandings, riddles and word-games. In the first half of the novel, techniques such as riddles and verbal ambiguities are used with great effect to exploit the comic misunderstandings between Emma and Mr Elton. The novel's engagement with a more sophisticated exploration of language and communication coincides, however, with the arrival of Frank Churchill, who is the prime exemplar of verbal charm and social manipulation.

From the outset, the Knightley brothers are associated with a lack of gallantry and a love of plain-speaking. For instance, when the brothers meet, they welcome each other in the 'true English style', which though plain and unaffected is not lacking in feeling: "'How dy'e do, George?, and John, how are you?" . . . burying under a calmness that seemed all but indifference, the real attachment which would have led either of them, if requisite, to do every thing for the good of the other' (*E*, pp. 99–100). But whereas John Knightley's forthrightness often verges on rudeness, George's rarely does. Furthermore, he is attuned to the fact that the language of gallantry used by other men, such as Frank and Mr Elton, is merely a means to an end. He warns Emma that Mr Elton speaks a different language in 'unreserved moments, when there are only men present'. Mr Elton's more private language reveals that 'he does not mean to throw himself away' (*E*, p. 66).

George Knightley is similarly intolerant of Frank Churchill's dandyish manners. His own bluntness, which is contrasted with Frank's excessive gallantry, conceals his genuine concern for others. For example, Frank's insin-uating praise and his importuning Jane Fairfax to continue singing, in spite of a hoarse voice, is contrasted with Mr Knightley's peremptory and blunt com-mand: 'That will do . . . You have sung quite enough for one evening—now, be quiet . . . Miss Bates, are you mad, to let your niece sing herself hoarse in this manner? Go, and interfere' (*E*, p. 229). As Emma observes of Mr Knightley, 'He is not a gallant man, but he is a very humane one' (*E*, p. 223).

Frank Churchill's gallantry and charm, on the other hand, are manifest-ed by his love and mastery of word-play. This is as its most skilful and scintil-lating when he is able to play Emma and Jane Fairfax off against each other, such as on the occasion when Emma discovers him mending Mrs Bates's spectacles, and at Box Hill. On both occasions, however, the verbal acrobatics and double-meanings are so brilliantly executed and multifaceted that they become almost mentally wearying, especially when Emma invariably takes up Frank's challenge. Mr Knightley's habitual brevity of speech, which usu-ally terminates the verbal games, is therefore welcomed. His barely concealed jealousy and disapproval of Frank Churchill, however, puts its own spin on the proceedings.

When Emma interrupts the lovers in the Bateses' sitting room to hear Jane Fairfax perform at her pianoforte, she mistakenly ascribes Jane's evident discomposure to nerves: 'she must reason herself into the power of perfor-mance'. However much Jane dislikes having to rouse herself to 'perform' a social lie, Frank relishes the opportunity to flex his verbal muscles by play-ing a flirtatious double game with the two women. He uses the opportunity to make love to Jane, whilst simultaneously continuing the Dixon pretence with Emma and using her as a blind. Thus he speaks of the pianoforte as a gift 'thoroughly from the heart. Nothing hastily done; nothing incomplete. True affection only could have prompted it' (*E*, p. 242). Emma, thinking he alludes to Dixon, is quick to reprimand Frank's indiscretion—'you speak too plain'—but he replies with insouciance, 'I would have her understand me. I am not in the least ashamed of my meaning' (*E*, p. 243).

When Mr Knightley passes the window on horseback, he is drawn into conversation with Miss Bates. Not only does his bluntness amidst so much verbal ambiguity come as a most welcome relief, but the highly comical dia-logue between him and the garrulous Miss Bates, which is audible to the small audience in the apartment, makes his feelings about Frank Churchill all too clear:

> [Knightley] cut her short with,
> 'I am going to Kingston. Can I do anything for you?'
> 'Oh! dear, Kingston—are you?—Mrs Cole was saying the other day she wanted something from Kingston.'

> 'Mrs Cole has servants to send. Can I do anything for you?'
>
> 'No, I thank you. But do come in. Who do you think is here?—
> Miss Woodhouse and Miss Smith . . . Do put up your horse at the
> Crown, and come in.'
>
> 'Well,' said he in a deliberating manner, 'for five minutes,
> perhaps.'
>
> 'And here is Mrs Weston and Mr Frank Churchill too!—Quite
> delightful; so many friends!'
>
> 'No, not now, I thank you. I could not stay two minutes.' (*E*,
> p. 244)

It is unsurprising that Mr Knightley, the advocate of forthrightness, dislikes Frank Churchill, although jealousy distorts his judgement. When he
and Emma discuss Frank's absence from Highbury, she shows herself to
be highly sensitive to the social pressures upon a young man who is almost
entirely dependent upon the will of a woman such as Mrs Churchill. As
she sharply reminds Knightley, 'You are the worst judge in the world of the
difficulties of dependence . . . You do not know what it is to have tempers
to manage' (*E*, p. 146). No doubt she is alluding to the management of the
more awkward members of her own family: 'Nobody, who has not been in
the interior of a family, can say what the difficulties of any individual of that
family may be' (*E*, p. 146).

Emma understands that forthrightness is a privilege of the powerful, not
the disenfranchised. When Knightley suggests to her the simple and resolute
speech that Frank should make to the Churchills in order to break free of
their claims, she mocks his social naivety:

> Such language for a young man entirely dependent to use!—
> Nobody but you, Mr Knightley, would imagine it possible. But you
> have not an idea of what is requisite in situations directly opposite
> to your own. Mr Frank Churchill to be making such a speech as
> that to the uncle and aunt, who have brought him up, and are
> to provide for him!—Standing up in the middle of the room, I
> suppose, and speaking as loud as he could! How could you imagine
> such conduct practicable? (*E*, p. 147)

Paradoxically, although Austen is sensitive to the idea that it is not always
'practicable' to be forthright, especially where there is an imbalance of
power, she also exploits the tragicomic possibilities of social decorum that
proscribes circumlocution. Emma's final and most painful misunderstanding occurs precisely because of social equivocations, which lead her to believe
that Harriet is in love with Frank Churchill rather than Mr Knightley.

Emma, resolving to herself that 'Plain dealing was always best' (*E*, p. 341), encourages Harriet to confess her new love, but adds an important codicil: 'Let no name ever pass our lips. We were very wrong before; we will be cautious now' (*E*, p. 342). The misunderstandings persist as the women, with due propriety, agree upon the superior merits of the 'gentleman' in question for rendering Harriet an elusive 'service':

> 'I am not at all surprised at you, Harriet. The service he rendered you was enough to warm your heart.'
>
> 'Service! oh! it was such an inexpressible obligation!—The very recollection of it, and all that I felt at the time—when I saw him coming—his noble look—and my wretchedness before. Such a change! . . . From perfect misery to perfect happiness.' (*E*, p. 342)

Emma, of course, refers to Frank's rescue of Harriet from the gypsies, whereas she remembers the far more painful social snub of being 'cut' by Mr Elton at the dance, and saved by Mr Knightley.

The confusion arises partly because social form dictates that the young women cannot be too explicit, that the man cannot be named. This is the sort of comic misunderstanding that is exploited in the drama. For example, in the *Clandestine Marriage* one of the best scenes involves a misunderstanding between the lovely young heroine and the lecherous Lord Ogleby. Fanny's equivocations on the delicate subject of her situation (she is secretly married and pregnant) mislead the debauched aristocrat to believe that she is in love with him. This is a classic example of the problems arising from the exigencies of female propriety. Of course, in *Emma*, the irony is intensified, as Emma is determined not to repeat her earlier misunderstanding with Harriet and Elton, and is therefore especially self-satisfied with her discretion and 'plain-dealing'. When the mistake finally comes to light, it is the catalyst for Emma's double epiphany: the revelation of her own love for Mr Knightley and the realisation of her own wrong-doing.

Jane Austen shows how language and propriety are vulnerable to evasions and misconstructions, but offsets this by demonstrating the unmistakable power of non-verbal communication. The most memorable moments in the novels are often those expressed by wordless actions. Few can forget the emotional impact of Captain Wentworth silently removing the small child from Anne's back in *Persuasion* or Mr Knightley almost kissing Emma's hand. Elinor Dashwood's tears of joy at the news that Edward is released from his engagement express her deep emotion, as do Emma's quiet, uncontrollable tears after Box Hill. Very often, strong feeling is rendered by the frequency with which characters look at each other. Darcy's love for Elizabeth is expressed by the manner in which he fixes his eyes upon her.

Mr Knightley rumbles Frank Churchill and Jane Fairfax long before anyone else does because he has noticed the way they look at each other: 'I have lately imagined that I saw symptoms of attachment between them—certain expressive looks, which I did not believe meant to be public' (*E*, p. 350).

In *Emma* Jane Austen explores the impact of a particular kind of telepathy between couples. When Harriet is snubbed by Mr Elton at the Crown Inn ball, it is made clear that Mrs Elton is complicit: 'smiles of high glee passed between him and his wife' (*E*, p. 328). But when Harriet is saved by Mr Knightley, we witness the loving telepathy between him and Emma: 'She was all pleasure and gratitude . . . and longed to be thanking him; and though too distant for speech, her countenance said much, as soon as she could catch his eye again' (*E*, p. 328). Later, 'her eyes invited him irresistibly to come to her and be thanked' (*E*, p. 330). Similarly, Knightley expresses his own approbation and strength of feeling non-verbally when he discovers that Emma has visited Miss Bates following the Box Hill episode: 'It seemed as if there were an instantaneous impression in her favour, as if his eyes received the truth from her's, and all that had passed of good in her feelings were at once caught and honoured.—He looked at her with a glow of regard' (*E*, p. 385).

Their mutual respect and compatibility are also revealed by the frankness of expression in their conversation. They quarrel and spar in private, showing they are intellectual equals. Emma refuses to be intimidated by Knightley's brusqueness. She dares to contradict him, to accuse him of being manipulative and very fond of 'bending little minds' (*E*, p. 147), and of being full of 'prejudice' against Frank Churchill. She deliberately provokes him by taking views opposite to his. She confesses that even as a young girl she called him George, 'because I thought it would offend you' (*E*, p. 463). In public, their dialogue is distinguished by an economy of expression, which contrasts refreshingly with the tortuous, circuitous way in which, for example, Frank Churchill and Jane Fairfax are forced to communicate in public.[9]

In the dialogue between Emma and Mr Knightley there is an easiness and familiarity, even when they touch upon delicate subjects. When Emma attempts to ascertain his feelings towards Jane Fairfax, with the words 'The extent of your admiration may take you by surprise one day or other', he blithely responds, 'Oh! are you there?—But you are miserably behindhand. Mr Cole gave me a hint of it six weeks ago' (*E*, p. 287). Strikingly, their romantic involvement is characterised by an absence of sentimental language and false courtesy:

> 'Whom are you going to dance with?' asked Mr Knightley.
> She hesitated a moment, and then replied, 'With you, if you will ask me.' 'Will you?' said he, offering his hand.

'Indeed I will. You have shown that you can dance, and you know we are not really so much brother and sister as to make it at all improper.'

'Brother and sister! no, indeed.' (*E*, p. 331)

Even when the lovers discuss their impending marriage, there is a distinct lack of sentiment: 'The subject followed; it was in plain, unaffected, gentleman-like English, such as Mr Knightley used even to the woman he was in love with' (*E*, p. 448).

The association of a particular kind of brusqueness and forthrightness with genuine feeling is used repeatedly in *Emma* to encapsulate the very essence of Englishness. The true affection that belies the gruff exterior of the language between the Knightley brothers, which Austen described as 'the true English manner', is now revealed in the union between Emma and Mr Knightley. It is, furthermore, Frank Churchill's language, expressed in a 'fine flourishing letter, full of professions and falsehoods', which enables Mr Knightley to clarify the indefinable 'something' that had previously eluded him in his early analysis of what constitutes right moral conduct: 'No, Emma, your amiable young man can be amiable only in French, not in English . . . he can have no English delicacy towards the feelings of other people' (*E*, p. 149). As in a long tradition within the drama, English plainness is contrasted with French affectation.

As Austen makes clear, this 'English delicacy' is not confined to rank or station. Even Emma recognises that Robert Martin and his sisters possess 'genuine delicacy', and that their exemplary conduct following Harriet's rejection is 'the result of real feeling' (*E*, p. 179). Yet this delicacy eludes the Eltons, who in particular show 'injurious courtesy' towards those who are socially inferior, and in need of protection, such as Jane Fairfax and Harriet Smith. Momentarily, Emma makes a similar transgression to this when she humiliates Miss Bates at Box Hill.[10] Mr Knightley duly emphasises the matter of social inequality when he censures Emma's treatment of Miss Bates: 'Were she your equal in situation—but, Emma, consider how far this is from being the case' (*E*, p. 375). Emma swiftly make reparations with the consciousness of his words guiding her response: 'It should be the beginning, on her side, of a regular, equal, kindly intercourse' (*E*, p. 377).

Austen's happiest alliances are those between equals, not necessarily social equals, but those in whom there is compatibility of mind, and mutual respect and understanding. In the union between Emma and Knightley there is the promise of an equal discourse. Integral to Austen's resolutions is the way that her spirited heroines, in the best tradition of the lively ladies of comic tradition, never relinquish their penchant for merriment. Those critics who insist that Emma's reformation is not genuine cite the impudence of her remark to her future spouse: 'I always expect the best treatment, because I never put up with any other' (E, p. 474). To regard this as merely a continuation of Emma's egotism is to misunderstand the workings of the lively lady, such as Austen's favourites, Lady G. and Lady Bell Bloomer: comedy proposes that a woman may marry a worthy and upright man without fear that her high spirits will be stifled.

* * *

Mr Knightley declares to Emma after Box Hill: 'I will tell you truths while I can.' There is only one final agonising encounter when they fail to communicate fully, a last misunderstanding when each believes the other to be in love with someone else. But this is short-lived, for Emma, having first begged Mr Knightley not to speak of his love, will not ultimately sacrifice their friendship: 'I will hear whatever you like. I will tell you exactly what I think' (E, p. 429). When the misunderstanding is happily resolved, he shows his characteristic awkwardness with the language of sentiment: 'I cannot make speeches . . . If I loved you less, I might be able to talk about it more. But you know what I am. You hear nothing but truth from me' (E, p. 430).

Paradoxically, however, Mr Knightley's pursuit of absolute truth is presented as touchingly idealistic: 'Mystery; Finesse—how they pervert the understanding! My Emma, does not every thing serve to prove more and more the beauty of truth and sincerity in all our dealings with each other?' (E, p. 446). His noble sentiment is ironically undercut by Emma's 'blush of sensibility on Harriet's account', for she is conscious that she is withholding the full truth of her friend's love for him, and her own part in it. It is only when Harriet is safely married to Robert Martin that 'the disguise, equivocation, mystery, so hateful to her to practise, might soon be over. She could now look forward to giving him that full and perfect confidence which her disposition was most ready to welcome as a duty' (E, p. 475). Whether or not Emma finally does reveal the whole truth to Knightley is left open. But this ambiguity should come as no surprise, for the authorial voice has already warned the reader: 'Seldom, very seldom, does complete truth belong to any human disclosure; seldom can it happen that something is not a little disguised, or a little mistaken' (E, p. 431). There is no escape from a little disguise, a little mistakenness: such is the lesson of the theatre.

The acknowledgement of the incompleteness of human disclosure strikes at the very heart of Jane Austen's creative vision. The novel, with its omniscient narrator, is in theory a genre that proposes the possibility of complete truth. Austen, however, is more akin to Shakespeare in her perception of the complexity and ambiguity of artistic truth. Her vision of how human beings behave in society is built on disguise and role-play, equivocation and mystery: arts inextricably associated with the dramatic tradition.

Jane Austen's insistence that all our disclosures are 'a little disguised' calls into question the argument of an influential line of critics who believe that she was suspicious of 'acting' because of the supposed insincerity of role-playing.[11] These critics maintain that the growth of the heroine towards authentic self-knowledge is the key to the moral world of the novels. Such critics are themselves more Knightleys than Austens: they are susceptible to an ideal of truth that is surely unattainable. Rather, from Jane Austen's earliest beginnings in the amateur theatricals at Steventon and her experiments with dramatic form in the juvenilia to her systematic engagement with the drama in the mature novels, we find an implicit belief that the social self is always *performed*. The ultimate model for this way of seeing is the theatre.

NOTES

1. Mr Weston comes from a 'respectable family, which for the last two or three generations had been rising into gentility and property' (*E*, p. 15). His fortune, acquired by trade, has enabled him to purchase a small estate. See Juliet McMaster, 'Class', in *The Cambridge Companion to Jane Austen*, ed. Edward Copeland and Juliet McMaster (Cambridge: Cambridge University Press, 1997), pp. 115–30.

2. Emma is delighted when Mrs Weston gives birth to a daughter: 'She would not acknowledge that it was with any view of making a match for her, hereafter, with either of Isabella's sons' (*E*, p. 461).

3. *The Clandestine Marriage* and *A New Way to Pay Old Debts* held the stage with notable success throughout Austen's lifetime.

4. This technique has been much discussed by critics. See especially A. Walton Litz, *Jane Austen: A Study of her Artistic Development* (London: Chatto and Windus, 1965), pp. 146–47.

5. Julia Prewitt-Brown has noted that Miss Bates's small apartment joins the older gentry (Woodhouses and Knightleys), the new rich (Coles), and the lower-middle to lower-class townspeople and clerks: 'She represents Highbury's fluidity and mobility'. See Prewitt-Brown, 'Civilizations and the Contentment of *Emma*', in *Modern Critical Interpretations: Jane Austen's Emma*, ed. Harold Bloom (New York and Philadelphia, 1987), p. 55.

6. In Burney's play *A Busy Day* the heroine is devoted to her servant, Mungo, whereas her newly rich family treat him with contempt.

7. Critics have noted the similarities between Emma and Mrs Elton, but, as Claudia Johnson suggests, Austen contrasts them to distinguish between the proper and improper use of social position. Mrs Elton's leadership, for example, depends upon the insistent publicity of herself as Lady Patroness, and the humiliation of those who are socially inferior to her. See Claudia L. Johnson, *Jane Austen: Women, Politics and the Novel* (Chicago: University of Chicago Press, 1988), pp. 129–30.

8. One exception is when she enters a private discussion with her trusted friends, Mrs Weston and Mr Knightley, concerning Mrs Elton's injurious treatment of Jane Fairfax (*E*, pp. 286–89).

9. They conduct a polite row on Box Hill, unbeknown to the rest of the party: 'How many a man has committed himself on a short acquaintance, and rued it all the rest of his life' (*E*, p. 372). Jane replies: 'I would be understood to mean, that it can be only weak, irresolute characters (whose happiness must be always at the mercy of chance), who will suffer an unfortunate acquaintance to be an inconvenience, an oppression for ever' (*E*, p. 373).

10. 'There is a pattern in the novel of vulnerable single woman, whom it is the social duty of the strong and the rich to protect': Marilyn Butler, *Jane Austen and the War of Ideas* (Oxford: Clarendon Press, 1975; repr; 1987), p. 257.

11. Lionel Trilling remains especially influential in this regard. See, in particular, his *Sincerity and Authenticity* (London: Oxford University Press, 1972), pp. 75–78. My own reading of Austen is closer to that of Joseph Litvak in his *Caught in the Act: Theatricality in the Nineteenth-Century Novel* (Berkeley: University of California Press, 1993). Jane Austen's characters act all the time, so even Fanny Price cannot help but play a part: 'All along in eschewing acting, Fanny has in fact been playing a role, albeit "sincerely" . . . From Henry's performance she learns not the necessity of acting, but the impossibility of *not* acting.' Litvak, *Caught in the Act*, p. 21.

GLORIA SYBIL GROSS

"Pictures of perfection as you know make me sick & wicked": Persuasion

Writing jauntily to favorite niece Fanny Knight, Austen flouts the pris-
siness of one, Mr. Wildman (Fanny's suitor), who apparently dipped into
her works and blanched: "I *hope* I am not affronted & do not think the
worse of him for having a Brain so very different from mine, . . . Do not
oblige him to read any more.—Have mercy on him, . . . He & I should not
in the least agree of course, in our ideas of Novels and Heroines; pictures
of perfection as you know make me sick & wicked" (Austen, *Letters*, JA to
Fanny Knight, Friday 14 March 1817, 486–87, no. 142). Perfect heroines
or, at least, exemplary ones, were indeed the rage from the mid-eighteenth
century forward,[1] though Johnson sometimes took nice exception. As we
have seen, when Mrs. Thrale proposed Richardson's Clarissa as "a perfect
character," he contradicted: "On the contrary (said he), you may observe
there is always something which she prefers to truth."[2] What lurks beneath
the surface of character piqued his avid curiosity. How sporting then a
challenge for Austen to invent another "perfect" heroine, whose inward life
belies the public shining example. Not Fanny Price, whose motives proved
too limp and hampered, but Anne Elliot is her contribution to the genre. If
Emma was the "heroine whom no one but myself will much like,"[3] Anne
conversely is the one whom everyone will like but she. As the author pre-
views the leading lady of *Persuasion* to Miss Knight in the same letter, "You

From *In a Fast Coach with a Pretty Woman: Jane Austen and Samuel Johnson*, pp. 164–186.
© 2002 by AMS Press.

may perhaps like the Heroine, as she is almost too good for me" (487), we anticipate an ambitious performance.

Following on the heels of the exuberant *Emma*, *Persuasion* was written quickly in twelve months, from August 1815 to July 1816.[4] Never thoroughly revised, the novel churns with raw feeling and naked revelation. Customarily Austen wrote carefully and revised intensively, as she famously describes "the little bit (two inches wide) of Ivory on which I work with so fine a Brush" (Austen, *Letters*, JA to J. Edward Austen, Monday 16 December 1816, 467, no. 134).[5] By contrast, *Persuasion* occupied her less than a year, its composition marred by the bankruptcy of brother Henry and by the onset of her illness.[6] Far from the deft handiwork of light ironic comedy, the levity and the gay burlesque of polite society, it often leans toward pathos, even melodrama. Its explicit realism stresses blasted hopes and a world without pity, where characters stoop and stumble in largely unrelieved, unenlightened bondage. An infernal vision intrudes on the high bourgeoisie, as Austen brings us closer and closer to catastrophe. Comparable to Shakespeare's dark comedies, the ordered conventional ethos, whatever its flaws and peccadillos, mutates into the grotesque. She visits the lower depths of satire, the place where jeering idiots and madmen hold sway. We are close to the world of Rabelais, Dante, or Pope and Swift's most gruesome caricature. Here Austen imagines an ideal heroine brought so low, she becomes a travesty. Oftentimes she parodies the very goodness she wants to protect.[7]

Not surprisingly, Johnson's essays on marriage and courtship, and not least the plight of single women, were on Austen's mind when she undertook *Persuasion*. Possibly Tranquilla, the mellow and mature "correspondent" who offers the advice of waiting for "a suitable associate," despite the drawbacks of single life, began as the model for Anne. Admitting the reckless way of the beau monde, the *Rambler*'s woman of experience urges not to quit the field nor take refuge in cynicism: "As, notwithstanding all that wit, or malice, or pride, or prudence, will be able to suggest, men and women must at last pass their lives together, I have never therefore thought those writers friends to human happiness, who endeavour to excite in either sex a general contempt or suspicion of the other." On balance, she counsels moderation and cautious optimism:

> That the world is over-run with vice, cannot be denied; but vice, however predominant, has not yet gained an unlimited dominion. Simple and unmingled good is not in our power, but we may generally escape a greater evil by suffering a less; and therefore, those who undertake to initiate the young and ignorant in the knowledge of life, should be careful to inculcate the possibility of virtue and happiness, and to encourage endeavours by prospects of success.

From Tranquilla's story, we gather that Johnson's greater evil is a bad marriage, his lesser spinsterhood, reversing conventional wisdom. On the verges of feminist manifesto, she declares resistance to requisite matrimony, telling of a succession of fops and jilts. The female counterpart to Hymaneus (see *Rambler* 113 and 115), she resists the bridechamber in the face of wounding disrespect. Hers "are the sentiments of one who has been subject for many years to all the hardships of antiquated virginity; has been long accustomed to the coldness of neglect, and the petulance of insult." Compounded by social ostracism, her dismal prospects make his seem rosy. Still she clings to a glimmer of hope, spoken peculiarly in negatives: "I do not yet believe happiness unattainable in marriage, though I have never yet been able to find a man, with whom I could prudently venture an inseparable union" (*Rambler* 119; Yale *Works*, IV, 270–75).

Sentimentally, Johnson marries Tranquilla to Hymaneus, both past their prime, in tribute, so it seems, to the cardinal virtues: discretion, fortitude, temperance, judgment, and the like. Having survived blunders enough and to spare, the two join in holy wedlock to their mutual relief. They boast a union, also oddly stressed in negatives: they were not rash, not impetuous, not bewitched. In the wedding announcement to Mr. Rambler, they congratulate themselves as a couple who "sought happiness only in the arms of virtue" (*Rambler* 167; Yale *Works*, V, 125). They represent the triumph of good over moral obliquity. "Too good." If anyone could catch this smidgeon of smugness, it is Austen. The two represent a bulwark against villainy, but their self-approving joy is simply not to be borne. Perhaps the story of Hymaneus and Tranquilla sparked the plan for *Persuasion*, but like Johnson, Austen so feasts on the negative that the positive is unpalatable. Anne is the prim and prudent heroine who is always right. "No one so proper, so capable as Anne" (*P*, vol. 1, chap. 12; Austen *Works*, V, 114), as Captain Wentworth succinctly, if ambiguously, puts it. A model of imperturbability, her character represents the over-the-hill schoolmarm whose lips are permanently pursed. From being finicky about the untidy life style at Uppercross, squeamish at the rough familiarity of the Crofts or the Harvilles' close quarters, tsk-tsking Mr. Elliot's Sunday travel, she takes a dim view of indecorum. More fatefully, her discipline counters the law of the jungle, where natives grow increasingly restless and bloodcurdling. The swine and brutes of *Persuasion* hardly bother to apply camouflage. So first to the charming menagerie.

Alongside General Tilney, Mrs. Ferrars, Lady Catherine, Aunt Norris, and Mrs. Churchill (among the eeriest for never being seen), Sir Walter Elliot dominates Austen's hall of monsters. While the latter interact with people, however acrimoniously, as we first lay eyes on Sir Walter, he interacts with the numinous Baronetage. Mirrors everywhere, staring down everyone only to remark appearance and rank, he assumes the freakish proportions that Oscar Wilde was to represent at the end of the century in *The Picture of Dorian Gray* (1891). Austen suffers no scruples in making Anne's father as repellent as possible: "Vanity was the beginning and the end of Sir Walter Elliot's character; vanity of person and of situation" (vol. 1, chap. 1; V, 4). Quitting the ancestral home at Kellynch only ruffles his feathers, which are instantly smoothed by being assured a tony position at Bath: "He might there be important at comparatively little expense" (vol. 1, chap. 2; V, 14). As he leaves in a fanfare, having been disgraced by profligate spending and primal stupidity, Austen describes the departure with acid contempt: "The party drove off in very good spirits; Sir Walter prepared with condescending bows for all the afflicted tenantry and cottagers who might have had a hint to shew themselves" (vol. 1, chap. 5; V, 36).

Goaded by gratuitous cruelty, Sir Walter insults two most hallowed institutions: family and country. As a parent, he is sinister, having ruined his best daughter's happiness. When Anne was engaged to Wentworth at nineteen, he abandoned the girl with chilling nonchalance: "Sir Walter, on being applied to, without actually withholding his consent, or saying it should never be, gave it all the negative of great astonishment, great coldness, great silence, and a professed resolution of doing nothing for his daughter. He thought it a very degrading alliance" (vol. 1, chap. 4; V, 26). In the equally repellent Elizabeth, a mirror image, he takes narcissistic gratification; to whiny Mary, who fancies herself frequently ill, he can only remark on the redness of her nose. As a citizen and peer, no less, Sir Walter dishonors patriotism by disparaging the navy: "The profession has its utility, but I should be sorry to see any friend of mine belonging to it." And he amplifies with appalling equanimity: "Yes; it is in two points offensive to me; I have two strong grounds of objection to it. First, as being the means of bringing persons of obscure birth into undue distinction, and raising men to honours which their fathers and grandfathers never dreamt of; and secondly, as it cuts up a man's youth and vigour most horribly; a sailor grows old sooner than any other man; I have observed it all my life." His sentiments reach an ungodly pitch when recalling "a certain Admiral Baldwin, the most deplorable looking personage you can imagine, his face the colour of mahogany, rough and rugged to the last degree, all lines and wrinkles, nine grey hairs of a side, and nothing but a dab of powder at top. . . . I know it is the same with them all: they are knocked about, and exposed to every climate, and every weather, till they are not fit to be seen. It is a pity they are not knocked on the head at once, before they reach Admiral Baldwin's age [forty]" (vol. 1, chap. 3; V, 19–20). This, after the bloodiest campaigns of naval history in defense of King and country, and when every English citizen knew by heart James Thomson's rallying battle cry, "Rule, Britannia, rule the waves; / Britons never will be slaves."[8] Not to mention the military service of Austen's two brothers, Sir Francis, Admiral of the Fleet, and Charles, Rear Admiral and Commander-in-Chief of the East India Station.

At Bath, Sir Walter convivially strolls the streets in search of eyesores. "He had counted eighty-seven women go by, one after another without there being a tolerable face among them. There certainly were a dreadful multitude of ugly women in Bath; and as for the men! they were infinitely worse. Such scarecrows" (vol. 2, chap. 3; V, 141–42). Fancying himself irresistible, he struts like a superannuated peacock. Elizabeth is no better. Flagrantly slighting Anne, she takes up the compliant, if devious, Mrs. Clay, who flatters and cajoles her way into Sir Walter's and her own unendearing graces. The latter accompanies the entourage to town instead of Anne, "for nobody will want her in Bath" (vol. 1, chap. 5; V, 33). Upon her sister's delayed coming and Mrs. Clay's posturings to go, Elizabeth underscores the preference: "'She is nothing to me, compared to you'" (vol. 2, chap. 4; V, 145). The groveling and slavering after Lady Dalrymple and Miss Carteret are rendered in nauseous detail. As high and mighty relations, they represent parodic deities, something akin to Pope's goddess Dullness and her court. Their procession through the concert hall is a sorry spectacle of knaves and fools: "The entrance door opened again, and the very party appeared for whom they were waiting. 'Lady Dalrymple, Lady Dalrymple,' was the rejoicing sound; and with all the eagerness compatible with anxious elegance, Sir Walter and his two ladies [Elizabeth and Mrs. Clay] stepped forward to meet her. Lady Dalrymple and Miss Carteret, escorted by Mr. Elliot and Colonel Wallis, who had happened to arrive nearly at the same instant, advanced into the room. . . . Elizabeth, arm in arm with Miss Carteret, and looking on the broad back of the dowager Viscountess Dalrymple before her, had nothing to wish for which did not seem within her reach" (vol. 2, chap. 8; V, 184–85). Needless to say, the object of her reach would have been more graphically represented by Pope.

If Anne is "ashamed," her estimate of "good company" begs to differ with the rest. Earlier reflecting on her cousin's Chesterfieldian code, she suggests:

> "My idea of good company, Mr. Elliot, is the company of clever, well-informed people, who have a great deal of conversation; that is what I call good company."
>
> "You are mistaken," said he gently, "that is not good company, that is the best. Good company requires only birth, education and manners, and with regard to education is not very nice. Birth and good manners are essential. . . . You may depend upon it, that they [Lady Dalrymple and Miss Carteret] will move in the first set in Bath this winter, and as rank is rank, your being known to be related to them will have its use in fixing your family (our family

let me say) in that degree of consideration which we must all wish for." (vol. 2, chap. 4; V, 150)

Austen clearly skewers the old saws of patrician education and code of gentlemanly conduct taught by Lord Chesterfield, Johnson's old nemesis. With fifteen editions published by 1800,[9] Chesterfield's *Letters to his Son* (1774) was still widely circulated, offering recommendations of social dissimulation and suave sexual morality. Also known was Johnson's famous takedown that "'they teach the morals of a whore, and the manners of a dancing master.'"[10] Another time, he remarks sardonically: "Every man of any education would rather be called a rascal, than accused of deficiency in *the* graces."[11] Rest assured that Johnson's and Austen's sneer comprehends the odious Elliots.

Next to Anne's abominable family, the Musgroves would appear the salt of the earth. Not really. The skeleton in their closet is a dead reprobate offspring, about whom Austen is at once grinning and severe:

> that the Musgroves had had the ill fortune of a very troublesome, hopeless son; and the good fortune to lose him before he reached his twentieth year; that he had been sent to sea, because he was stupid and unmanageable on shore; that he had been very little cared for at any time by his family, though quite as much as he deserved; seldom heard of, and scarcely at all regretted when the intelligence of his death abroad had worked its way to Uppercross, two years before. (vol. 1, chap. 6; V, 150–51)

The discovery of his serving under Captain Wentworth prompts his mother's mammoth outpourings: "Mrs. Musgrove was of a comfortable substantial size, infinitely more fitted by nature to express good cheer and good humour, than tenderness and sentiment." As she blubbers on the sofa with Anne scrunched to one side and out of view, "Captain Wentworth should be allowed some credit for the self-command with which he attended to her large fat sighings over the destiny of a son, whom alive nobody had cared for." If this were not enough, the narrator annotates: "Personal size and mental sorrow have certainly no necessary proportions. A large bulky figure has as good a right to be in deep affliction, as the most graceful set of limbs in the world. But, fair or not fair, there are unbecoming conjunctions, which reason will patronize in vain,—which taste cannot tolerate,—which ridicule will seize" (vol. 1, chap. 8; V, 68).

It may be Johnson also eavesdrops on this blatant episode of fat grief. While honest cause for sorrow earned his compassion and respect, beggarly tales of woe were laughed to scorn. At Mrs. Thrale's presuming a friend's commiseration over a will, he snaps: "'She will suffer as much perhaps (said he) as your horse did when your cow miscarried.'"[12] Another time, shown a letter in which friend Tom Davies, professing to lose sleep over mutual friend Baretti's murder trial, also recommends a young man in a pickle shop, he scoffs: "'Ay, Sir, here you have a specimen of human sympathy; a friend hanged, and a cucumber pickled. We know not whether Baretti or the pickle-man has kept Davies from sleep; nor does he know himself.'"[13] When the spirit moves them, Johnson and Austen expertly cut through the chaff. The kernel of fakery and self-deceit shows us life as a macabre comedy.

The Musgrove girls, granted more benign than the Miss Bertrams, the youngest Miss Bennets, let alone the Miss Steeles, nonetheless come across as nuisances. Another couple of primping poppets itching for marriage, they shimmy to the rhythm of gossip, balls, and beaus. When Captain Wentworth drops anchor, rich, handsome, and bedecked with naval insignia, they besiege him like groupies. To her credit, Henrietta withdraws, reminded of a semi-betrothal to the déclassé but acceptable Cousin Charles Hayter. Of course the one reminding her was sister Louisa, who now has Captain Wentworth to herself. In Austen's upside-down commentary on Anne's unfortunate defection eight years earlier, Louisa, of the rock-solid intellect, boasts pertinacity and self-will, no matter the opposition: "What!—would I be turned back from doing a thing that I had determined to do, and that I knew to be right, by the airs and interference of such a person [the hoity-toity Mary]?—or, of any person I may say. No,—I have no idea of being so easily persuaded. When I have made up my mind, I have made it. And Henrietta seemed entirely to have made up hers to call at Winthrop today—and yet, she was as near giving it up, out of nonsensical complaisance!" (vol. 1, chap. 10; V, 87). Déjà vu for Wentworth, and he launches into a fulsome encomium on the mincing girl's seriousness of purpose: "Happy for her, to have such a mind as yours at hand! ... *Yours* is the character of decision and firmness, I see." Commending a spirit of "fortitude and strength of mind," he alludes, no doubt from wounded ego and more than a little bitterness, to Anne, who overhears the whole exchange: "It is the worst evil of too yielding and indecisive a character, that no influence over it can be depended on.—You are never sure of a good impression being durable. Every body may sway it; let those who would be happy be firm." (V, 88) Then pontificating on a shrub, he illustrates: "'Here is a nut ... a beautiful glossy nut, which, blessed with original strength, has outlived all the storms of autumn. Not a puncture, not a weak spot any where.—This nut,' he continued with playful solemnity,—'while so many of its brethren have fallen and been trodden under foot, is still in possession of all the happiness that a hazel-nut can be supposed capable of'" (V, 88). Driveling on, he lavishes the rapt young thing with more praise: "My first wish for all, whom I am interested in, is that they should be firm. If Louis Musgrove would be beautiful and happy in her November of life, she will cherish all her present powers of mind" (V, 88). He is dangerously close to proposing.

Following such accolades to brainpower and a break-proof noggin, Louisa's cracking her head at Lyme is a masterful stunt. Literally throwing herself at Wentworth, she lands not him, but on the pavement. The near catastrophe befits all the lunacy of the mismatch: her childish fluster and his foolish indiscretion: "In all their walks, he had had to jump her from the stiles; the sensation was delightful to her. The hardness of the pavement for her feet, made him less willing upon the present occasion; he did it, however; she was safely down, and instantly, to shew her enjoyment, ran up the steps to be jumped down again" (vol. 1, chap. 12; V, 109). That Louisa's close call is farcical bares another lineament of *Persuasion*'s ghoulish, gallows humor. Indeed Anne has the last laugh, having wanted to bonk Louisa on the head for a long time and presently, observing Wentworth, she "wondered whether it ever occurred to him now, to question the justness of his own previous opinion as to the universal felicity and advantage of firmness of character" (V, 116).

Maiming and murderous impulses toward her notwithstanding, Louisa survives to find another lover and eventually a husband in the equally capricious Captain Benwick. While the good citizens of the Cobb gathered near the accident "to enjoy the sight of a dead young lady, nay, two dead young ladies [Henrietta fainted], for it proved twice as fine as the first report" (vol. 1, chap. 12; V, 111), they are rudely disappointed. But Fanny Harville is truly dead. Her fiancé Benwick first enters center stage inconsolable, sullen, and withdrawn, with "a melancholy air, just as he ought to have" (vol. 1, chap. 11; V, 97). All but neglected by the others, Anne gravitates to him only to hear more than she ever wanted of Scott's and Byron's poetry: "He shewed himself so intimately acquainted with all the tenderest songs of the one poet, and all the impassioned descriptions of hopeless agony of the other; he repeated, with such tremulous feeling, the various lines which imaged a broken heart, or a mind destroyed by wretchedness, and looked so entirely as if he meant to be understood" (V, 100). From the late lamented Fanny, not more than three or four months gone, he attaches himself to Anne, then casually drops her for Louisa, who obligingly and just as casually drops Wentworth. The hypocrisy of sentimental avowals recalls Johnson's retort to Boswell, who expresses qualms: "I have often blamed myself, Sir, for not feeling for others as sensibly as many say they do" whereupon that stalker of cant growls, "Sir, don't be duped by them any more. You will find these very feeling people are not very ready to do you good. They *pay* you by *feeling*."[14] Evidently Austen responds the same.

At Bath, infidelity, lies, and double-dealing run no less rampant. Falling in with the unsavory Mrs. Smith and the aptly dubbed Nurse Rooke, two denizens of the demimonde, Anne glimpses life in the sewers. For once, Sir Walter waxes correctly: "'Westgate-buildings!' said he; 'and who is Miss Anne Elliot to be visiting in Westgate-building?—A Mrs. Smith. A widow Mrs. Smith,—and who was her husband? One of the five thousand Mr. Smiths whose names are to be met with every where. . . . Upon my word, Miss Anne Elliot, you have the most extraordinary taste! Every thing that revolts other people, low company, paltry rooms, foul air, disgusting associations are inviting to you'" (vol. 2, chap. 5; V, 157). To be sure, Anne visits her father's *persona non grata*, an old schoolfellow who once befriended her in need and is presently unwell and near penniless. But one more conniver, Mrs. Smith has a secret agenda, hoping to make her fortune by Anne's presumed engagement to Mr. Elliot. With smooth indifference to a loyal girlhood chum's welfare, she encourages a match to a man whom minutes later she decries as Satan incarnate:

> Mr. Elliot is a man without heart or conscience; a designing, wary, cold-blooded being, who thinks only of himself; who, for his own interest or ease, would be guilty of any cruelty, or any treachery, that could be perpetrated without risk of his general character. He has no feeling for others. Those whom he has been the chief cause of leading into ruin, he can neglect and desert without the smallest compunction. He is totally beyond the reach of any sentiment of justice or compassion. Oh! he is black at heart, hollow and black! (vol. 2, chap. 9; V, 199)

This is too much. Downright un-Austenian, the evil is over the top, much as Johnson would occasionally overdo righteous indignation in pieces written in haste or invested with overzealous portions of injustice-collection.[15] Left unrevised but for the last two chapters, uncompleted owing to the author's advancing illness, *Persuasion* eventually founders in shoals of emotionalism, never genuinely fulfilling its promise of grand demonic epiphany. While the portrait of Sir Walter comes close, the rest falls short of the goal, and we lapse into melodrama, at times, bathos. That is probably one reason why Austen derides Anne as "almost too good for me," in effect, a parody of goodness. For a heroine she is overdrawn and inconsistent: a veteran of wars past, battles lost but herself honorably acquitted, she alters unconvincingly from rage and sexual longing to priggery, meekness, and servility. While often likened to Fanny Price, here is no seventeen-year-old cowering in the corner, baffled by chaotic sexual drives, but a mature woman unabashed by a frank passion for Wentworth. With patent eroticism, Austen describes how she watches his handsome face, the curl of his mouth, and thrills at his touch. Taking Mary's brat off her back, he arouses "sensations on the discovery [that] made her perfectly speechless" (vol. 1, chap. 9; V, 80), and handing her into the Crofts' carriage, she "felt that he had placed her there, that his will and his hands had done it" (vol. 1, chap. 10; V, 91).

But other times Anne is a stifled subordinate, mopping up after other people's messes. Careworn and self-effacing, she packs belongings, catalogues books, makes the rounds of official farewells at Kellynch, caters to Mary's prima-donnish conceits, and nurses her unadorable offspring. Humbly she forgives everyone's obnoxious behavior. To her father and Elizabeth, it goes without saying, she makes nary a complaint. To Lady Russell, a meddlesome old snoop, who originally vetoed the engagement to Wentworth under pretext of maternal affection, she acquiesces still. Apparently Anne's life for the last eight years has accommodated the usual superfluous offices of a spinster. Shunted back and forth between Kellynch, London, Bath, and Uppercross (where at least Mary finds her useful), Anne consoles herself by the older woman's attentions, "think[ing] with heightened gratitude of the extraordinary blessing of having one such truly sympathising friend as Lady Russell" (vol. 1, chap. 6; V, 42).

The soundness of Lady Russell's sympathy is sorely tested at Bath, when Captain Wentworth steps forward as the two women take a morning walk. Anne distinguishes him in a heartbeat:

> She looked instinctively at Lady Russell; but not from any mad idea of her recognising him so soon as she did herself. No, it was not to be supposed that Lady Russell would perceive him till they were nearly opposite. She looked at her however, from time to time, anxiously; and when the moment approached which must point him out, though not daring to look again (for her own countenance she knew was unfit to be seen), she was yet perfectly conscious of Lady Russell's eyes being turned exactly in the direction for him, of her being in short intently observing him.

Trusting to her confidant's felicitations, Anne lingers sensually on his physical charm: "She could thoroughly comprehend the sort of fascination he must possess over Lady Russell's mind, the difficulty it must be for her to withdraw her eyes, the astonishment she must be feeling that eight or nine years should have passed over him, and in foreign climes and in active service too, without robbing him of one personal grace!" All for naught, because the soul of tender loving care happened to be staring at window curtains. Zinging Lady Russell blows the lid off her patronage, self-absorbed and boorish. Even her protégé gets thrown off balance: "Anne sighed and blushed, and smiled, in pity and disdain, either at her friend or herself" (vol. 2, chap. 7; V, 179).

But Anne forgives Lady Russell, lamely explaining to Wentworth in an apology padded with special pleading: "I have been thinking over the past, and trying impartially to judge the right and wrong, I mean with regard to myself; and I must believe that I was right, much as I suffered from it, that I was perfectly right in being guided by the friend whom you will love better than you do now." Glossing over a monstrous error in judgment, she gets them both off innocent: "I was right in submitting to her, and that if I had done otherwise, I should have suffered more in continuing the engagement than I did even in giving it up, because I should have suffered in my conscience. I have now, as far as such a sentiment is allowable in human nature, nothing to reproach myself with" (vol. 2, chap. 11; V, 246). Exonerating one and all, she buries the hatchet she might well have wielded. She forgives the sniveling Captain Benwick and Captain Wentworth himself, originally out to even the score. Moody and spiteful, he either had smirked or frowned or flirted in her face with the giggly Musgrove girls.

Whether Anne's absolution extends to Mr. Elliot and Mrs. Clay, we never learn. By Austen's design, the former is perhaps too readily relegated to the dungheap, to abscond with the malodorous, now-it-can-be-told kept woman. That melting gaze at the Cobb was worthy of a Willoughby or Henry Crawford. Like them, he cuts a dashing figure and first appraises the heroine's sexual appeal. Ascending steps from the beach, she meets him at the top: "Anne's face caught his eye, and he looked at her with a degree of earnest admiration, which she could not be insensible of. She was looking remarkably well; her very regular, very pretty features, having the bloom and freshness of youth restored by the fine wind which had been blowing on her complexion, and by the animation of eye which it had also produced. It was evident that the gentleman, (completely a gentleman in manner) admired her exceedingly" (vol. 1, chap. 12; V, 104). At the family's grandiose abode at Bath, he has the good sense to prefer her to Elizabeth, seeking an honorable attachment. Another rake on the mend, he shows delicacy, poise, and grace, lacking only the love of Anne. Well, there is no accounting for taste: she prefers Wentworth.

While Anne's forbearance, multiple pardons, the affective elegies to nature (coming dangerously close to Fanny P.'s), and the mournful reflections on constancy are sincere enough, they are not at the center of *Persuasion*. More Richardson than Austen, they weigh onerous and register overwrought, often collapsing into melodrama. When Captain Wentworth finally succumbs and hands Anne his written proposal, we are in the clime of *Clarissa*, or worse, with the plaintive cry: "On the contents of that letter depended all which this world could do for her!" (vol. 2, chap. 11; V, 237). Austen tries to redress the gaffe by making Anne look so unwell that Mrs. Musgrove inquires if she got bonked on the head, like Louisa. But melancholy too often deflects the real goal. At the real center of *Persuasion* is hatred.[16] Had she the time and energy to revise, the novel might have bared in bold relief a most leering and grotesque epiphany of human nature. As such, it seethes with everything she fears and loathes: mercenary ambition, brutality, and violence.

Neither did Johnson shrink at representing human nature in all its primitive unmajesty. Addressing the young and naive, he warns:

> He surely is an useful monitor, who inculcates to these thoughtless strangers, that the "majority are wicked"; who informs them, that the train which wealth and beauty draw after them, is lured only by the scent of prey; and that, perhaps, among all those who croud about them with professions and flatteries, there is not one who does not hope for some opportunity to devour or betray them, to glut himself by their destruction, or to share their spoils with a stronger savage. (*Rambler* 175; Yale *Works*, V, 161)

And he could be killingly satirical. In the original *Idler* 22 on the vultures, suppressed when the essays were collected in book form, undoubtedly because he or his printer thought it too shocking for the general public, a mother vulture instructs her charges on the arts of seeking prey. With cool deliberation, she describes man as a beast of

> strange ferocity, which I have never observed in any other being that feeds upon the earth. Two herds of men will often meet and shake the earth with noise, and fill the air with fire. When you hear noise and see fire which flashes along the ground, hasten to the place with your swiftest wing; for men are surely destroying one another; you will then find the ground smoking with blood and covered with carcasses, of which many are dismembered, and mangled for the convenience of the vulture. (Yale *Works*, II, 319)

While Johnson is reviling the Seven Years' War (1756–63), Austen lived most her life through the long drawn-out agony of the French Revolution (1789–99) and Napoleonic Wars (1803–15).[17] Well may we suspect the reputable characters in *Persuasion*, career navymen and women (e.g., Wentworth's sister, the martial Mrs. Croft), who, having won fortunes through looting and plunder, whet their appetites for carnage and drool for more.

Attending to domestic life, Austen reproduces the sound and fury of a world bent on destruction. Through socially accepted outlets, the lust for power drives the bourgeois excellencies of rank, wealth, and possession. Hence *Persuasion* winds down with the author's lethal gibe at the ultimate bourgeois coup, marriage, as usual professing not to teach a lesson: "Who can be in doubt of what followed? When any two young people take it into their heads to marry, they are pretty sure by perseverance to carry their point, be they ever so poor, or ever so imprudent, or ever so little likely to be necessary to each other's ultimate comfort. This may be bad morality to conclude with, but I believe it to be truth (vol. 2, chap. 12; Austen *Works*, V, 248).

Austen's "bad morality" erodes a trust in what is right and proper. The mordant portrayals of personal and social deviancy appear to revoke any possibility of safe passage. Once more the ship of conscience careens in shark-infested waters. Neither is marriage a safety island for Anne, who trembles at the prospect of another war. Of all Austen's "happy endings," Anne's alliance affords the least security. When all is said and done, she is still the heroine mocked as "too good," who ironically loses peace of mind. Past endurance, it is the offensive cult of matrimony that emboldens Austen in *Persuasion* so to counter attack and draw blood. "You pierce my soul" (vol. 2, chap. 11; V, 237), writes Captain Wentworth, but his is not untainted nor can we wholly vouch for his integrity. The treacly denouement weakens Austen's fierce demand for answers. If venality spoils a perfect heroine's wedding garlands, and others grow foul by their own device, where then, as Rasselas also demands, is happiness to be found? Johnson's debate on marriage holds a key in Nekayah's snide challenge. We have come a long way from St. Paul's exhortation to the Corinthians, "It is better to marry than to burn." Future founder of "a college of learned women," the feisty princess speaks her mind: "How the world is to be peopled . . . is not my care, and needs not be yours. I see no danger that the present generation should omit to leave successors behind them. We are not now inquiring for the world, but for ourselves" (*Rasselas*, chap. 28; Yale *Works*, XVI, 106).

Notes

1. For a variety of ideals of womanhood, see Mary Poovey, *The Proper Lady and the Woman Writer: Ideology as Style in the Works of Mary Wollstonecraft, Mary Shelley, and Jane Austen* (Chicago: University of Chicago Press, 1984) and particularly Penelope Joan Fritzer, *Jane Austen and Eighteenth-Century Courtesy Books* (Westport, Conn.: Greenwood Press, 1997).

2. George Birkbeck Hill, ed. *Johnsonian Miscellanies*, 2 vols. (Oxford: Clarendon Press, 1897), I, 297.

3. James Austen-Leigh, *Memoirs of Jane Austen*, ed. R.W. Chapman (Oxford: Clarendon Press, 1926), 157.

4. John Halperin, *The Life of Jane Austen* (Baltimore: Johns Hopkins University Press, 1984), 278, 296–99.

5. We know, for example, that *Sense and Sensibility* and *Pride and Prejudice* were rewritten several times, *Mansfield Park* required two and a half years, and *Emma*, written at the height of her powers and in her most characteristic style, took well over a year. See introductory notes to Chapman's edition of the novels.

6. Halperin, *Jane Austen*, 292, 296.

7. For the experiment of an ideal heroine who redeems a fallen society, one thinks particularly of Shakespeare's Isabella in *Measure for Measure*. Like Anne Elliot's, her virtue, put to the test, distorts into over-nice scruples and self-righteousness.

8. *Alfred* (1740), Act 2, Scene 5.

9. *English Prose and Poetry, 1600–1800*, ed. Odell Shepard and Paul Spencer Wood (Cambridge, Mass.: Houghton Mifflin, 1934), 592.

10. James Boswell, *Life of Samuel Johnson*, ed. George Birbeck Hill; rev. L.F. Powell, 6 vols. (Oxford: Clarendon Press, 1934–50), I, 266.

11. Boswell, Life, III, 54.

12. *Johnsonian Miscellanies*, ed. George Birkbeck Hill, 2 vols. (Oxford: Clarendon Press, 1897), I, 207.

13. Boswell, *Life*, II, 94.

14. Ibid. 95.

15. See, for example, the *Life of Savage* (1744), written quickly after his beloved friend's demise in a Bristol debtor's prison. He channels his emotions into a lurid tale of Savage's mother, who allegedly disowned him. Johnson is stupefied "that she would look upon her son from his birth with a kind of resentment and abhorrence; and, instead of supporting, assisting, and defending him, delight to see him struggling with misery; or that she would take every opportunity of aggravating his misfortunes, and obstructing his resources, and with an implacable and restless cruelty continue her persecution from the first hour of his life to the last" (*Lives of the Poets*, II, 323–24). Resurrecting Savage as a sacrificial victim, Johnson analogizes from the atrocities of parents who murder their children to Savage's mother, a fiend who

> forbears to destroy him only to inflict sharper miseries upon him; who prolongs his life only to make it miserable; and who exposes him, without care and without pity, to the malice of oppression, the caprices of chance, and temptations of poverty; and who rejoices to see him overwhelmed with calamities; and, when his own industry or the charity of others, has enabled him to rise for a short time above his miseries, plunges him again into his former distress. (338)

Of the frantic emotionalism and bombast of his early efforts at dramatic tragedy, *Irene* (1736), he appears embarrassed in later life. Hearing it read in company, he left the room: "I thought it had been better" (Boswell, *Life*, IV, 5).

16. See D. W. Harding's seminal essay, "Regulated Hatred: An Aspect of the Work of Jane Austen" *Scrutiny* 8 (1940): 346–62. Rpt. in *Regulated Hatred and Other Essays by D.W. Harding*, ed. Monica Lawlor (London: Athlone Press, 1998), 5–26.

17. See Warren Roberts, *Jane Austen and the French Revolution* (New York: St. Martin's Press, 1979).

PATRICIA MENON

Sense and Sensibility *and* Mansfield Park:
"At Once Both Tragedy and Comedy"

Had *Sense and Sensibility* and *Mansfield Park* been the only two of her
novels to have survived, perhaps Austen would have evoked affection from
fewer readers. *Mansfield Park*, with a hero and heroine who are themselves
hard to love, is knotty and elusive in its complexity, while the earlier novel
often seems defiantly unsubtle, from the brilliant black farce of Fanny
Dashwood's education of her husband in the art of meanness (an unambigu-
ously nasty, if peripheral, example of the mentor-lover) to the unrepressed
emotion of Marianne's near-screams of agony at the loss of Willoughby
(105). Each of these two "darker" novels is noted for causing discomfort in
the course of its reading and dissatisfaction at its end, but there is another
resemblance other than Austen's refusal to beguile. Anticipating *Mansfield
Park*, the earlier novel is notable for the way in which its structure tends to
ensnare readers into the condition of inattentive proofreaders who find not
what is there, but rather what they expect—desirable mentor-lover relationships—even though in the earlier novel the promise of such relationships
fizzles to nothing while in the later it leads to tragedy.

Austen's obsession with age in *Sense and Sensibility* both suggests the
need for, and disappoints expectations of, successful mentorship. Every character of significance has a stated or calculable age, age is often the subject
for humour, and discrepancies between chronological age and moral and

From *Austen, Eliot, Charlotte Brontë and the Mentor-Lover*, pp. 47–79, 194. © 2003 by
Patricia Menon.

219

emotional development are part of an insistent pattern, though the characters prove immune to even the narrative's assertion that improvement has taken place. Many are simply childish in their self-absorption, while others show Austen working out more complex variations on the theme. Marianne, for example, as John Wiltshire points out, appears never to be emotionally weaned from her mother who, in turn, lives vicariously through her (29–30). At the same time, the forty-year old Mrs Dashwood is in effect another sister—"Indeed a man could not very well be in love with either of her daughters, without extending the passion to her" (90)—with judgment less mature than that of her oldest daughter. And Elinor, at nineteen, begins and remains a generation older than everyone else, the only adult in a novel that specializes in making children, and the blind indulgence with which they are treated, the butt of many a dark joke.

Though Elinor's calendar age makes her a rather unconventional candidate to be anyone's mentor, there is a figure who promises to fit the stereotype more closely. Joseph Weisenfarth is not alone in describing Colonel Brandon as such when he includes (among a pattern of Austen's "Pygmalions" and "Galateas") his "shaping of Marianne Dashwood" (*Emma*: point counterpoint" 216–17). The Colonel is an obvious choice by reason of his gravity and age—he is five years younger than Marianne's mother, as the reader is often reminded—and this is how he is usually perceived. But despite Marianne's convalescent resolve to draw on his library for books that will provide her with "a great deal of instruction" (343), he is, in fact, a testament to the power of cliché to shape expectations. As Laura Mooneyham White points out, "Marianne and Brandon do not educate each other. How can they when they do not even have one instance of reported dialogue in all of the novel?" (78).

In any case, Brandon isn't up to being a mentor, for, flannel waistcoat notwithstanding, he has never grown up. It is apparent from his falling in love with Marianne after the tragedy of Eliza, that the "romantic refinements of a young mind" (56), "the same warmth of heart, the same eagerness of fancy and spirits" (205) that appealed to him as a seventeen-year old are the very characteristics he continues to find attractive in Marianne, now the same age. His unwillingness to agree with Elinor that her sister would be the better for being disabused of "the prejudices of a young mind" through "a better acquaintance with the world" (56) is founded in a distrust of experience and of the ability to learn from it. In his view, disillusionment can only lead to moral breakdown and experience of the disasters ensuing from youthful romanticism has done nothing to temper his commitment to it. A romantic himself, the tale Austen gives him to tell is a signal of his condition, a standard from popular fiction (the kind she announced her own emancipation from in *Northanger Abbey*) covering all the angles: an elopement betrayed; a greedy guardian and lascivious husband; a woman deceived, debauched and impregnated; her mandatory end in rescue from the sponging house, repentance and death—with, of course, an echo in her daughter's own fall from innocence. The tale is interlaced with his account of his own naivety, first in his "noble" decision to take service in India leaving the girl he loves unprotected in the hands of a greedy father and brother, and then in the imprudence in his care for Eliza's daughter. The whole is crowned by the culmination of high romance, the step that Eleanor sighs over as a "fancied necessity" (211), a duel with Willoughby. Even the "impossibility" of the romantic's forming a "second attachment", one of the running jokes in the work, is not so much denied as supported by her likeness to Eliza, the first love whom, in effect, the romantic Brandon finally succeeds in marrying (227). Jocelyn Harris suggests that *Sense and Sensibility* is a multiple retelling of *Clarissa*: "The Eliza scenes fail for closely copying their original, the Marianne scenes, which scrutinize and rework *Clarissa*, convince and move" (59). But if the Eliza scenes are seen as criticism of a motif long fallen into cliché rather than failures in themselves, then the reworking of the tale takes on greater import.

If Austen fails to divest readers of their expectations of Brandon's role as mentor, she also fails to convince them (if indeed she tries very hard) of his role as lover. At the close, the narrative voice (sounding suspiciously tongue-in-cheek) asks us to accept that Marianne comes to love the Colonel. Generations of readers have failed to be convinced, in part because the process is couched in ominously sacrificial phrases that engender uneasiness at her conversion. Mrs Dashwood, Edward and Elinor "each felt [Colonel Brandon's] sorrows, and their own obligations, and Marianne, by general consent, was to be the reward of all. With such a confederacy against her, what could she do?"; "that she found her own happiness in forming his, was equally the persuasion and delight of each observing friend" (378–9). It isn't clear whether we are to laugh at Marianne's former convictions or at the transparent machinations of her "friends". Nor is it clear how hollow our laughter is expected to be.

There is no doubt about Marianne's love for Willoughby. It is, however, a love motivated by egotism, directed towards a man who "thought the same" as she (53). It is Austen's demonstration of the vulnerability of egocentrics to manipulation by those who confirm their worth, made possible, as Susan Morgan points out, by Willoughby's familiarity with the code of sensibility, which enables him to know in advance exactly what will please Marianne ("Letter Writing" 107). Although, unlike Willoughby, she is undoubtedly sincere, each lover adjusts to resemble the other in behaviour, endorsing the other's judgments and sharing an immature conviction of knowing everything. The potential dangers of this reciprocal education are clear: a mutual admiration society with the potential to injure the naively self-centred Marianne, while being insufficient to sway Willoughby from his absorption in his own desires.

As to her older sister's situation, no reader can long hold on to the hope that Edward will have anything to teach Elinor, nor does he. Glenda Hudson makes an attempt to rescue him from complete moral and emotional idiocy, arguing that "Edward's fraternal love is not metamorphosed into passionate love until Lucy elopes with Robert" (*Sibling Love*, 57). But the novel belies this when Edward admits "I *was* wrong in remaining so much in Sussex", persuading himself that "The danger is my own; I am doing no injury to anybody but myself" (368, emphasis in original). If Edward has nothing to teach Elinor, signs of her influence upon him are no more believable than the possibility that she might find lasting satisfaction with a thickhead who requires Lucy's elopement to convince him that his fiancée isn't just a simple good-hearted girl. When, at the novel's conclusion, Elinor criticizes the way he had behaved at Norland, the scolding is cast as love-talk, "as ladies always scold the imprudence which compliments themselves" (368), an indulgent recognition of his naivety that does nothing to reconcile the reader to him, convince us that he is mature enough to merit her "tears of joy" (300), or show him to have learned anything from Elinor. Indeed, his position, if not his personality, makes him an echo of the other idle males including Robert Ferrars, John Dashwood, Mr Palmer, Brandon's brother and Willoughby who are, as Claudia Johnson shows, part of a pattern in the novel of "weak, duplicitous and selfish" men who have little purpose in life but to await, and then spend, the money that they acquire through inheritance or marriage (*Jane Austen* 57–8).

An immature romantic, a manipulative egocentric and an irresponsible naif—the leading males in this novel have little to offer the sisters or receive from them in the way either of love or of mentorship. If we ask where the strongest drive to educate and the most intense love come together in the work, it becomes clear why Brandon and Edward are of so little account. They cannot help but be nullities in the face of Elinor's love for Marianne. Eve Kosofsky Sedgwick, citing the bedroom scene in which Elinor observes Marianne writing to Willoughby, claims it manifests elements of hetero-, homo- and autoerotic love (138–9). However, Elinor's love seems not so much sexual as an emotion of such intensity that it preempts the development of an intense loving relationship of any other kind, including the sexual, with the men the sisters marry. Motivating her pressing desire to educate her younger sister aright, it is the strongest emotion in the work, leaving room for very little else. It may be measured by the need that Elinor feels to conceal its strength, the fear that this bond may be threatened by love for others being the most convincing explanation for Elinor's continued unwillingness to ask Marianne about Willoughby, as well as for her decision, which she justifies as due to her promise to Lucy, to keep Edward's situation a secret. Following Elinor's confession of her own misery, it seems her devotion is reciprocated though to a lesser degree—Marianne's is the love of a creature stunned and damaged. Furthermore, as Marianne's mentor, Elinor has apparently been only too successful. All egoism drained, a young woman with a relationship to her husband more characteristic of a George Eliot heroine emerges: "Marianne found her own happiness in forming his" (379). It is a depressing prospect, but it is also an unconvincing one, for, insofar as the novel can be said to end happily, it does so because the sisters are not parted by marriage. The emphasis of the final paragraph is skewed towards the relationship of the sisters, to which all others are presented as adjuncts: "among the merits and happiness of Elinor and Marianne, let it not be ranked as the least considerable, that though sisters, and living almost within sight of each other, they could live without disagreement between themselves, or producing coolness between their husbands" (380).

With the dubious exception of the sisters' relationship, *Sense and Sensibility* treats the possibility of love and mentorship with the dismissive savagery of black humour. By contrast, *Mansfield Park* with its infinite range of greys seems—and is—a very different type of work. Yet in its concerns with sibling affection and its suspicions of love and mentorship, it shows Austen working with similar issues although to very much more subtly conceived ends.

* * *

Mansfield Park is the novel that provokes the most disagreement among Austen's readers, both as to its merits and its author's intentions. An examination of the pattern of the mentor-lover relationships within it suggests that in part this is due to the fact that Austen, who elsewhere proved herself aware of the potential for a darker side to such relationships by evading the difficult questions, here risked exploring that darkness more fully. That in neither the earlier *Sense and Sensibility* nor the later *Persuasion* does she make the mentor-lover relationship central suggests the difficulty she found in dealing with its challenges in those novels in which light-footed diversionary tactics could not be employed under the guise of comedy. The problem she faced has its parallel in an episode inside the novel itself when, in the absence of Sir Thomas, Mr Yates infects the susceptible young people of Mansfield Park with the compulsion to put on a play. The project almost stalls over their inability to agree on an appropriate genre: there was "such a need that the play should be at once both tragedy and comedy" (130).

But in *Mansfield Park*, comedy is relegated to the readers' expectations and the edges of the work: it ceases the moment the brisk and distanced summary of the Ward sisters' history modulates, in the course of a discussion of the possibility of fostering Fanny, into the exposure of an unhealthy and contagious mentor-lover relationship. It commences again only in the last chapter with its apparent endorsement of the belief that it really is possible to sort characters into those "not greatly at fault themselves" and "the rest" (461).

However, this shift into a comic closure leads to a related cause of controversy encouraged by Austen's closing designation of characters as sheep or goats. Repeatedly critics reject Fanny for Mary, or Edmund for Henry (or vice versa), or characterize Mansfield, in Trilling's words, "for the author as well as the heroine [as] the Great Good Place" (169). Indeed one of the most striking features of much of the published criticism of the work is that, although there are changes in interpretation and preferences over time, the assumption that characters and places of *Mansfield Park* should be considered symbols of good or evil is remarkably persistent. Like all Austen's novels, however, *Mansfield Park*, at least when shorn of its closing, resists, as I shall argue, all attempts to read it in a schematic way.

Given her desire (even at the cost of evasion) to demonstrate the possibility of achieving equality of love and moral stature by a passage through and beyond mutual mentorship in *Pride and Prejudice*, Austen might have been expected, in her next novel *Mansfield Park*, to push towards the same satisfying resolution. And, as in the case of its predecessor, much in the work suggests this is her purpose. Yet, ironically, the only example in the novel of achieved mutuality in love and mentorship is kept in the wings, hinted at through references to the play *Lover's Vows*. "As you have for a long time instructed me, why should I not now begin to teach you?" appeals Amelia as she manoeuvres her tutor into admitting he reciprocates her love. But this is a relationship that Austen keeps off the stage of the novel and, although rehearsed by Edmund and Mary, is not finally enacted, either in the drama or in their lives. The couple who appear to be the closest approximation to Inchbald's lovers, despite the differences in temperament between the aggressive Amelia and the passive Fanny, are the cousins of the concluding chapter. But theirs is a union requiring a more suspicious examination than is often given, an examination Austen discourages both through the appealing symmetry of their relationship and through belated assertions of its desirability.

Pervading the novel is Austen's development of a complex pattern of fractured mentor-lover relationships: overlapping three-way combinations in which a central figure of each trio cannot find in any one person the satisfaction of both moral and passionate needs and who suffers as a consequence by being divided between two people, one a lover and the other a mentor. Consideration of the intertwined relationships of Edmund, Fanny, Mary, Henry, Maria, Julia, Rushworth and Yates would illustrate many variations on this theme, but the initial pattern may be traced to their elders, for the novel is a cross-generational exploration of the relationship of mentorship and love. In the triangle of Sir Thomas, Lady Bertram and Mrs Norris, lie the origins of the moral, emotional and sexual disjunctions that corrupt the inhabitants of Mansfield Park.

The conditions for tragedy in this relationship are early demonstrated during the discussion of Fanny's "adoption". Sir Thomas Bertram is an Aristotelian figure, neither vicious and depraved nor, despite his pretensions, preeminent in virtue and justice. His tragic error has been his marriage to a woman inadequate as both a lover and a mentor, with superficial sexual charms but neither energy nor intelligence. The defence offered by the narrative voice, that she "did not think deeply, but, guided by Sir Thomas, she thought justly on all important points" (449), is less a compliment than a condemnation, for this denies her fallible husband any response that might challenge his moral complacency. Had he sufficient insight, Sir Thomas might well lament, in the words of the stage baron of *Lovers' Vows*, the consequences of choosing a moral nullity for a wife: "I had no instructor but my passions; no governor but my own will" (*LV* in *MP* 500).

But this would not be entirely true, for Sir Thomas has a sister-in-law who, though lacking sexual appeal, has both energy and an intense desire to manage others. Austen demonstrates, in the first discussion of Fanny's future, how the moral vacuum consequent on Sir Thomas's choice of wife enables Mrs Norris, while offering no overt challenge to his self-image as Grandisonian mentor, to seize the wifely role for herself. The conquest is achieved through the guise of submission, shared understanding and repeated flattery, "I perfectly comprehend you, and do justice to the generosity and delicacy of your notions" (6), embodying Austen's caricature of the courtesy book recommendations for the capture and pleasing of a husband in the interest of securing one's own aims. In fact, in her relationship with Sir Thomas, Mrs Norris has taken to heart the defence of conjugal obedience expressed in Hannah More's *Coelebs in Search of a Wife*:

> this scrupled "obedience" is so far from implying degradation, that it is connected with the injunction to the woman to "promote good works" in her husband; [suggesting] a degree of influence that raises her condition, and restores her to all the dignity of equality; it makes her not only the associate but the inspirer of his virtues. (I:5)[1]

Mrs Norris's particular talent is to corrupt Sir Thomas's better intentions in the interest of gaining and holding power within his household. Because it threatens her plans, she determinedly sweeps away his nervous, but justifiable, concern not to do a "cruelty instead of kindness" to a foster child (6) by playing on his pride of blood: "I could never feel for this little girl the hundredth part of the regard I bear your own dear children, nor consider her, in any respect, so much my own" (7). Indeed, while her own husband is a cypher who conveniently dies after only a shadowy appearance in the novel, she often speaks as if she is actually the baronet's wife: "A niece of our's, Sir Thomas. . ."—and when she corrects herself at such a time, it is more a matter of flattery than abdication of the wifely role: "or, at least of *your's*, would not grow up in this neighbourhood without many advantages" (6, emphasis original). Equally striking is Sir Thomas' responsiveness to this treatment, sometimes giving the momentary impression of speaking as husband to wife: "There will be some difficulty in our way, Mrs. Norris. . . . as to the distinction proper to be made between the girls as they grow up" (10). As his speech (an appropriate term) continues, Austen carefully lays bare the sources of his vulnerability: the blend of justifiable delicacy (Fanny will not have the financial expectations that will make his own daughters more marriageable) with sheer snobbery, concluding in a request that disguises his submission to his mentor as a courtly invitation:

> "It is a point of great delicacy, and you must assist us in our endeavours to choose exactly the right line of conduct."
>
> Mrs. Norris was quite at his service; and though she perfectly agreed with him as to its being a most difficult thing, encouraged him to hope that between them it would be easily managed. (11)

The reminder of the existence of another wife ("assist us") is no more than a token; a nullity can have no place "between them".

Austen creates an odd trio who are not only morally but emotionally deficient, so that even the three "parents" together cannot provide the love necessary for the children to thrive. Lady Bertram knows no other love than self-love while Mrs Norris, as substitute mother, considers love to be a combination of indulgence and flattery. As Austen insists, and as the clumsy attempts of Sir Thomas to overcome his emotional woodenness show, good intentions are not enough to counteract this destructive situation, and often he is simply blind to the disastrously incremental effects of the contradictory methods employed in his children's upbringing.

But, most significantly, Austen suggests that Sir Thomas continues to be in the power of sexual impulses of which he is only intermittently aware, and is still prone to be affected by the charms of a young woman, or, negatively, by their absence. Leaving for Antigua, he tactlessly expresses the hope that William will find Fanny not "entirely without improvement—though I fear he must find his sister at sixteen in some respects too much like his sister at ten" (33). Though the meaning of this reproach is initially obscure, it may be understood in the light of his reaction when he returns. For, while readers often give him moral credit for softening towards Fanny soon after his return, Austen suggests that this is in considerable part due to his niece's improved physical charms. His first reaction is his "observing with decided pleasure how much she was grown!" (178). And lest "grown" is thought to be merely a recognition that she is taller, Austen has Edmund assure Fanny, soon after,

> "Your uncle thinks you very pretty, dear Fanny—and that is the long and the short of the matter ... the truth is, that your uncle never did admire you till now—and now he does. Your complexion is so improved!—and you have gained so much countenance!—and your figure—Nay, Fanny, do not turn away about it—it is but an uncle." (197–8)

The deftness with which Austen so neatly skewers not only Sir Thomas but the insensitive son who teasingly quotes him, while allowing the reader to feel Fanny's surprise, embarrassment and hurt, is characteristic of the dense texture of the work.

Austen offers a portrait not so much of a man harbouring incestuous lust but rather of one whose perception of any woman is shaped by her sexual appeal, and who, because of his susceptibility, is fearful of the effects of sexual attraction. His being "an advocate for early marriages" (317) implies not only a distrust of Henry's ability to remain faithful, but a more general concern that male sexuality requires the containment of wedlock. He imputes Fanny's resistance to Henry Crawford, accurately, but against all appearances, to an absence in his niece of what "a young, heated fancy imagines to be necessary for happiness" (318) while he finds reassurance in the evidence that Maria plans to marry Rushworth "without the prejudice, the blindness of love" (201), his relief suggesting a distrust of sexual attraction based on his own experience, at some level regretted, with the former Maria Ward.

The evidence for Sir Thomas being a man emotionally improved by his new awareness of Fanny following his return from Antigua is ambiguous at best. Austen makes it clear that his recent awareness of Fanny as a sexual being also prompts his recognition that Henry is sufficiently attracted to her to offer her an advantageous marriage. While the impetus of his own pleasure in her "figure" might not have done more than propel her to an occasional parsonage party, the possibility of Henry's interest leads to the ball, and finally to the exertion of pressure on Fanny to ensure she accepts this financially desirable match.

Seen in this light, the episode of the schoolroom fire and Sir Thomas's half apology for Mrs Norris appear the result of Fanny's new consequence, rather than of avuncular tenderness on her uncle's part. In his altered view of the past, now illumined by Henry's interest, it appears to him that his mentor Mrs Norris has encouraged a "misplaced distinction" and he therefore urges Fanny to understand—adding distance to his apology by his use of the third person—that "Though their caution may prove eventually unnecessary, it was kindly meant" (313). His is a performance of self-deceiving shiftiness that becomes despicable when combined with the alternations of cruelty and "kindness" to which he subjects her. The hurtful accusations

> that you can and will decide for yourself, without any consideration
> or deference for those who have surely some right to guide you—
> without even asking their advice (318)

are so undeserved yet so accurately aimed at Fanny's greatest fears that they seem deliberately chosen to cause the greatest pain to a girl he acknowledges to be "very timid, and exceedingly nervous" (320). The accusations roll on, prudently suspended for tactical reasons to be replaced by the provision of warmth in the schoolroom and the partial (but only partial) shielding from Mrs Norris, acts that make Fanny's unmerited sense of guilt all the greater, while revealing how even genuine (if limited) sympathy and awareness can be perverted. At the very moment when Sir Thomas, unwilling to tell Mrs Norris about Henry's proposal for tactical reasons, appears most clearly to separate himself from his mentor, Austen allows him to reveal that he has actually taken on his sister-in-law's role, pointing up the similarity through commentary:

> Sir Thomas, indeed, was, by this time, not very far from classing
> Mrs Norris as one of those well-meaning people, who are always
> doing mistaken and very disagreeable things. (332)

After a tirade from Mrs Norris against Fanny's "independence" it seems to Sir Thomas, motivated by a Norris-like conviction of rightness, that "nothing could be more unjust, though he had been so lately expressing the same sentiments himself" (324). And Fanny is assured "You cannot suppose me capable of trying to persuade you to marry against your inclinations" (330) even as he plans to transfer the task of overt persuasion to Henry Crawford, and, later, to Edmund.

The best light in which Sir Thomas's scheme for the Portsmouth trip can be seen is another act of "well-meaning zeal", carried out in ignorance of the conditions there and of how oppressive his niece will find them. What cannot be justified is his abandonment of Fanny: it is only after Maria and Julia have run off that he sends for her, and then not for her own good but, as Edmund correctly thinks, "for my mother's sake" (442) and to have an excuse to get Edmund away from London (452). At the end of the penultimate chapter there is no evidence he has unlearned his mentor's lessons in his own treatment of Fanny, although that mentor, having done all the damage of which she is capable, has been reduced to an impotence that makes her, when not "irritated . . . in the blindness of her anger" at Fanny, a parody of her placid sister: "quieted, stupefied, indifferent" (448).

* * *

This primary triangle, with Sir Thomas at its apex, is the source of the moral and emotional corruption of the Bertram children in *Mansfield Park*, and as such is fully worked out in the course of the novel in such a way as to make a very persuasive case for the dangers resulting from the separation of the roles of lover and mentor and upon deficient love and mentorship. In Edmund's case his Aristotelian fall is not due, any more than his father's, to vice and depravity. He has been protected from the worst of the influences shaping his siblings by the long-understood need for him to take up a profession and his solid, quiet temperament leading to his interest in the Church. The inheritance of some characteristics from his father, a seriousness and an acceptance of established principles, has contributed to an easier relationship between them, freeing Edmund to some extent from the fear and resentment that the other children feel. And Austen both names and reveals Edmund's best quality, "the gentleness of an excellent nature" (15) when, at sixteen, he perceives and soothes some measure of his cousin's misery. Sir Thomas's damaged impulses to kindness have clearly survived in Edmund in a stronger and more admirable form, capable of open expression. From the beginning he becomes Fanny's mentor, giving her "a great deal of good advice" and she feels she has "a friend" (17). The echoes of Grandison's inscription of himself to Clementina as "*Tutor, Friend, Brother*" (616) ring warmly here until one remembers what a tangle Richardson's pair got themselves into.

But Austen suggests that Edmund has acquired some of his father's conventionality and emotional blindness, as capable as everyone else of expecting Fanny to adjust with ease to her new life until he is forced into awareness by finding her crying. From the beginning, he establishes a pattern that is to be a constant in their relationship. He attempts to shape her responses for her, simplifies the causes of her misery to fit the orthodox terms he expects, and then, ostensibly for her own good, gently gives a conventional reason to behave as the family desires while falsifying their feelings out of a convenient blindness:

> "You are sorry to leave Mamma, my dear little Fanny," said he,
> "which shows you to be a very good girl; but you must remember
> that you are with relations and friends, who all love you, and wish
> to make you happy." (15)

That this is no isolated response is clear when Austen provides a later parallel in the less forgivable advice he offers Fanny when she is fifteen and expected to move to the home of the newly widowed Mrs Norris. Fanny, "in distress", tells him of the shocking news: "Well, Fanny, and if the plan were not unpleasant to you, I should call it an excellent one" (25). In a lengthy series of justifications, Edmund shows he is as gullible as his father in thinking that his aunt will take Fanny on. Worse still, he is either capable of deceiving himself about his aunt's character and the benefits to Fanny from the scheme or of lying to his cousin, instead of attempting to protect her from the future she dreads. Some of his father's insensitivity to the depth of another's feelings must play a part, along with a convenient allegiance to the principle of filial respect that excuses him from considering the possibility of challenging a parental decision. Fanny's protests punctuate his advice, but by the end he brings her to concede:

> "I cannot see things as you do; but I ought to believe you to be right
> rather than myself, and I am very much obliged to you for trying to
> reconcile me to what must be." (27)

Austen draws a parallel here to Mrs Norris's flattering treatment of Edmund's father, but Fanny's response is in some ways more dangerous by reason of its differences. Its very sincerity, her belief she should trust to his view rather than her own endanger Edmund's ability to examine his motives critically. His "excellent nature" makes him more subtly vulnerable: a Mrs Norris, though capable of manipulating his father, could not overset his judgment of himself as Fanny can.

In both of these instances, Austen shows Edmund's habitual mode, even when uninfluenced by such special circumstances as the willed blindness induced by having fallen in love. But once he has met Mary, the moral weak spots in Edmund crack open to reveal, not merely a loss of sensitivity to Fanny's welfare and feelings, but a willingness to employ tactics strongly resembling his father's. Alone, unsupported, guilty, Fanny has withstood every pressure to accept Henry Crawford. Edmund, the only person who might sustain her, apprised of the situation by his father, responds manipulatively (and characteristically):

> "So far your conduct has been faultless, and they were quite mistaken
> who wished you to do otherwise. . . . But (with an affectionate smile),
> let him succeed at last, Fanny, let him succeed at last. . . ."

> "... I wish he had known you as well as I do, Fanny. Between us, I
> think we should have won you.... I cannot suppose that you have
> not the *wish* to love him—the natural wish of gratitude. You must
> have some feeling of that sort. You must be sorry for your own
> indifference." (347, 348, emphasis original)

Hoping, as on previous occasions, for his support, she is thrown what looks
like a lifeline, only to find herself pulled deeper into guilt and isolation.
Austen's unusual interpolation of a stage direction in the form of his "affectionate smile", draws attention to the theatricality of his performance, the
refusal to recognize Fanny's anguish and the artificial insistence on a warm,
shared, understanding. Fanny's objections are swept away as they always
have been, Edmund "scarcely hearing her to the end" (349). Austen shows
that all that is new since their very first conversation is Edmund's unconscious incorporation into the argument of his own concerns about Mary
Crawford. It may be too much to expect of Edmund that he recognize that
Fanny loves him, but Austen suggests it isn't modesty that blinds him, but
insensitivity. The dreadful blundering joviality of "Between us, I think we
might have won you" in reference to Henry echoes his earlier heavy-handed
account of the nature of his father's admiration, and offers a reminder of his
father's blindness to others' feelings.

Austen marks the episode from its beginning to its end with signs of
Edmund's treachery. He is clearly aware of the emotional satisfaction attached
to the role of mentor and he attempts to use it to further Henry's cause:

> "a most fortunate man he is to attach himself to such a creature—to
> a woman, who firm as a rock in her own principles, has a gentleness
> of character so well adapted to recommend them.... I know he will
> make you happy; but you will make him every thing."
>
> "I would not engage in such a charge," cried Fanny in a shrink-
> ing accent, "in such an office of high responsibility!"
>
> "As usual believing yourself unequal to anything!" (351)

It is a well-honed routine, but one to which Fanny no longer responds to with conviction: "Fanny could with difficulty give the smile that
was here asked for. Her feelings were all in revolt" (354); her smile, again
scripted by Edmund, is as artificial as his had been. Austen signals that
the betrayal is complete when Edmund, recognizing further talk is useless
"led her directly with the kind authority of a privileged guardian into the
house" (355). The identification of father and son is confirmed when they
agree on the same tactics, Edmund subsequently showing no more interest
in her welfare than his father, making contact only in so far as his need for
a confidante arises.

But the resemblances between father and son as mentors also have some disconcerting echoes in their nature as lovers. In Mrs Norris's favour it should be noted that she had been psychologically correct in predicting that Fanny's position would prevent Tom or Edmund falling in love with his cousin. For Edmund, as Mrs Norris predicts, Fanny remains friend, cousin and, after his rejection of Mary, "My Fanny—my only sister—my only comfort now" (444); it is the un-sisterly and un-Fanny-like Mary Crawford with whom he falls in love:

> Active and fearless, and, though rather small, strongly made, she seemed formed for a horsewoman; and to the pure genuine pleasure of the exercise, something was probably added in Edmund's attendance and instructions. (66–7)

Mary's physical vitality and confidence, her conscious pleasure in her own sexual attractiveness, and a willingness to take the lead (it is she who suggests they "rise to a canter" although Edmund is nominally giving "instructions") make Edmund her very willing pupil (67).

Indeed, in this couple Austen initially presents a wholly engaging depiction of mutual sexual attraction. But she also shows Edmund to be son to Sir Thomas and Lady Bertram, and as such, shaped by their marriage. For this very reason, Mary's active self-assertion, so unlike his mother's manner, both attracts and frightens him. Son, too, of Mrs Norris, he struggles to dissociate Mary from a kind of "liveliness" he has learned to dislike: "there is . . . nothing sharp, or loud, or coarse. She is perfectly feminine, except in the instances we have been speaking of. *There* she cannot be justified." His frequent discussions with Fanny are designed to elicit a reassurance from her that he is right to judge Mary's "lively mind" to be "untinctured by ill humour or roughness" even before he knows her views on marriage or the clergy. But his uncertainty necessitates a preemption of criticism, "I am glad you saw it all as I did". As Austen begins the long process of testing the reader's judgment of Miss Crawford in all her complexity, she is careful to offer a reminder that Fanny is no unbiased observer. Even if jealousy played no part, she could not follow Edmund in "a line of admiration" powered by the magnetic force of sexual attraction (64, emphasis original).

Mary, despite her good qualities, is deeply flawed as a result of her upbringing by an unfaithful uncle and an unhappy aunt: unthinkingly mercenary and cynical in her view of marriage and frighteningly willing to abet her brother's campaigns of emotional plunder. When she speaks to Fanny of Henry's courtship, her willingness to do so in terms of power—"your conquest", "your power over Henry" who "glories in his chains" (360), and "the glory of fixing one who has been shot at by so many; of having it in one's power to pay off the debts of one's sex" (363)—reveals not only her acceptance of power as the basis of relations of men and women, but also her low valuation of love, which to her is worth only the most hackneyed of clichés. She is obsessed with attacking Edmund's chosen profession, in part for worldly reasons and in part in reaction against the example of her brother-in-law. Yet, despite all her defences, conscious and unconscious, she, like Fanny, is attracted to Edmund by his virtues: "There was a charm, perhaps, in his sincerity, his steadiness, his integrity, which Miss Crawford might be equal to feel, though not equal to discuss with herself" (65).

If Edmund is to make headway as Mary's mentor as well as her lover, it seems more likely that his conduct rather than his speech will convert her. Austen neatly has him both enunciate and illustrate this point as he defends the clergy:

> "The *manners* I speak of, might rather be called *conduct*, perhaps, the result of good principles; the effect, in short, of those doctrines which it is their duty to teach and recommend; and it will, I believe, be every where found, that as the clergy are, or are not what they ought to be, so are the rest of the nation."
>
> "Certainly," said Fanny with gentle earnestness.
>
> "There," cried Miss Crawford, "you have quite convinced Miss Price already." (93, emphasis original)

The carefully constructed pronouncements provoke flippancy from his newest pupil and at their last meeting, when Mary lashes out defensively under his rebuke: "A pretty good lecture upon my word. Was it part of your last sermon?" (458), it is his propensity to preach and his choice of the role of public mentor that she chooses to insult.

In the end, Edmund's conduct and character aren't sufficient to combat the effects of Mary's preconceptions and the influence of her upbringing and friends, although her wit and liveliness appeal as much to the reader as to Edmund. Indeed, Austen herself seems to have realized the reader might have difficulty with, in the phrase of Samuel Johnson, such a "mixed character" and, anxious to preclude confusion, to have been guilty of putting her own finger unnecessarily on the scales when she has Mary write to Fanny of the possible advantages of Tom's death.

Edmund's reactions to Mary in their final meeting are not just a simple victory of right over wrong. Something seems amiss when he repeats a charge he formerly denied in the early stages of his love when he had defended her as "feminine" against his own doubts of her propriety. Repelled by Mary's worldly attempts to hush matters up and designate the elopement "folly" he struggles to express his sense of her failings: "No reluctance, no horror, no feminine—shall I say? no modest loathings!" (454–5). For Edmund, the word "feminine" indicates a belief in a double standard, not only of speech but of moral judgment, although nothing else in Austen's work suggests that she herself believed standards of judgment should differ by gender. This must be Edmund's problem, one more inheritance from his father.

It is at his final meeting with Mary, or at least in his retrospective account of it to Fanny, that Edmund, so appealingly open to Mary's sexual attraction in the course of the novel, appears to revert under stress to something more resembling Sir Thomas's distrust:

> "I had gone a few steps, Fanny, when I heard the door open behind me. 'Mr. Bertram,' said she, with a smile—but it was a smile ill-suited to the conversation that had passed, a saucy playful smile, seeming to invite, in order to subdue me; at least, it appeared so to me. I resisted. . . ." (459)

As Anne Mellor notes, Mary is "finally depicted as little better than a prostitute, beckoning seductively from a doorway" (58). It's impossible to know whether Edmund's impressions correspond to Mary's intentions; he himself is unsure. More significant is the fact that he interprets the appeal as a sexual one, designed to override his moral judgment, to "invite" and "subdue". His disgust makes him particularly susceptible to the attractions of a docile, sisterly creation of his own who will not, like Mary, attempt to "subdue" him through sexual attraction: "Fanny's friendship was all that he had to cling to" (460). Austen, of course, is already setting us up for another world, the world of comedy in the last chapter in which, to the hero's surprise, he unexpectedly finds love where he least expects it, but this should not obscure her delineation of Edmund's revulsion from an apparent sexual appeal as an inheritance from his father.

No critic denies that either Sir Thomas or Edmund has his faults; the more usual response is to judge those faults as forgivable. Fanny, however, has frequently been seen (with admiration or horror) as being intended by Austen to be perfect.[2] Even the Bakhtinian Baldridge denies the novel the dialogic status it so richly deserves: "the static career of whose immaculate heroine stands at cross purposes with the formal requirements of the genre she inhabits" (62). It is a relief, therefore, to find critics resisting the pressure of the novel's closing to discuss Fanny as a complex human being. Roger Gard, for example, maintains that "Fanny's judgments (those that have a hint of the mean-minded or mealy-mouthed) and her excessive decorum, are typically responses to threats to her precariously held calm" (131–2). John Wiltshire argues that "Jane Austen's representation of Fanny's psychology is so full and intricate that it causes conflict within the novel's ethical, and ultimately conventional, structure" (108), a statement that can equally well be applied to Austen's representation of its mentor-lover relationships. The outward manifestations of Fanny's insecurity have, through time, appealed or repelled depending on both the individual and cultural predilections of the reader. But Austen explores more complex issues: whether, with Fanny's particular combination of interrelated weaknesses and strengths, she can live an independent moral life, whether her relationship with Edmund is advantageous to both, and whether she will share Edmund's ambivalent attitude to sex.

Though the detrimental effects of Fanny's admiration on her mentor are clear, his care for her seems, initially at least, to be wholly beneficial. But, just as the consequences of her grateful devotion enable Edmund to avoid judging himself by calling on her approval, so the relationship has risks for Fanny, for whom his love and his mentorship have always been linked. It isn't surprising, then, to find a seventeen-year-old Fanny hastening to agree with Edmund that Miss Crawford is "very indecorous" (63), both out of a desire to demonstrate she has learned her lessons in propriety as well as out of inklings of rivalry. Nor is it unexpected that she should learn with pain that her role is not to agree with his criticisms but to refute them.

But, as a consequence of Fanny's demure demeanour, what is easier to miss (at least on the evidence of most critical readings) is how quickly after the Crawfords' arrival, Fanny's love for Edmund develops a sexual element. Tony Tanner, for example, considers that the closing of the novel demonstrates Austen's "purposeful—deliberate—intentions to abstain from the whole realm of sexual feelings" (173). Roger Gard believes that Fanny is "neither saintly nor sexy" although, as he points out, some find saintliness erotic (130), a position supported by Hannah More's recommendation in *Coelebs* that modesty is sexually exciting (I:89). But although Sir Thomas and Henry Crawford (undoubtedly both supporters of the conduct-book ethos) are reassured and excited by what they see as a contrast between her unfeigned modesty and her sexual development, Austen goes further than this, showing that Fanny, though unaware others might find her sexually attractive until Edmund teases her about his father, is certainly conscious of her own sexuality. The situation is complicated by Fanny's status. Mrs Norris's belief that the cousins, having been brought up as "brothers and sisters" (6) will not fall in love, while true of Edmund, has been nullified for Fanny by her sense of herself as an outsider, ironically perpetuated by Mrs Norris herself (the issue of whether such love is incestuous is best considered later in this chapter).

Austen's willingness to allow Fanny a sexual life is further impressive testimony to an authorial interest that most critics have denied or ignored. On the second day of Mary's riding lessons, the waiting Fanny is forgotten,

and she walks to where she can see the cheerful group admiring the riding of
the physically intrepid Mary:

> [Fanny] could not turn her eyes from the meadow, she could not
> help watching all that passed.... Edmund was close to [Mary], he
> was speaking to her, he was evidently directing her management of
> the bridle, he had hold of her hand; she saw it, or the imagination
> supplied what the eye could not reach. (67)

As she watches, Fanny passes from child to sexually aware woman, from
sulkiness to jealousy. That she is capable not just of seeing, not even just of
imagining, but of recognizing the possibility she is imagining, that Edmund
"had hold of [Mary's] hand" marks her sexual awareness though she is quick
to attempt to deny significance to what she sees:

> She must not wonder at all this; what could be more natural than
> that Edmund should be making himself useful, and proving his
> good nature by any one? (67)

But the statement is concluded with a question mark; Edmund's interest,
though "natural", is not simple "good nature"; and Miss Crawford is not
"anyone", as Fanny now very well knows. There really is no possibility for
Fanny to retreat back to childhood from this moment.

And, indeed, the atmosphere of Mansfield, liberated from the oppression
of Sir Thomas's presence, is permeated with sexuality released and encouraged
by the arrival of the Crawfords, and given expression through the decision to
enact *Lovers' Vows*. Mary, much against her will, is unable to maintain the sexual
and emotional detachment that has hitherto protected her from more than a
mercenary interest in men, while Henry's skilful playing of one sister against
the other flourishes on his indifference and their self-centred inability to resist
his manipulations. That a good deal of both Edmund's hostility and attraction
to the play can be seen in terms of hostility and attraction to the atmosphere
of sexual excitement it promotes is clear. But what Austen also suggests is that
Fanny's contribution to their shared but faltering resistance is driven by the
same mixed motives as her mentor's. This isn't, of course, what Fanny admits
to herself: "For her own gratification she could have wished that something
might be acted, for she had never seen even half a play, but every thing of
higher consequence was against it" (131). But she is alert, with the empathy of
a fellow-sufferer "connected only by [her] consciousness" (163) to Julia's "agita-
tions of *jealousy*" (136, emphasis original), while her astonishment at the choice
of play when she reads it can only be exacerbated by the recognition that her
predicament would be even more "improper for home representation" (137)

than that of the play's heroine, Amelia. Like the character, she is in love with her mentor but without Amelia's belief that the emotion is reciprocated or her superior social standing. But it is the expression of love rather than the feelings themselves that Fanny consciously repudiates: "the language of [Amelia], so unfit to be expressed by any woman of modesty" (137).

Austen doesn't simplify Fanny's reaction to acting to virtuous or priggish distaste, instead revealing the mixture of moral qualms, disappointment, jealousy and self-pity she feels when Edmund "consults" her about his taking a role:

> Her heart and her judgment were equally against Edmund's decision; she could not acquit his unsteadiness; and his happiness under it made her wretched. She was full of jealousy and agitation. Miss Crawford came with looks of gaiety which seemed an insult. . . . She alone was sad and insignificant. (159)

But Austen goes further, offering a much more ambiguous account of Fanny's "innocent" reaction to the highly charged rehearsals, once they begin, when she, unlike Julia, becomes involved in them:

> Fanny believed herself to derive as much innocent enjoyment from the play as any of them;—Henry Crawford acted well, and it was a pleasure to *her* to creep into the theatre, and attend the rehearsal of the first act—in spite of the feelings it excited in some speeches for Maria.—Maria she also thought acted well—too well;—and after the first rehearsal or two, Fanny began to be their only audience, and—sometimes as a prompter, sometimes as spectator—was often very useful.—As far as she could judge, Mr. Crawford was considerably the best actor of all. (165, emphasis original).

From the retrospective position of Henry's reading of *Henry the Eighth*, Fanny's fascination with the rehearsals is passed off (by Fanny or the narrative voice) as a simple attraction to the theatre:

> His acting had first taught Fanny what pleasure a play might give, and his reading brought all his acting before her again; nay, perhaps with greater enjoyment, for it came unexpectedly, and with no such drawback as she had been used to suffer in seeing him on the stage with Miss Bertram. (337)

But "drawback" seems a mild term in view of the fact that even the sophisticated Mary finds the performance of Maria and Henry ("one of the times when they were trying *not* to embrace") so blatantly erotic that she feels she must protect her brother from even the imperceptive Rushworth's growing suspicions by pretending to admire the *"maternal"* in Maria's performance (169, emphases original). Justified by being "useful", "Fanny believed herself to derive as much innocent enjoyment from the play as any of them", but, in the ferment of strong sexual and emotional excitement that the play engenders, the comparison says nothing more of Fanny's innocence than that the others are far from innocent and she wishes to deceive herself, a self-deception that strongly resembles that of her mentor Edmund. Her discernment of the situation is too sharp for an innocent, but she cannot keep away, drawn to the overtly sexual spectacle.

The climax comes with the arrival (tellingly in Fanny's domain-by-default, the schoolroom) of Mary asking that Fanny read Edmund's part so that Mary can practise Amelia's speeches of love to her stage (and would-be real) mentor-lover, then of Edmund himself with the mirror image of this request. The convergence of real and theatrical roles are painfully appropriate punishment for Fanny's having been tempted into the role of voyeur in the scenes between Maria and Henry. It is a scene in which Austen makes every detail count. Mary's assumption that Fanny can have no sexual interest in Edmund, "But then he is your cousin, which makes all the difference" and her conflation of the two: "You must rehearse it with me, that I may fancy *you* in him, and get on by degrees, You *have* the look of *his* sometimes" (168–9, emphases original) puts Fanny in the discomfiting position of taking the role of the mentor who has moulded her in his likeness, as well as reminding her of her questionable position in loving a cousin. Her awareness is reinforced by Edmund's arrival and his delight in being able to alter his plan from rehearsing with Fanny to using her as prompt for his acting as mentor with Mary, doubly ironic in view of his final return to Fanny. Even Mary's conversion of the schoolroom chairs, "not made for the theatre" but "more fitted for little girls", into furniture supporting declarations of theatrical love and real sexual interest serves as a reminder of the discontinuity between the maturity of Fanny's emotions and the family's consignment of her to the limbo of the ex-schoolroom and being neither "in" nor "out" (48–9). Only a renewed request that she take a role in the play forces her to articulate the strength of the unsuspected power that drew her to the rehearsals, while leaving her unable, or unwilling, to admit to herself the strength of the compulsion: "She was properly punished" (172).

Though Sir Thomas's return provides a brief respite for Fanny, it is followed by the much greater ordeal of being subjected to pressure from all those who claim to know best on Fanny's behalf, to accept an unwelcome suitor. That Austen intended to point a parallel between Sir Thomas the slave-owner and his desire to "sell" Fanny to the highest bidder has become part of the critical argument deriving from the Antiguan visit (Sutherland xxiii–xxv) and Brian Southam provides details of Austen's personal connections with Antiguan estates that make it difficult to argue that Austen was not aware of the implications of choosing such a destination ("Silence" 493–8).

More hotly disputed is the significance of the visit as an indicator of Austen's own assumptions. We never learn Sir Thomas's attitude to the slave *trade* as such, as his reply to Fanny is not reported (the family's "dead silence" and Fanny's diffidence cause the subject to be dropped, 197–8) although, given the date, he is certainly a slave *owner*, and, as Southam suggests, perhaps his uncharacteristic failure to pursue the conversation denotes his embarrassment. But is Austen on Sir Thomas's side? Edward Said believes she is (*Culture* 80–97), but his reading of the novel in the tradition of Trilling's "Great Good Place" ("*Mansfield Park*" 169), as if Mansfield Park and its owner (and therefore the wealth from the West Indian plantation) are endorsed by Austen, is an oversimplification dependent on giving the closing chapter more weight than the remainder of the novel.[3] On the other hand, sweeping statements of any kind concerning Austen's intentions to condemn slavery and suggest Fanny herself is enslaved seem out of place here. The actions of the navy to which Austen's admired brothers belonged, and into which Anne Elliot so joyfully married, contributed to defence of colonies that had long depended on slavery. And while Austen's references to Sir Thomas's source of wealth implicitly criticize his assumption of a right and duty to think for others, including finding his children homes with a wealthy "bidder", it is too crude a formulation to equate Fanny directly with Sir Thomas's enslaved workers. The echoes from those distant plantations, however, may be heard (though perhaps with more resonance by readers today) in Fanny's recognition that her duty as a dependent is to obey her uncle, and they provide an appropriate backdrop to her inner conflict. As Maaja Stewart points out, the "real issue in the drawing room [is] Fanny's wish to please Sir Thomas" (122). Her resistance to him over Henry's proposal is therefore all the more impressive.

Henry's first urge to make "a small hole in Fanny Price's heart" is initiated by his response (resembling that of Sir Thomas) to "the wonderful improvement" in her looks (229), strengthened by an egotistical desire to overcome her manifest dislike of him (230). It is at this point, with evident intent, that Austen suggests the resemblance between sexual and sibling love, bringing Fanny and William together in a relationship which, were it not identified by the context as fraternal, would surely be difficult for a reader to distinguish from the sexual. Often considered a creator of cool love scenes, Austen ensures that this reunion is all warmth, lit by "the glow of Fanny's cheek, the brightness of her eye...." It is a scene in which Austen explores the complex effects on the watching Henry Crawford, who has "moral taste enough to value" her obvious capacity for "feeling, genuine feeling" while her physical attractions pique his desire to "excite the first ardours of her young, unsophisticated mind" (235).

Austen must know what she is doing here, deliberately evoking a watcher's sexual response to the intensity of this sibling love, a step particularly daring because the narrative voice has just been praising the "fraternal" over the "conjugal tie":

> Fanny had never known so much felicity in her life, as in this unchecked, equal, fearless intercourse with the brother and friend . . . with whom . . . all the evil and good of their earliest years could be gone over again, and every former united pain and pleasure retraced with the fondest recollection. An advantage this, a strengthener of love, in which even the conjugal tie is beneath the fraternal. Children of the same family, the same blood, with the same first associations and habits have some means of enjoyment in their power, which no subsequent connections can supply. (234–5)

Of course, it is notoriously difficult in an Austen novel to find the exact point at which the narrative voice or the character's thoughts take or give up control, but it seems to me that "An advantage this . . ." has too generalizing a tone to be Fanny's, the question being, rather, whether the narrative voice is endorsed by Austen, which can best be decided by the course of the work as a whole.

This is a part of the novel that has provoked a variety of responses. In a detailed reading, attentive to the complexities of a very knotty passage (one that he finds "profoundly unsettling") Brian Crick suggests that it might be paraphrased as "can the estrangement between a brother and sister who have been especially fond of one another ever be justified by marrying someone from outside the family circle?" (81), tracing the implications of this passage for the relative valuing of familial and marital love through the work to the novel's close, where "the tell-tale signs of irresolution" (104–5) mark Austen's treatment of Fanny's marriage to her surrogate brother. Glenda Hudson, however, has no qualms at all about the appropriateness of "fraternal love" as the basis for marriage, believing Austen intends us to see Mansfield Park as preserved and revivified, concluding that "the incestuous marriage of Fanny and Edmund is healing and curative . . . a retreat to family life is appropriate and necessary to solidify moral standards" ("Consolidated Communities" 109).

With a view that is radically different from Hudson's, Claudia Johnson discerns in the work Austen's creation of a pattern of incestuous eroticism displayed in references throughout the work, not only in Fanny's interest in

William (easily transferred to Edmund) but also the comments of both Sir Thomas and Fanny's own father, the latter making his daughter the "object of a coarse joke" (*MP* 389). Johnson links fraternal and cousinly affection to the erotic interest shown by these father figures, maintaining that Austen builds up "a sustained body of detail that invites us to reconsider conservative political arguments which idealize familial love" (Johnson, *Jane Austen* 117–18).

However, though there are, as I have argued, striking parallels between Edmund and his father, there are also significant differences. To treat the two as one, and then to conflate both with William on one hand and Mr Price on the other neglects Austen's carefully drawn distinctions—we surely do not feel the same distaste for William and Fanny's love that we feel for Mr Price's joke nor Sir Thomas's stiffer admiration. Nor does a wholesale attack on familial love explain the troubling endorsement of the cousins' marriage at the close of the work. I also find it difficult to read the passage on the "conjugal" and "fraternal" ties as ironic to the discredit of the fraternal. It seems to me that Austen does indeed find Fanny's love for William attractive and does rate "fraternal" love so highly that she wishes to bestow its attributes on the "conjugal", in so doing recognizing the element of the sexual that is a component of such a strong emotion.

There are a number of responses the reader may make to this messy problem. It would be easy to simply dismiss this sibling love as "incestuous" and thus automatically objectionable (subsequently either condemning Austen for endorsing it or arguing, as Johnson does, that Austen herself condemns it). But as Sybil Wolfram has demonstrated in her study of kinship, the definitions of incest and arguments usually advanced against it vary from one society to another and each argument can in turn be shown to be illogical (137–96).[4] She points out that the most common popular objection is that the offspring are likely to be defective, a view she counters by arguing from genetics that "inbreeding intensifies characteristics, but good as well as bad" (145). As a justification of Fanny's marriage to Edmund, however, this may prove no defence at all if the intensified characteristics (symbolic rather than genetic) are indeed "bad" and the relationship is based on a retreat from maturity.

The problem of "fraternal" love adds to the reader's difficulty in assessing the intricately linked causes of Fanny's resistance to Henry Crawford and the pressures brought to bear on her by Sir Thomas and Edmund, revealing just how complicated, difficult, and sometimes fortuitous Austen perceives human choice to be. Fanny, with great difficulty given her desperate need to please, withstands the accusations of ingratitude and selfishness, and the implicit threats to deprive her of all she cares about. She asserts by her resistance that her judgment is superior to that of Sir Thomas who has permitted his daughter to marry Rushworth and to that of Edmund who, in his pursuit of Mary, has compromised his principles. That the same principles have proved ineffectual to guide the other young people suggests that it is Fanny's exclusion from Mrs Norris's indulgence that has helped to safeguard her, but the matter is not entirely straightforward, for Fanny's greatest protection has been her hidden love for Edmund, and her high valuation of mutual love. Moral integrity and love together give Fanny strength to overcome her weaknesses, but Austen makes no claim here that the connection between passion and judgment is anything but coincidental, for, while love gives Fanny strength because it supports her principles, it weakens Edmund because it runs counter to his.

When Fanny is recalled to Mansfield Park from Portsmouth, her moods swing violently: initially considering "the greatest blessing to every one of kindred with Mrs. Rushworth would be instant annihilation" (442), she subsequently feels "in the greatest danger of being exquisitely happy, while so many were miserable" (443). Edmund's arrival at Portsmouth and his "violent emotions", "brought back all her own first feelings" (445, 444)—but soon she feels "enjoyment" in seeing the beauties of the Mansfield grounds, followed by "melancholy again" (447). Such mixed and fleeting reactions are both natural and understandable, but, when Edmund comes to unburden himself, declaring he "would infinitely prefer any increase of the pain of parting, for the sake of carrying with me the right of tenderness and esteem" (458), Fanny's resolve hardens. Edmund's self-centred reiteration of his miseries is certainly irritating (and Mary's revelations to Fanny outrageous, if unconvincingly out of character), but what follows is a ruthlessness worthy of Mrs Norris:

> Fanny ... felt more than justified in adding to his knowledge of [Mary's] real character.... He submitted to believe, that Tom's illness had influenced her; only reserving for himself this consoling thought, that considering the many counteractions of opposing habits, she had certainly been *more* attached to him than could have been expected, and for his sake had been more near doing right. Fanny thought exactly the same; and they were also quite agreed in their opinion of the lasting effect, the indelible impression, which such a disappointment must make on his mind ... and as to his ever meeting with any other woman who could—it was too impossible to be named but with indignation. Fanny's friendship was all that he had to cling to. (459–60)

The nature of Fanny's triumph is dubious, her actions suggesting not only a decision to cause pain in order to speed up the cure, but, much worse, also a smug conviction of rightness: "more than justified". Her actions here present a contrast to her earlier refusal to use her knowledge of Henry's behaviour with Maria to discredit him and release herself from Sir Thomas's pressure. Fanny, whose changing language has charted her course from the alternations of the "girlish" and "bookish" to the maturity of Portsmouth, as Kenneth Moler demonstrates (172–9), now regresses to the dangerous role of admirer though now sustained by hypocritical reassurances: "Fanny thought exactly the same, and they were also quite agreed in their opinion". But there is a difference: that "they were quite agreed" becomes "he submitted to believe" and their relationship completes the shift into what it had always had the potential to be: a vehicle for ruthless management methods resembling, though more subtle than, those of Mrs Norris. To say that Mrs Norris and Sir Thomas are finally united in Fanny and Edmund is too crude a formulation to take into account what remains genuinely admirable in the cousins, but enough elements of that earlier "marriage" are present to cause disquiet.

Edmund of the "strong good sense" (21) now appears as the foolish male, a victim of wounded vanity whose self-centred conviction that he will be forever tragically inconsolable will soon be disproved by his recognition that Fanny is "only too good for him" (471). His love and current disillusionment are belittled by the language of this account: "not an agreeable intimation", "it would have been a vast deal pleasanter" (459). The closing paragraph of the penultimate chapter thus provides a transition into the determinedly comic resolution of the last, a chapter denying two conclusions Austen has already demonstrated: that the world is a great deal too complex to be divided into those "not greatly in fault themselves" and "the rest" (461), and that, while the division between mentor and lover is destructive, the coming together of the two roles may be as dangerous in its own way if it involves the mutual reinforcement, rather than the questioning, of the lover's worst qualities.

The difficulty of judging Austen's relationship to the events and to the narrative voice in the final chapter is considerable, partly because the tone, even within the chapter, is uneven, patches of flippancy alternating with passages that are unmistakably serious and appropriate to the tone of the novel as a whole. In fact it seems that Austen, very late in the game, has set herself, unsuccessfully, to satisfy the same apparently conflicting purposes that gave the young people such difficulty when they chose *Lovers' Vows*—to combine both "tragedy and comedy" (130). On the one hand, the narrative voice in the final chapter imitates the "rhyming butler" of the play, comically simplifying the moral complexity of the novel in the same terms: "And if his purpose was not fair, / It probably was base" (*LV* in *MP* 518) with cursory claims to have cleansed the infection, the neat classification of the characters into "fair" sheep and "base" goats, and the perfunctory distribution of the appropriate rewards and punishments. On the other hand, despite the narrative voice's disavowal, there is a good deal of "guilt and misery" (461) in the last chapter that is indeed consonant with what has gone before, although even here the treatment is inconsistent. Tom and Julia are dismissed with conventional tokens of penitence that suggest complete lack of interest on Austen's part, while the accounts of the fates of Mary and Henry Crawford and of Maria and Mrs Norris, though summary, are nevertheless appropriate to the tragic tenor of the work as a whole.

But it is on behalf of the remainder that falsification and special pleading occur. Sir Thomas becomes "poor Sir Thomas" (461), recognizes his past inadequacies as a parent, and is freed from the "hourly evil" of Mrs Norris, who, in an echo of her wifely status, had "seemed a part of himself, that must be borne for ever" (465–6) but is now dismissed as if divorced, ostracized in the company of "their" cast-off daughter. The serious analysis of his failures mixes oddly with the ease with which he is permitted to recognize and repudiate them (along with the adulterous daughter of his own creating). The convincing relapse into cynicism of Mr Bennet after the flurry of Lydia's elopement has no counterpart in consistency here. Furthermore, Sir Thomas's treatment of Fanny is dishonestly trivialized: "He might have made her childhood happier; but it had been an error of judgment *only* which had given him the *appearance* of harshness" (472, emphases mine). The narrative voice allows good intentions to excuse the errors that have led directly to Maria's downfall and a great deal of misery besides: his "liberality had a rich repayment" in the form of both a replacement daughter and a substitute niece (472). But even those good intentions are carelessly recast in a way not supported by the prior text: "He saw how ill he had judged, in expecting to counteract what was wrong in Mrs. Norris, by its reverse in himself" (463), a false claim of deliberate policy indirectly contradicted soon after: "His opinion of [Mrs. Norris] had been sinking from the day of his return from Antigua" (465), by which time, as Austen had demonstrated, his children's characters had been long formed.

Like "poor" Sir Thomas, Fanny is also taken under protection of the narrative voice of the final chapter, as "My Fanny", before the difficult business of describing her equivocal state is glossed over: "sorrow so founded on satisfaction, so tending to ease, and so much in harmony with every dearest sensation, that there are few who might not have been glad to exchange their greatest gaiety for it" (461). Her state is presented not only as emotionally understandable but also as morally unproblematic.

But the final betrayal of Austen's prior revelation of the dangers of Edmund's relationship to Fanny as mentor-lover comes in the nonchalant justification of their marriage:

> With such a regard for her, indeed, as his had long been, a regard founded on the most endearing claims of innocence and helplessness, and completed by every recommendation of growing worth, what could be more natural than the change? Loving,

guiding, protecting her, as he had been doing ever since her being ten years old, her mind in so great a degree formed by his care, and her comfort depending on his kindness, an object to him of such close and peculiar interest, dearer by all his own importance with her than any one else at Mansfield. . . .

. . . there was nothing on the side of prudence to stop him or make his progress slow; no doubts of her deserving, no fears from opposition of taste, no need of drawing new hopes of happiness from dissimilarity of temper. (470, 471)

If Pygmalion does not marry his own creation, the narrative voice implies, his only other choice is a woman with alien and dangerous values. Moreover, the nature of Edmund's "change" towards Fanny is not specified as a change from familial to sexual love but is blurred by the use of the more general "care": "Edmund did cease to care about Miss Crawford, and became as anxious to marry Fanny, as Fanny herself could desire", while flippancy discourages serious reflection on the reader's part: "I purposely abstain from dates on this occasion . . ." (470). This is a cosy union of mutual admiration all the more distressing because it presents as desirable those aspects of the relationship that Austen has clearly revealed in Edmund's father's situation, as in his own, to be morally and emotionally dangerous. Julia Prewitt Brown goes further, arguing that "At the close of *Mansfield Park*, Fanny is as much married in mind to her surrogate father Sir Thomas as she is in fact to her substitute brother Edmund. . . . Anticipating Freud, Austen implies that for the woman, the classic sex partners are father and daughter" (*Jane Austen's Novels* 99), but striking as this statement is, I think it over-schematizes the more complex pattern of resemblances and differences for which I have argued.

Although to trust the tale but not the teller in regard to *Mansfield Park* is, in most areas, to free the body of the work from the narrative voice of the final chapter, some problems in that chapter stem not so much from the betrayal of earlier insights, but from the culmination of contradictions already established. Fanny completes her transmutation to sister-mother, making up for the emotional and moral deprivations of Edmund's childhood and Edmund becomes her brother-child, a replacement for William and her Portsmouth siblings. The confusion over "fraternal" and "conjugal" love, earlier highlighted by the unironic treatment of Fanny's relationship to William, is thus perpetuated. The potential of "incest" to intensify characteristics, "good as well as bad" here works against the couple, intensifying the worst. Unfortunately, the pressure to bring fraternal and conjugal love together results in the undercutting of the central insight of the work, that to marry your own admiring creation is a terrible moral risk for both of you. And yet, denial of this recognition is what the last chapter demands.

But there is yet another problem that cannot be blamed on the closing chapter. From the beginning Austen has shown what is wrong with the particular situation of Edmund and Fanny and suggested the temptations to which the mentor-lover is in general prone; however, by exploring the dangers of dividing lover from mentor she has set up a logical structure that presses towards uniting the two in one person. As a result, Edmund in the last chapter is so clearly less mature than Fanny that Austen's determination to achieve moral equality for her couples as a prerequisite for marriage, central to her work (although, as noted, not achieved in *Sense and Sensibility*), is undermined. Regrettably, as Julia Prewitt Brown argues, part of Edmund Bertram is annihilated when he marries Fanny ("Civilization" 95).

Although a familiar problem from *Emma* and to a lesser extent from the other novels discussed, the question as to how to explain the flippancy that characterizes parts of the closing chapter[5] cannot be evaded in the predominantly serious *Mansfield Park*. Is it the consequence of Austen's loss of interest once the traditional closure of the marriage plot has been reached? Is it a test of the sentimental reader, with covert warnings about life's uncertainty? Is it a general recognition that the complex questions raised in the novel are not subject to any form of conclusion, and that, therefore, a happy ending is no more true or false than any other? Is it an unsuccessful attempt to yoke a tragedy with a comic finale to placate her readers? As such it would be consistent with the would-be actors' motive in choosing *Lovers' Vows*: "There were . . . so many people to be pleased" (130).

The truth probably consists of some combination of all of the above. As mentor, Austen declines to pose true/false questions, and while this refusal has much to recommend it as a pedagogical device, it brings with it the ancillary "benefit" of blurring her own uncertainties and difficulties. What is clear, however, is that in her relationship to her readers in all but the last chapter of *Mansfield Park*, Austen is less interested in pleasing them than in any other of her novels and even less willing to lead them to the recognition of a definitive ideal, a change that helps to account for the acute discomfort many feel with the work of a writer they expect to be both charming and assured. It is much harder to love the author of *Mansfield Park* than of *Pride and Prejudice* or *Persuasion*, and in this novel Austen relinquishes flirtation to Mary Crawford.

* * *

Though the complexities of *Mansfield Park* challenge any too-simple formulation, Austen's treatment of the mentor-lover in her works as a whole suggests that she is principally interested in the mentor-lover relationship as it contributes to, or works against, what she sees as an ideal end: a marriage founded on both moral equality and mutual sexual love, on both judgment and passion. This is true both when passion is ultimately feared or denigrated as it is, for example, in Abelard's presentation of it—attitudes Austen clearly condemns in Sir Thomas, Edmund, or Mr Bennet—and also when a character such as Fanny is tempted to adopt Heloise's self-denying devotion. Austen's attitude remains steady whether the mentor-lover relationship is marginal as in *Northanger Abbey* and *Sense and Sensibility*, (supposedly) mutual as in *Pride and Prejudice*, perilous as in *Mansfield Park*, or something to be outgrown as in *Emma*. This is an ideal she never abandons, despite her partial recognition that judgment and passion, though not automatically opposed, are also not amenable to being neatly integrated with or balanced against each other, and despite the unsolved difficulties arising from the conflict of this insight with the comic endings of the various novels.

In fact, it is Mr Bennet, speaking out of his recognition of the ideals he has betrayed, who reveals just this problem as he seeks to counsel Elizabeth after Darcy requests her hand for a second time:

> I know that you could be neither happy nor respectable, unless you truly esteemed your husband; unless you looked up to him as a superior. Your lively talents would place you in the greatest danger in an unequal marriage. You could scarcely escape discredit and misery. My child, let me not have the grief of seeing *you* unable to respect your partner in life. (376, emphasis original)

While there is no difficulty in prefacing either "respect" and "esteem" with a word such as mutual, the difficulty lies in reconciling a desire both to "look up" to a "superior" and to repudiate an "unequal marriage". We applaud Mr Bennet's words without examining too closely their inherent contradiction. That Austen reaches for the goal of mutual love combined with moral equality, however impossible to perfect in life as in art, is what makes her view of the responsibilities and rewards of marriage so attractive; that her closings claim success in the endeavour remains problematic.

* * *

In 1814, soon after she had begun *Emma*, Austen wrote to Cassandra, "Do not be angry with me for beginning another letter to you. I have read the Corsair, mended my petticoat, & have nothing else to do" (*Letters* 257: 5 March 1814). Less than three years later, in "Sanditon", Austen began a caricature of a would-be-Byron, Sir Edward Denham, whose account of his favourite reading materials marked him as one whose ideals were totally antipathetic to hers:

The Novels which I approve ... are such as exhibit the progress
of strong Passion from the first Germ of incipient Susceptibility
to the utmost Energies of Reason half-dethroned,—where we see
the strong spark of Woman's Captivations elicit such Fire in the
Soul of Man as leads him—(though at the risk of some Aberration
from the strict line of Primitive Obligations)—to hazard all, dare
all, achieve all, to obtain her ... and even when the Event is mainly
anti-prosperous to the high-toned Machinations of the prime
Character, the potent, pervading Hero of the Story, it leaves us full
of Generous Emotions for him;—our Hearts are paralized—....
            (*Minor Works* 403–4, punctuation and spelling as shown)

A little over thirty years later, Charlotte Brontë would write of Jane Austen,
in language almost as fevered as Sir Edward's, and with only slightly less
reliance on capital letters:

The Passions are perfectly unknown to her; she rejects even a
speaking acquaintance with that stormy Sisterhood; even to the
Feelings she vouchsafes no more than an occasional graceful but
distant recognition; too frequent converse with them would ruffle
the smooth elegance of her progress. Her business is not half so
much with the human heart as with the human eyes mouth hands
and feet; what sees keenly, speaks aptly, moves flexibly, it suits her
to study, but what throbs fast and full, though hidden, what the
blood rushes through, what is the unseen seat of Life and the
sentient target of death—this Miss Austen ignores; she no more,
with her mind's eye, beholds the heart of her race than each man,
with bodily vision sees the heart in his heaving breast. (Southam,
CH 1:128)

But there was another link between the two authors besides Brontë's
repugnance for what she perceived to be Austen's ignorance of "The Passions". Sir Edward Denham's future was secured by an irony of fate: he was
to be reincarnated repeatedly in Brontë's juvenilia, and, as "the potent, pervading Hero of the Story", would reappear in the person of another Edward—Edward Rochester. As if looking forward in time, Austen, in whose
works mentorship was a relationship best left behind in the growth to mutual
maturity, provided a criticism of Brontë sharper than any Brontë would make
of her. The worlds Brontë created had more in common with the schoolroom
of Abelard than Austen's "elegant but confined houses" (Brontë in Southam
1:126), schoolrooms where teaching and learning were erotic activities likely
to lead to "Aberration from the strict line of Primitive Obligations", where

judgment and passion were opposed, and passion was a cause of elation and fear because it threatened annihilation rather than mutual completion.

NOTES

1. Cassandra had encouraged an apparently unenthusiastic Jane to read this work in 1809 (*Letters* 170, 172: 24 and 30 January 1809).

2. For critics who have bestowed angelic or demonic status on Fanny over the years see, for example, Harding in 1940 ("Regulated Hatred" 358), Trilling in 1955 ("*MP*" 155, 160), Tanner in 1986 (*JA* 143, 148–9), Auerbach—"vampire", "Grendel", "cannibalistic"—in 1983 ("Charm" 212–13), Mellor in 1993 (58), Baldridge in 1994 (62).

3. For a thoroughgoing response to Said's reading, covering more material than is relevant here, see Susan Fraiman, "Jane Austen and Edward Said ... ": "Slavery functions ... as a trope ... to argue the essential depravity of Sir Thomas's relations to other people. I agree with Said that they are largely elided and always subordinated to the English material. The imperialist gesture is to exploit the symbolic value of slavery while ignoring slaves as suffering and resistant historical subjects" (Fraiman 213).

4. In her study of kinship and marriage, Sybil Wolfram argues that though marriage between cousins had been legal from the time of Henry VIII, opposition to such marriages has nevertheless survived into the present, on the "unfounded assumption" that they commonly produce "idiot children". She points out that while this case is usually argued today on genetic grounds, in the eighteenth century the wrath of God was adduced, to the extent that at least one cattle-breeder of the time kept quiet about his practice of inbreeding to improve his stock (21, 38, 138, 145). On a personal level, Jane Austen's brother Henry married his father's sister's daughter, the widowed Eliza de Feuillide (née Hancock).

5. This is, of course, an issue that has been much discussed in connection with Austen's novels in general and *Mansfield Park* in particular. For a helpful summary of various views, see Pam Perkins (21–5).

EMILY AUERBACH

An Excellent Heart:
Sense and Sensibility

For there is no friend like a sister
In calm or stormy weather;
To cheer one on the tedious way,
To fetch one if one goes astray,
To lift one if one totters down,
To strengthen whilst one stands.
                    —Christina Rossetti, *Goblin Market*

... my troubles are two.
But oh, my two troubles they reave me of rest,
The brains in my head and the heart in my breast.
                    —A. E. Housman, *Additional Poems*: XVII

She had an excellent heart;—her disposition was affectionate, and
her feelings were strong; but she knew how to govern them: it was a
knowledge which her mother had yet to learn, and which one of her
sisters had resolved never to be taught.
                    —Jane Austen, *Sense and Sensibility*

As Jane Austen worked to transform "Elinor and Marianne" into what
would become *Sense and Sensibility*, she must have wondered whether any

From *Searching for Jane Austen*, pp. 100–127, 314–316. © 2004 by the Board of Regents
of the University of Wisconsin System.

manuscript of hers would ever reach a readership or generate an income. Austen knew she could write novels with "genius, wit, and taste to recommend them," as she noted in the unpublished *Northanger Abbey*, but would any publisher agree (*NA*, 37)? Was there a public discriminating enough to prefer them to the improbable, sensational bestsellers of the day?

The changed title suggests that Austen perhaps added philosophical depth to what began primarily as a sketch of two characters. The new title, however, has in some ways hindered readings of *Sense and Sensibility*. Yes, Austen links Elinor to sense ("Her own good sense so well supported her") and Marianne to sensibility ("too great importance placed by her on the delicacies of a strong sensibility"), but she continually muddies the semantic waters, using not just the title words but terms like sensitive, sensible, and sensation (141, 201). Marianne is "sensible and clever," Elinor is "most feelingly sensible," and Marianne ironically becomes *"insensible* of her sister's presence" when she focuses on the sensations of her own romance (6, 134, 175). Austen carefully crafts her fiction so that readers cannot, in all fairness, reduce these two sisters to mind and emotion. As Carol Shields observes, "we have real sisters here, not convenient contrarieties."[1] Furthermore, Austen presents a large cast of characters, both male and female, possessing varying degrees of sense and sensibility. By so doing, she joins Mary Wollstonecraft in inviting readers to reconsider the standard assumption that men have sense, women have feeling.

Though her narrative voice is less pronounced in *Sense and Sensibility* than in *Northanger Abbey*, Jane Austen still remains ever present between the lines of her novel. If you think this female character in *Sense and Sensibility* is an unbelievably greedy, selfish, mercenary schemer, be advised that she is better than half her sex, Austen asserts with acerbic irony. If you find this marriage loveless, this man's will and testament unfair, this woman insipid, this card party dull, this man idle, or this group's conversation boring, remember that they are typical, Austen insists. Phrases such as *no traits at all unusual, like every other place, like half the rest of the world, as usual,* and *often* dot the pages of this biting novel. The Jane Austen we discover in *Sense and Sensibility* indicts her era's anti-intellectualism, commercialism, and selfishness. Through her narrative voice, she reminds readers that scoundrels, wastrels, philistines, and bores are the norm, not the exception, in real life—a dark, cold, almost-tragic real life offset only by instances of individual growth and genuine affection.

As Eva Brann notes in an article about *Sense and Sensibility* entitled "Whose Sense? Whose Sensibility? Jane Austen's Subtlest Novel," Austen asks "the frequent question, unique to this book: Who is its heroine?"[2] Some critics find the easy answer to be Elinor: "*Sense and Sensibility* is the story of Elinor Dashwood. The action of the novel is hers; it is not

Marianne's."[3] Yet two women move across center stage in this novel. What exactly are we meant to conclude about the differences between "Elinor and Marianne," the novel's original title? If Elinor is the heroine, do we automatically assume that her husband is more heroic than Marianne's? What does John Hardy lose by excluding Marianne from his collection of Austen heroines?[4] In our search for Jane Austen, do we find her more on one heroine's side than the other? Some have argued that Marianne is in fact "the life and center of the novel."[5] Biographers alert us to the fact that there may be greater similarities between Jane Austen and Marianne, Cassandra Austen and Elinor. According to a relative, Jane Austen reported that, faced with the death of her fiancé, Cassandra behaved "with a degree of resolution and Propriety which no common mind could evince in so trying a situation."[6] Could the book have started out as a tribute to Cassandra Austen's propriety and ended as a celebration of Jane Austen's vitality? As early as 1866 a reviewer noted, "Elinor is too good; one feels inclined to pat her on the back and say, 'Good girl!' but all our sympathy is with the unfortunate Marianne."[7] Other critics claim that Jane Austen meant for Elinor to be the heroine but that Marianne took on a life and power of her own: "Marianne . . . has our sympathy: she, and our response to her, are outside Jane Austen's control"; "The true heroine of *Sense and Sensibility* is Marianne. . . . The result is that a perfect comedy of manners was spoilt, and a great flawed novel written."[8]

I believe that Jane Austen deliberately constructs a tale of two heroines—or rather, two young women. The narrator shifts readers back and forth between the two sisters and everything they represent. To exclude Marianne from *Jane Austen's Heroines* shortchanges Austen's dual accomplishment in *Sense and Sensibility*—in particular, her ambivalent feelings toward revolutionary ideals, romantic notions, and youthful illusions.

If *Northanger Abbey* demonstrated that, had she chosen, Jane Austen could have written a gothic potboiler, then *Sense and Sensibility* proves that she could have created a romantic tragedy. The word *heart* appears in this novel far more than in any other she would write, often accompanied by adjectives such as *anguished, broken, sinking, wrung, wounded, sick,* and *heavy.* Austen censured and laughed at humiliated, desperate young women in her adolescent sketches (like Emma, who "continued in tears the remainder of her Life" after Edgar departs [*MW*, 33]), but in *Sense and Sensibility* she tempers her criticism with empathy. Marianne Dashwood may be silly at times ("I must feel—I must be wretched") but her heartache is raw—and real (190). As Victorian novelist George Moore notes, in *Sense and Sensibility* Austen "gives us all the agony of passion the human heart can feel" because "it is here that we find the burning human heart in English prose for the first, and alas, for the last time."[9]

Why might Austen delve more deeply into emotional states in this novel? As she worked on revising "Elinor and Marianne" into *Sense and Sensibility*, Austen encountered suffering too real to be ignored: her sister's loss of a fiancé to yellow fever in 1797, the death of a cousin in a road accident in 1798, her family's decision to leave their home in 1801, her father's death in 1805 and the corresponding need for Mrs. Austen, Jane, and Cassandra to find smaller living quarters (much like Mrs. Dashwood and her daughters moving to a smaller cottage), and Jane Austen's possible disappointments in love, whatever they may have been, before reaching the decision to don the garb of an old maid. Perhaps seeing grieving fiancées and devastated widows so close to home left Austen unwilling to write yet another light-hearted spoof of the sentimental heroine.

Austen's portrayal of Marianne's romanticism differs in tone from her derision of Catherine Morland's fascination with the gothic. After all, Austen liked the same writers as Marianne: Austen praises Cowper and Scott in her letters, as well as Gilpin's writings on the picturesque.[10] Like Marianne, Austen enjoyed music and felt less restrained and proper than her elder sister, who preferred painting. In one letter Jane Austen jokes that Cassandra has more "starched Notions" than her own (4 February 1813). An acquaintance of the family praised Jane Austen's sparkling eyes and energy but observed, "her sister Cassandra was very lady-like but *very prim*."[11] By using adjectives such as *striking, brilliant, eager*, and *animated* to describe Marianne but never Elinor, Austen suggests that Marianne's romanticism gives her a fire lacking in her tamer sister. True, by staying inside during inclement weather rather than running wildly down a steep slope Elinor avoids spraining her ankle and getting thoroughly drenched, but one suspects she could have used the fresh air and the liberty.

Liberty seems central to Marianne's character—and perhaps to her name. At the time Austen began "Elinor and Marianne" in the mid-1790s, she would have been well aware that Marianne stood for France—in particular, revolutionary France—and was being captured in the iconography of the time as a half-clothed, vibrant young woman whose youth and spirit conveyed the dawning of a new era. In *Marianne into Battle*, Maurice Agulhon traces the official link between the female symbol of liberty and the French republic to 1792, just a few years before Austen began "Elinor and Marianne." Statues of Louis XV gave way to statues of Marianne; paintings depicted her as "young, active, with a short dress (that leaves her legs bare at least below the knee, and sometimes also a breast bared); rather a tomboy in short."[12] As Lynn Hunt observes, by the end of the 1790s, "Liberty was indelibly associated with the memory of the Republic she had represented. In collective memory, *La Republique* was 'Marianne.'"[13] Characters named Marianne figure prominently in French literature, often as young women of common origins who stand up to their so-called aristocratic betters.

Could Austen have chosen the name Marianne because she wanted readers to consider both the good and the bad side of French revolutionary ideals? Austen copied out the Marseillaise, dotted her letters and novels with French phrases and allusions, and was acutely aware through her brothers of military conflicts between France and England.[14] I disagree with George Moore, who patronizingly creates an apolitical, demure, sheltered voice for Jane Austen: "I know nothing . . . of politics. . . . I am a maiden lady, interested in the few people with whom my life is cast. If you care to know how So-and-so marries So-and-so, I will tell you."[15] Austen tells her readers far more than that. We recognize Marianne's idealism and scorn of outmoded conventions, but also her impracticality and zeal. Consider the words of Marat-Mauger, a French revolutionary, who wrote in 1793, "A revolution is never made by halves; it must either be total or it will abort."[16] This sounds much like Austen's comment about Marianne, "She could never love by halves" (379). Marat-Mauger also offers a definition—"Revolutionary means outside of all forms and all rules"—that seems to fit Marianne's proud disregard of propriety. Marianne's fervor is refreshing yet disturbing, admirable yet off-putting.

There also is a French connection the only other time that Austen chooses the name Marianne: Austen dedicates her juvenile sketch "Love and Freindship," composed as a series of letters to Marianne, to her flamboyant cousin Eliza de Feuillide, then married to a French count. When Austen wrote "Love and Freindship" in 1792, Count de Feuillide had not yet lost his head to the guillotine, so perhaps Austen felt freer to send her cousin this light-hearted burlesque. In "Love and Freindship," Laura tells Marianne that she and Sophia successfully persuaded a young woman to reject a sensible man because of his lack of romantic appreciation: "They said he was Sensible, well-informed, and Agreable; we did not pretend to Judge of such trifles, but as we were convinced he had no soul, that he had never read the Sorrows of Werter, & that his Hair bore not the slightest resemblance to Auburn, we were certain that Janetta could feel no affection for him, or at least that she ought to feel none. The very circumstance of his being her father's choice too, was so much in his disfavour, that had he been deserving of her, in every other respect yet *that* of itself ought to have been a sufficient reason in the Eyes of Janetta for rejecting him. . . . It was her Duty to disobey her Father" (*MW*, 91–92). Austen's readers would have known that Goethe's *Sorrows of Werther* (1774) epitomized romanticism and had already caused a rash of suicides. Tormented by passions and lost in dreams, Goethe's artistic hero eventually shoots himself in the head. As Marianne recognizes near the end of *Sense and Sensibility*, she comes perilously close to following after Werther: She exclaims, "Had I died—it would have been self destruction" (345). Austen must have sensed that one danger of European romanticism—whether French, English, or German—was its morbidity.

The passage from "Love and Freindship" describing Janetta's rejection of a man because he is Goethe-less and because he is her father's choice seems an exaggerated version of scenes Austen would later include in *Sense and Sensibility*. Marianne believes Elinor should reject Edward because he reads Cowper so lamely, and she and Willoughby scorn the fatherly Colonel Brandon because others respect him. People in love must be afflicted, Marianne suggests, and she assumes that Elinor cannot possibly love Edward because she acts so sensibly: "When is she dejected or melancholy?" (39). Although Marianne is not a mere caricature as are Laura and Sophia of "Love and Freindship," she displays some of the same affectations.

In passages in *Sense and Sensibility* giving voice to Marianne, Austen summons the affected diction, punctuation, and martyred tone of romantic poetry. Marianne's lyrical address to Norland expresses her regret that her childhood home cannot feel her pain and that the trees will not visibly register grief over the departure of owners with such good taste: "Oh! happy house, could you know what I suffer in now viewing you from this spot, from whence perhaps I may view you no more!—And you, ye well-known trees!—but you will continue the same.—No leaf will decay because we are removed, nor any branch become motionless although we can observe you no longer!— ... No, you will continue the same; unconscious of the pleasure or the regret you occasion, and insensible of any change in those who walk under your shade!—But who will remain to enjoy you?" (27). Austen may be smiling here at Marianne's overblown use of language, but she also lets readers know that Marianne's feelings are real. Marianne does appreciate nature more than the new inhabitants do. The answer to her question of who will remain to enjoy nature is no one: later in the novel we discover that John and Fanny Dashwood, the new owners of Norland, have chopped down the old walnut trees to make room for a greenhouse.

Elinor twits her younger sister for delighting in romantic agony—her love of things desolate, dying, and dead. If Edward were at death's door, maybe Marianne would be attracted, Elinor jokes: "Had he been only in a violent fever, you would not have despised him half so much. Confess, Marianne, is not there something interesting to you in the flushed cheek, hollow eye, and quick pulse of a fever?" (38). Marianne, one suspects, could have written a moving "Ode to Autumn" à la Keats, "Ode to Dejection" à la Coleridge, or "Ode to the West Wind" à la Shelley ("the leaves dead / Are driven, like ghosts from the enchanter fleeing"):

"And how does dear, dear Norland look?" cried Marianne.

"Dear, dear Norland," said Elinor, "probably looks much as it always does at this time of year. The woods and walks thickly covered with dead leaves."

"Oh!" cried Marianne, "with what transporting sensations have I formerly seen them fall! How have I delighted, as I walked, to see them driven in showers about me by the wind! What feelings have they, the season, the air altogether inspired! Now there is no one to regard them. They are seen only as a nuisance, swept hastily off, and driven as much as possible from the sight."

"It is not every one," said Elinor, "who has your passion for dead leaves."

"No; my feelings are not often shared, not often understood." (87–88)

Marianne cries; Elinor says. Autumn brings Marianne "transporting sensations" and exclamations, while Elinor sees piles of dead leaves. In conversations like this one, Austen places readers in the middle with her, irritated that Marianne is carrying on excessively yet conscious that she genuinely delights in nature and spends more time outdoors than Elinor does.

Part of Marianne's appeal is her frankness, her lack of guile and concealment. In a society of fawning hypocrites and greedy schemers, Marianne is refreshingly open. Marianne has "neither shyness nor reserve" when, talking to Willoughby and scorns her sister's suggestion that she has been too unrestrained: "'Elinor,' cried Marianne, 'is this fair? is this just? are my ideas so scanty? But I see what you mean. I have been too much at my ease, too happy, too frank. I have erred against every common-place notion of decorum; I have been open and sincere where I ought to have been reserved, spiritless, dull, and deceitful:—had I talked only of the weather and the roads, and had I spoken only once in ten minutes, this reproach would have been spared'" (47–48). Marianne believes that she can do no wrong because she can feel no wrong. Perhaps Austen felt that one limitation of romantic literature was its amorality. When Marianne asserts of a man, "Whatever be his pursuits, his eagerness in them should know no moderation," she little realizes that Willoughby has indeed followed just such a credo, seducing young women and pursuing women of fortune with plenty of eagerness and immoderation (45). Marianne has to learn that one can be eager, handsome, spirited, lively, passionate, musical, and well spoken—but despicable.

Austen clearly saw that too great an emphasis on feeling leaves one self-absorbed, uncontrolled, and vulnerable. Too great a faith in imagined worlds guarantees disillusionment. Those who embrace liberty may become libertines; instincts are not always divine. Colonel Brandon's melodramatic Tale of Two Elizas (is it coincidence Austen chose the name of her cousin?) stands as a warning to Marianne. Like Marianne, Eliza had a "warmth of heart" and "eagerness of fancy and spirits" that caused Colonel Brandon to fall in love with her (205). Scorning the values of their society, the romantic colonel and Eliza tried unsuccessfully to elope in order for Eliza to escape forced marriage to the colonel's older, more prosperous brother. Faced with disappointment, Eliza responds by becoming a fallen woman subject to her passions. As Colonel Brandon reports, "I could not trace her beyond her first seducer, and there was every reason to fear that she had removed from him only to sink deeper in a life of sin. . . . So altered—so faded—worn down by acute suffering of every kind!" (207). After Colonel Brandon rescues her from prostitution and imprisonment for debt, Eliza dies of consumption. There is real death, disease, poverty, and sex in *Sense and Sensibility*. Eliza's pursuit of sensuality leads to a real child, "a little girl, the offspring of her first guilty connection" (208). This second Eliza, also subject to "the violence of her passions," falls victim to Willoughby's seduction (322).

Although Marianne scorns Elinor for suggesting that it is improper for her to be wandering alone with Willoughby through the rooms of his relative's house and scoffs at the need for a formal engagement, the Tale of Two Elizas suggests that Marianne is foolish to discard rules designed not for her oppression but for her protection. Austen censures those like Lady Middleton who are too priggish to hear talk of pregnancy or illegitimacy, but she also warns against promiscuity, anarchy, and the unbridled pursuit of sensation.

Austen demonstrates that Marianne, despite her romantic taste and personal beauty, evinces antisocial behavior at times, making no effort to flatter others: "'What a sweet woman Lady Middleton is!' said Lucy Steele. Marianne was silent; it was impossible for her to say what she did not feel, however trivial the occasion; and upon Elinor therefore the whole task of telling lies when politeness required it, always fell" (122). Is Marianne's refusal to lie a refreshing sign of her integrity, winning our admiration? Or is it a sign that she has not learned to be an adult member of a community? Perhaps both: Austen simultaneously praises and censures the romantic emphasis on spontaneous, uninhibited emotion.

If Marianne illustrates the unbridled zeal of French revolutionaries, perhaps Elinor embodies the enduring British tradition of remaining composed under pressure, of keeping a stiff upper lip. Passages describing Elinor are dotted with words like *judgment, reason, duty, principle, observation, thought, restraint, command, civility, decorum*, and *knowledge*. Stay calm, she tells herself: "For a few moments, she was almost overcome—her heart sunk within her, and she could hardly stand; but exertion was indispensably necessary, and she struggled so resolutely against the oppression of her feelings, that her success was speedy, and for the time complete. . . . Elinor [spoke] with a composure of voice, under which was concealed an emotion and distress beyond any thing she had ever felt before" (134–35). Like the British explorer Stanley, Elinor might have observed calmly, "Dr. Livingstone, I presume?" when encountering a countryman in the heart of an African jungle.

Elinor uses her calm, steady, reasoned judgment to keep her family functional throughout the novel. With a mother acting like little more than a teenager, two younger sisters whose eyes are glazed over with romance, and a father so cheerfully sanguine that he dies without obtaining written documentation providing adequately for his widow and daughters, Elinor must become wise beyond her nineteen years. She seems the calm, rational head of the household. Calmness does not win as many admirers as passion, though: as one critic laments, "Elinor, not to mince words, is what some have forthrightly called a stick."[17] Mark Twain crowned Elinor the queen of waxwork, unable to warm up and feel a passion.[18]

Elinor is no prudent stick without emotion, however. Austen first introduces Elinor as a woman of feeling—a loving daughter and sister with an "excellent heart" and "affectionate but genuine feeling" (6). Elinor falls in love with Edward before Marianne ever meets Willoughby. What draws us to Elinor is her genuine concern for her family, her ability to suffer without wallowing in misery, her pride when she faces rejection or disappointment, her discernment, her skill at handling awkward social situations, her empathy for others, and her masterful efforts at self-control.

Yet Austen shows that Elinor is not as objective as she thinks. Because she is attracted to Edward Ferrars with a "blind impartiality," she invests him with artistic potential: "Had he ever been in the way of learning, I think he would have drawn very well" (19). Austen will later give this silly thought to Lady Catherine de Bourgh in *Pride and Prejudice*, who insists that she and her daughter are naturally musical, though neither can play (*PP*, 173). Elinor's keen eyes seem to play tricks on her at times. When Elinor sees Edward wearing a ring with hair in it and hears him falsely assert that the hair is his sister's, Elinor jumps to a conclusion without evidence: "That the hair was her own, she instantly felt" (98). Like Marianne, Elinor indulges in instant feelings and, like Marianne, her judgment can thus be wrong. The hair is not hers, nor is Edward free to propose marriage.

Austen gives readers no answer as to what an intelligent, sensitive woman with sense and sensibility ought to do when forced to spend evenings with tasteless, insensitive neighbors and relatives. Marianne withdraws; Elinor adapts. While Marianne solipsistically pours out her emotions into the piano, Elinor "joyfully profit[s]" from the subterfuge of using "the powerful protection of a very magnificent concerto" to hide her secret conversation with a rival, "and thus by a little of that address, which Marianne could never condescend to practise, gained her own end" (149, 145). Are we to admire Elinor for using a hypocritical means to a social end, or applaud Marianne for refusing to play the game?

Marianne needs to be more like Elinor in order to find a welcome place in society, yet along with Colonel Brandon we applaud Marianne's audacity, ardor, and candor. We all, in a sense, would like to tell the Mrs. Jennings, Mr. Palmers, Lady Middletons, and Mrs. Ferrars of the world that they are nosy, rude, boring, and mean, rather than continuing to exchange Christmas cards and pleasantries with them. Of course Marianne should not be as rude as Mr. Palmer, who perhaps stands as a warning of social "honesty." Mr. Palmer calls his mother-in-law "ill bred," labels Willoughby's house "as vile a spot as I ever saw in my life," and constantly opposes his wife, who informs him, "My love, you contradict every body. . . . Do you know that you are quite rude?" (111–12). Marianne's bluntness and contrariness place her in danger of becoming as outspoken and opinionated as Mr. Palmer.

Both sisters have affectionate hearts, but Elinor masks hers and strains for social correctness, even if it means dissembling. When Marianne makes blunt remarks, Elinor assumes "the whole task of telling lies when politeness required it" (122). Elinor stands somewhere in the middle between the open, direct Marianne and the manipulative Lucy Steele, an artful woman who skillfully and insincerely uses the art of flattery to worm her way into favor. Austen invites readers to compare differing social responses by having Elinor, Marianne, Lucy and Nancy Steele (as eldest, called Miss Steele) all present when Lady Middleton and Fanny Dashwood argue over the earthshaking matter of their sons' comparative heights:

> One subject only engaged the ladies till coffee came in, which was the comparative heights of Harry Dashwood, and Lady Middleton's second son William, who were nearly of the same age. . . .
>
> Lucy, who was hardly less anxious to please one parent than the other, thought the boys were both remarkably tall for their age, and could not conceive that there could be the smallest difference in the world between them; and Miss Steele, with yet greater address gave it, as fast as she could, in favour of each.
>
> Elinor, having once delivered her opinion on William's side, by which she offended Mrs. Ferrars and Fanny still more, did not see the necessity of enforcing it by any farther assertion; and Marianne, when called on for her's, offended them all, by declaring that she had no opinion to give, as she had never thought about it. (233–34)

A key question here is *what does Austen think?* Which approach does she recommend? The Steele sisters are social hypocrites, but it is precisely Lucy's cunning use of flattery that will land her a wealthy husband by the novel's end. Did Elinor need to give an opinion about the boys' heights at all? Was Marianne's approach—to abstain entirely and display obvious indifference—the only one with integrity?

I see no "triumph of politeness over sincerity" here, to use Susan Morgan's phrase; no clear victor or clear heroine.[19] In a later scene at the Palmer house as the other women do carpet-work and chat of children and social engagements, Austen again shows two sisters responding differently to vapid conversation: Elinor "however little concerned in it, joined in their discourse," while Marianne makes a bee line for the library (304). Who made the right decision? Where is our heroine? Elinor maintains a civility sorely absent in Marianne, yet she lacks Marianne's refreshing openness.

Since pain triggers growth, Marianne emerges the most altered of the two sisters by novel's end. As if to underscore the idea of character development, Austen leaves Marianne at the same age (nineteen) as Elinor was at the novel's beginning. How much can happen in just two years if people are open to learning from their erroneous judgment and behavior, Austen implies.

Elinor's stance at the end of the novel differs dramatically from her earlier complacency. In an early chapter, she had smugly observed of Marianne, "A few years will settle her opinions on the reasonable basis of common sense and observation. . . . A better acquaintance with the world is what I look forward to as her greatest possible advantage" (56). By the novel's end Elinor has dropped this irritatingly parental tone because she knows that her own maturing process was far from over. Perhaps she might now admit the truth of Blaise Pascal's remark, "Le coeur a ses raisons que la raison ne connait point" (The heart has its reasons which reason knows nothing of).[20] Readers, too, may feel differently now about that earlier moment in the novel when Marianne and Elinor parted from their mother before heading for London for a few weeks. At the time, the narrator implied that Elinor was the only reasonable one: "Elinor was the only one of the three, who seemed to consider the separation as anything short of eternal" (158). But by showing readers that this almost *was* a final farewell, Austen invites reconsideration of Elinor's perceptions.

In a novel with two heroines rather than one, it is interesting that the only time the term "heroism" appears is when *both* sisters are present—and both progressing. When Marianne stifles the spasm in her throat and does *not* burst out passionately, Elinor hails this evolution in her sister: "Such advances towards heroism in her sister, made Elinor feel equal to any thing herself" (265). Austen celebrates the growth (or "advances") of both heroines. To leave out either Elinor or Marianne from a discussion of Austen's heroines does an injustice to Austen's dual focus. *Sense and Sensibility* invites readers to compare and contrast Elinor and Marianne, not choose between them.

Similarly, *Sense and Sensibility* emerges as the only Austen novel to present two men running for election as the hero. Some vote for Colonel Brandon; others for Edward Ferrars. If real life has more than one central character, why not a novel, Austen seems to suggest. To reinforce the realism of her art, Austen contrasts both men with John Willoughby, a man resembling "the hero of a favourite story" (43). Contemporary moviemakers miss the point of Austen's characterization when they give white horses, soul-searching glances, or a taste for poetry to Colonel Brandon or Edward, as if distrusting audiences ever to accept an unheroic hero.[21] Austen asks more of her readers.

Austen ironically demonstrates that although John Willoughby has "manly beauty" and reads Cowper "with all the sensibility and spirit" Edward lacked, he apparently has ignored the poet's message (42, 48). Did Austen hope readers would think of the following Cowper lines, which contain the title words of her novel?

> I would not enter on my list of friends
> (Though graced with polish'd manners and fine sense,
> Yet wanting sensibility) the man
> Who needlessly sets foot upon a worm.[22]

Willoughby definitely is "graced with polish'd manners and fine sense," yet even he admits that he has trampled on Marianne's feelings: "It is astonishing . . . that my heart should have been so insensible!" (320).

During Marianne's illness, Colonel Brandon both feels and thinks, cares and acts. With quick helpfulness, he brings Mrs. Dashwood to her daughter's bedside: "*He*, meanwhile, whatever he might feel, acted with all the firmness of a collected mind, made every necessary arrangement with the utmost dispatch, and calculated with exactness the time in which [Elinor] might look for his return. Not a moment was lost in delay of any kind" (312). I disagree with those who find Colonel Brandon a disappointing match for Marianne. Poor Colonel Brandon has been called a "wooden and undeveloped character . . . unexciting and remote," a "vacuum," and a "stolid sad sack."[23] Colonel Brandon's primary fault resembles that of British colonialists in general, even those claiming to be enlightened: he has a paternalistic tendency to enjoy rescuing the weak and less fortunate. But Colonel Brandon's character is hardly "undeveloped." True, he is an awkward narrator, but he admits this about himself. His inarticulateness hints at depth not dearth of feeling: "it would be impossible to describe what I felt," he tells Elinor (199). As Austen notes of this man who uses both his head and his heart, "Colonel Brandon . . . was in every occasion *mindful* of the *feelings* of others" (62; my italics).

In fact, one begins to wonder along with Mrs. Jennings why Austen did not pair this chivalrous man of action with Elinor. The two spend far more time talking to each other than to their prospective mates. So what does Edward Ferrars add to the novel, and why might Elinor prefer him? We have our dastardly villain (Willoughby) and our manly hero (Colonel Brandon) paired literally in a duel: "we met by appointment, he to defend, I to punish his conduct" (211). Willoughby marries for money while Colonel Brandon marries for love. Willoughby looks the part of the perfect gentleman; Colonel Brandon acts like one. Why might Austen have added Edward Ferrars to her gallery of gentlemen?

Although Edward may seem weak, inexperienced, or idle compared to the older, well-traveled Colonel Brandon, he possesses at least one trait Austen knows is lacking in both the Colonel and in Marianne: wit. Edward has self-deprecating humor and can banter with the ever-serious Marianne in a way slightly reminiscent of Henry Tilney's exchanges with Catherine Morland and Eleanor Tilney in *Northanger Abbey*. Instead of praising the picturesque as Henry does, Edward dryly mocks the affectations of its sentimental proponents: "I have no knowledge in the picturesque . . . I shall call hills steep, which ought to be bold, surfaces strange and uncouth, which ought to be irregular and rugged, and distant objects out of sight, which ought only to be indistinct through the soft medium of a hazy atmosphere" (96–97). Marianne takes Edward seriously and wonders why he boasts of his ignorance, but Elinor recognizes his pose. When Edward continues to assert, "I do not like crooked, twisted, blasted trees . . . ruined, tattered cottages . . . nettles, or thistles, or heath blossoms" and boasts that he would prefer "a troop of tidy, happy villagers" to "the finest banditti in the world," Marianne looks at him with amazement while Elinor laughs (98). Throughout the novel only Elinor and Edward—and of course the narrator—display the ability to see life ironically.

If we free ourselves from the image of Edward as a dull, mother-dominated milquetoast and look carefully at his conversation, we see that he displays a flair for discerning character. In a conversation with Marianne, he drolly imagines what she would do if she inherited a fortune: "And books!— Thomson, Cowper, Scott—she would buy them all over and over again; she would buy up every copy, I believe, to prevent their falling into unworthy hands; and she would have every book that tells her how to admire an old twisted tree. Should not you, Marianne? Forgive me, if I am very saucy. But I was willing to shew you that I had not forgot our old disputes" (92). Marianne replies in utter seriousness, failing to catch Edward's friendly jibes. Although Edward tells Elinor that "gaiety never was a part of *my*

character," one senses that the esprit he displays here while unhappily engaged to Lucy has the potential to turn to genuine mirth once he is blessed
with a happy marriage (93).

Our final view of Edward shows him with greater integrity than his
more pragmatic wife-to-be. Edward refuses to cave in to his mother: "I can
make no submission—I am grown neither humble nor penitent," he insists,
but Elinor argues that "a little humility may be convenient." Although finally
he agrees to visit his mother, he "still resisted the idea of a letter of proper submission" (372). Throughout, Edward displays democratic notions, observing
that he feels more at home among the lower classes than with the gentility.
Edward remains steady in his principles, secure in his exceptional decision to
forfeit the right of eldest son, and happily engaged in his parish duties. Austen turns her milquetoast into a mensch.

As narrator, Austen reserves some of her censure for her minor characters, particularly for those who do not grow. Edward Ferrars's younger brother
has become a pretentious dandy who regards his decorated toothpick case as
a necessity of life:

> The correctness of his eye, and the delicacy of his taste, proved to
> be beyond his politeness. He was giving orders for a toothpick-case
> for himself; and till its size, shape, and ornaments were determined,
> all of which, after examining and debating for a quarter of an
> hour over every toothpick-case in the shop, were finally arranged
> by his own inventive fancy, he had no leisure to bestow any other
> attention on the two ladies, than what was comprised in three or
> four very broad stares. . . . At last the affair was decided. The ivory,
> the gold, and the pearls, all received their appointment, and the
> gentleman having named the last day on which his existence could
> be continued without the possession of the toothpick-case, drew on
> his gloves with leisurely care, and bestowing another glance . . . as
> seemed rather to demand than express admiration, walked off with
> an happy air of real conceit and affected indifference. (220–21)

This passage perhaps hints at the devastating effects of "empire" on those
who decadently reap its rewards without possessing any awareness of the
labor and injustice supporting their own luxurious lifestyle. We see Robert
Ferrars giving orders and making demands. The repetition of words like
"leisure" and "bestow" captures his idleness and imperiousness. Austen's
readers would have recognized that ivory, gold, and pearls were among the
fruits of colonialism. Although this passage contains the only reference to
ivory in Austen's novels, there are other brief allusions to the slave trade and
to the West and East Indies. Earlier in *Sense and Sensibility* Willoughby's

references to "nabobs, gold mohrs, and palanquins" would similarly have reminded readers that British extravagance came only through the harsh labor of others (51).[24]

Robert Ferrars thinks only of himself, not those exploited for the sake of his country's wealth. He loves ornaments and is "adorned in the first style of fashion." Little else occupies his time. He reminds one of Mary Wollstone-craft's depictions of women more interested in what they will wear on a trip than in where they will go. In a chapter called "The State of Degradation to Which Woman is Reduced," Wollstonecraft asks, "Can dignity of mind exist with such trivial cares?" She concludes that rich men have become honorary women: "Women, in general, as *well as the rich of both sexes*, have acquired all the follies and vices of civilization, and missed the useful fruit."[25] An idle, wealthy gentleman like Robert Ferrars is ladylike in the worst sense of the epithet. Robert Ferrars's act of drawing on his gloves "with leisurely care" shows his uselessness. Austen's oxymoronic description of Robert Ferrars's "sterling insignificance" captures the link between British imperialism ("sterling" suggests the British unit of value) and the pettiness of its leisured, pampered upper class (221).

Austen includes many other sterling examples of insignificant men and women in this novel. Mr. Palmer "idled away the mornings at billiards, which ought to have been devoted to business" and displays "Epicurism ... selfishness ... conceit" (305). Sir John Middleton has no resources for solitude, displays a "total want of talent and taste," and feels no purpose in life beyond hunting, shooting, and throwing pleasure parties (32). Nancy Steele uses bad grammar and thinks of nothing but herself, her pink ribbons, and her conquest of beaux, while the vulgar Lucy Steele schemes her way up the social ladder. A dense woman, the "everlasting talker" Mrs. Jennings fails to see that her raillery causes pain or that her comments lack depth ("Mrs. Taylor did say this morning that one day Miss Walker hinted to her, that she believed Mr. and Mrs. Ellison would not be sorry to have Miss Grey married") (54, 194). Both her daughters are vapid, uneducated, frivolous women who display a few trivial "accomplishments" for the sake of catching a husband, then promptly drop the effort: Lady Middleton celebrates her marriage by giving up music and now passes the time elegantly "saying little and doing less"; Charlotte Palmer hangs above her mantlepiece "a landscape in coloured silks of her performance, in proof of her having spent seven years at a great school in town to some effect" and now spends her time lounging, dawdling, laughing, and whiling away the time while her servants do the work (175, 160).

Why are Lady Middleton, Charlotte Palmer, Fanny Dashwood, the Steele sisters, and women of their ilk so insipid and illiberal? Again, Austen suggests that idleness and lack of education are much to blame, just as in the case of the many dissipated and indolent men in this novel. Wollstonecraft had warned of self-indulgent fine ladies "brimful of sensibility, and teeming with capricious fancies" as well as "mere notable women" with "a shrewd kind of good sense, joined with worldly prudence" who possess "neither greatness of mind nor taste."[26] Without ever writing a line of a political treatise as Wollstonecraft had done, Austen offers an equally revolutionary argument for educating both men and women to be whole human beings. Only then can they live in harmony and fulfillment.

Like Wollstonecraft, Austen rejects the notion that "man was made to reason, woman to feel."[27] Perhaps Austen was tired of reading passages in conduct books suggesting that young women were innately sensitive, quivering, emotional messes, such as the Reverend John Bennett's *Letters to a Young Lady, on a Variety of Useful and Interesting Subjects, Calculated to Improve the Heart, to Form the Manners, and Enlighten the Understanding*: "The timidity, arising from the natural weakness and delicacy of your frame; the numerous diseases to which you are liable; that exquisite sensibility, which, in many of you, vibrates to the slightest touch of joy or sorrow . . . the sedentariness of your life, naturally followed with low spirits or *ennui*; whilst we are seeking health and pleasure . . . will expose you to a number of *peculiar* sorrows."[28] Austen also might have objected to Tennyson's later lines, "Man with the head and woman with the heart: . . . All else confusion."[29] In *Sense and Sensibility* Austen insists that all will be confusion unless *both* men and women possess *both* sense and sensibility.

John Halperin writes, "Somewhere between *Sense and Sensibility* lies what is just plain *sensible*, and it is here that Jane Austen wishes us to stand."[30] Austen argues this not only in *Sense and Sensibility* but in all her other novels: as Joan Ray notes, "the phrase *sense and sensibility* is key to reading Austen, whichever of her novels we pick up."[31] Sensibility need not be delicate weakness or self-indulgence, but rather a genuine ability to feel for others. Sense need not be cunning or narrow pragmatism but rather an enlightened use of one's mind. In Austen's world, any *human* needs both. As Joseph Wiesenfarth observes, "to be a whole person, one must have sensibility enlightened by sense."[32]

Austen suggests that it may be particularly difficult to achieve such wholeness, such humanity, in an economically exploitative society. For many men and women, sense becomes little more than a calculated self-interest in obtaining cents and percents for oneself. In *Sense and Sensibility* more than in any other novel, Austen links the pursuit of money to the destruction of finer feelings.

This novel is permeated with remarks about fortunes, annuities, moieties, inheritances, salaries, and livings, as if each character comes with a price tag attached. From start to finish, money determines behavior. Money, not love, seems to make most of the world of *Sense and Sensibility* go round.

Perhaps W.H. Auden had *Sense and Sensibility* in mind when he wrote these lines about Jane Austen:

> You could not shock her more than she shocks me;
>   Beside her Joyce seems innocent as grass.
> It makes me most uncomfortable to see
>   An English spinster of the middle class
>   Describe the amorous effects of "brass",
> Reveal so frankly and with such sobriety
> The economic basis of society.[33]

We certainly see the amorous effects of brass in the loveless marriages of Lucy Steele, Colonel Brandon's brother, and John Willoughby. As Willoughby admits, "My affection for Marianne . . . was all insufficient to outweigh that dread of poverty, or get the better of those false ideas of the necessity of riches, which I was naturally inclined to feel, and expensive society had increased" (323) Willoughby has managed to hit the jackpot, snaring Miss Grey and her fifty thousand pounds. As he notes in a rare moment of integrity, "In honest words, her money was necessary to me" (328). Edward Ferrars could have been the equivalent of a millionaire as well, for if he had married Miss Morton he "would settle on him the Norfolk estate, which, clear of land-tax, brings in a good thousand a-year," land her thirty thousand pound fortune, gain a wife with a title, and be assured of receiving his inheritance from his pleased mother (266). Mrs. Jenning's "ample jointure" (a financial settlement providing for a widow) allows her to see both her daughters "respectably married" with expensive and extensive estates (36). If money can't buy you love, it certainly can buy you marriage.

In *Sense and Sensibility* we meet a society so based on economics that it uses income to measure the worth not only of prospective marriage partners but also of people in general. John Dashwood would probably approve of having people wear name tags saying "Hello, my name is ___ and I make ___ pounds a year." He compliments Mrs. Ferrars because she has "such very large fortune" and indeed "never wished to offend anybody, especially anybody of good fortune" (222, 267). When Colonel Brandon arrives, John Dashwood "only wanted to know him to be rich, to be equally civil to him" (223). As the grieving Marianne declines in health, John Dashwood ticks off her declining market value: "I question whether Marianne *now*, will marry a man worth more than five or six hundred a-year, at the utmost" (227). The only purpose of John Dashwood's life seems to be to acquire money, spend it on himself and his immediate family, and keep it away from others, including the relatives he had promised to help. His concept of the ultimate spiritual horror is the loss of property: "Can anything be more galling to the spirit of a man than to see his younger brother in possession of an estate which might have been his own?" (269).

Is John Dashwood's first name of significance? In a novel where "Marianne" may symbolize revolutionary France, does Austen invoke the spirit of John Bull—the prosaic, mercenary, soulless symbol of England—by naming three of her English gentlemen "John"? John Dashwood is a selfish materialist, Sir John Middleton an aristocrat without taste or inner resources, and John Willoughby an idle, dissipated, extravagant "gentleman" who marries for money and seduces for pleasure, leaving broken hearts and lives in his wake. Young John Middleton, a boy of six, monopolizes the conversation, harasses his female cousins, searches their bags, steals their belongings, and displays his "spirits" by "monkey tricks" such as throwing Lucy's handkerchief out the window—hardly a good omen of little John Bulls to come (121). If we add to Austen's collection the crass, philistinistic, fortune-hunting John Thorpe of *Northanger Abbey*, the dissolute "Honorable" John Yates of *Mansfield Park*, the rather dour, reserved attorney John Knightley of *Emma*, and the "civil, cautious" lawyer John Shepherd in *Persuasion*, John Bull definitely comes out in need of amendment.

Austen heightens the contrast between those with and without feeling by presenting two Mrs. Dashwoods. As Isobel Armstrong observes, "The novel imagines a world with too much sensibility in Mrs. Dashwood, and too little in the other Mrs. Dashwood, Fanny."[34] The first Mrs. Dashwood's warm-blooded personality and possession of "a sense of honour so keen, a generosity so romantic" make her a far cry from the coldly objective and selfishly calculating Mrs. John Dashwood (6). Austen shows how Fanny perverts the language of maternal feelings ("our poor little boy") to talk her easily convinced husband out of any sense of charity, duty, or justice (9). The original plan to give three thousand pounds to needy relatives is reduced in just a few minutes to nothing more than an occasional present of fish and game, when in season. Fanny succeeds as a mother in looking out for the interests (literally) of her child, but at what social and moral cost?

Using words like *observe, certainly, undoubtedly, to say the truth*, and *I am convinced*, John and Fanny Dashwood conclude that the late Mr. Dashwood was not "in his right senses" when he asked his son to share his fortune (9). By sprinkling the word *sense* throughout this novel, Austen demands that we question its meaning. When Colonel Brandon decides to give Edward a living as rector that he could have sold for profit, John Dashwood responds with utter amazement: "This living of Colonel Brandon's—can it be true?—has he really given it to Edward? . . . this is very astonishing! . . . and now that livings fetch such a price! . . . a man of Colonel Brandon's *sense*! . . . It is truly astonishing! . . . what could be the Colonel's motive?" (294–95). John Dashwood's definition means it makes *sense* for Willoughby to marry the heiress Miss

Grey. It makes *sense* for Mrs. Ferrars to want Edward to marry the wealthy, titled Miss Morton. As Miss Steele observes, "Miss Godby told Miss Sparks, that nobody in their *senses* could expect Mr. Ferrars to give up a woman like Miss Morton, with £30,000 to her fortune, for Lucy Steele that had nothing at all" (273; my italics).

As narrator, Austen pretends to admire the fact that Lucy's sense pays off: "The whole of Lucy's behaviour ... the prosperity which crowned it ... may be held forth as a most encouraging instance of what an earnest, an unceasing attention to self-interest ... will do in securing every advantage of fortune, with no other sacrifice than that of time and conscience" (376). Why might Austen call this behavior "encouraging" or refer to John Dashwood as "respectable"? Austen pretends as narrator to adopt her era's prevailing opinions—to assume the majority voice of her era. Yet by ironically praising characters with obviously flawed values, Austen invites her readers to go against the norm. She demonstrates that those with a "sensitive conscience" like Marianne, a respect for principles like Edward and Elinor, or a generosity of spirit like the brotherly Colonel Brandon must look senseless to the Steeles and John and Fanny Dashwoods of the world (350).

While Austen attacks the money-mindedness of society, she also exposes the vulnerability of those too romantic to cope with financial reality. Mrs. Dashwood's inability to save money in the past makes her ill equipped to handle her newfound adversity. Marianne's naivete about money matters makes her too blind to Willoughby's expensive lifestyle and the lengths he will go to preserve it. At least Elinor and Edward face real life: "They were neither of them quite enough in love to think that three hundred and fifty pounds a-year would supply them with the comforts of life" (369). The happiest characters in Austen's fictional world are those who understand money but are not destroyed by its corrupting power. Colonel Brandon's act of giving a living to Edward Ferrars may not make "sense" to John Dashwood, but it is consistent with the ideals of brotherhood celebrated in this novel.

Austen does not come in as narrator to tell us her ideals or even to indicate whether we are to prefer Elinor to Marianne, Edward to Colonel Brandon. Instead of intruding as she did in *Northanger Abbey* to tell us about the hero and heroine of her "tale," she inserts her presence in *Sense and Sensibility* for a different purpose: to remind readers that her seemingly exaggerated characters and events are *not unusual*. All of society stands indicted here through Austen's frequent references to the characters' resemblance to others of their sex, class, or era.

Throughout this novel, Austen reminds us that selfish, unfair people will be deemed respectable if they have money. Rather than presenting the unfair disinheritance of Mrs. Dashwood and her daughters as unusual, Austen informs us in the opening chapter that such occurrences are the norm: "The old Gentleman died; his will was read, and *like almost every other will*, gave as much disappointment as pleasure" (4; my italics here and in the next quotation). Rather than expressing surprise at Fanny and John Dashwood's selfish disregard for the claims of their relatives, Austen matter-of-factly states, "It was *very well known* that no affection was *ever* supposed to exist between the children of *any man* by different marriages" (8). Throughout *Sense and Sensibility*, Austen sprinkles in clauses such as *still more common, in many cases of a similar kind, like many others, too common, in common use, the common opinion, in the common phrase, as any other man, as ladies always [do], by no means unusual, in the usual style, like other parties, like the half the rest of the world, like every other place*. Austen makes her opinion clear that mean-spirited, crass, tasteless people, loveless marriages, and boring events are the norm, not the exception.

What are we to think of the state of women if the illiterate Lucy Steele (described as "capable of the utmost meanness of wanton ill-nature") is pronounced to be "superior in person and understanding to half her sex"? (366). What are we to think of men if our narrator tells us that the rude, hedonistic Mr. Palmer possesses "no traits at all unusual in his sex and time of life"? (304).

The dreadful marriage of the Palmers—one of insults and abuse on the one hand and escapist oblivion on the other—is described as too usual, too common, to make Elinor wonder about it. Indeed, Elinor considers "the strange unsuitableness which *often* existed between husband and wife" (118; my italics). She mistakenly assumes that since Mr. Palmer's mistaken reasons for marriage are *common*, it must not do any harm: Mr. Palmer's "temper might perhaps be a little soured by finding, *like many others of his sex*, that through some unaccountable bias in favour of beauty, he was the husband of a very silly woman,—but she [Elinor] knew that this kind of blunder was too common for any sensible man to be lastingly hurt by it.—It was rather a wish of distinction she believed, which produced his contemptuous treatment of everybody, and his general abuse of every thing before him. It was the desire of appearing superior to other people. The motive was too *common* to be wondered at" (112; my italics). This is a fascinating passage. Mr. Palmer, like Mr. Allen in *Northanger Abbey* and like Mr. Bennet in *Pride and Prejudice*, has joined "many others of his sex" in valuing beauty at the expense of sense, a far "too common" blunder. Austen implies that many men marry inferior women, and that this action reflects a more universal desire of looking superior to others. Austen seems to separate herself from Elinor Dashwood in this paragraph. Elinor stops wondering about Mr. Palmer because his circumstances seem so common. But readers are left to conclude that a man of sensibility may indeed be lastingly and devastatingly hurt by a bad marriage and by inflated egotism.

Perhaps more than in any book she would write, Austen aims her satiric gaze at the ignorance, dullness, and tastelessness of *the public*—of everyone. If the empty-headed Robert Ferrars is "as well fitted to mix in the world as any other man," God help the world (251). The ostentatious residence of the Palmers is "like every other place of the same degree of importance" (302). When Austen describes a "musical" party consisting of people who talk through performances and have no real taste or appreciation for the music, she points out that such events are "not very remarkable" because they are "like other musical parties" in general where the majority of listeners have no taste and the "performers themselves were, as usual" arrogant in assuming themselves the best performers in England (250). John Middleton's vapid pleasure parties are conducted in "the usual style." Lady Middleton utters "the most common-place inquiry or remark," and Mrs. Jennings offers "common-place raillery." The "common cant" usually distorts the truth, Austen notes. Austen indicts all people as empty talkers with her comment about Mrs. Ferrars's concise use of words: "She was not a woman of many words: for, *unlike people in general,* she proportioned them to the number of her ideas" (232; my italics). Rather than singling out the selfish Fanny Dashwood as unusual, Austen relates her cruelty to her relatives to the behavior of people in general.

Throughout *Sense and Sensibility* Austen categorically suggests that something profound is *wanting* in society. Mrs. Ferrars evinces a "want of liberality," Mrs. Palmer a "want of recollection and elegance" (90, 304). Lucy Steele evinces a "want of real elegance and artlessness" and "want of information in the most common particulars," as well as a "thorough want of delicacy, of rectitude, and integrity of mind" and "want of liberality" stemming from her "want of instruction" and "want of education" (124, 127, 367). Sir John and Lady Middleton resemble each other only "in that total want of talent and taste," and the audiences at their musical parties show a "shameless want of taste" (32, 35). The cumulative effect of all these references to wants is to leave readers deeply aware that something is lacking in human society.

Austen's narrative intrusions point out that her society lacks not only culture but also morality. Although critics have sometimes faulted Austen for creating a stage villain in Willoughby, she seems to me to have gone to great lengths to make Willoughby quite unsurprising to those around him.[35] She reduces him at the end not to shameful ignomiy or penitent remorse, but just to ordinariness. True, once he finds out that Mrs. Smith might have left him her fortune even if he had married Marianne, he regrets choosing a woman for money rather than love. Yet he expresses no concern about his seduction of Eliza, and he goes on to lead an unremarkable life: "But that he was for ever inconsolable, that he fled from society, or contracted an habitual gloom of temper, or died of a broken heart, must not be depended on—for he did neither. He lived to exert, and frequently to enjoy himself. His wife was not always out of humour, nor his home always uncomfortable; and in his breed of horses and dogs, and in sporting of every kind, he found no inconsiderable degree of domestic felicity" (379). Willoughby will fit in fine. Maybe Sir John Middleton will stop labeling him "as good a kind of fellow as ever lived," but he still will take him out hunting (43). Lady Middleton decides to visit rather than snub Mrs. Willoughby because she is rich enough to be elegant. Like spraying air freshener on the source of a bad odor rather than removing it, society masks over any stink, any scandal (if the perpetrator be male), any injustice, and proceeds with elegance. The well-bred Lady Middleton may rush out of the room to avoid hearing talk of a love-child or a pregnancy, but the true horror lies in her own indifference, ignorance, and false elegance.

Although Marianne stands out as exceptional, striking, and refreshingly unconventional compared to the Lady Middletons of her milieu, even she becomes less extraordinary in the hands of our ironic narrator. When Marianne misjudges others, falls for the superficially graceful, polished Willoughby, or displays selfishness, she merely resembles many others in the world: "Elinor [was] ... assured of the injustice to which her sister was often led in her opinion of others, by the irritable refinement of her own mind, and the too great importance placed by her on the delicacies of a strong sensibility, and the graces of a polished manner. *Like half the rest of the world, if more than half there be that are clever and good*, Marianne, with excellent abilities and an excellent disposition, was *neither reasonable nor candid*. She expected from other people the same opinions and feelings as her own, and she judged of their motives by the immediate effect of their actions on herself" (201; my italics). Does Austen insert this perplexing passage to inform readers that most of us, Marianne included, are neither reasonable nor candid in its earlier sense of being unprejudiced and, as Dr. Johnson puts it in his famous dictionary, "free from malice; not desirous to find fault"? Even those who are clever and good with excellent dispositions and abilities may fall victim to irrationality and partiality, she suggests. Through an inserted "if" clause, Austen makes us question whether the majority of people are clever and good. By this point in the novel, Austen has demonstrated that more than half the characters are silly and selfish. The whole world seems implicated here, since even a character with cleverness and feelings judges others according to "the immediate effect of their actions on herself."

Such narrative potshots at the world perhaps explain why many critics are quick to call *Sense and Sensibility* a bleak book written in a foul mood by an embittered spinster.[36] Perhaps Austen's anger stemmed not from her inability to find a mate but to find a readership. How did she feel as lightweight pulp fiction brought fame and fortune to lesser writers while her manuscripts of *First Impressions* and *Susan* remained unpublished? Did her experience of watching across the Channel as the French Revolution dissolved into the

Reign of Terror leave her convinced of the selfishness of all concerned? As her family moved from Steventon to Bath, did she find herself condemned to a hollow life of unbearably petty activities in the company of stupid people? Did Austen's acquaintance with real emotional pain (as in the case of Cassandra's loss of a fiancé) darken her vision?

Although Marianne in *Sense and Sensibility* comes closer to death than any other Austen heroine does, it is interesting that even in this novel Austen refuses to write unadulterated tragedy. The word "almost" occurs at climactic moments. Feeling "almost choked by grief," Marianne "almost screamed with agony" when confronting Willoughby's rejection (182). In turn Willoughby "almost ran out of the room" when departing forever from Marianne and Elinor, "almost ran out of the room" when responding to the news of Edward's liberty (332, 360). Through qualifiers like these, Austen keeps her narrative reins in check, giving us something that is almost tragedy, almost melodrama. The same Jane Austen who burlesqued fainting heroines in "Love and Freindship" perhaps still distrusts tear-jerking sentimental fiction but knows that life really does contain tragic losses and dark despair. As Eudora Welty put it, Jane Austen's novels are "profound in emotion" for "in her writing there deeply lies, as deeply as anything in her powers, a true tenderness of feeling."[37] *Sense and Sensibility* leaves us no doubt that Austen could have written a poignant deathbed scene, with Mrs. Dashwood and Elinor consumed with grief at the side of a lifeless Marianne, with a power that would have rivaled the ability of Charles Dickens to describe Little Nell's final moments or Louisa May Alcott to describe the loss of Beth March.

In our search for Jane Austen, we often found her in *Northanger Abbey* using the personal pronoun "I," whether telling us of "my heroine" or delivering her ironic opinions. For the most part, that "I" voice is gone from *Sense and Sensibility*. The only direct use of the narrative "I" in this novel appears at the beginning of a passage describing Fanny Dashwood's frustration at having to send a carriage for Marianne and Elinor. I quote this passage at length because it illustrates several features of the narrator:

> I come now to the relation of a misfortune, which about this time befell Mrs. John Dashwood. It so happened that while her two sisters with Mrs. Jennings were first calling on her in Harley-street, another of her acquaintance had dropt in—a circumstance in itself not apparently likely to produce evil to her. But while the imaginations of other people will carry them away to form wrong judgments of our conduct, and to decide on it by slight appearances, one's happiness must in some measure be always at the mercy of chance. In the present instance, this last-arrived lady allowed her fancy so far to outrun truth and probability, that on merely hearing

the name of the Miss Dashwoods, and understanding them to be Mr. Dashwood's sisters, she immediately concluded them to be staying in Harley-street; and this misconstruction produced within a day or two afterwards, cards of invitation for them as well as for their brother and sister, to a small musical party at her house. The consequence of which was, that Mrs. John Dashwood was obliged to submit not only to the exceedingly great inconvenience of sending her carriage for the Miss Dashwoods; but, what was still worse, must be subject to all the unpleasantness of appearing to treat them with attention. . . . The power of disappointing them, it was true, must always be her's. But that was not enough; for when people are determined on a mode of conduct which they know to be wrong, they feel injured by the expectation of any thing better from them. (248–49)

This "I" ironically adopts Fanny's point of view by pretending that the obviously trivial incident of sending a carriage is a "misfortune," an "evil," and an "exceedingly great inconvenience." This same narrator refuses to let readers put Fanny's selfish, snobbish behavior at arm's length from their own. She interrupts this account to talk about "our conduct" and ends with a general comment on "*people.*"

The final chapters of *Sense and Sensibility* provide further glimpses of Jane Austen, simply from the emphasis she chooses to give at the end. To the irritation of many critics, Austen chooses to withdraw as narrator rather than give us tender romantic scenes between her two pairs of lovers. When Edward finally has the freedom to propose to Elinor, Austen states matter-of-factly, "How soon he had walked himself into the proper resolution, however, how soon an opportunity of exercising it occurred, in what manner he expressed himself, and how he was received, need not be particularly told" (361). Why need it not particularly be told? Why do we also hear no spoken words between Marianne and Colonel Brandon in the final chapter?

Some have speculated that Austen distances herself from such romantic moments because, as an unmarried woman, she had no familiarity with such scenes and a prudish reluctance to dwell on them. Yet since she displayed no such inhibition in giving us Marianne's passionate outburst to Willoughby or Colonel Brandon's narrative of his attachment to Eliza, one suspects a different reason. Could it be that in a novel exploring the relationship between solitude and society, between intimacy and public life, Austen demonstrates through her respectful silence that there are some emotions and moments understood only in private? She need never back off from dialogue between Sir John and Lady Middleton, for Sir John's idea of intimacy is a noisy crowd.

We know that John and Fanny Dashwood will never talk of anything un-related to money and property. Perhaps Austen leaves readers outside the homes of Edward and Elinor, Colonel Brandon and Marianne, to signal that indoors these two couples have found their own very private domestic happi-ness—the exchange of ideas and reciprocity of affection possible only to men and women with both sense and sensibility. Her stance as author—respectful of her lovers' privacy—places her in diametric opposition to Nancy Steele, hovering outside the door to eavesdrop on her sister's conversation with Ed-ward. "La! . . . do you think people make love when any body else is by? . . . all I heard was only by listening at the door. . . . And I am sure Lucy would have done just the same by me" (274). Nancy and Lucy Steele will listen through the door; Austen will not.

In the final paragraph of *Sense and Sensibility*, Austen delivers an in-junction to her readers: "Between Barton and Delaford, there was that con-stant communication which strong family affection would naturally dic-tate;—and among the merits and the happiness of Elinor and Marianne, let it not be ranked as the least considerable, that though sisters, and living almost within sight of each other, they could live without disagreement between themselves, or producing coolness between their husbands" (380). The narrator ranks as considerably important the fact that the sisters remain close to their mother and to each other; their two husbands have warmth between them. The final image is of a world of rational discourse ("constant communication") *and* natural emotion (the "happiness" resulting from the natural dictates of "strong family affection"). Austen ends her novel about the prevalence of cold, selfish, dull people bickering over money and status with the image of a close-knit family.

Even though that final sentence suggests that the main characters lived happily ever after in perfect harmony, Austen does not lapse into saccharine Walt Disney–like writing here. She could have written, "because they were sisters, they lived within sight of each other in harmony and their husbands enjoyed a warm relationship." Instead, she writes "*though* sisters, and living *almost* within sight of each other, they could live *without disagreement* between themselves, or producing *coolness* between their husbands." Just as when we are told "whatever you do, do not think of an elephant" we must think of the elephant, so here by being reminded of disagreement and coolness, we keep those problems with us as we close the pages of the novel. Austen continues to the end to insert into *Sense and Sensibility* her biting perception that the majority of human beings—and their countries—lack the true sense and sen-sibility needed to live in harmony.

Perhaps in *Sense and Sensibility* more than in any other novel she would write, Austen opines that most men and women are selfish, competitive, dull, greedy, petty, vain, and insufferably insipid. Create your own oasis of family warmth, intellectual stimulation, personal growth, and social altruism, Austen suggests in the conclusion to *Sense and Sensibility*, for little hope exists of reforming or even escaping "the rest of the world."

NOTES

1. Shields, *Jane Austen*, 48.

2. Eva Brann, "Whose Sense? Whose Sensibility?" *Persuasions* 12 (1990): 131.

3. Stuart Tave, *Some Words of Jane Austen* (Chicago: University of Chicago Press, 1973), 96.

4. John Hardy, *Jane Austen's Heroines: Intimacy in Human Relationships* (London: Routledge, Kegan & Paul, 1984).

5. Marvin Mudrick, *Jane Austen: Irony as Defense and Discovery* (Princeton: Princeton University Press, 1952), 93.

6. Eliza Hancock to Philadelphia Hancock, 3 May 1797, in Richard Austen-Leigh, *Austen Papers* (London, 1942), 159, cited in Le Faye, *Family Record*, 94.

7. *Englishwoman's Domestic Magazine*, 1866, cited in Southam, *Critical Heritage*, 1: 206.

8. Marilyn Butler, *Jane Austen and the War of Ideas* (Oxford: Clarendon Press, 1975), 196; Lawrence Lerner, "*Sense and Sensibility*: A Mixed-Up Book," in *The Truthtellers: Jane Austen, George Eliot, and D. H. Lawrence* (London: Chatto & Windus, 1967), 166.

9. George Moore, *Avowals* (1919; reprint, London: Heinemann, 1924), 39–40.

10. See Tony Tanner, *Jane Austen* (Cambridge, Mass.: Harvard University Press, 1986), 91.

11. Le Faye, *Jane Austen*, 178.

12. Maurice Agulhon, *Marianne into Battle: Republican Imagery and Symbolism in France, 1789–1880*, trans. Janet Lloyd (Cambridge: Cambridge University Press, 1981), 16. Also see the discussion of Marianne's dangerous name in Margaret Anne Doody's introduction to *Sense and Sensibility* (Oxford: Oxford World Classics, 1990), xvii.

13. Lynn Hunt, *Politics, Culture, and Class in the French Revolution* (Berkeley: University of California Press, 1984), 62.

14. See Honan, *Jane Austen*, 98.

15. George Moore, "Turgueneff," *Fortnightly Review*, February 1888, cited in Southam, *Critical Heritage*, 2: 188.

16. Marat-Mauger's remarks are cited in Hunt, *Politics, Culture, and Class in the French Revolution*, 27.

17. Steele Gibbons, Introduction to *Sense and Sensibility* (New York: Heritage Press, 1957), x.

18. For the complete text of Twain's remarks in "Jane Austen," an unpublished essay about *Sense and Sensibility*, see my appendix.

19. Susan Morgan, "Polite Lies: The Veiled Heroine of *Sense and Sensibility*," *Nineteenth-Century Fiction* 31 (September 1976): 191.

20. Blaise Pascal, *Pensées*, section 4, line 277 (New York: Dutton, 1958), 79.

21. See the discussion of Ang Lee's *Sense and Sensibility* in *Jane Austen in Hollywood*, ed. Linda Troost and Sayre Greenfield (Lexington: University Press of Kentucky, 1998). For example, Cheryl Nixon notes that "the film remakes Brandon into

a standard-bearer of true emotion" and "a courtship hero" (39), and Nora Nachumi observes that "the movie works hard to create the impression that Brandon is the perfect romantic hero for Marianne" (133).

22. William Cowper, *The Task*, book 4, line 560, in *Poetical Works*, ed. H. S. Milford (London: Oxford University Press, 1967), 231.

23. Honan, *Jane Austen*, 275, 278; Marvin Mudrick, *Jane Austen*, 88; Louis Menand, "What Jane Austen Doesn't Tell Us," *New York Review of Books* (1 February 1996), 14.

24. *Nabobs* were wealthy, important colonists; *mohrs* were coins used in British India; *palanquins* were closed litters on which several natives would transport VIPs.

25. Mary Wollstonecraft, *Vindication of the Rights of Woman* (1792; reprint, London: Penguin, 1985), 151–52.

26. Ibid., 158.

27. Ibid., 154.

28. John Bennett, *Letters to a Young Lady* (Warrington: W. Eyres, 1789), 7.

29. "The Princess," 5: 439–41, in *The Poems of Tennyson*, ed. Christopher Ricks (London: Longmans, 1969), 815.

30. Halperin, *Life of Jane Austen*, 91.

31. Joan Ray, "Code Word Jane Austen, or How a Chinese Film About Martial Arts Teaches Life Arts," *Persuasions* 22 (2000): 10.

32. Joseph Wiesenfarth, *The Errand of Form: An Assay of Jane Austen's Art* (New York: Fordham University Press, 1967), 55.

33. W.H. Auden, "Letter to Lord Byron, Part 1," in *Letters from Iceland* (London: Faber & Faber, 1937), 21.

34. Isobel Armstrong, *Sense and Sensibility* (London and New York: Penguin Books, 1994), 81.

35. "Willoughby is a stage villain," notes William Lyon Phelps in his introduction to the 1906 New York Holby edition of *Sense and Sensibility* (xxxvii).

36. See, for instance, Halperin's description of *Sense and Sensibility* as "bleak and black and nasty" in *Life of Jane Austen*, 84.

37. Eudora Welty, "The Radiance of Jane Austen" (1969), in *The Eye of the Story: Selected Essays and Reviews* (New York: Random House, 1978), 8–9.

SARAH EMSLEY

Learning the Art of Charity in Emma

But lovely as I was the Graces of my Person were the least of my
Perfections. . . . In my Mind, every virtue that could adorn it was centered;
it was the Rendezvous of every good Quality & of every noble sentiment.
—Jane Austen, "Love and Friendship,"
Volume the Second (*MW* 77–78)

Emma is about the process of learning to respect other people, to tolerate
differences, and to be charitable to others, and it is about the role of misery
in the process of education. Although Emma Woodhouse never suffers
severe physical pain or loss, in the course of the novel she is required to
undergo suffering that contributes to her education, and the kind of pain
she endures is the torment of coming to consciousness of her own errors.
In contrast to Fanny Price, who possesses a firm knowledge of herself,
but struggles to act with confidence, Emma acts confidently but has to
learn to think about the consequences of her actions; she thus resembles
Elizabeth Bennet. The novel describes how a young woman who appears
to have everything comes to realize that she does not quite have it all, and,
moreover, that she definitely does not know everything. Some have suggested that the process she has to go through to arrive at that realization
is education by humiliation, and that she is required to submit to the better knowledge of her moral superior, her friend/brother/father-surrogate,

From *Jane Austen's Philosophy of the Virtues*, pp. 129–144, 181–182. © 2005 by Sarah
Emsley.

whose testing of her moral worth is rewarded by her hand in marriage. A number of critics have objected to the idea that Emma must be disciplined by Mr. Knightley in order to be worthy of becoming his bride.[1] In contrast, I read Emma as primarily responsible for her own moral education, an education into charitable thought. Her education is dependent on her choosing to change, not on her submitting to Mr. Knightley's wishes. I see Emma as independent, even in her education in recognizing her own errors, and there is evidence that Mr. Knightley himself sees her as capable of recognizing her own errors.

Unlike Marianne Dashwood, who learns mostly from her sister, and Elizabeth Bennet, who learns primarily from the process of reading Darcy's letters, and Fanny Price, who learns from her cousin and her reading of Samuel Johnson and other writers, Emma Woodhouse does not listen and she does not read. How, then, does she learn? What is it that brings her to understanding and humility, and how does she discover what is missing from the "best blessings of existence" that her life at the start of the novel seems to incorporate? Emma has "some" of the "best blessings of existence" (*E* 5) from the opening sentence onward, but what does she lack? What she starts with is that she is "handsome, clever, and rich, with a comfortable home and happy disposition," and the added comfort that her life thus far has been unruffled by bad fortune of any form: she "had lived nearly twenty-one years in the world with very little to distress or vex her" (*E* 5). But although she seems to have everything, what is missing is charity.[2] To some extent this absence recalls the lack of love in *Lady Susan*, but whereas love never gains prominence in Lady Susan Vernon's life, it gradually does in Emma's. At the beginning of the novel, Emma has not yet either had to experience the charity of others, or had to learn how to practice charity toward others. And as Paul says in 1 Corinthians, "though I have all faith, so that I could remove mountains, and have not charity, I am nothing" (13:2b). Emma needs to learn what charity is, and to do so she must struggle to achieve self-knowledge.

Education and the Dangers of Solitude

At the beginning of the novel, having lost the constant companionship of her governess and friend Miss Taylor, who has now become Mrs. Weston, Emma is "in great danger of suffering from intellectual solitude" (*E* 7). Austen's irony is directed at Emma here, as Emma will not really be cut off from all social discourse, but to what extent does intellectual solitude constitute real danger? The focus here is on Mr. Woodhouse, whose valetudinarian habits prevent him from engaging in any "activity of mind or body," and thus he is "no companion" for his daughter (*E* 7). She will have to look outside her home for intellectual companionship, then, because what she fears, though she may not be fully aware of the fact, is the reality of being left with her own mind. Emma claims to be quite able to depend on her own mind for strength, but one of the things she has to learn is that she is not self-sufficient. When Harriet Smith presses her for her reasons for not marrying, and her plans for the future in lieu of marriage, Emma says confidently that "'If I know myself, Harriet, mine is an active, busy mind, with a great many independent resources'" (*E* 85); however, she does *not* know herself yet, and that is part of the point of the novel. Does Emma have to come to terms with society's expectation of her, and reshape her conception of her own strength to fit a model that requires her to be supported by a much stronger and more independent gentleman? Does Austen require that Mr. Knightley learn anything, or is he permitted to be genuinely self-sufficient? Unlike Mr. Darcy, who has to adjust his perspective when he falls in love, Mr. Knightley represents a static, unchanging standard of gentleman-like virtue. To what extent is he Emma's teacher, and to what extent is her judgment independent?

Emma's fear of loneliness means that she welcomes company, even if it is not quite up to the standard of Mrs. Weston's friendship. Facing another of the "long evenings" in which her only company is hearing Mrs. Goddard, Mrs. Bates, and Miss Bates in conversation and "quiet prosings" with her father over cards, she welcomes the introduction of Harriet Smith to the circle at Hartfield (*E* 22). The addition of Harriet appears to promise a kind of relief from intellectual solitude. Harriet is a distraction, and Emma can take her on as a project, and improve her, despite the fact that "She was not struck by any thing remarkably clever in Miss Smith's conversation" (*E* 23). What Harriet mainly alleviates is the problem of lonely exercise, not the problem of intellectual solitude. The conversation may not be challenging, but "As a walking companion, Emma had very early foreseen how useful she might find her .... She had ventured once alone to Randalls, but it was not pleasant; and a Harriet Smith, therefore, one whom she could summon at any time to a walk, would be a valuable addition to her privileges" (*E* 26). Although Emma tells herself that the appeal of Harriet's companionship is that "Harriet would be loved as one to whom she could be useful" (*E* 26–27), it is clear that the real appeal is that Harriet is useful to Emma, as a kind of decorative, serviceable addition.[3]

What might be more useful to Emma at this point in her career is a little more intellectual solitude. She has little time for contemplation of her own mind or her place in the world, partly because she is richly blessed with the outward markers of what her place in the world is—beauty, money, and independence—and partly because she is too busy participating in society, laughing at the mistakes of others. When her brother-in-law Mr. John Knightley suggests to her that Mr. Elton "'seems to have a great deal of good-will towards *you*'" (*E* 112), she does not even consider the possibility that her confident assessment of her social life might be wrong, and receives this warning simply as a joke: "she walked on, amusing herself in the consideration of the blunders which often arise from a partial knowledge of circumstances, of the mistakes which people of high pretensions to judgment are for ever falling into" (*E* 112). She is certain that Mr. Elton should marry Harriet.

Knowing One's Own Mind

Emma does, however, see some things clearly, early on; she is not entirely blind to the meaning of the workings of society. Although she does not judge herself, she does judge Frank Churchill to be in error for not visiting his new stepmother (Austen's term is "mother-in-law") Mrs. Weston (*E* 122), even though she later defends Frank Churchill's behavior to Mr. Knightley, arguing that dependence and indebtedness to others can make it difficult to do what is right in a given situation (*E* 146). She finds herself "taking the other side of the question from her real opinion, and making use of Mrs. Weston's arguments against herself" (*E* 145). It could be argued here that her judgment of Frank's nonappearance in Highbury has to do with her own interest in seeing him, and finding out whether her imagined connection with him has any basis in reality, but it is also important that she can see that it is the right thing to do for him to visit his father's new wife. She can see this well before Mr. Knightley stresses to her that "'There is one thing, Emma, which a man can always do, if he chuses, and that is, his duty. . . . It is Frank Churchill's duty to pay this attention to his father'" (*E* 146).

One of the ways in which Emma shows that she does know her mind is that it is very difficult for her to pretend that she is in love with Frank Churchill, even after she has met him and been charmed by him. She may not be able to see that she loves Mr. Knightley, but she is intellectually and emotionally aware of the fact that she is not in love with Frank Churchill. Emma thinks through her flirtation with Frank, and her self-knowledge in this situation makes it possible for her to think through other aspects of her own behavior and feelings. It is through her analysis of where her love lies that she begins to know more about how she engages with other people in society. When Frank leaves Highbury after his first visit, Emma spends time alone thinking about her feelings, and after examining her reaction to his departure she concludes that "'I do suspect that he is not really necessary to my happiness. So much the better'" (*E* 264). She sees that he is changeable and that she does "'not altogether build upon his steadiness or constancy,'" and that "'Every consideration of the subject, in short, makes me thankful that my happiness is not more deeply involved'" (*E* 265). She knows herself too well to play at lovesickness, and she knows something about her own happiness. The problem, still, is that she has difficulty knowing the happiness of others.

The roots of this problem lie in her initial conception of what charity is. She has thought that it would be charitable to be useful to Harriet (when in fact she uses Harriet as a pawn in her own matchmaking game), that it would be charitable to Mr. Elton to find him a pretty wife (when she has used him as the object of that game), and also, that it would be charitable to Frank Churchill for her to bestow her affections on him. This is charity conceived of as condescension. Emma Woodhouse, proud, elegant, and benevolent, might condescend to treat "a Harriet Smith" as a friend, to arrange the local clergyman's love life for him, and to fall in love with a long-lost neighbor. But, as Emma needs to learn, charity is not about power.

In contrast to Elizabeth Bennet and Catherine Morland, whose revelations of self-knowledge come quite late in their respective novels, Emma has her first encounter with the pain of enlightenment relatively early, in Chapter 16. Marilyn Butler argues that it is not until Emma learns that Frank Churchill and Jane Fairfax are engaged that she finally judges herself clearly.[4] But Emma is forced to criticize her own mind well before the climax of the novel. After Mr. Elton has proposed to her—"actually making violent love to her" (*E* 129)—in the carriage on the way home after the Westons' Christmas Eve party, she is obliged to acknowledge her blindness regarding the object of her charitable matchmaking scheme. She does not yet know how blind she has been to Harriet's feelings in the whole affair with Robert Martin, or how reprehensible it is that she has directed Harriet to love Mr. Elton, but she does see how wrong she has been about interpreting Mr. Elton's behavior, and how her encouragement of his attentions could have been misinterpreted as welcoming his affection for her.

When she arrives home that night she is obliged to compose herself for her family's sake, and to wait until she is alone to think things through: "her mind had never been in such perturbation, and it needed a very strong effort to appear attentive and cheerful till the usual hour of separating allowed her the relief of quiet reflection" (*E* 133). Quiet reflection—being alone with her own mind—may be a relief of sorts, but it is not comfortable, as "Emma sat down to think and be miserable.—It was a wretched business, indeed!" (*E* 134). Thinking about one's own mistakes is difficult, painful, and miserable. It is something Mr. Woodhouse almost never does—later in the novel Emma blesses his "favouring blindness" to her interest in Frank Churchill's attentions to her, and Austen says that "the entire deficiency in him of all such sort of penetration or suspicion, was a most comfortable circumstance" (*E* 193). In this case his deficiency provides comfort for Emma, but presumably in most cases it provides comfort for him: he worries, but he does not think, and thus even his complaints are part of the comfort of his own complacency. With such a father it is either surprising or inevitable, depending on the influence granted to genes or the exigencies of circumstance, that Emma does have to think for herself.

When she does, she is thoroughly miserable. She forces herself to look back "as well as she could; but it was all confusion. She had taken up the idea, she supposed, and made everything bend to it" (*E* 134). The more she thinks about the past, the more she realizes her responsibility for what has happened: "If *she* had so misinterpreted his feelings, she had little right to wonder that *he*, with self-interest to blind him, should have mistaken her's" (*E* 136). The result of her miserable intellectual solitude is that she sees that

> The first error and the worst lay at her door. It was foolish, it was wrong, to take so active a part in bringing any two people together. It was adventuring too far, assuming too much, making light of what ought to be serious, a trick of what ought to be simple. She was quite concerned and ashamed, and resolved to do such things no more. (*E* 136–37)

This language suggests that Emma begins to see herself as chief among sinners,[5] and that she is contrite about her sin. In taking blame upon herself, she is beginning to acknowledge that she cannot do everything right by herself, but needs help. She is not wholly self-sufficient.

Following the debacle with Mr. Elton, Emma is angry not with him, but with herself. "She wished him very well; but he gave her pain, and his welfare twenty miles off would administer most satisfaction" (*E* 182). Although she would be more comfortable if he never returned to Highbury, she knows the value of seeing him as a reminder of her faults. Austen says that "his sight was so inseparably connected with some very disagreeable feelings, that except in a moral light, as a penance, a lesson, a source of profitable humiliation to her own mind, she would have been thankful to be assured of never seeing him again" (*E* 182). Seeing him is painful, but morally useful.

As far as Harriet is concerned, Emma is obliged to think again about separating her from Robert Martin. When Harriet sees Mr. Martin and his sister in Ford's, she is flustered and does not know what to do, especially when they are kind to her despite her rejection of the proposal and the family as beneath her. At Hartfield, Harriet turns automatically to Emma to assuage her nervousness, saying "'Oh! Miss Woodhouse, do talk to me and make me comfortable again'" (*E* 179). But Miss Woodhouse, having had to acknowledge her error about Mr. Elton, is a little more wary of providing immediate comfort without thinking carefully about the consequences: "Very sincerely did Emma wish to do so; but it was not immediately in her power. She was obliged to stop and think. She was not thoroughly comfortable herself" (*E* 179). As in *Sense and Sensibility* and *Pride and Prejudice*, the desire to be amiable and make others comfortable conflicts with the desire to be wholly truthful. Emma's discomfort at this point is not enough to make her seriously reexamine her initial judgment that Robert Martin is not good enough for Harriet, but it is enough to make her stop and think. And if she does this often enough, Austen implies, she will approach a better understanding of truth, and will be better equipped to behave charitably to others.

Charity as Style

What charity is not, therefore, is looking after others by telling them how to live. This is Mrs. Elton's idea of charity, and it is clearly shown to be misguided, as her officious exertions on behalf of Jane Fairfax demonstrate. In addition to directing the lives of the less fortunate, Mrs. Elton also sees charity as a matter of style. In her estimation, charity is what those in power offer to those without power: it both assists the beneficiary, and increases the positive social image and self-image of the benefactor. Early in the novel, Emma is guilty of conceiving of charity in just this way, and the introduction of Mrs. Elton to Highbury is a reminder to her of how charity should not be conducted. For example, Emma feels for Jane when Mrs. Elton insists that her servant will pick up Jane's mail, or when she insists on arranging a governessing position for Jane. Even when Mrs. Elton is planning her part in the strawberry party, her focus is on her image, and her ability to make Jane over in her own image. She tells Mr. Knightley that "'I shall wear a large bonnet, and bring one of my little baskets hanging on my arm. Here,—probably this basket with pink ribbon. Nothing can be more simple, you see. And Jane will have such another'" (*E* 355). But this kind of charity—"Look, you too can be perfectly stylish just like me—it's easy"—is vanity, as Mrs. Elton's repeated insistence on image at the expense of feeling shows. Similarly, she opines, "'I wish we had a donkey. The thing would be for us all to come on donkies [*sic*], Jane, Miss Bates, and me—and my caro sposo walking by. I really must talk to him about purchasing a donkey'" (*E* 356). As Marcia McClintock Folsom points out, "The artificiality of Mrs. Elton's vision is revealed by her thought of pestering her husband to *buy* the donkey to complete this imaginary scene of country life."[6] Mrs. Elton is clearly thinking more of the picturesque image of herself on a donkey than of providing any help to Jane or Miss Bates. At the strawberry-picking party at Donwell, "Mrs. Elton, in all her apparatus of happiness, her large bonnet and her basket, was very ready to lead the way in gathering, accepting, or talking" (*E* 358), and her insistence on being first in everything belies her attempts to provide charity to others.

Is it necessary to have equipment for virtue, apparatus for happiness? It is easier, no doubt, to offer charity to others if one has much to offer, but charity resides more in the disposition of a person than in objects or wealth to be dispensed. The question of external circumstances necessary to the virtuous life arises when Emma and Harriet discuss the situation of Miss Bates. Emma is defending the idea that she herself proposes to remain single, and argues that while "'a very narrow income has a tendency to contract the mind, and sour the temper,'" "'a single woman, of good fortune, is always respectable, and may be as sensible and pleasant as anybody else'" (E 85). She acknowledges that Miss Bates does not fit in the category of miserly old maid, however: "'Poverty certainly has not contracted her mind: I really believe, if she had only a shilling in the world, she would be very likely to give away sixpence of it'" (E 85). Like Mrs. Smith in Persuasion and like the biblical widow who gives her last mite to those poorer than herself, Miss Bates is an exemplar of charity.[7] Thus although Emma professes to believe that it is necessary to have wealth in order to be generous and good-natured, she has to except Miss Bates, the example of the single woman's life that is closest to home, because Miss Bates does not lack charity. She is "'only too good natured and too silly to suit'" Emma (E 85), but she is not uncharitable. Equipment and material resources for promoting virtue may make charity easier, as Aristotle proposes, and as Austen suggests in other novels, especially earlier novels such as Sense and Sensibility, but they are not always necessary, as characters in both Emma and Persuasion demonstrate.[8]

Emma has drawn on the resources of Hartfield in order to offer charity to Mrs. and Miss Bates, in much the same way that she visits the poor. She sends Hartfield pork to the Bates household—as her father says, "'Now we have killed a porker, and Emma thinks of sending them a loin or a leg; it is very small and delicate'"; Emma replies that she has done more than that: "'My dear papa, I sent the whole hind-quarter. I knew you would wish it'" (E 172). She is generous, but her charity here is mostly action, not thought. Although she has to be thoughtful enough to go to the trouble of sending this gift to them, the action does not really alter her attitude toward the recipients of her charity. It is more a matter of form than of goodwill to others.

In her conversation with Harriet, just after they have established that Miss Bates is not an uncharitable old maid, Emma speaks uncharitably of Jane Fairfax—"'I wish Jane Fairfax very well; but she tires me to death'" (E 86)—and then she moves easily into the role of Lady Bountiful, visiting the poor of the parish and dispensing tangible charity. There is no irony, however, in Austen's description of Emma's attitude toward the people she visits here: "Emma was very compassionate; and the distresses of the poor were as sure of relief from her personal attention and kindness, her counsel and her patience, as from her purse" (E 86).[9] So it is not empty action, but compassionate aid, as she "entered into their troubles with ready sympathy, and always gave her assistance with as much intelligence as good-will" (E 86). It is Emma's own ironic observation after they have left the cottage that it can be difficult to fix one's mind on the sufferings of others when there are potential distractions in one's own life, as she says smilingly, "'I hope it may be allowed that if compassion has produced exertion and relief to the sufferers, it has done all that is truly important. If we feel for the wretched, enough to do all we can for them, the rest is empty sympathy, only distressing to ourselves'" (*E* 87). She does not believe that sympathy alone will help: action and benevolence in proportion to the need of those in distress will be helpful, but thinking without acting will not.

That Emma knows the difference between the sentimental pretensions of claims to suffer along with others in distress, and the more realistic attempt to help others without drowning in their misery with them, suggests that she is critical of the idea of charity as style. She is not, of course, as stylishly charitable as Mrs. Elton, and she does offer real help. Yet like Mrs. Elton, she also claims to offer help to those whose social situation is not quite so distant from her own. Mrs. Elton fixes on Jane; Emma fixes on Harriet, and then tries to help Jane as well. In both of her fixations, Emma is attracted to the object of her charity partly because of the idea of helping a beautiful young woman who appears to need help. This attraction makes Emma resemble the eponymous hero of George Eliot's *Daniel Deronda*, heroic and sympathetic rescuer of beautiful women in distress. Harriet is not as desperate as Mirah Lapidoth, and Jane is not as tragic as Gwendolen Harleth, but nevertheless the rescuer in each case is predisposed to offer help because of the beauty not of the action of rescue, but of the recipient. As in the epigraph I have chosen for this chapter, from "Love and Friendship" (*MW* 77–78) the graces of the person are conflated with the graces of the mind; and thus the beauty of the woman in question makes charity that much more appealing.

In *Emma*, Austen is concerned with the difference between charity as love and charity as image. The issue is highlighted in an exchange between Emma and Frank Churchill in which Frank proposes to purchase gloves at Ford's as proof that he is "'a true citizen of Highbury'"; he says, "'It will be taking out my freedom'" (*E* 200). Emma laughs that "'You were very popular before you came, because you were Mr. Weston's son—but lay out half-a-guinea at Ford's, and your popularity will stand upon your own virtues'" (*E* 200). It is not that it would be charitable of Frank to support the business of Ford's, but that to be seen to patronize the same shop as everyone else would serve as a sign that he subscribes to the image of Highbury society. Frank proves his virtues by exercising the power of purchasing. But this is not a version of virtue Austen condones: for her, virtue has to do with consistency between charitable thought and charitable action.

Benevolence and Friendship

Frank needs to prove his virtues, because not everyone in Highbury is convinced that he has them. Prior to his arrival there, Emma and Mr. Knightley have speculated on his character, with the latter insisting, on the basis of

Frank's seeming reluctance to visit Mrs. Weston at the proper time, that he will prove to be "'a very weak young man'" (*E* 148). Mr. Knightley's opinion is that Frank "'can be amiable only in French, not in English. He may be very "amiable," have very good manners, and be very agreeable; but he can have no English delicacy towards the feelings of other people: nothing really amiable about him'" (*E* 149). Amiability, as I have suggested in previous chapters, is an important virtue for Austen because it is so closely connected with charity. Emma teases Mr. Knightley that this kind of amiability might be enough for Highbury, as "'We do not often look upon fine young men, well-bred and agreeable. We must not be nice and ask for all the virtues into the bargain'" (*E* 149).

Their conversation raises the question of the difference between good will and friendship, an issue that recurs in the novel. Although Emma says she does not expect all the virtues, she does appear to imagine that Frank will be everyone's friend: she says that "'My idea of him is, that he can adapt his conversation to the taste of every body, and has the power as well as the wish of being universally agreeable'" (*E* 150). Mr. Knightley objects to this description as the ideal of amiability, because if true it would mean that Frank would adapt his character so well to the demands of those around him that he would be insufferable: "'What! At three-and-twenty to be the king of his company—the great man—the practised politician, who is to read every body's character, and make every body's talents conduce to the display of his own superiority'" (*E* 150). Mr. Knightley is already jealous of Frank, but his objection holds, and the kind of universal goodwill that caters to every individual while serving primarily to emphasize the charitable person's own superiority is insufferable in the great as well as in the inexperienced twenty-three-year old.

Emma experiences the problem of an older man's universal amiability later in the novel when she realizes that Mr. Weston does not discriminate among his acquaintants, even though he treats them each as a particular and exclusive friend. When it comes to the evening of the ball at the Crown, it turns out that he has invited a large number of friends to come early to inspect the rooms, giving each to believe that he relies on his or her taste alone. It is not Emma's vanity alone that is damaged by being considered "the favourite and intimate of a man who had so many intimates and confidantes" (*E* 320); although her vanity is hurt here, she is right to see the contradictions inherent in this way Mr. Weston has of treating everybody. Consciously or not, she recalls the earlier conversation with Mr. Knightley, and reflects that "General benevolence, but not general friendship, made a man what he ought to be.—She could fancy such a man" (*E* 320).

Where is tolerance and where is charity, in the debate about the difference between benevolence and friendship? How does one determine who one's friends are, and how treatment of a friend differs from treatment of everyone else? Does one merely tolerate all others, or does tolerance also require one to be amiable, charitable, and benevolent? Charity involves more than just the right attitude toward giving gifts and paying visits. In *Emma*, Austen suggests that an understanding of charity also involves careful judgments about friendships and intimate relationships. Tolerating everyone or everything will not always be the charitable thing to do, so distinctions may be necessary. It seems exclusive to gather a small group of friends, and leave the rest to chance and charity, and yet this is what Austen leaves us with at the end of the novel: a "small band of true friends" who witness the wedding of Emma and Mr. Knightley (*E* 484). She does not say exactly who makes it into that category, but there is no question that it is an exclusive group. Although to a certain extent the distinctions Emma and Mr. Knightley make about the small band of friends have to do with class, such judgments also have to do with charity. Austen suggests that while one may cultivate a charitable attitude and a healthy respect for other people, one need not treat everyone as a "favourite" or an "intimate." Some people will form closer ties than others, and both this love that binds together a small band of friends, and the kind of love one offers to broader numbers of people are central aspects of charity. In *Emma*, charity is not defined simply as either good works performed for other people, or as love offered to one's intimates: romantic love, the love of friendship, and the love of benevolent good works are all part of Austen's understanding of charity. The process of learning to be charitable, therefore, is more than an education in good works or social justice, as it can help characters work toward happiness as well as goodness.

"Perfect Happiness"

A number of critics have discussed the concept of "perfect happiness" in Jane Austen's novels, especially in *Emma*. Rachel Brownstein suggests, rightly, that "The gap between 'real' Austen heroines like Catherine or Emma or Fanny and the ideal mere picture of perfection Jane Austen thought other people admired too much is in effect the subject of all her novels."[10] "Pictures of perfection as you know make me sick & wicked," Austen wrote (*Letters*, March 23, 1817; 335), and it is worth remembering this statement of hers when we find Fanny especially "too perfect" or "too good." Even Austen's most virtuous heroines are not always perfect. Elaine Bander makes the distinction that "Perfection, for Austen, is not being but becoming."[11] Through their contemplation of what it means to live a good life, Austen's heroines work toward practicing, exercising, or becoming virtuous.

Julia Prewitt Brown argues that "when we close the pages of *Emma* we have learned enough about Emma and Mr. Knightley and Highbury and life in general there to know exactly how much perfection and how much happiness are included in the narrator's 'perfect happiness.'"[12] Yet while Austen surely recognizes the limitations of the "perfect happiness" and wedded bliss that she alludes to in the concluding paragraph of *Emma*, it seems unlikely that she intends her readers to shake their heads sadly over the disillusionment that awaits Emma and Mr. Knightley. On the contrary, her earlier description of Mr. Knightley offers a better way of understanding her choice of these words: when he and Emma reach an understanding, "Within half an hour, he had passed from a thoroughly distressed state of mind, to something so like perfect happiness, that it could bear no other name" (*E* 432). Their life together, therefore, promises to be, like Emma, "faultless in spite of all [its] faults" (*E* 433). The virtuous life is not a perfect life, but in attempting to learn, exercise, and practice the virtues, Austen suggests, one may achieve something like perfect happiness, not happiness as an end result, but as a process open to revision.

In *Emma*, Austen suggests that the practice of charity is part of the process of learning, in Mrs. Dashwood's terms, to know one's own happiness. Charity is not about one's own image, one's condescension to others, but about generosity of spirit and genuine love and grace toward other people, whether those people are intimates or strangers. How does one achieve the right attitude toward one's self and others, and how would one know exactly when it was right? As in *Sense and Sensibility*, the awareness of the right balance that constitutes happiness is difficult to achieve. And as in *Pride and Prejudice*, practicing charity at the right time, and in the right manner, toward the right persons, can be challenging. Emma's reaction following Mr. Elton's proposal to her causes her to repent her errors, and to resolve to behave better and more carefully in the future. She confesses to Harriet that she was wrong to have encouraged the pursuit of Mr. Elton, and this confession "completely renewed her first shame" (*E* 141). Emma thinks that "It was rather too late in the day to set about being simpleminded and ignorant; but she left [Harriet] with every previous resolution confirmed of being humble and discreet, and repressing imagination all the rest of her life" (*E* 142). Her repentance is genuine, and the turn to humility is part of the traditional response of the contrite sinner following confession, although her vow to repress imagination forever is more along the lines of Marianne Dashwood's sober plans for her cheerless virtuous future than along the pattern of Christian confession. The person confessing prays to be granted "that this day we fall into no sin, neither run into any kind of danger; but that all our doings may be ordered by thy governance,"[13] all the while knowing that the fallen nature common to all will mean that each day we fall into some kind of sin. The prayer is part of the process. Emma repents, knowing that she will not be able to avoid being wrong about something else yet again. But in this situation, she confesses to Harriet, and she worries that "she should never be in charity with herself again" (*E* 141). Is it the aim of virtue to be in charity with one's self?

Uncharitable Emma

When Emma infamously chides Miss Bates at Box Hill for having to limit herself to saying only three dull things at once in response to Frank Churchill's game (*E* 364), she does not at first realize that she has been uncharitable. She carries on blindly with her conversation with Frank and Mr. Weston, and it does take Mr. Knightley's later reprimand to cause her to review her conduct. At first she "tried to laugh it off," saying that "'It was not so very bad. I dare say she did not understand me'" (*E* 374), but he explains to her the implications of her insult to someone like Miss Bates whose "'situation should secure [Emma's] compassion'" (*E* 375). Would Emma have realized this herself? Having recognized in the situation with Harriet and Mr. Elton just how wrong her behavior could be, is Emma any more likely to see clearly the occasions on which she condescends to those around her? Perhaps she would in time have come to see the folly of treating Miss Bates this way, but moral education is slow and time-consuming as well as painful. Would it have taken her years or at least months to learn where her charity is deficient?

When during the ball at the Crown Mr. Knightley and Emma had discussed the problem of Emma's attempt to marry Harriet to Mr. Elton, Mr. Knightley had said, "'I shall not scold you. I leave you to your own reflections'" (*E* 330), and Emma had asked, "'Can you trust me with such flatterers?—Does my vain spirit ever tell me I am wrong?'" (*E* 330). His reply was that she could be trusted to distinguish between her vain spirit and her serious spirit: "'If one leads you wrong, I am sure the other tells you of it'" (*E* 330). He knows that she is capable of thinking through moral decisions.[14] Yet at Box Hill, he sees that her serious spirit has not told her of it, as he witnesses her continued attempts at amusement with the others, with no sign of apology to Miss Bates. Is he trying to save her the trouble of having to learn to come to a consciousness of her mistakes? In trying to teach her virtue, is he making her moral education less painful, or more? Or is his reprimand partly the result of his own vanity: he wants Emma to be perfect too, despite his objection to Mr. Weston's clever remark that the letters "'M. and A.—Em—ma'" stand for perfection (*E* 371)? The reason he reprimands her is that he knows she will not learn by reading. She does learn by thinking things through, but it took Mr. Elton's outburst to provide the occasion for her to reconsider that situation, and there is no way that Miss Bates would ever confront Emma. There needs to be something that instigates Emma's thinking about her conduct. Mr. Knightley's speech here parallels Mr. Elton's declaration of love in that it prompts Emma to think.

There is no need for Mr. Knightley to continue to argue the point, as Emma immediately sees "[t]he truth of his representation" (*E* 376). And from here on, she is left in intellectual solitude, despite Harriet's presence in the carriage, and "Time did not compose her. As she reflected more, she seemed but to feel it more. She had never been so depressed" (*E* 376). Once she gets home, she realizes that her attitude toward her father ought to have guided her attitude toward Miss Bates. To him, she has been patient and kind in thought as well as in action. Toward Miss Bates, "She had been often remiss, her conscience told her so; remiss, perhaps, more in thought than fact; scornful, ungracious" (*E* 377). Mr. Knightley has chided her only for the one public remark, but Emma's conscience tells her that she has been thinking scornfully of Miss Bates all along, even while sending her pork and paying her visits. And she has spoken of her ungraciously to Harriet. In fact, Emma's own conscience is more severe in judging her thought and action than Mr. Knightley is. The realization that she has not loved her neighbor as herself is Emma's second moment of revelation, and it is far more painful than the earlier revelation that she has misjudged the situation with Mr. Elton.

Charity and Romantic Love

Emma's third revelation is the recognition "that Mr. Knightley must marry no one but herself!" (*E* 408). Once again, however, it takes someone else's prompting to get her to examine her own perceptions. As soon as Harriet has revealed that she not only aspires to love Mr. Knightley, but actually has some idea that he returns her affections, Emma's mind starts working, and "A mind like her's, once opening to suspicion, made rapid progress" (*E* 407). This description is important: Emma has the kind of quick mind that can analyze behavior thoroughly. Her intelligence is sharp, but her initial perceptions are a little dull, perhaps because she is so confident of her social position that she lacks the critical impulse. From the moment Harriet tells her love, thinking is painful once more for Emma. While Harriet "give[s] the history of her hopes with great, though trembling delight," Emma's "mind was in all the perturbation that such a developement [*sic*] of self, such a burst of threatening evil, such a confusion of sudden and perplexing emotions, must create" (*E* 408–09). Intellectual self-examination may be painful, whether one is analyzing the difficulties of acting charitably toward other people, or the complexities of romantic love.

In the opening paragraphs of the novel, Jane Austen reveals that the "real evils" of "Emma's situation were the power of having rather too much her own way, and a disposition to think a little too well of herself" (*E* 5). Added to these evils, or perhaps a result of them, has been a resistance to thinking very deeply. The things that need to be adjusted to make the "best blessings" of her life more complete are the way she treats others, and the way she thinks of herself. Yet while it sounds reasonable, as Mr. Knightley says elsewhere in the novel, that "'Fine dancing, I believe, like virtue, must be its own reward'" (*E* 258), virtue in *Emma* is rewarded with more material blessings, just as fine dancing is often rewarded with a fine partner. Virtue may be worth pursuing for its own sake, but it does not hurt that one's reputation improves, or that benefits accrue to virtuous behavior. Parallel to the two things that need to be adjusted in Emma's world are two possible definitions of charity: Emma needs to learn to be charitable to others in thought as well as in action, and to be less forgiving of her own faults. Thinking makes her miserable, especially when she's thinking of her own errors, but careful thought is essential to the practice of charity, and Emma comes to understand not only what her blessings mean for her own life, but also what these blessings require of her in her attitude toward those who are less blessed and who suffer more. Emma has to learn to love her neighbor as herself, and to be in love and charity with her neighbors rather than simply with herself.

Like Fanny Price, Emma has to think hard, and negotiate the tension between knowing her own mind and heart and knowing how to behave to relatives and friends around her. Self-knowledge can conflict with charity toward one's neighbors, but in *Emma*, Austen proposes that it is important to endeavor both to know one's self and to love God and neighbor. Emma Woodhouse experiences moments of moral recognition, and each of these three major revelations causes her to think carefully and to challenge her usual view of the world. In contrast to Elizabeth Bennet, who experiences one significant epiphany after reading Darcy's letter, Emma undergoes three revolutions of mind in order to effect her moral education. Like Elizabeth, however, she finds that her education is prompted by the reminders the hero gives her to revisit her interpretation of the world. In *Emma*, Austen focuses on the theological virtue of charity, and explores its meaning as the Christian love of neighbors as well as its role in romantic love. Through intellectual suffering, Emma Woodhouse learns how to think about charity, and how she may live out charity in action.

NOTES

1. Mark Schorer describes "The Humiliation of Emma Woodhouse." Gilbert and Gubar, e.g., argue that Emma is humiliated and "must accept the fate of being mastered" (*Madwoman in the Attic*, 161–62), and Edward Neill criticizes the "ultra-patriarchal Mr Knightley" (*Politics of Jane Austen*, 95).

2. Michael Giffin argues that in addition to the novel's focus on the education of an individual into charity, Austen explores the predicament of the fallen community of Highbury (*Jane Austen and Religion*, 150). Jane Nardin also argues that *Emma* is about charity, but she emphasizes the narrower definition of charity as "the act of

giving material aid or advice to those, especially those in a worse social or financial position, who seem to need it" ("Charity in *Emma*," 66).

3. Barbara K. Seeber argues that Harriet is the "other heroine" of the novel, and that "the dominant narrative tries to naturalize Harriet's exclusion and to naturalize her inferior class position as her inferior personal worth." Seeber suggests that "Harriet, like Frankenstein's monster, takes on a life of her own and it is precisely this that the main narrative cannot accommodate" (*General Consent*, 43). While Emma does make use of Harriet more as an accessory than as a friend, Harriet is not monstrous, she is just ordinary. Upon their marriages both she and Emma take up new responsibilities that mean their parting is not "The 'unmerited punishment' of Harriet Smith" that Seeber's chapter title claims it to be. When Seeber argues that Harriet is "exiled to the periphery of Highbury" (*General Consent*, 45), she cites the passage in which Emma thinks that "every blessing of her own seemed to involve and advance the sufferings of her friend, who must now be even excluded from Hartfield" (*E* 450). But in this passage Emma still believes that Harriet is in love with Mr. Knightley, and she imagines the exclusion of Harriet as necessary to spare Harriet the pain of seeing Emma and Mr. Knightley happy together. Once Emma discovers that "Harriet had always liked Robert Martin" (*E* 481), their friendship begins to "change into a calmer sort of goodwill" (*E* 482), but there is no banishment, no punishment here.

4. Butler, *Jane Austen and the War of Ideas*, 258.

5. Compare 1 Timothy 1:15, where the Apostle Paul writes, "This is a faithful saying, and worthy of all acceptation, that Christ Jesus came into the world to save sinners; of whom I am chief." On the relation between embarrassment and shame, see David Southward, "Jane Austen and the Riches of Embarrassment."

6. Folsom, "'I Wish We Had a Donkey,'" 160.

7. Miss Bates is the only Austen character who quotes—in her case, misquotes—from the Bible: commenting on Emma's kind gift of Hartfield pork, she says, "We may well say that 'our lot is cast in a goodly heritage'" (*E* 174). The reference is to Psalm 16:7. As Margaret Doody points out, Miss Bates has no heritage, no estate to inherit, and her good fortune here is that she is the recipient of charity ("Jane Austen's Reading," 348). It is typical of her good nature, however, to see even the smallest kindnesses, whether given or received, as examples of Christian charity. Koppel contrasts Miss Bates's Christian charity with the negative version of Christian perfection represented by the Eltons (*Religious Dimension*, 26).

8. See Aristotle, *Nicomachean Ethics*, 1099a.31–1099b.2.

9. Emma is less charitable in her attitude toward Robert Martin and his family than she is to the poor, however. David Wheeler attributes her snobbery toward manual laborers to her "old-fashioned attitudes toward agrarian economy," and points out that she seems unaware of recent economic changes in her society ("Jane Austen and the Discourse of Poverty," 253). For a discussion of the relation between economics and virtue in Austen, see also Elsie B. Michie, "Austen's Powers: Engaging with Adam Smith in Debates about Wealth and Virtue."

10. Brownstein, "England's *Emma*," 233.

11. Bander, "The Pique of Perfection," 161.

12. Brown, *Jane Austen's Novels*, 69–70.

13. The Order for Morning Prayer, in *The Book of Common Prayer*. Koppel also argues that Emma's repentance and desire to reform can best be understood with reference to the Christian ideal of moral behavior; he suggests that Emma is

"by Christian standards the most deeply flawed of Jane Austen's heroines" (*Religious Dimension*, 31; 37).

14. Patricia Menon suggests that Austen downplays Mr. Knightley's role as a mentor, as she does in the case of Henry Tilney in *Northanger Abbey* and Mr. Darcy in *Pride and Prejudice* as well, because these novels propose a model of marriage in which moral equality is necessary for "perfect happiness" (*Mentor-Lover*, 45).

Chronology

1775	Jane Austen is born on December 16 in the village of Steventon, Hampshire, to George Austen, parish clergyman, and Cassandra Leigh Austen. She is the seventh of eight children. She and her sister Cassandra are educated at Oxford and Southampton by the widow of a principal of Brasenose College, and then they attend the Abbey School at Reading. Jane's formal education ends when she is nine years old.
1787–93	Austen writes various pieces for the amusement of her family (collected in the three volumes of *Juvenilia*), the most famous of which is *Love and Friendship*. She and her family also perform various plays and farces, some of which are written by Jane.
1793–97	Austen writes her first novel, the epistolary *Lady Susan*, and begins the epistolary *Elinor and Marianne*, which will become *Sense and Sensibility*.
1796–97	Austen completes *First Impressions*, an early version of *Pride and Prejudice*. Her father tries without success to get it published. Austen begins *Sense and Sensibility* and *Northanger Abbey*.
1798	Austen finishes a version of *Northanger Abbey*.
1801–02	George Austen retires to Bath with his family. Jane probably suffers from an unhappy love affair (the man in question is believed to have died suddenly), and also probably becomes engaged for a day to Harris Bigg-Wither.

1803	Austen sells two-volume manuscript titled *Susan* to a publisher for £10. It is advertised but never printed. This is a version of *Northanger Abbey*, probably later revised.
1803–1805	Austen writes ten chapters of *The Watsons*.
1805–1806	George Austen dies. Jane abandons work on *The Watsons*. She, her mother, and her sister live in various lodgings in Bath.
1806–1809	The three Austen women move to Southampton, living near one of Jane's brothers.
1809	Jane, her sister, and her mother move to Chawton Cottage, in Hampshire, which is part of the estate of Jane's brother Edward Austen (later Knight), who has been adopted by Thomas Knight, a relative. Edward has just lost his wife, who died giving birth to her tenth child, and the household has been taken over by Jane's favorite niece, Fanny.
1811	Austen decides to publish *Sense and Sensibility* at her own expense and anonymously. It appears in November in a three-volume edition.
1811–12	Austen is probably revising *First Impressions* extensively and beginning *Mansfield Park*.
1813	*Pride and Prejudice* is published in January. A second edition of it, as well as a second edition of *Sense and Sensibility*, come out in November.
1814	*Mansfield Park* is published anonymously. Austen begins *Emma*.
1815	Austen completes *Emma* and begins *Persuasion*. *Emma* is published anonymously by a new publisher.
1816	A second edition of *Mansfield Park* is published.
1817	A third edition of *Pride and Prejudice* is published. Austen begins *Sanditon*. She moves to Winchester, where she dies, after a year-long illness, on July 18. She is buried in Winchester Cathedral.
1818	*Persuasion* and *Northanger Abbey* are published posthumously together, their authorship still officially anonymous.

Contributors

HAROLD BLOOM is Sterling Professor of the Humanities at Yale University. He is the author of 30 books, including *Shelley's Mythmaking*, *The Visionary Company*, *Blake's Apocalypse*, *Yeats*, *A Map of Misreading*, *Kabbalah and Criticism*, *Agon: Toward a Theory of Revisionism*, *The American Religion*, *The Western Canon*, and *Omens of Millennium: The Gnosis of Angels, Dreams, and Resurrection*. *The Anxiety of Influence* sets forth Professor Bloom's provocative theory of the literary relationships between the great writers and their predecessors. His most recent books include *Shakespeare: The Invention of the Human*, a 1998 National Book Award finalist, *How to Read and Why*, *Genius: A Mosaic of One Hundred Exemplary Creative Minds*, *Hamlet: Poem Unlimited*, *Where Shall Wisdom Be Found?*, and *Jesus and Yahweh: The Names Divine*. In 1999, Professor Bloom received the prestigious American Academy of Arts and Letters Gold Medal for Criticism. He has also received the International Prize of Catalonia, the Alfonso Reyes Prize of Mexico, and the Hans Christian Andersen Bicentennial Prize of Denmark.

MARY POOVEY is a professor at New York University, where she is also the director of the Institute for the History of the Production of Knowledge. Her publications include *A History of the Modern Fact* and *Making a Social Body: British Cultural Formation, 1830–1864*.

E.B. MOON has been associated with the University of New England in Armidale, New South Wales, Australia.

ANNE K. MELLOR is a distinguished professor of English and women's studies at the University of California at Los Angeles. She has edited and/or written several texts, including *Mothers of the Nation: Women's Political Writing in England, 1780–1830* and *Passionate Encounters in a Time of Sensibility,* both of which she authored.

CYNTHIA WALL is a professor at the University of Virginia. She is the author of *The Prose of Things: Transformation of Description in the Eighteenth Century* and *The Literary and Cultural Spaces of Restoration London.* Additionally, she has edited or coedited several titles.

WILLIAM DERESIEWICZ is an associate professor at Yale University. He is the author of *Jane Austen and the Romantic Poets.*

JO ALYSON PARKER is chair and professor of English at St. Joseph's University. She is the author of *Narrative Form and Chaos Theory in Sterne, Proust, Woolf and Faulkner* and coeditor of *Time and Memory.*

IVOR MORRIS has been a university lecturer and is the author of *Shakespeare's God: The Role of Religion in the Tragedies* and *Hamlet, King of Denmark,* an alternative tragicomical ending to Shakespeare's play.

PAULA BYRNE is the author of *Perdita: The Literary, Theatrical, Scandalous Life of Mary Robinson* and editor of *Jane Austen: A Sourcebook.*

GLORIA SYBIL GROSS is a professor of English at California State University, Northridge. She has written *The Invisible Riot of the Mind: Samuel Johnson's Psychological Theory.*

PATRICIA MENON has taught at Niagara College in Southern Ontario, Canada.

EMILY AUERBACH is a professor of English at the University of Wisconsin at Madison. She is the author of *Maestros, Dilettantes, and Philistines: The Musician in the Victorian Novel* and *The Courage to Write I and II: Women Novelists of 19th-Century Europe and America.* Additionally, for Wisconsin Public Radio she is the project director of "The Courage to Write," an award-winning series of documentaries on women writers released nationally.

SARAH EMSLEY teaches in the Expository Writing Program at Harvard University. She is the editor of *Jane Austen and the North Atlantic Essays from the 2005 Jane Austen Society Conference in Halifax, Nova Scotia, Canada.*

Bibliography

Bander, Elaine. "The Other Play in *Mansfield Park*: Shakespeare's *Henry VIII*," *Persuasions* 17 (December 1995): pp. 111–20.

Bautz, Annika. *The Reception of Jane Austen and Walter Scott: A Comparative Longitudinal Study*. London; New York: Continuum, 2007.

Beer, Patricia. "Elizabeth Bennet's Fine Eyes." In Enright, D. J., ed., *Fair of Speech: The Uses of Euphemism*, pp. 108–121. Oxford: Oxford University Press, 1985.

Benedict, Barbara M. "Jane Austen's *Sense and Sensibility*: The Politics of Point of View," *Philological Quarterly* 69, no. 4 (Fall 1990): pp. 453–70.

Bilger, Audrey. *Laughing Feminism: Subversive Comedy in Frances Burney, Maria Edgeworth, and Jane Austen*. Detroit: Wayne State University Press, 1998.

Bourdeau, Debra Taylor, and Elizabeth Kraft, ed. *On Second Thought: Updating the Eighteenth-Century Text*. Newark: University of Delaware Press, 2007.

Breunig, Hans Werner. "Jane Austen: Romantic? British Empiricist?" In Bode, Christoph and Neuman, Fritz-Wilhelm, eds. *Re-Mapping Romanticism: Gender Text-Context*, pp. 163–81. *Studien zur Englischen Romantik*. 14. Essen, Germany: Blaue, Eule, 2001.

Brownstein, Rachel M. *Becoming a Heroine: Reading about Women in Novels*. New York: Columbia University Press, 1994.

Byrne, Paula, ed. *Jane Austen's "Emma": A Sourcebook*. London; New York: Routledge, 2004.

Copeland, Edward and Juliet McMaster. *The Cambridge Companion to Jane Austen*. Cambridge, England: Cambridge University Press, 1997.

Correa, Delia Da Sousa, ed. *The Nineteenth-Century Novel: Realisms*. London: Routledge for Open University, 2000.

Dabundo, Laura, ed. *Jane Austen and Mary Shelley, and Their Sisters.* Lanham, Md.: University Press of America, 2000.

Ferguson, Frances. "Jane Austen, *Emma*, and the Impact of Form," *Modern Language Quarterly* 61, no. 1 (March 2000): pp. 157–80.

Fraiman, Susan. *Unbecoming Women: British Women Writers and the Novel of Development.* New York: Columbia University Press, 1993.

Galperin, William. "Byron, Austen and the 'Revolution' of Irony," *Criticism: A Quarterly for Literature and the Arts* 32, no. 1 (Winter 1990): pp. 51–80.

———. *The Historical Austen.* Philadelphia: University of Pennsylvania Press, 2003.

———. "The Picturesque, the Real, and the Consumption of Jane Austen," *Wordsworth Circle* 28, no. 1 (Winter 1997): pp. 19–27.

Galperin, William, ed. *Re-Reading Box Hill: Reading the Practice of Reading Everyday Life.* College Park, MD: University of Maryland, 2000.

Garber, Marjorie. *Quotation Marks.* New York: Routledge, 2003.

Giffin, Michael. *Jane Austen and Religion: Salvation and Society in Georgian England.* Houndmills, Basingstoke, Hampshire; New York: Palgrave Macmillan, 2002.

Giles, Paul. "The Gothic Dialogue in *Pride and Prejudice.*" *Text and Context* 2, no. 1 (Spring 1988): pp. 68–75.

Gill, Richard, and Susan Gregory. *Mastering the Novels of Jane Austen.* Houndmills, Basingstoke, Hampshire; New York: Palgrave Macmillan, 2003.

Harmsel, Henrietta Ten. "The Villain-Hero in *Pamela* and *Pride and Prejudice.*" *College English* XXIII (November 1961): pp. 104–108.

Havely, Cicely Palser. "*Emma*: Portrait of the Artist as a Young Woman," *English: The Journal of the The English Association* 42, no. 174 (Fall 1993): pp. 221–37.

Hawkridge, Audrey. *Jane and Her Gentlemen: Jane Austen and the Men in Her Life and Novels.* London; Chester Springs, Pa.: Peter Owen, 2000.

Heydt-Stevenson, Jillian. *Austen's Unbecoming Conjunctions: Subversive Laughter, Embodied History.* New York: Palgrave Macmillan, 2005.

Jenkyns, Richard. *A Fine Brush on Ivory: An Appreciation of Jane Austen.* Oxford; New York: Oxford University Press, 2004.

Jones, Darryl. *Jane Austen.* Houndmills, Basingstoke, Hampshire; New York: Palgrave Macmillan, 2004.

Knox-Shaw, Peter. *Jane Austen and the Enlightenment.* Cambridge, U.K.; New York: Cambridge University Press, 2004.

Kramp, Michael. *Disciplining Love: Austen and the Modern Man.* Columbus: Ohio State University Press, 2007.

Lambdin, Laura Cooner, and Robert Thomas Lambdin, eds. *A Companion to Jane Austen Studies.* Westport, Conn.: Greenwood, 2000.

Lau, Beth. "Jane Austen, *Pride and Prejudice.*" In Wu, Duncan, ed. *A Companion to Romanticism,* pp. 219–226. Oxford, England: Blackwell, 1998.

Lessing, Doris. *Time Bites: Views and Reviews.* New York: HarperCollins, 2005.

Littlewood, Ian, ed. *Jane Austen: Critical Assessments.* Mountfield: Helm Information, 1998.

Looser, Devoney, ed. *Jane Austen and Discourses of Feminism.* New York: St. Martin's, 1995.

Mandal, Anthony. *Jane Austen and the Popular Novel: The Determined Author.* Basingstoke : Palgrave Macmillan, 2007.

Marsh, Nicholas. *Jane Austen: The Novels.* New York: St. Martin's, 1998.

McMaster, Juliet. *Jane Austen, the Novelist: Essays Past and Present.* London: MacMillan Press; New York: St. Martin's Press, 1996.

McMaster, Juliet and Bruce Stovel, eds. *Jane Austen's Business: Her World and Her Profession.* Hampshire, England; New York: Macmillan, St. Martin's, 1996.

Miller, D. A. *Jane Austen, or, The Secret of Style.* Princeton, N.J.: Princeton University Press, 2003.

Morrison, Robert, ed. *Jane Austen's "Pride and Prejudice": A Sourcebook.* New York: Routledge, 2005.

Newman, Karen. "Can This Marriage Be Saved: Jane Austen Makes Sense of An Ending," *ELH* 50, no. 4 (1984): pp. 693–710.

Newton, Judith Lowder. *Women, Power and Subversion.* Athens: University of Georgia Press, 1985.

Perkins, Moreland. *Reshaping the Sexes in "Sense and Sensibility".* Charlottesville: University Press of Virginia, 1998.

Rigberg, Lynn R. *Jane Austen's Discourse with New Rhetoric.* New York: P. Lang, 1999.

Ruderman, Anne Crippen. *The Pleasures of Virtue: Political Thought in the Novels of Jane Austen.* Lanham, Md.: Rowman & Littlefield Publishers, 1995.

Southam, Brian. *Jane Austen: A Students' Guide to the Later Manuscript Works.* London: Concord, 2007.

Tandon, Bharat. *Jane Austen and the Morality of Conversation.* London: Anthem, 2003.

Waldron, Mary. *Jane Austen and the Fiction of Her Time.* Cambridge, England: Cambridge University Press, 1999.

Wallace, Tara Ghoshal. *Jane Austen and Narrative Authority.* New York; Hampshire, England: St. Martin's, Macmillan, 1995.

Acknowledgments

Mary Poovey, "Ideological Contradictions and the Consolations of Form: The Case of Jane Austen" From *The Proper Lady and the Woman Writer: Ideology as Style in the Works of Mary Wollstonecraft, Mary Shelley, and Jane Austen.* © 1984 by the University of Chicago. Reprinted by permission.

E.B. Moon, "'A Model of Female Excellence': Anne Elliot, *Persuasion,* and the Vindication of a Richardsonian Ideal of the Female Character." From *AUMLA* 67 (May 1987): 25–42. © 1987 by the Australasian Universities Language and Literature Association. Reprinted by permission.

Anne K. Mellor, "Why Women Didn't Like Romanticism: The Views of Jane Austen and Mary Shelley." From *The Romantics and Us: Essays on Literature and Culture,* edited by Gene W. Ruoff. © 1990 by Rutgers, The State University. Reprinted by permission of Rutgers University Press.

Cynthia Wall, "Gendering Rooms: Domestic Architecture and Literary Acts." From *Eighteenth-Century Fiction,* vol. 5, no. 4 (July 1993): 349–372. © 1993 by McMaster University. Reprinted by permission.

William Deresiewicz, "Community and Cognition in *Pride and Prejudice.*" From *ELH* 64, no. 2 (1997): 503–535. © 1997 by the Johns Hopkins University Press. Reprinted with permission of the Johns Hopkins University Press.

Index

Characters in literary works are indexed by first name (if any), followed by the name of the work in parentheses.